Whole Earth Ecolog

THE BEST OF ENVIRONMENTAL TOOLS AND IDEAS

HARMONY BOOKS/NEW YORK

PURPOSE

We are as Gods and might as well get good at it. So far remotely done power and glory — as via government, big business, formal education, church — has succeeded to the point where gross defects obscure actual gains. In response to this dilemma and to these gains, a realm of intimate, personal power is developing — the power of individuals to conduct their own education, find their own inspiration, shape their own environment, and share the adventure with whoever is interested. Tools that aid this process are sought and promoted by the Whole Earth Catalogs.

FUNCTION

The **Whole Earth Ecolog** is an evaluation and access device. We're here to point, not to sell. We have no financial obligation or connection to any of the suppliers listed. We only review stuff we think is great; why waste your time with anything else?

UPDATES

Our listings are continuously revised and updated according to the experience and suggestions of our readers and staff. The latest news is in our magazine, **Whole Earth Review**. (For subscription information, see p. 127.)

HOW TO SUBMIT STUFF TO US

You are invited to submit comments, ideas, articles, reviews, photographs, and suggestions. We pay for what we use. For details, send SASE to Assistant Editor, 27 Gate Five Road, Sausalito, CA 9496;. (415) 332-1716.

HOW TO ORDER FROM SUPPLIERS REVIEWED IN THE ECOLOG

Consider these points of mail-order etiquette essential; they'll make shopping by mail much more pleasant for you and the supplier. This advice is distilled from the requests of many of the firms listed, and from our own 20 years of experience.

I. **Do not order anything from us at the Whole Earth Ecolog!** (Except our own publication, of course. See p. 127.)

2. **Don't order from the excerpts of catalogs we review.** Send for their brochure or catalog, and order from that.

3. **Include payment with your order.** Use a money order or personal check; cash or stamps won't do. You may be able to do charge card orders — ask first. Don't send personal checks or U.S. Money Orders overseas.

4. **Include sales tax** if the supplier is in your state.

5. **Use International Money Orders (IMO) to send money abroad.** You get them at the Post Office. To send money to the U.S. *from* abroad, use IMO or a bank draft in U.S. dollars.

6. **Expect prices to rise.** The prices shown in the **Ecolog** are accurate as of July 1990. Most firms will write you back if you don't send enough money. Some will bill you for the extra amount.

7. **Expect prices to be higher if you live outside the continental U.S.** It's best to write for the overseas price before ordering. Enclose an International Reply Coupon (available at your Post Office). Be sure and ask about the price difference between sea mail (cheaper, but slow and prone to theft) and air mail (quick and expensive). We recommend air for most items.

8. **Write legibly.** Block print or type. Use printed address labels if you have them. That way if your scribble can't be read, at least they'll know where it came from.

9. **Write what you want on the envelope.** "Mail order" or "catalog request" or "subscription order" will help prevent the loss of your order.

10. **Be patient.** It takes at least two weeks for your goods to arrive. Four to six weeks is normal, especially if you've paid with a personal check. Don't worry too much unless it's taken more than two months. Keep a record of the date of purchase, and a photocopy of your check, so if your order is lost, you can give specific details. Include your full name and address (and zip) and order number, if any, every time you write.

11. **Be considerate.** Don't send for catalogs just to keep your mailbox full. Small companies may be swamped by frivolous requests; large ones may respond with big minimum orders if harassed by dilettantes. If you ask for free information, send a stamped, self-addressed envelope (SASE).

You probably don't have to buy that book! Most libraries can get just about any book if you're willing to wait for the interlibrary loan network to go through its rituals.

And don't forget your local bookstore. You can support your local economy, and probably save postage and handling charges, by ordering through them.

HOW TO ORDER FROM WHOLE EARTH ACCESS COMPANY (✳WEA)

Any book that has indicated ✳WEA under the book ordering information may be ordered by mail or telephone from the Whole Earth Access in Berkeley, California. This company was originally inspired by the Whole Earth Catalog more than 20 years ago but has always been a separate and independent company with no financial ties to us. We list them as a convenience to our readers, who may want to order from a single source instead of dealing with various publishers. To order from them:

1. Start with the list price (not the postpaid price). Total the prices of the book(s). Add $3 to each order of up to five books, and 50 cents for each additional book for postage. Orders over 20 books will be charged actual UPS shipping rate. For delivery in California, add local sales tax.

2. Beside listing the title and quantity of books you want, it is helpful to indicate the page number they appear on in the **Ecolog**.

3. Include your street address. All orders are shipped UPS, and UPS does not deliver to P.O. box numbers.

4. For foreign orders shipping is $5 for the first two books and $1 for each additional book. Send check or money order in U.S. dollars.

5. Enclose payment in full with check or money order. VISA/MasterCard customers print name from card, account number, expiration date, and sign your name.

Send orders, or call in with a credit card, to:

**Whole Earth Access
2990 Seventh Street
Berkeley, CA 94710**

(800) 845-2000; (415) 845-3000

Copyright © 1990 by Point Foundation

Published by Harmony Books, 201 East 50th Street, New York, New York, 10022. Member of the Crown Publishing Group.

HARMONY and colophon are trademarks of Crown Publishers, Inc.

Manufactured in the United States of America

Library of Congress Cataloging in Publication Data

Whole earth ecolog: tools and ideas for earth-conscious living/edited by J. Baldwin. p. cm.
    Includes index.
    1. Human ecology.   2. Environmental protection.
I. Baldwin, J. (James)
GF50.W46 1990   90-42917
363.7—dc20   CIP

ISBN: 0-517-57658-9

BOMC offers recordings and compact discs, cassettes and records. For information and catalog write to BOMR, Camp Hill, PA 17012.

Bigger, finer, slower

Start with the city.

In Christopher Alexander's **New Theory of Urban Design**, reviewed on p. 78, is a guiding rule: "*Every increment of construction must be made in such a way as to heal the city.*"

It's not hard to do that. When it's done, even just a little, people in the cities — where civilization's decisions are made — can see the benefits of scaling up the rule: "*. . . as to heal the bioregion;*" "*. . . as to heal the Earth.*"

For the last three decades one of the most successful (and least lauded) joint efforts of government, local business, philanthropists, environmentalists, and volunteers has been the preservation and reviving of historic city centers. Even government sponsored low-cost housing works in those neighborhoods, if — as in Charleston, South Carolina — it is salted around in rehabilitated old buildings and scattered new buildings designed to fit in with the old.

Paradoxically, when you increase the density of urban activity, and mix together working and dwelling places, then mass transit also can work, and the general amenity level goes up.

One of the attractions of well-preserved, lively cities is that they give a surface of familiarity over the seething, surging currents of change in technology and commerce that show no sign of settling down in the coming decades.

Well-preserved, living rural landscapes and wildernesses offer the same comfort. Rafting a wild river makes the body sing with the old dangers, gives the body a sure sense of itself and frees it to explore unfamiliar hazards such as immersion in computerized "virtual reality."

The extremely new and the deeply old inform and cure and maintain each other.

A direct and beneficial product of the 45-year Cold War, now over, was the globalizing of human attention. Fear of nuclear war led to the space race and the photos from space of Earth that the Whole Earth Catalogs have been named after since 1968. Fear of "Nuclear Winter" led to studies of the

Stewart Brand

atmosphere that produced concerns about Global Warming and an unprecedented degree of international collaboration on the most fundamental of environmental issues.

With the passing of the threat of nuclear annihilation (though probably an increased chance of localized nuclear warfare), people lifted the iron curtain from their sense of future time. Future generations became something to think seriously about and work for. As the year 2000 approaches, people are making the crucial jump from thinking in decades to thinking in centuries forward.

Costa Ricans refer to their rain forests as cathedrals of the 21st Century, requiring generations of work to preserve and enhance. The satisfactions of huge, slow projects like that are enormous. The actual process consists of countless detailed, local actions of refinement, each rewarding in itself — for its own sake and for its reference to the larger task.

This is a book of tools for saving the world at the only scale it can be done, one hand at a time.

—Stewart Brand

(Founder and editor of Whole Earth Catalogs from 1968 to 1985)

What's an Ecolog?

Old friends will note that the **Ecolog** resembles the original Whole Earth Catalogs from twenty years ago. It's equally big and floppy, with similar spirit, intent, and utility. What's different is the focus — in this case on environmental and ecological matters. But attempting to include *everything* in one huge paper Catalog is no longer practical (although we've made a start at doing that electronically with the **1988 Electronic Whole Earth Catalog.** See p. 127). There were hard choices to be made; it's literally the nature of things that nearly everything is in some way involved with the environment.

This **Ecolog** is a metaphorical snapshot of some of the interesting action in applied ecology. Like any snapshot, it can't show more than a freeze-frame of a scene that is actually seething. As is our custom, we review what's deemed important and interesting by our staff and our friendly experts, many of whom are readers of our quarterly magazine, **Whole Earth Review** (see p. 127). We tend to show typical — but not all — examples of a breed. If your wonderful enterprise or one you love isn't here, it's probably because we aren't covering that subject this time, we can't show 'em all, we thought everybody already knew, or — horrors — we missed it (let us know!).

Following our Whole Earth tradition, the **Ecolog** does not attend to what's wrong in the world — a host of other publications (and your intuition) do that very well. Nor do we give bad reviews to things we don't like. Negative reviews tend to focus on how smart the reviewer is, and just bring further publicity to things best left to decompose quietly. Positive reviews introduce readers to the good stuff, which is what we're all here for. Items are selected for review because they're exemplary, basic, unique, unproven-but-worth-watching, or combinations thereof. We are

not interested in political correctness of any sort.

You may have noticed that bookstores are stacked high with Earth-Saving fare these days. We looked at 'em all (up until our July deadline, that is), then made sure ours isn't just another verse of 99 (Recyclable) Bottles Of Beer On The Wall. We particularly celebrate those individuals and groups undertaking work that is essential, but initially unlikely to attract the sponsorship of business, government, and universities. With few exceptions, that's where the real pioneering is taking place. As usual, we gleefully report successful enterprises, things that work, and even some brave tries.

J. Baldwin

We note with satisfaction (and an occasional wry cackle), that many causes we've championed in past Whole Earth Catalogs are now mainstream or getting close to it. When we started twenty-one years ago, phenomena such as photovoltaics, commercial organic food raising, ecological restoration, and grade school ecology classes were rare. Replacing confrontation with cooperation was considered a sellout to the blackhats. Now it's widely realized that the "enemy" is hard to define without self-incrimination — the contents of the Exxon Valdez oil tanker was enroute to *our* gas tanks. In 1970, it was almost unthinkable that a private, environmentally oriented organization like RMI (p. 57) would soon be advising multinational corporations, the United States Government, and the Kremlin (simultaneously!) on energy and resource

conservation. And who would have expected to see the day when realty interests and the Chamber of Commerce helped pass environmental laws such as Proposition 70 (p. 104)? This is no time for smuggery, though. As one of our friends — it may have been Steve Baer (Zomeworks p. 53) — once said, "If you're not in the Sears catalog, you're probably irrelevant." Metaphor again, but close enough.

The question is whether our best efforts at what is still regrettably dubbed *environmentalism* will "make it to Sears" or otherwise sufficiently affect mainstream worldwide thought in time. Innovation isn't enough; there's inertia to be overcome. You'd think that the undisputed success of the energy-saving, natural-everything Village Homes neighborhood (p. 74) would have cloned imitators by now, but it hasn't. Maybe that's because it was hard to accomplish, like all complex "solutions." Simple solutions always leave out something important; slogans like "Sustainable Development" are dangerous. Any solutions are going to be a bit messy and incremental. Uncounted ignorant personal acts brought us to the present situation; countless personal actions of a well-informed world citizenry are the only way out.

It takes high spirits to do that in the face of accelerating degradation and an apparently increasing kakistocracy (government by a society's worst elements). The **Ecolog** shows some spirited folks at work. It's high time for more to join the fray. There's plenty to do. Professional recycler Linda Christopher put it neatly to local university students: "The goal isn't just a successful *program*, we want it to be the way people normally do things around here!"

—J. Baldwin (—JB)

✱WEA — Available from Whole Earth Access, see p. 2.

Understanding Whole Systems means looking both larger and smaller than where our daily habits live and seeing clear through our cycles. The result is responsibility, but the process is filled with the constant delight of surprise. Neither the Earth nor our lives are flat. What happened in the 20th century? The idea of self — the thing to be kept alive — expanded from the individual to the whole Earth.

—Stewart Brand

The Thousand-Yard Model,
or the Earth as a Peppercorn

Try this for size: Imagine a bowling ball (representing the sun) and a peppercorn (Earth, in proper scale) sitting on your table. How far apart would you separate the ball and the peppercorn to give the true scale distance? Answer: 26 yards! I invite you to actually try this physically. I'll bet that when you do, you'll feel, rather then merely accept (gee whiz) the scale of the solar system for the first time. This nifty booklet takes you through the entire exercise all the way out to Pluto, which is correctly represented by a pinhead more than a thousand yards away. The administrative details are worked out in detail so your demonstration — with kiddies or adults — will go smoothly. (Remember, you have participants strung out over half a mile). It's all utterly convincing; you'll feel it in your bones. Education at its best. The author should get a prize or something. —JB

The Thousand-Yard Model
Guy Ottewell; 1989; 15 pp.
$5 postpaid from:
Astronomical Workshop
Furman University
Greenville, SC 29613; (803) 294-2208 ✱WEA

•

First, collect the objects you need. They are:

Sun—any ball of diameter 8 inches.

Mercury—a pinhead, diameter .03 inch.

Venus—a peppercorn, diameter .08 inch.

Earth—a second peppercorn.

Mars—a second pinhead.

Jupiter—a chestnut, pecan, or gooseberry, diameter .9 inch.

Saturn—a filbert (hazelnut) or acorn, diameter .7 inch.

Uranus—a peanut or coffeebean, diameter .3 inch.

Neptune—a second peanut or coffeebean.

Pluto—a third pinhead (smaller, if possible, since Pluto is the smallest planet).

You may suspect it is easier to search out pebbles of the right sizes. But the advantage of distinct objects such as peanuts is that their rough sizes are remembered along with them. It does not matter if the peanut is not exactly .3 inch long; nor that it is not spherical.

Put the Sun ball down, and march away as follows. (After the first few planets, you will want to appoint someone else to do the actual pacing — call this person the "Spacecraft" or "Pacecraft" — so that you are free to talk.)

*10 paces. Call out "Mercury, where are you?" and have the Mercury-bearer put down his card and pinhead, weighting them with a pebble if necessary.

*Another 9 paces. Venus puts down her peppercorn.

*Another 7 paces. Earth.

Already the thing seems beyond belief. Mercury is supposed to be so close to the Sun that it is merely a scorched rock, and we never see it except in the Sun's glare at dawn or dusk — yet here it is, utterly lost in space! As for the Earth, who can believe that the Sun could warm us if we are that far from it?

The correctness of the scale can be proved to skeptics (of a certain maturity) on the spot. The apparent size of the Sun ball, 26 paces away, is now the same as that of the real Sun — half a degree of arc, or half the width of your little finger held at arm's length. (If both the size of an object and its distance have been scaled down by the same factor, then the angle it subtends must remain the same.)

*Another 14 paces. Mars.

Now come the gasps, at the first substantially larger leap:

*Another 95 paces to Jupiter.

Here is the "giant planet" — but it is a chestnut, more than a city block from its nearest neighbor in space!

From now on, amazement itself cannot keep pace, as the intervals grow extravagantly:

*Another 112 paces. Saturn.

*Another 249 paces. Uranus.

*Another 281 paces. Neptune.

*Another 242 paces. Pluto.

You have marched more than half a mile. (The distance in the model adds up to 1,019 paces. A mile is 1,760 yards.)

To do this, to look back toward the Sun ball which is no longer visible even in binoculars, and to look down at the pinhead Pluto, is to feel the terrifying wonder of space.

Below From Above

The best book of aerial photographs ever (133 — in color). What is unique is the captioning — Gerster knows what he is floating over, or he studies it until he does. He knows the history of places, and why the farmers do odd things, and what the tribe is after, and how to keep sand dunes from covering the oasis. The book is a tour de force of form and content.

The range is so worldwide and culturally rich that no reader-flier can escape wanting to try things differently. That's the yield of perspective. I've seen no other book — not even the space satellite ones — with perspective like this. —Stewart Brand

Below From Above
Georg Gerster
1985; 133 plates
$50 ($53.50 postpaid)
from:
Abbeville Press
488 Madison Ave.
New York, NY 10022
(800) 227-7210 ✱WEA

(Left) Battling wind erosion on a field near Wichita, Kansas. A sudden May wind spurred the farmer into action. He roughened up the soil with a spring-tooth harrow by driving haphazardly over the field. He simply wanted to secure the largest possible amount of land against the wind in the shortest possible time and with the least fuel consumption. Uncultivated fields lack sufficient protective surface cover of crop residue. The dry, whitish crust indicates just how vulnerable they are when bare. In Kansas every year the wind blows away an average of three tons of soil per acre — only about four-fifths of a ton less than what is lost through water erosion.

(Right) The village of Labbézanga, on an island in the Niger River, Mali. The granaries wind through the village like strings of beads. In them, millet and rice keep for up to three years, though in the recent past, during the seemingly endless droughts, the harvest has rarely been sufficient to maintain full capacity. The amphora-shaped mud containers, some as high as the houses, are filled and emptied through an opening at the top. Stone slabs and fragments, jutting out from the body of the granaries like spikes, make them easier to climb. The villagers, settled, non-nomadic members of the Songhai tribe, live mainly in the traditional round mud huts with domed thatched roofs. In Labbézanga, however, terrace-roofed square houses of Islamic-Arabic origin are on the increase. Owning one boosts a family's social standing.

I have explained in the introduction why I felt like Columbus when I found Labbézanga. Beyond being "the most beautiful village in Africa," it is also, according to the cyberneticist Frederic Vester, a shining example of an inter-connected system. For the unassuming Labbézangans almost too much praise.

Simply stated, the (Gaia) hypothesis says that the surface of the Earth, which we've always considered to be the environment of life, is really part of life. The blanket of air — the troposphere — should be considered a circulatory system, produced and sustained by life. —Lynn Margulis

— From Elmwood Institute (an ecological think tank founded by Fritjof Capra, 415/845-4595) Newsletter, Volume 5, Number 2.

The Ages of Gaia

James Lovelock has upgraded his notion of the Earth as living organism from hypothesis (testable speculation) to theory (persuasive explanation). One might have expected him to modify its radical nature at this stage. He did not. Instead, in this book he extends its ramifications, arguing convincingly that Earth's personality — its ocean character, the ingenious delivery of its water as rain over dry land, its transparent, blue-air skin, and perhaps the very mold of the land itself — are all caused by life. In the biography he tells of Gaia, life is not a fragile weakling, but a hardy, indomitable force that awakens Gaia herself. This is science writing at its best, and the boldest earth-science book in decades.
—Kevin Kelly

The Ages of Gaia
James Lovelock
1988; 252 pp.
$16.95 postpaid from:
W.W. Norton & Co., Inc.
Keystone Industrial Park
Scranton, PA 18512
(800) 233-4830 ✴WEA

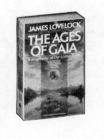

●

At the risk of having my membership card of the Friends of the Earth withdrawn, I say that only by pollution do we survive. We animals pollute the air with carbon dioxide, and the vegetation pollutes it with oxygen. The pollution of one is the meat of the other.

●

Much more probably, "Earth's fragile shield" is a myth. The ozone layer certainly exists today, but it is a flight of fancy to believe that its presence is essential for life. My first job as a graduate was at the National Institute for Medical Research in London. My boss was the courteous and distinguished generalist, Robert Bourdillon. I was privileged to watch, and later participate in, the experiments that he and my colleague, Owen Lidwell, made as they tried to kill bacteria by exposing them to unfiltered ultraviolet radiation. Our practical objective was the prevention of cross infection in hospital wards and operating theatres. We were seeking a way to kill airborne bacteria and so prevent the spread of infection. Naked washed bacteria of some species, when suspended in the air as fine droplets, were easily destroyed by ultraviolet. It was impressive, though, how small a film of organic matter would almost entirely protect even these sensitive species. In the real world outside the laboratory, bacteria do not exist suspended in distilled water or a saline solution. In their normal habitats, bacteria are clothed in mucus secretions or the organic and mineral constituents of their environment. They do not live naked anymore than we do. Many practical trials were made before it was realised that ultraviolet radiation is not an effective method of eliminating from the hospital environment the tender fragile pathogens. It takes almost no clothing to stop ultraviolet radiation.

Gaia: An Atlas of Planet Mangement

This book is the result of an ambitious project to map and analyse the effects of human activities on the planet. Though it was one of the first attempts at a general overview, the data-backed, clear analyses remain valid today. The book is divided into major areas: Land, Ocean, Elements, Evolution, Humankind, Civilization, and Management. Each chapter deftly outlines the present situation and how it got that way, illustrating everything with photographs and big, colorful drawings. What we had better do next is discussed calmly but candidly, letting the chips fall where they may. This realistic attitude, unusual in scholarly books, bestows a credible urgency to academic and layperson alike. I've not seen the Big Picture more accessibly presented. —JB

●

We face a situation in which the mega-corporations are coming to wield virtual monopoly power over key sectors of the food trade. And their desire for more control over our food-producing systems is expanding even further. Since 1970, a few giant petro-corporations have quietly taken over more than 400 small seed businesses; businesses that hitherto produced seeds with vast variety to suit diverse environments, tastes, and price ranges. By controlling the production of seeds, a petro-corporation can breed crops that need extra-large dollops of synthetic fertilizer, pesticides, and other petroleum-based additives, regardless of more desirable trends for future agriculture (viz. away from reliance on fossil-fuel inputs). What happens when the oil wells run dry? The corporation answers that it will tackle those problems as they arise, but meanwhile it is a private profit-making concern, not a public charity.

Probably even more insidious in its ultimately

GAIA (An Atlas of Planet Management)
Norman Myers
1984; 272 pp.
$22.95 ($24.95 postpaid)
from: Doubleday & Co.
P.O. Box 5071
Des Plaines, IL
60017-5071
(800) 223-6834 ✴WEA

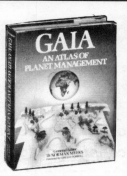

EATING OIL. Since 1950, population growth has reduced grain land per head by a third, but per capita fertilizer use has risen five-fold. Grain production per capita rose steadily until the 1973 oil crisis, then leveled off. In 1983, it actually fell.

4.66 billion
3.88 billion
2.51 billion

Population
Grain per capita
5 kg fertilizer per capita
Area of harvested grain land per capita

20 kg
25 kg
5 kg

0.24 ha   0.19 ha   0.16 ha
1950   1973   1983

detrimental impact on agriculture is the support provided by giant corporations to the "farmers' lobby" in developed nations. The Common Agricultural Policy of the EEC causes governments to pay out $14 billion a year to encourage farmers to produce butter mountains and milk lakes. Similarly, American farmers are subsidized to the tune of around $40 billion a year. One "solution" proposed for these grotesque surpluses is to turn the milk lakes into powdered milk, and feed it back to the cows that gave the milk in the first place! By contrast, the World Bank estimates that the sum required to supply Third World subsistence farmers with the means to lift themselves out of self-reinforcing poverty is only $8 billion a year.

Mind and Nature

Mind and Nature addresses the hidden, though unoccult, dynamics of life — the misapprehension of which threatens to unhorse our civilization. Bateson doesn't have all the answers, he just has better questions — elegant, mature, embarrassing questions that tweak the quick of things.

One of the themes that emerges is the near identity between the process of evolving and the process of learning, and the ongoing responsibility they have for each other which includes our responsibility, which we have shirked. We shirked it through ignorance. **Mind and Nature** *dispels that.*
—Stewart Brand

●

It is a nontrivial matter that we are almost always unaware of trends in our changes of state. There is a quasi-scientific fable that if you can get a frog to sit quietly in a saucepan of cold water, and if you then raise the temperature of the water very slowly and smoothly so that there is no moment *marked* to be the moment at which the frog should jump, he will never jump. He will get boiled. Is the human species changing its own environment with slowly increasing pollution and rotting its mind with slowly deteriorating religion and education in such a saucepan?

●

Human sense organs can receive *only* news of difference, and the differences must be coded into events in *time* (i.e. into *changes*) in order to be

Mind and Nature (A Necessary Unity) Gregory Bateson, 1972, 1988; 272 pp.
$9.95 ($11.95 postpaid) from:
Bantam Books
414 E. Golf Road
Des Moines, IL 60016; (800) 223-6834 ✴WEA

perceptible. Ordinary static differences that remain constant for more than a few seconds become perceptible only by scanning.

●

Ross Ashby long ago pointed out that no system (neither computer nor organism) can produce anything new unless the system contains some source of the random. In the computer, this will be a random-number generator which will ensure that the "seeking," trial-and-error moves of the machine will ultimately cover all the possibilities of the set to be explored.

●

I do not believe that the original purpose of the rain dance was to make "it" rain. I suspect that that is a degenerate misunderstanding of a much more profound religious need: to affirm membership in what we may call the *ecological tautology*, the eternal verities of life and environment. There's always a tendency — almost a need — to vulgarize religion, to turn it into entertainment or politics or magic or "power."

Biosphere II

By Kevin Kelly

In southern Arizona, a band of dedicated mavericks are quietly erecting the most gutsy science experiment since the days of the first moon landing. It's a brilliant, bold, harebrained, and completely gonzo undertaking: A sealed, self-sustaining ark for human living. The Arizona group calls it Biosphere II, a bonsai version of Biosphere I, our Earth.

Small compared to Earth, this self-contained terraquarium is awesome at the human scale. Biosphere II (Bio2) is a gigantic glass ark the size of an airport hangar. It's airtight to the outside. Sealed at the bottom, too, with a stainless-steel tray 25 feet under the soil to prevent seepage of air from below.

In September 1990, eight volunteers — four men, four women — will walk through the air-locks, and seal themselves in for two years.

Inside there is a soaking-wet rain forest at one end, a desert savanna at the other, and a coral reef and marsh in the middle. Off to one side is

an intensive agriculture area where the eight will grow all their own food for two years. Like Noah's boat there will be animals aboard: some for meat, some for pets, and some on the loose: lizards, fish, birds, and bats roaming about the wild parts. There are honey bees, papaya trees, a beach, TV, and a laundromat.

The Biospherians (as they call themselves) will recycle 100 percent of what they breathe, drink, and eat. For two years they will live in a closed mini-world, a dramatic surrogate of our home planet. They see Bio2 as a double-sided investigation: how to live off the Earth and how to live on the Earth.

There is a green faction within the Bio2 group that sees this experiment as an emblem of Gaian awareness, an icon with as much spiritual power as the image of the whole Earth from space. And there is a space-cowboy faction within Bio2 that sees this as a pragmatic step on a spiritual journey off the planet into the galaxies. ∎

The rock wall in this picture separates two of the seven biomes enclosed under the glass canopy being erected. On top of the cliff will be the African thornshrub savanna; at the base of the cliff, the ocean with Caribbean coral reef. (An underwater viewing port is being constructed in the foreground.) Under the framework lies the future Baja fog desert. At the junction where framework shown is over the cliff, a waterfall drops to a Florida mangrove swamp. The water will come from a tropical cloud forest, out of the picture to the right; its highest point will be five stories tall. In the background are the domes of the agricultural area. And the seventh biome, an urban human habitat, will house *Homo sapiens Americanus* with conventional materials.

(Right) Constructing a wetlands by reassembling a natural one is the analog method of biome building. It seems to work fine. "If we were really doing this right, we would be piping in thunder for the frogs," says Warshall. "But we are not really modeling the earth, we are modeling Noah. How many links can we break and still have a species survive? In reality that's our question." "Well, we haven't had a crash yet!" Walter Adey chuckles. He has built two living coral reefs and a mangrove swamp. His analog swamp gets a thunderstorm when someone turns a gushing water hose onto it. Living mesocosms, even synthetic ones, are hard to break.

(Below) "Designing a biome is an opportunity to think like God," Peter Warshall points out with a smile. Says Tony Burgess, "You can go two ways with this. Mimic an analog of a particular environment you find in nature, or invent a synthetic based on many of them. Bio2 is definitely a synthetic ecosystem. But so is California by now." Redundancy of pathways in the foodchain is the great challenge for would-be Gods. With multiple food chains, if the sandflies die off, then there'll still be a second choice of food for the lizards. Humans are "keystone predators," acting as checks of last resort (The 14 candidates are shown here.) Populations of plants or animals that outrun their niches can be kept in reasonable range by human "arbitration." If the ocotillo shrub takes over, the bionauts will hack it away. Adey says, "You can build synthetic ecosystems as small as you want. But the smaller you make it, the greater role human operators play because they must act out the larger forces of nature beyond the ecological community. The subsidy we get from nature is incredible."

Photos by Kevin Kelly except where noted.

(Above) Of all the myriad parts making up Bio2, the most well-researched is the intensive agriculture area. The total area available for food crops is about 1/2 acre. Domesticated plants are bred for more sheltered climates so the entire atmosphere of the agricultural area under these domed structures will be air-conditioned to some extent. The garden's air will be dehumidified year-'round, and cooled during the summer. While water for use inside the farm will be recycled, water for the evaporation cooling towers will be drawn from wells outside. Research done by Environmental Research Laboratory (ERL) has shown that it is possible to grow enough food for one person for one year on as little as 250 square meters, your basic tennis court size. And to do this year after year.

(Above) Combination water purifier and aqua-farm. Here's a multilevel tub system for growing rice, green compost, and fish on "waste" water. The rice is grown paddy-style in flooded beds. On the water surface a mat of azolla, a tiny flat water fern that is high in nitrogen, floats between stalks of rice. It is collected after the rice is harvested and composted for fertilizer. Under the water, tilapia fish proliferate. Tilapia, a tropical carp-like fish from the inland lakes of Africa, have an unusually high percentage of protein, reproduce rapidly, and are excellent restaurant fare. "Waste" water from the rice/fish tubs spills into water-hyacinth tubs which begin a biological clearing of the water, a job picked up with gusto by microbial bacteria adhering to a drum spun by the water movement. Since everything is recycled, there is no garbage.

(Left) To entirely feed one person indefinitely on a backyard-sized plot requires that nutrition be maintained for both soil and human. ERL has worked out a rotation of cultivars for a small plot that produces a varied human diet which exceeds the minimum RDA for calories and all nutrients, except for vitamin B12. It is not boring food: oats, wheat, rice, sweet potatoes, squashes, sunflower seeds, various beans and peas, peanuts, lots of leafy greens, root crops like beets and carrots, the usual garden veggies like tomatoes, cukes, eggplant, peppers, and some fruit such as melons and strawberries.

Peter Menzel

See Also...
For a tiny basic Biosphere see page 120.
For more ERL work see page 49.

World Game ®

"To make the world work
For 100% of humanity
In the shortest possible time
Through spontaneous cooperation
Without ecological offense
Or the disadvantage of anyone"

—Buckminster Fuller

A big order. Buckminster Fuller initiated the World Game in 1969 as one means of accomplishing this worthy goal, to which he dedicated his life. He insisted that with enough accurate data on world resource distribution and use — including human skills and accumulated knowledge — the world's citizens would conduct their lives in a way that was best for all. Fuller's own investigations proved that there was enough of virtually every resource if people would learn "to do more with less" by using their minds for "comprehensive, anticipatory design." Once people began to see the big picture, they would stop fighting and get to work making the world work — if not as a utopia, then at least in a way that was not suicidal. But how to deliver the big picture in a comprehensible way?

Bucky (*everyone* called him Bucky) realized that global problems were enormous, complicated and difficult to comprehend even with the aid of computers. To make things easier to visualize, he proposed a "Geoscope", an enormous globe — one of his materials-efficient geodesic structures, of course — skinned with thousands of lamps. The idea was to show worldwide data, animated by lighting the appropriate bulbs in a manner rather like that used on the sides of the Goodyear Blimp. For example, you might ask to see the seasons, locations and quantities of the world's rice crops. With bulbs of a contrasting color, you could then superimpose population data, annual rainfall, shipping patterns and tonnage, cash flow and endemic beri-beri. Seen on the Geoscope, the data could be understood well enough to suggest strategies that might help alleviate hunger and poverty. Of course, data could also be simulated, allowing World Gamers to try a variety of ideas. Bucky assumed that the participants would eventually come up with a scheme that would maximize benefits for all. He expected that if all factors were considered, selfishness would obviously be of advantage only in the short term, and thus would no longer be a useful policy. A bit idealistic perhaps, but a concept that certainly had to be tried.

World Game got off to a shaky start about 20 years ago, the grand scheme smothered by a pleasant, utterly ineffective touchie-feelie crowd that felt personal enlightenment had to be realized before larger problems could be addressed. However commendable that goal, it was not the purpose of World Game. Bucky was too nice to put his foot down, but it wasn't long before the Game got serious under the guidance of Medard Gabel, its present director. His team has staged many World Game sessions addressing real problems — unfortunately without the aid of a Geoscope. With limited time and budget, and with (paying) participants of diverse and not necessarily germane experience, the Game has so far come up with few results that have enjoyed widespread, practical implementation. Nonetheless, with twenty years of persistent and clever development, World Game has become a powerful and increasingly influential teaching tool. Many presentations

feature a startling basketball court-size "Big Map" (Fuller's patented Dymaxion projection shown on this page) as an aid to clarity. Participants representing various data move about on the huge map as required, making the exercise dynamic and unforgettable.

As World Game has become more effective, demand for its services has risen sharply. This year schedules 180 Workshops, up from 100 in 1989. They'll play to universities, high schools, and a wide variety of mostly non-governmental organizations. World Game is getting some high-level attention too: sessions have been

Fuller's Dymaxion Map writ large (35 by 70 feet) in highway marking paint, the Big Map is the center for learning about world resources, problems and prospects on a global scale. Activities range from the simplest "Simon Says" through role playing games and actual drawing of cultural or natural features on the map in chalk. Students standing on the map enjoy a view the equivalent of that from a satellite in orbit 1500 miles above the Earth. Small Dymaxion Maps & other geodesic artifacts available from: **Buckminster Fuller Institute, 1743 South La Cienega Blvd., Los Angeles, CA 90035 (213) 837-7710.**

well-received on Capitol Hill. Next year, the Rockefeller Brothers Fund will sponsor a series of World Game Workshops for the U.N., Ambassadors, Consulates and their staffs. Big-time at last!

But perhaps the best news is that a sort of Geoscope — an 80 by 60 foot wall map — is under construction at the new St. Louis Science Center. It isn't Bucky's geodesic sphere (alas), but it promises to be very effective anyway. It's called "Macroscope", an appropriate name for a device that looks at huge things. World Game's formidable and ever-expanding Global Data Manager software (see below), will instantly laser-project the requested information onto the map. It's scheduled to open next year. When it does, we'll do a full report in Whole Earth Review.

Another version of the same scheme is under study for a World Game Pavilion at EXPO 1992 in Seville. If built, it will include an interactive theater for 540 delegates, each one representing 10 million of the world's 5.4 billion people. Now *that* would be a World Game to see! By the time you read this, the decision will have been made. Let's hope it's yes, but if not, a big, interactive, truly international

Geoscope is certain to be realized soon. It's an idea whose time has come. *—JB*

World Game Goods and Services

World Game sessions come in many shapes and sizes; from multi-subject overview to a sharply focussed look at a single issue or geographic area (including your own locale). It can be a couple hours for a small group, or an 8-hour, multimedia blowout for thousands. Semester programs can be arranged. They do computer labs and public school assemblies, too. All can be tailored to fit your needs. Anywhere in the world, of course.

In addition to presenting sessions, the World Game Institute offers a variety of goods and services. Chief among these is their peerless **Global Data Manager** software, available for MS-DOS and Apple machines. It combines numbers from the U.N., World Bank, World Resources Institute, and several other world-class data collections. At this time, the Global Data Manager is available as separate disks for Basic World Data (180 variables, correct to 1989), World Development Indicators 1970-1983 (371 variables from the World Bank on economics and development), World Social Development Indicators (100 variables from UNESCO, World Bank and others on health, education, defense, justice etc.), World Minerals Data (150 variables on production and reserves and reserve bases), and World Energy Data (190 variables 1950-1987). An interactive disk called **Global Recall** combines many features from the Data Manager disks into a single-disk quick review for research, analysis, education or media needs. Why guess, when this disk can whip out the facts you need so quickly?

The data are presented in spreadsheet form. It can be manipulated into graphs, onto maps, compared, correlated and added to. Matching teacher's manuals are available. The Global Data Manager now has about 1000 variables listed for every country, and will soon have 5000. The goal is 100,000 per country! Under development: a CD-ROM version enabling all the data to be manipulated on one disk.

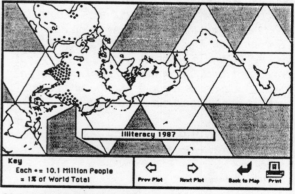

Global Recall for the Macintosh.

The Hitachi Fund recently funded a monster stencil for the **Big Map**, making it possible to have one done in durable, skid-proof paint on the floor, wall, or (most commonly) playground of your choice. The contract price includes the fairly tricky installation. Kids love it.

Aaaaand, you can support and keep up with the exploits of World Game by joining it as a member. That brings you their newsletter, **Macroscope**, plus price breaks on some of the offerings which include the usual T-shirt type stuff too. Help a unique, much-needed world-wide service grow.

Information **free** from: World Game Institute, 3508 Market Street, Philadelphia, PA 19104; (215) 387-0220

State of the World

Who has time to read all available environmental and ecological news? Not me, certainly. If we subscribed to every available magazine, and bought all the books published each month, we'd soon be buried in an environmentally unseemly pile of paper, much of it destined to remain unread. Yet it is good to keep up with the latest ideas and events. We are in luck: All we have to do is pay attention to, or better, join Worldwatch Institute. Since 1974, their publications have proven to be a comprehensive, reliable and often prescient look at the world's problems and possible solutions thereto. Each year since 1984, Worldwatch has delivered another book in their remarkable State of the World *series. This year's edition is labelled as a "report on progress toward a sustainable society." It must be the best single look at what is and is not being done about the world's major problems. The information is presented by a cadre of Worldwatch authors, all of whom know how to write. The general tone is energetic and instistent, but not hysterical. Partisan politics are absent, but are reported as fact where necessary. Copious footnotes (mercifully located at the back of the book) assure credibility. Some of the articles are shortened versions of recent* Worldwatch Papers *(see below).*

If you read just one ecobook a year, this is certainly it. You'll be in good company; many governments, schools and organizations use the book as a principal resource. Since Worldwatch is truly a global organization, State of the World *is now published in Arabic, Chinese, English, French, German, Indonesian, Italian, Japanese, Polish, Portuguese, Russian, and Spanish, with Dutch, Hungarian, Korean, Norwegian, and Swedish versions coming soon. I keep a copy (in English, yes?) nearby. —JB*

World•Watch

You don't need to wait until next year to find out what's going on. The redoubtable Worldwatch crew also puts out a magazine six times a year. It covers pretty much the same stuff as the annual State of the World *book. Editorial policy aims the magazine at the task of providing good information, as you'd expect. It is also intended "to provide a global framework for the thousands of organizations throughout the world that work on energy, environmental, food, population, and peace issues." Editing is deliberately done in a way that provides a quick, accurate source of information for us media hacks. I appreciate the effort a lot, and use the magazine in courses I teach. —JB*

State of the World
Lester R. Brown, editor
$9.95 ✱WEA
World•Watch
Lester R. Brown, editor
$15/year (six issues)
Worldwatch Papers
Lester R. Brown, editor
$4/single copy; $25/year
membership includes
State of the World)
all from: Worldwatch Institute, 1776 Massachusetts Avenue, NW Washington, DC 20036

•

Norplant consists of six rubber capsules, each the size of a matchstick. The capsules contain levonorgestrel, the synthetic hormone found in birth control pills. In a brief surgical procedure performed with the patient under a local anesthetic,

Trade-offs Between Military and Environmental Priorities:

Military Priority	Cost	Social/Environmental Priority
Trident II submarine, F-16 jet fighter programs	$100 billion	One-third of estimated clean-up cost for U.S. hazardous waste dumps, over 50 years
Stealth bomber program	$79 billion	80 percent of est. costs to meet U.S. clean water goals by 2000
German outlays for military procurement and R&D, FY 1985	$10.75 billion	Estimated clean-up costs for West German sector of the North Sea
Approx. 2 days of global mil. spending	$4.8 billion	Annual cost of proposed U.N. Action Plan to halt Third World desertification, over 20 years
MK-50 Advanced Light Weight Torpedo	$6 billion	Annual cost to cut sulfur dioxide emissions by 8-12 million tons/year in the U.S. to combat acid rain, over five years

Source: Worldwatch Institute

—World•Watch

the six capsules are inserted in a woman's upper arm. The time-released hormone provides effective contraceptive protection for up to five years, primarily by inhibiting ovulation and thickening cervical mucus to prevent sperm from reaching the egg. When the implants are removed, fertility returns almost immediately.

The main advantages of Norplant are its effectiveness, convenience and longevity. With less than 0.5 percent risk of pregnancy in the first year of use, and 1 percent risk even in the fifth year, Norplant is more effective than either the pill or the IUD and rivals the record of sterilization. Unlike the pill, it does not require daily discipline; unlike the condom or diaphragm, it is not awkward or disruptive; and unlike sterilization, it is easily reversed.

All of which makes Norplant sound like a wonder contraceptive, but it does have drawbacks. First, it is less effective in women who weight more than 150 pounds. More important, it causes menstrual irregularity, ranging from prolonged bleeding to no bleeding at all (side effects that usually subside by the end of the first year). While many women find the bleeding merely bothersome, others consider it serious enough to have their implants removed.

Clearly, no contraceptive, Norplant included, can compensate for a lack of family planning services. The success of Norplant is pinned to the expansion of these services.

Worldwatch Papers

Six or eight times a year, Worldwatch publishes a paper on one of the topics that Worldwatch watches. These papers take the form of paperbound booklets offering concise background information on the subject under discussion.
Check our reviews of #84 Rethinking the Role of the Automobile (p. 70), and #90 The Bicycle: Vehicle for a Small Planet (p. 67). If you join Worldwatch Institute, your annual fee includes all the Papers for that year, plus a copy of the latest State of the World. *All are available separately, too. —JB*

•

Staggering as the absolute quantities of debt are, however, the pivotal question is which way resources are moving across the North-South boundary. Until 1984, industrial countries gave more to developing countries in loans each year

than they took back in interest and principal payments. At that point, the flow become a backward torrent; by 1988, the poor were paying the rich $50 billion a year. The massive diversion of resources to the North has taken a toll not only on the people of developing lands, but on the land itself. Forests have been recklessly logged, mineral deposits carelessly mined, and fisheries overexploited, all to pay foreign creditors.

•

Nepal exemplifies the way sheer growth of human numbers fuels the spiral, as human practices at a given level of technology exceed a local environment's carrying capacity. As population swells, peasants in highland valleys are forced to expand their plots onto steep forested hillsides, extending women's journeys to gather fuel and fodder. Over the past decade, during which forests have receded to half their original extent, women's daily journey has increased by more than an hour, their workday in the fields has shortened, family incomes have fallen, and diets have deteriorated.

Shubh Kumar and David Hotchkiss of the International Food Policy Research Institute (IFPRI) in Washington report not only that food consumption in the region has fallen by 100 calories per person on average, but that in village after village childhood malnutrition rates and deforestation rates are

Table 3-3. Water Scarcity, Selected Countries and Regions

Africa, North and East	Ten countries likely to experience severe water stress by 2000; Egypt, already near its limits, could lose vital supplies from the Nile as upper-basin countries develop the river's headwaters.
China	Fifty cities face acute shortages; water tables beneath Beijing are dropping 1–2 meters per year; farmers in Beijing region could lose 30–40 percent of their supplies to domestic and industrial uses.
India	Tens of thousands of villages throughout India now face shortages; plans to divert water from Brahmaputra River have heightened Bangladesh's fear of shortages; large portions of New Delhi have water only a few hours a day.
Mexico	Groundwater pumping in parts of the valley containing Mexico City exceed recharge by 40 percent, causing land to subside; few options exist to import more fresh water.
Middle East	With Israel, Jordan, and the West Bank expected to be using all renewable sources by 1995, shortages are imminent; Syria could lose vital supplies when Turkey's massive Ataturk Dam comes on-line in 1992.
Soviet Union	Depletion of river flows has caused volume of Aral Sea to drop by two thirds since 1960; irrigation plans have been scaled back; high unemployment and deteriorating conditions have caused tens of thousands to leave the area.
United States	One fifth of total irrigated area is watered by excessive pumping of groundwater; roughly half of western rivers are overappropriated; to augment supplies, cities are buying farmers' water rights.

SOURCE: Worldwatch Institute, based on various sources.

—State of the World

closely coupled. In the hills of Nepal, in other words, the health of a village's children can be read in the retreating tree line on surrounding slopes.

Nothing incites people to deplete forests, soils, or water supplies faster than fear they will soon lose access to them.
—State of the World

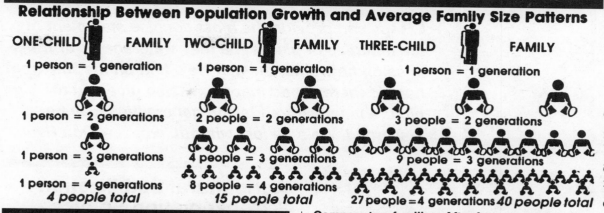

Relationship Between Population Growth and Average Family Size Patterns

ONE-CHILD FAMILY	TWO-CHILD FAMILY	THREE-CHILD FAMILY
1 person = 1 generation	1 person = 1 generation	1 person = 1 generation
1 person = 2 generations	2 people = 2 generations	3 people = 2 generations
1 person = 3 generations	4 people = 3 generations	9 people = 3 generations
1 person = 4 generations	8 people = 4 generations	27 people = 4 generations
4 people total	*15 people total*	*40 people total*

The Population Explosion

It must give Paul Ehrlich grim satisfaction to see that so much of what he worried about in 1968 has come to pass. That year, he published his famous **The Population Bomb,** *an early warning of what would happen (including global warming!) if we did not act to reduce population growth. It was widely influential, and it did make a difference — a respectable accomplishment for one book. But it clearly wasn't enough. Just as he said it would, and despite the counterclaims of his detractors, the situation has become much worse.* **The Population Explosion** *opens fire with nine depressingly well-argued chapters outlining the problems in principle and fact. Every major aspect of population growth and its effects is examined. The Ehrlichs take special care to dismantle the arguments of those who say that overpopulation is not a problem. The hopeful claims of moralists and other pro-natalists are exposed as being unsupported by the facts of what is actually happening.*

Unlike many authors, the Ehrlichs do not leave us to writhe in guilty despair. They come through with a plan of action which, if taken right now, will at least hold the line. It is an insistent call to action, strengthened by being integrated with the concerns of virtually all other environmental workers. This encourages the cross-disciplined efforts that must occur if population control is to be accomplished without drastic coercion or die-offs.

The book concludes with a rousing section on what you can do as an individual (complete with sample letters to people in power), an appendix amounting to a quick course in ecology, and a formidable wad of footnotes to hold off those critics who still think science is vulgarized by making it accessible to normal citizens. Read it soon. —JB

●

The impact of any human group on the environment can be usefully viewed as the product of three different factors. The first is the number of people. The second is some measure of the average person's consumption of resources (which is also an index of affluence). Finally, the product of those two factors — the population and its per-capita consumption — is multiplied by an index of the environmental disruptiveness of the technologies that provide the goods consumed. The last factor can also be viewed as the environmental impact per quantity of consumption. In short, Impact = Population x Affluence x Technology, or I = PAT.

The I = PAT equation is the key to understanding the role of population growth in the environmental crisis. It tells us why, for example, rich nations have such serious population problems (because the A and T multipliers for each person are so large). That is why it is so important that those nations begin shrinking the size of their populations by lowering birthrates until they are below death rates. It also tells us why a little development in poor nations with big populations like China can have an enormous impact on the planet (because the P multiplier on the A and T factors is so large).

●

Those who believe in the intrinsic good of having large numbers of people (for instance, as future souls to be processed into a better world) clearly should wish for a population size stabilized at well below the carrying capacity at any given time. Having, say, one billion people alive all the time for four million more years obviously would create a greater cumulative total than topping out at 10 billion in the next century and then dying out or collapsing to a population of a few hundred thousand people eking out a livelihood on an impoverished planet for the next four million years. Is it somewhere written that a major goal of humanity should be maximize the number of human beings living *all at once?*

The Population Explosion ✳ WEA
Paul R. Ehrlich & Anne H. Ehrlich 1990; 320 pp.; **$18.95** ($21.95 postpaid) from: Simon & Schuster 200 Old Tappan Road, Old Tappan, NJ 07675; (800) 223-2336

Compare two families: After four generations, a family with a three-child tradition will consume 160 percent more resources (including fish, meat, wood, and vegetable products) than a two-child-per-generation family.

Zero Population Growth

ZPG hatched in 1968. Its main goal: to stabilize the population of this country just after the year 2000. Their long-term goal is, as you might guess, to stabilize world population as soon as possible. To accomplish this difficult task, ZPG engages in a wide variety of activities — all essentially educational. One of their strongest programs helps teachers present population matters without creating a storm at the school board. Their work is frequently controversial; not surprising where there is sex, religion, and no-growth policy involved. (Also not surprising where there is Paul Ehrlich involved — he's a co-founder.) —JB

Zero Population Growth
ZPG does favor unlimited population increase of their membership. **$20**/year (includes subscription to ZPG Reporter) from: Zero Population Growth, Inc., 1400 16th Street, NW Washington, DC 20036; (202) 332-2200

USA by Numbers

ZPG looks at our population statistics. The unmentionable facts of immigration and teen pregnancy are here — without polemics or political comment — for all to see. The numbers are official evidence that there is a lot of denial going on in places both high and low. This book is a fine reference, it'd take you weeks to dredge up all this stuff yourself. —JB

USA by Numbers (A Statistical Portrait of the United States) Susan Weber, Editor; **$8.95** ($10.45 postpaid) from: ZPG Publications, 1400 16th Street, NW Suite 320, Washington, DC 20036

●

Public Cost of Teenage Childbearing: It is estimated that a family begun by a first birth to a teenage mother in 1986 will cost taxpayers $14,852 by the time that child reaches age 20. Families begun by first births to adolescents in 1986 alone will cost taxpayers a total of $5.3 billion over the next 20 years.

Planned Parenthood

As you can see on the evening news several times a week, Planned Parenthood brings population management to the personal level, right into your bedroom (or the back seat of a '56 Chevy, for that matter). It's not an enviable vocation — the flak comes from all sides — but the work gets done. A visit to your local Planned Parenthood clinic will show you the realities a lot faster than listening to the babble of all the factions for and against. Planned Parenthood also carries their work worldwide through Family Planning International Assistance (FPIA), an organization supporting voluntary family planning. They help governments and private organizations (including churches) with grants, materials and management advice. They've become adept at nurturing programs to where assistance is no longer needed — the best (and hardest) way to long-term success. —JB

Planned Parenthood
Contributions tax deductible; Information **free** from: Planned Parenthood
810 Seventh Avenue
New York, NY 10019

The Insider's Guide to Demographic Know-How

Monitoring how money swirls in, around, and out of populations is what modern demographers are really after. Of course, purely social and political currents can also be queried and tracked. There is no end of numbers available, many for free. Making sense of statistics requires carving them up with insight. You can get them sliced by commercial companies for a nice fee, or you can dice them up yourself. This excellent manual guides you through the wonderland of databases, most of them public. Although computers are increasingly pertinent (and often vital) in analyzing demographics, this handbook also shows you how to tackle the job yourself with printouts and a calculator. Happy trend hunting. —Kevin Kelly

The Insider's Guide to Demographic Know-How; Penelope Wickham, Editor; 1988; 246 pp. **$21.95** ($24.95 postpaid) from: Probus Publishing Co.; 118 N. Clinton Street, Chicago IL 60606 (312) 346-7985 ✳WEA

Doubling Time

If something is increasing at the rate of 2% per year, in how many years will it double? That 2% sounds innocently small; need we worry? Here's a crude trick for figuring it out: Divide the annual percent increase into 70 (some people use 72). You get 35, so world population, now at 5 billion and increasing at 2% a year, will be ten billion in about 35 years — 2025. Many of us will live to regret it. —JB

✱WEA — Available from Whole Earth Access, see p. 2.

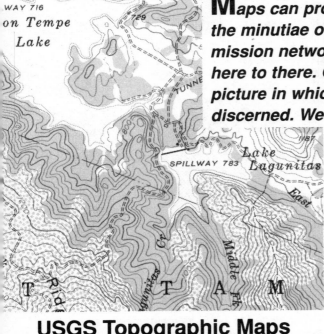

Maps can provide the most concise statement of the minutiae of places, be they watersheds, or transmission networks, or what we'll find on the way from here to there. Good maps may also give you the big picture in which trends and generalities may be discerned. We'd be lost without 'em. —Don Ryan

USGS Topographic Maps and Low-Altitude Aerial Photographs

THE basic maps. Contour-lined for elevations, they come in two basic scales (one inch equals 2,000 feet, and one inch equals about one mile).

For maps by mail, write to the USGS in Denver. They'll also send you a list of USGS regional offices. —Peter Warshall

USGS Topographic Maps and Low-Altitude Aerial Photographs; Index and Catalogs **free** from: Map Distribution/U.S. Geological Survey Box 25286, Denver Federal Center, Denver, CO 80225; (303) 236-7477

DeLorme Atlases

With their large format they look like road atlases, but if you're in a hurry to get to granma's house upstate they won't be much help. If you're like me you'll have long since turned off onto that fine red line that wanders off over hills you've never been behind to that town you never knew existed. These are serious maps, with the features you'd expect to find on a topographic map — great for field trip planning. In studying the areas I know well I've yet to find even the smallest track unrepresented on the page. Included in each is a large gazetteer listing categories such as bike routes, fishing piers, wilderness areas, etc. —Don Ryan

DeLorme Atlas & Gazetteer
S.& Cent.CA, N.CA, WA, MN, WI, MI, OH, PA, NY, VA, TN, FL, **$12.95**; VT, NH, ME, **$11.95** each (add $3 for postage & handling) from: DeLorme Mapping Company, P.O. Box 298, Freeport, ME 04032; (800) 227-1656, ext. 5500

See Also...
World Game, p. 7.
Bicycling maps, p. 67.

Agricultural Stabilization & Conservation Service

The ASCS has black-and-white photos for many seasons, with scales as large as 1"=400'. It's a branch of the Department of Agriculture with local offices in almost every county. (If you have no ASCS office near you, then contact your local State Forester or your County Extension Agent.) Request a photo by sending a map of the area (with the specific part you want clearly outlined) or the exact latitude and longitude. Ask for the scale you'd prefer or just the largest scale available.
—Peter Warshall

ASCS Aerial Photographs
10"x10", before 1987, **$3**; after, **$6**
24"x24", before 1987, **$12**; after, **$20**
38"x38", before 1987, **$25**; after, **$33**
All prices postpaid. Information **free** from:
ASCS Aerial Photography Division Field Office
2222 West 2300 South/P.O. Box 30010
Salt Lake City, UT 84130; (801) 524-5856

Raven Maps and Images

These smart cookies turned information-rich but deadly dull gray-brown almost embarrassing U.S. government maps into captivatingly lifelike shaded-relief wall maps of twelve western states. Because the maps are made from the Geological Survey's negatives all the minutiae in the originals are preserved. The addition of intelligent and subtly applied color enhances only, never obscuring the details.

These are the kinds of maps you want to fall face-down into. (Raven suggests you buy them in their optional laminated versions to protect against greasy faceprints.)

The same smart cookies produce a poster series of oblique views, computer-plotted from digital terrain information collected as part of mapmaking routine by government agencies. Again, the use of color and the design are the arresting attributes. Looking at their view over "The Rockies, the High Plains, and the Intermountain West," I found myself smelling distant pinyon smoke and feeling cool, high-altitude breezes. —Don Ryan

Raven Maps and Images, Catalog **free** from: Raven Maps & Images, 34 North Central Ave. Medford, OR 97501; (800) 237-0798

Globes

*For George F. Cram or Replogle globes in many sizes and price ranges (**$8.95-$5,000**), call or write: Rand McNally, 595 Market Street, San Francisco, CA 94105; (415) 777-3131.*

Map Use

If I had to limit myself to one book about mapmaking and map use, this would be it. The illustrations show cartographic concepts very well. The author does an excellent job, reminding the reader that the map is not the territory, and that maps can be used to abuse as well as to enlighten.
—Ron Hendricks

Map Use, Phillip C. Muehrcke; 1986; 525 pp. **$25** ($28 postpaid) from: J.P. Publications P.O. Box 4173 Madison, WI 53711 (608) 231-2373 ✱WEA

•

Simplicity, too, can be seen as a liability as well as an asset. Simplification of the environment through mapping is nothing but an illusion which appeals to our limited information-processing ability. By using maps, we avoid confronting reality in its overwhelming and confusing natural state. But the environment remains unchanged. It is just our view of it that lacks detail and complexity. If we are able to understand map information at a glance, it is only because the map is such a crude model of our surroundings. Yet it is the environment, not the map, which we want to understand.

•

Ordinarily a map or any picture with so much black at the top would be considered poor design, because it seems top-heavy, unbalanced. On this map from *Time* magazine, however, the intent was to show that South Africa was being hemmed in by black-ruled countries, and the map's design helps to maintain that impression. Poor South Africa looks as though it is being threatened, overcome by ominous forces. If we simply interchange the black and white colors, a totally different mood is created. The design slips into visual balance, and the feeling of menace disappears.

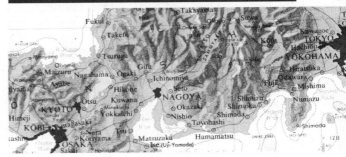

Goode's World Atlas

Per buck, this atlas has the most and the best — 368 pages of locational maps (from continent right down to city), landforms, climate, weather, vegetation, soil, population, agriculture, trade, language, resources, ocean floor — including a fine pronouncing index. When something in the newspaper puzzles you, check here. Well, well: about ten different languages are spoken in different regions of the Soviet Union. —Stewart Brand

Goode's World Atlas
Edward B. Espenshade, Jr., Editor; 1990; 368 pp.
$24.95 ($28.70 postpaid) from: Rand McNally & Co. Direct Mail, P.O. Box 1697 Skokie, IL 60076-9871 (800) 234-0679 ✱WEA

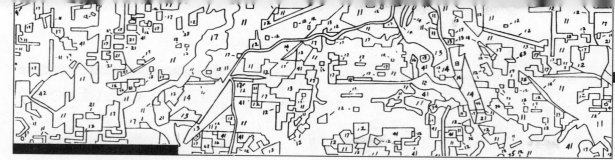

Access to USGS

The U.S. Geological Survey produces and distributes information on a wide variety of earth-science specialities such as geology, hydrology, cartography, geography, and remote sensing, as well as information on land use and energy, mineral, and water resources.

I have found the Geological Survey to be a very user-friendly organization. In most cases your first contact will be able to answer all your questions. There are Public Inquiries Offices in the downtowns of major cities, designed for walk-in custom-

ers but accessible by mail or phone. The USGS National Center in the D.C. area also has a PIO and can direct you to your local center as well as answer your questions. Check your own phone book under U.S. Government, Department of the Interior, for local offices. If you don't know what to ask for, start by asking for these **free** publications:

Catalog of maps — All the kinds of maps the Survey produces or distributes are described, illustrated, and accessed. This is in a poster format, very attractively designed and illustrated. If it is to be displayed on a bulletin board, get two copies so the back and front can both be seen.

Catalog of Cartographic Data — Things you didn't know you could get, like software for cartographic computer programs, advance prints of topographic maps in progess, land use (culture) and land cover (nature) maps for much of the U.S., access to the National High Altitude Photography Program — the USA from 40,000 feet.

Guide to Obtaining USGS Information (Circular 900). All the addresses and phone numbers you'll need to know. The various products are named but not described so you ought to have some idea of what you're looking for, derived from the above two publications. —Don Ryan

Public Inquiries Office, U.S.G.S., 503 National Center, Room 1-C-402, 12201 Sunrise Valley Drive, Reston, VA 22092; (703) 648-6892

Map Link

Suppose you're setting off on a trip to the mountains of Mexico and want a map for the region you're going to. You know that there are 1:250,000 scale topographic maps available, but you can't find any locally. Just imagine how useful it would be to be able to pick up the phone and order the map you need with only the coordinates of the town you're visiting, no catalog number or other information necessary. Such a service is offered by Maplink. They also have an impressive World Map Directory from all around the world, with short but detailed comments on each series that display a true love for the subject. They seem to carry the

6840 YUGOSLAVIA: GENERAL

Freytag Berndt's double sided map of Yugoslavia provides an amazing amount of road and village information. Included with the map are insets of the entire coast of Yugoslavia at 1:275,000. No other map compares!

Yugoslavia	FB YUG	$7.95	600K	1985
991, Yugoslavia	M 991	$4.95	1M	nd

largest scale and most informative available for both towns and regions. The mail-order service was excellent. —Jonathan Evelegh

The World Map Directory; Aaron Maizlish and William S. Hunt; 1990; 278 pp.; **$29.95** postpaid from: Maplink, 529 State Street, Santa Barbara, CA 93101; (805) 965-4402

Compasses

A good source for compasses is REI (Quality Outdoor Gear and Clothing). Catalog **free** from: REI, P.O. Box 88125, Seattle, WA 98138-2125, (800) 426-4840.

One Day Celestial Navigation

What if you miss Hawaii? It's just that sort of fear that drives folks to involve themselves with the traditional weighty volumes and complex worksheets that make Hegel seem simple by comparison. But you needn't fret. This skinny book gives you what you need to know to fetch Diamond Head, though you may have to do a bit of unprofessional dog-legging to do so. You'll be successful, which is more than you can be sure of using more complex techniques you don't fully understand. The methods shown here are simple enough, but you will have to make that "one day" a disciplined one. Two people learning together will help, and that'll give you the advantage of having more than one person aboard with navigation skills — a useful safety factor. The author also takes you through the steps for checking the accuracy of the ship's compass, and what to do if your clock stops. If you're going out of sight of land, all this is stuff you need to know. This book is about as simple a course as you're likely to find.
—JB

One Day Celestial Navigation (For Offshore Sailing), Otis S. Brown; 1984; 133 pp.; **$9.95** ($11.95 postpaid) from: Liberty Publishing, 440 South Federal Hwy, Suite 202, Deerfield Beach FL 33441; (305) 360-9000 ✱WEA

Celestaire

Navigation is still one of the basic skills of the true wanderer. There is discipline involved, and penalties for lack of it. There are instruments that must be mastered. Here's a selection of the instruments (traditional and electronic) and associated instruction. There's a kind of immanence to it all that you may find, as I do, strangely thrilling. —JB

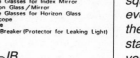

SEXTANT COMPONENTS

A)Frame   E)Tangent Screw
B)Limb   F)Release
C)Arc   G)Micrometer Drum
D)Index Arm   H)Vernier
I)Index Mirror
J)Shade Glasses for Index Mirror
K)Horizon Glass / Mirror
L)Shade Glasses for Horizon Glass
M)Telescope
N)Handle
O)Light Breaker (Protector for Leaking Light)

Celestaire (Marine and Air Navigation Instruments); Catalog **free** from: Celestaire 416 S. Pershing, Wichita, KS 67218 (800) 727-9785; in KS (316) 686-9785

The NC-77 is a permanently pre-programmed celestial navigation calculator. An easy to understand dialog system provided by the digital display tells you what to do step by step. This allows the infrequent navigator to begin using it without reviewing procedures. Values of latitude and longitude may be entered directly in degrees and minutes without the need for decimalization. Its basic navigation functions include:

- Sight Reduction
- Almanac for sun and stars (until 1999)
- Fix Computation
- Dead Reckoning
- Star Identification
- Refraction

In addition to a full range of scientific function keys, it has two user-accessible memories that can be used with a number of navigation programs. It is powered by four type-A batteries. An optional Nicad pack, DC adapter/charger (12-volt), and an AD adapter/charger is available. The calculator comes in a handsome felt-lined wooden case with comprehensive instruction manual.

NC-77 CALCULATOR

NC-77 #3001	$324

Land Navigation

We've run reviews of many "Where are we?" books over the years, but this one is easily the most clear and easy to use. Absolutely everything is explained in a way that does not subtly assume that you have a degree (so to speak) in advanced trigonometry. All those little symbols you see on maps are discussed, and after 25 years of trail experience I finally found out what those yellow square markers you see along trails are for. He even gets into navigation with an altimeter! And there's a good chapter on finding your way by the stars — even in the Southern Hemisphere in case you end up in New Zealand. All this stuff is presented in a commendably relaxed way that makes it easy to remember without the book. A sample topo map is included so you can try things in the safety of your own home. It'll be a long time before someone does this subject better. —JB

Land Navigation Handbook (The Sierra Club Guide to Map and Compass); W.S. Kals; 1983; 230 pp.; **$9.95** ($12.95 postpaid) from: Sierra Club Books, 730 Polk Street, San Francisco, CA 94109; (415) 923-5500 ✱WEA

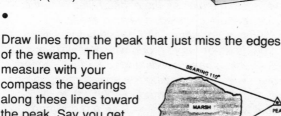

●

Draw lines from the peak that just miss the edges of the swamp. Then measure with your compass the bearings along these lines toward the peak. Say you get 60° and 110°.

You can approach the peak from any direction and be certain to avoid the swamp as long as the peak bears less than 60° or more than 110° from you. You can see from this drawing that you'd pass North of the swamp when the bearing is more than 110°.

● Strategy: If you can only obtain an accurate latitude, you must modify the approach to your island. You sail down (or up) to the latitude of the island. You intentionally miss it to the west (or east) by sixty miles. This is a dog leg, or "landfall" technique. Upon arrival at the island's latitude you will know in which direction to turn to arrive at the island. You will not know exactly how far you are from the island, but you will be certain to hit the island.

"Intentional Miss"
This assures you that Bermuda will be to the east of you.

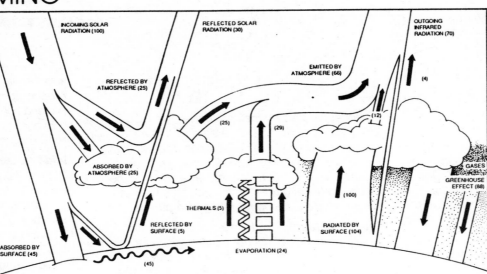

GLOBAL WARMING — the "Greenhouse Effect" — is hotly debated. The idea that human air pollutants might cause the Earth to warm is a century old. The high temperatures and drought of 1988 coincided with climatologist James Hansen, director of the NASA Goddard Institute For Space Studies, saying before a subcommittee of the Senate that he was very certain global warming was at hand. The ensuing controversy attracted the media, and we entered Stephen Schneider's era of "Mediarology."

The papers reviewed here are only a sampler from a wide spectrum of views. At one extreme one finds the "It's a Hoax" and the "Not to Worry" crowd. These writers tend to focus on some narrow aspect, for example the last 10 years of weather data, or confine their analysis to to impacts of CO_2 while ignoring other greenhouse gasses. At the other extreme are the "Worst-casers." Much of their fodder comes from taking the upper range of computer models, sometimes coupling this with the most drastic recent weather events. A minority — getting smaller — holds that an ice age will result from atmospheric pollution.

The majority view is that global warming is likely, but with much uncertainty about when, where, and what the impacts might be. Even if 1990 is another record year, it won't suffice as scientific proof.

My view is that the greenhouse effect must be taken seriously because if emerging trends become destiny, we won't be able to apply a quick fix to the ultimate commons, our atmosphere. To decide to do nothing is to decide something: business as usual. Tucked inside wait-and-see postures is the hope that things may not be so bad after all. Maybe, but I wouldn't bet the planet on it!

And I will be sorry if Global Climate Change headlines obscure solid information on smog, ozone increases at ground level, ozone depletion in the stratosphere, acid precipitation and adverse health effects from dirty air, all begging for action now.

—Dr. Jean A. Merriman, Professor
School of Environmental Studies and Planning
Sonoma State University, Rohnert Park, CA 94928

The Greenhouse Trap

Changing the basic human actions which cause air pollution means changing the basic human being, for there is nothing so fundamental about us as energy use, agriculture, and having children (the population factor). First in a series of World Resources Institute Guides to the Environment, The Greenhouse Trap is a very well-written book which provides a good balance between doubt and worst-case scenarios. Brief side-bar summaries on such topics as the ozone holes help the reader get up-to-speed in related areas. WRI (1709 New York Ave., NW, Washington, DC 20006) is a non-profit group which seeks ways to meet basic human needs and to nurture economic growth without degrading the environment and so half of the book is devoted to solutions to the global warming problem. —Jean A. Merriman

The Greenhouse Trap, Francesca Lyman; 1990; 190 pp.; **$9.95** ($12.70 postpaid) from: Beacon Press, 25 Beacon Street, Boston, MA 02108; (800) 631-8571 ✳WEA

(Above) The earth's radiation energy balance, which controls the way the greenhouse effect works, can be seen graphically here. The numbers in parentheses represent energy as a percentage of the average solar constant — about 340 watts per square meter — at the top of the atmosphere. Note that nearly half the incoming solar radiation penetrates the clouds and greenhouse gases to the earth's surface. These gases and clouds re-radiate most (i.e., 88 units) of the absorbed energy back down toward the surface. This is the mechanism of the greenhouse effect. —*Global Warming*

Global Warming

A look at the global warming issue through the eyes of a noted scientist in the field of climatology, Stephen Schneider.

Departing from the cloisters of science, he has appeared on television and authored non-technical books such as this one. In this book's dedication to his own children he expresses the hope "that their generation will be more creative in adapting to the greenhouse century than mine has been in preventing it." He is relentless in pointing out the scientific uncertainties, and there are many. Still, he brings us to the crux of the matter of how important is it? "A degree or two temperature change is not a trivial number in global terms and it usually takes nature hundreds to thousands of years to bring it about on her own. We may be doing that in decades. . . . Humans are putting pollutants into the atmosphere at such a rate that we could be changing the climate on a sustained basis some ten to hundred times faster than nature has since the height of the last ice age." —Jean A. Merriman

Global Warming: Are We Entering the Greenhouse Century? Stephen Schneider; 1989: 317 pp.; **$18.95** ($21.95 postpaid) from: Sierra Club Books, 730 Polk St., San Francisco, CA 94109; (415) 923-5500 ✳WEA

•

In 1989, the first "carbon offset" project was launched with considerable fanfare. The equivalent of the 15 million tons of carbon that will be emitted over 40 years from a coal-burning power plant built in Connecticut by Applied Energy Services will be absorbed by an enormous woodlot in a combined forestry and agricultural project in Guatemala. The energy company donated $2 million to this maiden effort, and CARE, the Peace Corps, the U.S. Agency for International Development, and the Guatemalan Forestry Department are also chipping in. Altogether, some 52 million trees will be planted in what the *National Geographic* calls "the most sensible and imaginative program yet conceived to put the industrialized world's money where its mouth is."

Least-Cost Energy

This book attracted little notice when it appeared in 1982 — the political climate on both sides of the fence made its importance hard to see. Too bad. If this analysis had been taken seriously then, we'd have a decade's experience solving the energy and pollution problems that are now so popular. The analysis is still valid, and continues to be the strongest credible argument for energy efficiency as the most effective means of reducing undesirable atmospheric changes. Equally important, nuclear power is shown to be an ineffective option despite finding new favor with certain prominent scientists. Indeed, the Lovinses and their colleagues show that investment in nuclear power would actually worsen global warming! As with everything published by Rocky Mountain Institute (see p. 57), this assertion is backed by solid facts and specific, realistic recommendations for action. I consider their tough talk damn near irrefutable, despite squeaks of protest from the opposition. Now we know what to do. —JB

Least-Cost Energy: Solving the CO_2 Problem Amory B.Lovins, L. Hunter Lovins, FlorentinKrause, Wilfrid Bach; 1989 (2nd ed.); 184 pp.; **$30** postpaid from: Rocky Mountain Institute 1739 Snowmass Creek Road Snowmass, CO 81654-9199

The Impacts of Global Warming On California

The California Energy Commission was mandated to carry out an assessment of the impacts of global warming on the state. The interim report does an outstanding job of bringing a global issue down to the level where we live. It is an excellent example for those states and regions which have yet to look down the road at the what-ifs of global warming. The report evaluates a range of projected impacts, both beneficial and adverse, upon water prices, agricultural output, investment risk, infrastructure needs, energy prices, transportation systems, and balance of trade. Good graphics make complex processes understandable. Such advance planning seems like taking out an insurance policy for something we hope won't happen and it seems prudent to consider the risks from global warming in this light. The politically sensitive final report has been delayed and may emerge in a watered down form. However, the very useful Interim Report is available.
—Jean A. Merriman

The Impacts of Global Warming on California (An Interim Report); California Energy Commission; 1989; 148 pp.; **free** (1 copy) from: California Energy Commission, Publication Office 1516 9th Street, Sacramento, CA 95814; (916) 324-3016

Typical Northern Sierra Watershed

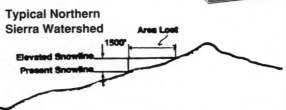

AREA LOST DUE TO SNOWPACK ELEVATION

The Coevolution of Climate and Life

Ah weather. It can irritate us so . . . being beyond our control. Yet, in one lifetime, we get so little feel for its true extremes — little Ice Ages, Greenhouse Effects, el Niño. These are but the passing children of biospheric evolution or rather a coevolution in which life itself helps steer the fickle unknown forces of climate. This tome analyzes the speculations of "new primitive" scientists trying to understand the sun god's spots or the heavens' and oceans' affinity for dancing carbon molecules. It covers four billion years and focuses on the I'm-going-to-scare-you issues of aerosols, nuclear winter, overheating, acid rains and droughts. It is, at times, tainted by a humorless, clawing "human-ism" and a college-sophomore attitude toward topics it cannot fully comprehend (history, Marx-ism, capitalism, the Gaia Hypothesis). But there is no other book so readable and complete. You leave it linked — by each breath, each eddy current created by your waving arm, each belch of your automobile — to the huge involvement of at-mosphere, planet spin, and life.

—Peter Warshall

The Coevolution of Climate and Life
Stephen H. Schneider & Randi Londer; 1984; 576 pp.; **$25** ($29.50 postpaid) from: Sierra Club Books, 730 Polk Street, San Francisco, CA 94109 (415) 923-5600 ✱ WEA

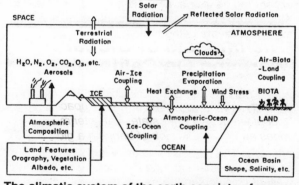

The climatic system of the earth consists of many interacting subsystems: the atmosphere, the oceans, the cryosphere (ice and snow), the bio-sphere (biota and their environment plus humans and their activities), the bottoms of the oceans, and some of the solid material below land and oceans. The interacting components of these subsystems are called the *internal* climate sys-tem, whereas those forces that drive the climate system, but are not an internal part of that system, are known as *external* forcing or *boundary* conditions.

Spacious Skies

"Whaddaya readin', JB?" "Cloud book." "One of those how-to-tell-one-type-cloud-from-another handbooks?" "Naw, those always have pictures that don't match what I'm looking at in the sky, and their weather predictions aren't much either." "What's so great about the one you're reading then — it's just cloud pictures and a lot of words like the others?"

Because it's extreme, it's written by people who are passionate about clouds. And it's not just identification, it's why the clouds look like they do and what made them that way, and what they're likely to do next, and there are a bunch of sequen-tial photos of clouds growing and swirling around, and generally acting like clouds really act when they're not in a book. But best is that this book is of a sort that I hold in high esteem; the authors are totally into the subject, and take you with them as they learn about stuff we normally just sort of let go by without much thought. They actually chase clouds by car and aircraft, madly photographing (much in color) and note-taking. The result is

Weather for the Mariner

I've been watching weather books since I was an obsessive teen. This one surpasses all the others as far as I'm concerned. It's sufficiently and fascinatingly technical without interrupting the comprehensive clarity that makes it so unique. It is a working text for people who live or die by the weather. No reason to limit its use to mariners.

—Stewart Brand

Weather for the Mariner
William J. Kotsch
1983; 315 pp.
$19.95 ($22.95 postpaid)
from: Book Order Dept.
U.S. Naval Institute
2062 Generals Hwy.
Annapolis, MD 21401
(800) 233-8764
(301) 224-3378 ✱ WEA

The Morning Glory. The fanciful name of this phenomenon conveys the feeling of elation which its passage arouses, but it does not begin to describe what it actually is. The near-est to it is the tidal bore on a river, which some-times comes as a single rather sudden rise in level, but on other oc-casions it is followed by a series of waves of de-creasing size.

So far it has only been reported in Australia, al-though in several different places there. It is par-ticularly interesting because it appears to travel large distances without much change in form: it is not dispersed like gravity waves.

Spacious Skies
Richard Scorer & Arjen Verkaik; 1989; 192 pp.
$35 ($37.50 postpaid)
from: Sterling Publishing Co., Inc., 387 Park Avenue South New York, NY 10016-8810 (800) 367-9692 ; in NY (212) 532-7160 ✱ WEA

probably more than you really wanted to know, but you'll likely be left truly appreciating clouds in a way you never did before. I read the handsome book cover to cover, fascinated. —JB

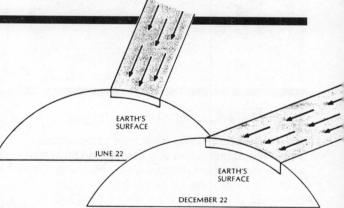

It is perhaps surprising to some individuals that the sun is nearest the earth during the Northern Hemisphere winter. Consequently, it is not dis-tance from the sun that is responsible for the difference in temperature during the different seasons. The reason centers on the altitude of the sun in the sky and the length of time the sun remains above the horizon. During the summer months, the sun's rays are more nearly vertical. Consequently, they are much more concentrated, as shown here. And since the sun is above the horizon more than half the time, heat is being added by absorption for a longer period than it is being lost by radiation. Astronomically, the sea-sons begin with the equinoxes and solstices. But meteorologically, they vary from place to place around the earth.

Wind & Weather Catalogue

You'd expect a selection of high quality weather instruments, and you won't be disappointed. Less expected is a remarkable array of sundials, including some very classy traditional designs. And then there are the weathervanes — including those huge, expensive, gorgeous three-dimen-sional copper birds and animals. All sharpen your awareness of the patterns, and remind you that there's no such thing as bad weather. —JB

Wind & Weather
Catalogue **free** from:
Albion Street Watertower
P.O. Box 2320
Mendocino, CA 95460
(707) 937-0323

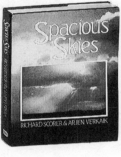
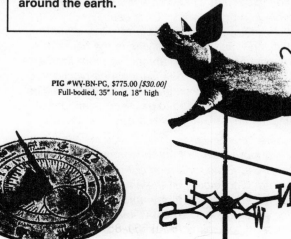

The west coast of Borneo.

The Home Planet

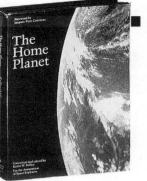

Here are 150 awesome color photographs of Earth from space (most previously unpublished) chosen from NASA and Soviet archives. The comments from the world's astronauts and cosmonauts are translated into the nine languages in which this book has been simultaneously published. Editor Kevin W. Kelley (no relation to our own Whole Earth Review's Kevin Kelly) has done us a great service by seeing this difficult international enterprise through to such a beautiful result. Most readers come away with a new feeling of what it means to say "our Earth." —JB

The Home Planet
Kevin W. Kelley; 1988; 149 pp.; **$8** (originally reviewed at $50; the publisher is closing out the stock) ($11.50 postpaid) from: Addison-Wesley, 1 Jacob Way Reading, MA 01867 (800) 447-2226 ✱ WEA

The Greenpeace Book of Antarctica (A new view of the seventh continent), John May 1989; 192 pp.; **$24.95** ($26.95 postpaid) from: Doubleday & Co., P.O. Box 5071, Des Plaines, IL 60017-5071 (800) 223-6834 ✱ WEA

The Greenpeace Book of Antarctica

The "Whole Antarctica Catalog" from Greenpeace. It's a wide-focus look at the Southern Continent — the land itself, its wildlife and the human impact of 200 years of exploration. What's fascinating about Antarctica is that it has become a laboratory where studies improving our scientific understanding of how the planet works are taking place amid a political experiment in international cooperation. How the experiment works, if, indeed, it's even possible, is of great significance in our changing world. With this volume, Greenpeace has made an important contribution to the process.

—David Burnor

Just passing through: A whalers' oil tank, now disused, forms the backdrop to a group of tourists visiting Deception Island. Chile has recently been expanding its tourist activities, flying tourists into King George Island where a hotel, bank and supermarket are being built.

The Big Outside

This book does with words what a satellite does with photographs, it lets you see the land whole, without man-made boundaries and divisions. The subject is wilderness in the continental U.S. — how much is left, and where. The criteria are roadless areas of at least 100,000 acres in the West and 50,000 acres for the East, and 368 of them are described and listed by state.

The last person to make this kind of inventory was the pioneering conservationist Bob Marshall in 1936. Since then, everyone has only been looking at and arguing over the pieces — this is Forest Service land, that's private, over there is BLM and back in those mountains is a Wilderness Area. Plenty of categories, lots of bureaucracies, but through the years an ever-shrinking pie.

This book looks at all those pies whole, including private roadless lands. It is full of surprising loopholes, each one contributing to the shrinking pie. The authors are two of the founders of the environmental group Earth First! (see p. 106), and they make it clear that what gets announced from Washington or shown on TV is usually not what actually is happening on the land. They argue that if all this dividing and identifying in the name of Conservation is going to amount to more than a roll-call of degraded and disappearing places, accompanied by the extinction of the rare species living on them, we need to get serious about truly protecting the few large wild areas that are left.

Of course this is radical, it was back in 1936 too. But is it more than just an environmentalist pipe dream? Set aside for a moment all the politics and people and consider just the animals. The central unanswered question today among population biologists trying to maintain viable numbers of threatened species is: "How much land is

The Big Outside, Dave Foreman and Howie Wolke 1989; 458 pp.; **$19** ($21 postpaid) from: Ned Ludd Books P.O. Box 5141, Tucson, AZ 85703; (602) 628-9610 ✱ WEA

enough?" Increasingly, the answer comes back: "More than we thought." Settling that score alone (assuming we really want to) may mean that the geographical prescriptions given in this book turn out to be more like blueprints, and less like fantasies.

—Richard Nilsen
[Suggested by Martha Weaver-Britell]

•

The livestock industry has probably done more basic ecological damage to the Western United States than has any other single agent. . . . In non-timbered areas, most "developments" on public lands — roads, fences, juniper chainings, windmills, pipelines, stock tanks and the like — benefit only a few ranchers.

Vast areas of the Great Basin and Southwest could be designated as Wilderness were it not for the livestock industry. Throughout the rural West, public lands ranchers are the most vocal and militant lobby against environmental protection or Wilderness designation. Sadly, designation of an area as Wilderness or National Wildlife Refuge does not restrict commercial livestock grazing. Even some National Parks are legally grazed. Of course, nearly all National Forest, BLM and state lands in the West are grazed by domestic livestock.

To make this situation more outrageous, all this is done to produce only 2% of the nation's red meat; 98% of US beef production is on private lands, mostly in the Eastern states. . . . All in all, the

Forest Service and BLM lose about $100 million a year with their grazing programs — and this does not count the costs of environmental degradation, which run into the hundreds of millions of dollars annually. The 22,000 ranchers with BLM or FS grazing leases are among the most accomplished welfare chiselers in the nation (perhaps only military contractors are more facile at living on the public dole).

•

McCormick 89,000 acres

Designated McCormick Wilderness Area

(Ottawa NF) **16,850** ac
Escanaba River State Forest roadless **8,320** ac
Private roadless **64,000** ac

Description: Upper Peninsula of Michigan east of L'Anse. The Sierra Club says, "McCormick is probably the best and largest living example of the original Michigan forest . . . Climax white pine and maple forests dominate the area . . . Disturbance in the area is minimal." Rocky outcroppings tower over lakes, streams and wetlands frequented by Moose, Black Bear, Bobcat, River Otter, Common Loon, Bald Eagle, Pileated Woodpecker and possibly Gray Wolf. The cascading Yellow Dog River is among the most pristine streams in the Upper Midwest and has a thriving trout population.

Status: The private lands and Escanaba State Forest are open to logging, but there is not much activity at this time. Protection of these roadless lands adjacent to the designated Wilderness, including acquisition of the private land, should be a high priority for conservationists. A dirt road is all that separates this area from the Huron Mountain roadless area. By closing it and several other old logging roads, a 200,000 acre Wilderness could be established.

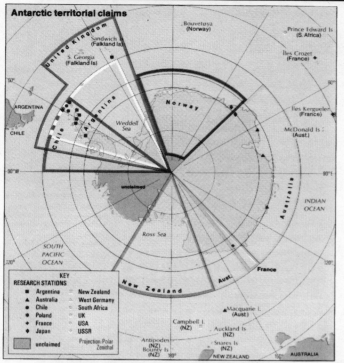

Antarctic territorial claims

KEY
RESEARCH STATIONS
■ Argentina   ● New Zealand
▲ Australia   ○ West Germany
▲ Chile   ○ South Africa
● Poland   ■ UK
◆ France   ● USA
◆ Japan   ● USSR
[ ] unclaimed   Projection: Polar Zenithal

The Times Atlas and Encyclopaedia of the Sea

Alastair Couper, Ed.;
1990; 272 pp.; **$65**
postpaid from: J.B. Lippincott, Route 3, Box B,
Hagerstown, MD 21740; (800) 638-3030 ✱ WEA

The Times Atlas and Encyclopaedia of the Sea
is a pure joy to behold. A comprehensive understanding of the ocean environment has become
critical as we learn more about the limits of the
once-boundless sea. **The Times Atlas** is well-
written, graphically pleasing, and logically organized — it includes ship-borne commerce, shoreline
development, pollution sources, military strategy,
sea law, etc. —David Burnor

The Beaches Are Moving • Living with the Shore Series

Beachfront buildings must be considered temporary. If you don't agree, **The Beaches Are Moving**
will probably change your mind. Oh, you can slow
the process down, probably, and the authors tell
you how. They also give good advice on locating
and strengthening your structure. But realism in
real estate must eventually defer to realism of the
physics of wind, wave, and sand. Predicting when
a shoreline change will occur isn't easy; predicting
whether it'll change is: it will.

The **Living with the Shore** series may include the
shore you know — there are fourteen books now.

A typical title, **Living with the California Coast**,
analyzes every beach from Oregon to Mexico,
showing (with maps) which are most and least
stable, what the local problems may be, the basic
geology, erosion patterns, wave action and the frequency and speed of the changes. Lots of photographs, many taken of specific locations at different dates, drive home the inevitability of natural
forces that operate despite the dreams of property
owners and the assurances of land sellers. Each
book in the series also presents most of the basic
information (and many of the same illustrations) as
the more general **The Beaches Are Moving**. If
you plan to buy or build near a shore, your research starts with these books. —JB

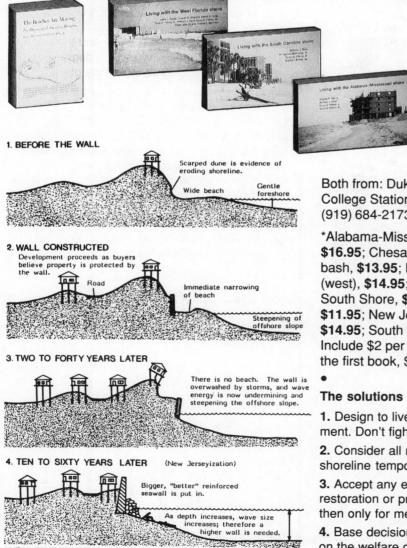

1. BEFORE THE WALL

Scarped dune is evidence of
eroding shoreline.
Wide beach   Gentle
              foreshore

2. WALL CONSTRUCTED
Development proceeds as buyers
believe property is protected by
the wall.
Road
Immediate narrowing
of beach
Steepening of
offshore slope

3. TWO TO FORTY YEARS LATER
There is no beach. The wall is
overwashed by storms, and wave
energy is now undermining and
steepening the offshore slope.

4. TEN TO SIXTY YEARS LATER (New Jerseyization)
Bigger, "better" reinforced
seawall is put in.
As depth increases, wave size
increases; therefore a
higher wall is needed.

ULTIMATE RESULTS: Development is behind wall, no beach is available, and
the sea floor is cluttered with fallen walls and groins.

**The saga of a seawall. —*Living with the South
Carolina Shore***

The Beaches Are Moving
(The Drowning of America's
Shoreline), Wallace Kaufman
and Orrin H. Pilkey, Jr.; 1983;
330 pp.; **$12.95** ($14.95
postpaid)

**Living with the Shore
Series,** Orrin H. Pilkey, Jr.
and William J. Neal, Editors;
(see * for prices)

Both from: Duke University Press, Box 6697,
College Station, Durham, NC 27706
(919) 684-2173 ✱ WEA

*Alabama-Mississippi, **$14.95**; California,
$16.95; Chesapeake, **$12.95**; Currituck-Cala-
bash, **$13.95**; Florida (east), **$14.95**; Florida
(west), **$14.95**; Lake Erie, **$14.95**; Long Island's
South Shore, **$14.95**; Louisiana, **$11.95**; Maine,
$11.95; New Jersey, **$14.95**; Puget Sound,
$14.95; South Carolina, **$14.95**; Texas, **$14.95**.
Include $2 per copy for postage and handling for
the first book, $.95 each additional title.
●

The solutions

1. Design to live with the flexible coastal environment. Don't fight nature with a "line of defense."

2. Consider all man-made structures near the
shoreline temporary.

3. Accept any engineering scheme for beach
restoration or preservation as a last resort, and
then only for metropolitan areas.

4. Base decisions affecting coastal development
on the welfare of the public rather than the minority of shorefront property owners.

5. Let the lighthouse, beach cottage, motel, or hot
dog stand fall when its time comes.

Plastics in the Ocean

Oil spills make headlines. As do the occasional
beach closures due to syringes and other medical
wastes washing ashore. But any beach visitor
knows that these are just some of the more
dramatic forms of ocean pollution. High tides bring
in a harvest of plastic trash: six-pack holders,
styrofoam pellets, plastic bags, tampon applicators
and more. Amidst the garbage on the sand are the
carcasses of some of the victims of these floating
killers. Fish and diving birds tangled in abandoned
nets; sea lions strangled, or nearly decapitated, by
six-pack rings; sea turtles and seals suffocated by
plastic sheeting and bags.

The sources of this pollution range from commercial fishing fleets to offshore trash dumping from
cargo ships and pleasure boats to overflow from
land-based disposal sites. Here are some resources you can use to educate yourself and your
community about the problem and what you can
do to help. —David Burnor

NOAA Marine Debris Information Offices
(Books, reports, coloring books, posters and
banners for community involvement)

West Coast:
312 Sutter Street, Suite 606, San Francisco
CA 94108; (415) 391-6204

East Coast:
1725 DeSales Street NW
Washington, DC 20036
(202) 429-5609

**Pacific Marine Fisheries
Commission**
Marine Debris Project
950 NW 10th
Newport, OR 97365
(503) 265-3262

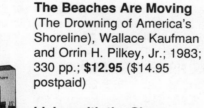

The Society of the Plastics Industry
1275 K Street NW, Suite 400, Washington, DC
20005; (202) 371-5200

Oceanic Society Expeditions

The Oceanic Society has been sponsoring educational natural history travel for almost 20 years. A
strict code of ethics minimizes unfortunate effects
of the visitors; indeed, travelers participate in
ongoing studies intended to improve matters. You
can study dolphins (and join their cavorting) in the
Bahamas. There will be a coral study in 1991. Not
all expeditions are strictly Oceanic; one of the most
interesting visits the rainforests of Peru's Manu
National Park. With respected experts as guides,
these expeditions are among the best learn-in-
stead-of-just-gawk available. —JB

Oceanic Society Expeditions; Information **free**
from: Fort Mason Center, Building E
San Francisco, CA 94123; (800) 326-7491

See Also . . . Ecotourism, pages 102-103.

✱WEA — Available from Whole Earth Access, see p. 2.

A Forest Journey

*John Perlin co-authored **A Golden Thread**, a history of the use of solar energy. Like that book, **A Forest Journey** began as an article in our magazine ("Running Out," CQ #37, p. 18). Perlin discovered that people historically turned to the sun to heat houses and water only when they ran out of wood. Working backwards, in this new book he looks at wood, from Bronze Age Mesopotamia up to America in the 1880s.*

For that vast span of time wood was the equivalent of oil, natural gas and uranium all rolled into one. Not only did all civilizations heat and cook with it, they also made weapons, wheels (including water wheels that allowed desert agriculture to blossom), merchant ships and navies out of trees. Today we speak of "strategic metals," but formerly it was the forests that were strategic. In this breezy history you can watch empires rise and fall based on who controls the woods, how long they last, who they get traded to and what does or doesn't get built out of them. Trees, it turns out, bear an inverse relationship to civilization, and vanishing forests are as old as the denuded hills.

—Richard Nilsen

A Forest Journey, John Perlin; 1989; 276 pp.; **$19.95** postpaid from:
W.W. Norton, 500 5th Ave.
New York, NY 10110
(212) 354-5500 ✱WEA

This is probably the earliest drawing depicting a reforestation project. It "shews how vacant forests and woods which have been cut down, may be replanted by their roots. . ." Portion *A* shows "(a) place where trees have been felled and where there are only stumps to be extirpated"; *B* depicts "a long and thick root which is sawed into many pieces"; *C-F* describe the process for preparing the root for replanting on the hills to the right.

•

The need to conserve wood stimulated the development of a lively market for recycled glass in the first century A.D. Poor Romans scoured the city for broken glass. The glass recyclers of Rome would trade their booty for sulfur matches and scrap dealers subsequently sold the used glass to local workshops. Artisans had to heat the recycled glass only moderately to turn out new glass products instead of to the higher temperatures required by furnaces producing glass from raw materials.

Culinary experts shared their expertise with housewives to show how they, too, could cut fuel bills and still prepare delicious meals. For example, one authority suggested adding stalks of wild fig while cooking beef, permitting the meat to be boiled to the desired soft texture with a great saving in fuel.

The more we begin to understand how forests function as ecological systems, the clearer it becomes that modern forestry is akin to mining, not resource management, and precludes any hope of sustainability.
—Richard Nilsen

The Redesigned Forest • Forest Primeval • From the Forest to the Sea

The more we begin to understand how forests function as ecological systems, the clearer it becomes that modern forestry is akin to mining, not resource management, and precludes any hope of sustainability. In the forefront of scientists doing the fieldwork to back up these kinds of assertions is Chris Maser. He writes books in a style equivalent to an ecological food web — a careful look at process via a tangential combination of hard science, history and humanistic psychology.

***The Redesigned Forest** contrasts the ecological needs of a forest with current short-rotation forestry practices. If you want to understand his basic argument, start here. **Forest Primeval** is a biography of an ancient forest in Oregon, from its beginnings in the year 988 up to the present. **From the Forest to the Sea** is an example of the fieldwork Maser was doing at the Bureau of Land Management before he left to become a private consultant. It examines what happens to the biomass of fallen trees, in the forest, in the watershed, and even on the seabed miles off the Oregon coastline.* —Richard Nilsen

The Redesigned Forest
Chris Maser; 1988; 234 pp.
$12.95 ($14.45 postpaid) from:
R. & E. Miles,
P. O. Box 1916
San Pedro, CA 90733
(213) 833-8856 ✱WEA

Forest Primeval
Chris Maser; 1989; 282 pp.
$25 ($29.50 postpaid) from:
Sierra Club Books
730 Polk Street
San Francisco, CA 94109
(415) 923-5600 ✱WEA

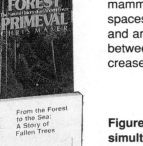

From the Forest to the Sea (A Story of Fallen Trees), Chris Maser, Robert F. Tarrant, James M. Trappe and Jerry F. Franklin
(stock #001-001-00642-4) 1988; 153 pp.
$15 (postpaid) from:
Superintendent of Documents, Government Printing Office, Washington, DC 20402-8325; (202) 783-3238

•

When we think of Nature's forest as a commodity, we treat it like one. Because we treat it like a commodity, we are trying to redesign it to become one. We take a system designed by Nature to run in 400- to 1,200-year cycles and attempt to replace it with recurring cycles of only the first 80 to

---

120 years. We do not see the forest. We are so obsessed with our small goals that we . . . redesign the forest with an instability that cannot be repaired with fertilizers, herbicides, or pesticides.

•

Decades of scientific research have concentrated on every possible cause of forest decline except that it might be the direct result of intensive plantation management based on ignorance of forest processes. The forests of central Europe are now dying . . . and we hear much about acid rain . . . .

I agree that atmospheric pollutants may well be playing a role in *Waldsterben* (the dying forest). Yet I cannot help but wonder how the cumulative effects of a century or more of intensive plantation management and use may have strained the forests of Central Europe, and thus predisposed them to the *"Waldsterben syndrome"* we see today. —*The Redesigned Forest*

•

The Douglas firs in the burn near the spring are now 250 years old and between 200 and 220 feet tall . . . .

By now, 1237, their crowns have lost much of the pyramidal form and have become rounded or somewhat flattened. And by the time they are 450 years old in 1437, their crowns will be cylindrical and resemble a bottle brush (albeit one missing many bristles). Their trunks will be clear of branches from 65 to 130 feet above the ground. . . .

The upper surfaces of the large branches will become covered with perched, organic "soil" several inches thick that will support entire communities of epiphytic plants (plants growing on other plants, in this case primarily mosses and lichens) and animals. Large branches will become the home for myriad invertebrates, as well as some birds and a few mammals. . . .

A single ancient tree can have over 60 million individual needles that have a cumulative weight of 440 pounds and a surface area of 30,000 square feet, or about 1 acre. —*Forest Primeval*

•

A fallen tree interacts with its environment through internal surface areas. A newly fallen tree is not yet a habitat for plants or most animals. But once organisms gain entrance to the interior, they consume and break down wood cells and fibers. Larger organisms — mites, collembolans, spiders, millipedes, centipedes, amphibians, and small mammals — must await the creation of internal spaces before they can enter. The flow of plant and animal populations, air, water, and nutrients between a fallen tree and its surroundings increases as decomposition continues (fig. 2.14).
—*From the Forest to the Sea: A Story of Fallen Trees*

Figure 2.14 — Fallen trees progress through two simultaneous successional processes — internal and external. —*From the Forest to the Sea: A Story of Fallen Trees*

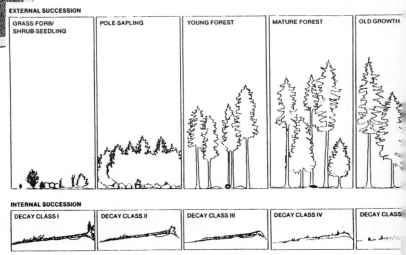

Secrets of the Old Growth Forest

How easy it is to look with scorn and frustration at the destruction of tropical rainforests today. How hard to recognize our own destruction of a comparable domestic treasure. The old-growth forest of the Pacific Northwest is Canada's and America's ancient biological wonder. Here are trees hundreds of feet high that aren't "mature" until 250 years and often live a thousand. We are destroying the last remnants of this treasure at a time when science is just beginning to understand how it functions and sustains itself as a biological system.

It's rare to find a book that instructs with as much eloquence and beauty as this one does. When information is also aesthetic — like the color photographs throughout this book — it makes a deeper impression. Peregrine Smith Books has made a business out of doing right by books on worthy subjects, and this volume is one of their best ever. —Richard Nilsen

•

As of 1988 most Americans had never even heard of old growth. Still, one wonders how many Americans besides the members of Ducks Unlimited and the Audubon Society could have defined habitat in 1932. It is interesting to note that FDR allowed Aldo Leopold to create the national wildlife

The largest trees of the Pacific Northwest old growth, redwoods commonly attain diameters of 10 feet and heights of 300 feet in a narrow zone in northern California and southern Oregon. This is the greatest forest on Earth in terms of total weight of plant life — twice as massive as the tropical forests. All but 4 percent has been logged off since the nineteenth century.

Secrets of the Old Growth Forest
David Kelly and Gary Braasch; 1988; 128 pp.
$15.95 ($17.95 post-paid) from: Peregrine Smith Books, P.O. Box 667, Layton UT 84041 (801) 544-9800 ✱ WEA

refuge system purely to get the duck hunters off his back. He never intended to fund it. He put the famous editorial cartoonist Ding Darling, who was a conservative Republican, in charge of the new U.S. Fish and Wildlife Service and gave him scarcely enough money for office supplies. Darling finally tricked the president by getting a rider attached to an omnibus bill that FDR signed, unread, just as he was leaving the White House for a fishing trip. It was weeks before anyone realized that Darling's rider was a appropriation of six million dollars for Leopold's refuges.

Darling's chicanery undoubtedly saved many species from extinction. Together with the Canadian lands bought or leased by a new private organization, Ducks Unlimited, the new refuges became the basis for what is by far the greatest international conservation success story in history.

•

The best knowledge we possess suggests that a short-rotation managed forest on these soils will become increasingly expensive to maintain by the artificial means required as the nutrient levels drop. . . . There is worldwide evidence that artificial forestry simply doesn't work. In parts of Europe three short rotations have been sufficient to thoroughly deplete the forest soil; while in much of China, it has taken only two.

The Forest and the Trees: A Guide to Excellent Forestry

In 1966 the Sierra Club hired their first professional forester in order to respond to the accelerating timber harvests of the U.S. Forest Service. Gordon Robinson, the author of this book, was that man. As chief forester of the Southern Pacific Land Company, he already had a whole career's experience with forest management. He also had a collection of index cards with relevant facts and citations about good forest practices. That experience and those index cards (nearly 400 of them), plus the history and science of American forestry, and Robinson's own philosophy, are all in this book.

What is meant by "excellent" forestry is uneven-aged harvesting of trees, not mono-cropping and

not clear-cutting. For anyone owning forested land or dealing with timber companies or the Forest Service, this is an essential and welcome book.
—Richard Nilsen

•

The Forest Service was once proud to implement the principles of multiple use and did so for many years. It is still bound by law to do so under the Multiple Use-Sustained Yield Act of 1960.

However, in recent years the Forest Service has turned its back on its tradition and substituted "dominant use" — timber production — in its management of the nation's commercial timberland. Clearcutting has become the norm rather than the exception. If the agency is allowed to continue on its present course, the nation's old-growth forests will vanish forever, perhaps as soon as the end of this century. . . . And when the old

growth is gone, surely there will be a concerted effort by the timber industry to log the wilderness areas and parks as well.

Is this the direction in which we want to go? Or can we citizens, the owners of these old-growth forests, using the information in this book and others and the findings from the Forest Service's own research stations, succeed in convincing the agency to take a more prudent path?

The Forest and the Trees
(A Guide to Excellent Forestry)
Gordon Robinson
1988; 257 pp.; **$19.95** ($21.95 postpaid) from: Island Press P.O. Box 7, Covelo, CA 95428 (800) 828-1302 ✱ WEA

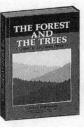

Woodland Ecology

Seventy-three percent of the forest land in the eastern United States is held by private, nonindustrial owners, according to the author. He considers the eastern hardwood forest types and explains very basic woodland ecology and discusses the options a small owner has in deciding how to maintain and use his woods. The book includes an extensive appendix of references, well annotated, and a section on growing and using wood for fuel.
—Richard Nilsen

•

(Far right) A forest managed for integrated uses. This scene shows improvement cutting on the left leaving the good immature trees to grow. Near the center a group of trees has been harvested, and sapling reproduction is occupying the opening. A

Woodland Ecology (Environmental Forestry for the Small Owner)
Leon S. Minckler; 1980; 241 pp.
$14.95 ($16.95 postpaid) from: Syracuse University Press, 1600 Jamesville Avenue, Syracuse, NY 13244-5160; (315) 443-5534 ✱ WEA

large den tree in the foreground, two beautiful white birch in the background, and a hemlock along the stream have been left. Note the piles of brush for wildlife. This is a northern hardwood forest, and trees of yellow birch, black cherry, beech, red oak, and sugar maple can be identified. The deer herd should also be managed because too many deer will consume new regeneration of forest trees. When woodlands are interspersed with fields, however, deer find much of their food,

outside the woodlands. The woodland owner lives in an idealized setting with a pile of wood for the fireplace from the thinnings and the tops of sawlog trees.

Visitors new to rainforests, primed by the purple prose that characterizes almost all writing on the subject, are often disappointed not to find the trees dripping with bizarre and brilliant flowers and the air reverberating with the cries and howls of exotic creatures. The forest does not advertise itself; the overwhelming impression is of a green stillness.
—*In the Rainforest*

The tropical humid forests, aka "rainforests," form a somber, green girdle around the equator. Shrouded in clouds, known for their steamy heat, they may support as many as one hundred species of trees in a single acre. Here is access to the fastest disappearing bioregion of the planet. —*Peter Warshall*

Rainforests

Rainforests

Rainforest Action Network

It's a pretty straightforward proposition: If we destroy our rainforests, and the millions of species of insects, birds, plants and trees that live in them, Earth will be uninhabitable, at least by people as we know us.

And we are, of course, killing the forests, at a horrendous rate. That much is beyond debate. The good news is that we can do something about it.

As with any self-cure, the first step is education. When Catherine Caufield's **In the Rainforest** appeared in 1984, most laypeople hardly knew what a rainforest was. That's changed, mightily, and due in no small part to Caufield's book (it's been translated into thirteen languages). Above all, she's a good reporter. In a hard-nosed, fact-filled, highly readable style she takes you into rainforests around the world — the Amazon, Indonesia, Malaysia, Africa. You get history, you get science, you get a close dissection of the colossally twisted workings of Big Business and the so-called "development" institutions that are the primary funders of rainforest destruction.

In the years since **In the Rainforest** was published, the numbers have changed — they're worse — but the paradigms have not. Meanwhile, our overall fund of rainforest knowledge has increased exponentially. **Lessons of the Rain-**

Rainforests

forest will bring you up to date. It's a tool chest of articles that offers the insights of biologist, ecologist, historian, anthropologist, lawyer, economist, and activist to find alternatives to rainforest destruction. Among the twenty-four contributors are Norman Myers, Anne and Paul Ehrlich, Frances Moore Lappé, and Jason Clay.

Lesson number one from the rainforest, as presented here, is: Everything is connected. We can't save the rainforests if we don't change how we live.

We change first as individuals, as consumers, by understanding how intricately our daily lives — starting with that wake-up cup of rainforest-bred coffee — intertwine with the rainforest itself, a world that at first thought might seem dark, gooey, and terribly remote. Then we change as a society. One of the hundreds of well-made points in **Lessons** is that the U. S. tax dollar, via the World Bank and such other highly secretive investment bodies as the Inter-American Development Bank, is still the principal destroyer of rainforests worldwide (though the Japanese timber industry is challenging for that position). But recently, in direct response to pressure from

Rainforests

outraged U. S. citizens, these institutions have finally begun to awaken to the environmental havoc they've caused.

Lessons of the Rainforest will teach you about the banks, about the forests themselves, about the people and plants and animals who live in them, and about what you can do to save what's left. And that may be the most important lesson: The rainforests can be saved, but only if we as individuals act. Start by reading these books, then swing into action. **Rainforest Action Network**, the U. S. wing of the World Rainforest Movement, will outfit you with all the info you need to organize a local, grassroots Rainforest Action Group, and every month their Action Alert will tell you about a rainforest crisis somewhere around the globe and what you can do personally to help remedy it.

Finally, and perhaps most importantly, try to see the rainforest for yourself. **Rainforests: A Guide to Research and Tourist Facilities** is the first reference book designed specifically for people who wish to visit a rainforest, whether to do research or simply to enjoy their beauty and biological diversity. Though it deals strictly with the New World tropics, it is quite thorough in describing locations, logistics, forest types, trail systems, and the costs of visiting sites in seven of the most accessible countries. It also tells you how to contact lodge owners and field-station directors and where to find relevant books and maps.
—*Joe Kane*

Rainforests

•

Veiled in the mysteries of ancient eras, the primeval rainforests seem to exist in a world apart, so remote that few temperate-zone dwellers have any appreciation of their value to our daily lives. Yet today and every day their disappearance is making our tax burdens heavier, the cost of living higher, the fascinating cultures of the world fewer, and the chances of survival on Earth slimmer.
—Randall Hayes, *Lessons of the Rainforest*

In the Rainforest, Catherine Caufield; 1984; 304 pp. **$11.95** ($13.75 postpaid) from: University of Chicago Press 11030 South Langley Ave. Chicago, IL 60628 (800) 621-2736 ✳WEA

Lessons of the Rainforest Suzanne Head and Robert Heinzman, Editors; 1990 275 pp.; **$14.95** ($17.95 postpaid) from: Sierra Club Books, 730 Polk Street San Francisco, CA 94109 (415) 923-5500 ✳WEA

Rainforest Action Network; $25/year (includes 12 monthly Action Alerts & 4 World Rainforest Reports) from: Rainforest Action Network 301 Broadway, Suite A San Francisco, CA 94133 (415) 398-4404

Rainforests (A Guide to Research and Tourist Facilities at Selected Tropical Forest Sites in Central and South America) James L. Castner, Ph.D 1990; 416 pp.; **$21.95** ($23.45 postpaid) from: Feline Press P.O. Box 7219, Gainesville, FL 32605 ✳WEA

•

The main canopy of the forest is formed by the crowns of the middle strata of trees, generally those from 100 to 130 feet high. A few taller trees of the forest emerge from this canopy, too widely separated to form a continuous layer. Below the canopy are the shorter trees, 50 to 80 feet high, and the relatively sparse understory, consisting of shrubs, nonwoody plants, seedlings, and young trees. The forest floor is often bare, save for a thin litter of dead leaves. Superimposed on this framework are climbers and epiphytes, plants that occupy all levels and even move back and forth from one to another. —*In the Rainforest*

•

Between 40 and 50 percent of all types of living

things — as many as five million species of plants, animals, and insects — live in tropical rainforests, though they cover less than 2 percent of the globe. . . .

A typical four-square-mile patch of rainforest, according to a report by the U. S. National Academy of Sciences, contain up to 1,500 species of flowering plants, as many as 750 species of trees, 125 species of mammal, 400 species of bird, 100 of reptile, 60 of amphibian, and 150 of butterfly, though some sites have more. Insects in tropical rainforests are so abundant and so little known that it is difficult to establish an average density. The same report cites a recent estimate that 2.5 acres might contain 42,000 species. Ten square feet of leaf litter, when analyzed, turned up 50 species of ant alone.
—In the Rainforest

•

PERU: Explorer's Inn

Logistics Guests are met at the airport in Puerto Maldonado by staff members of the Explorer's Inn. Transfer to the boat dock takes approximately 15 minutes via private bus or vehicle. Visitors then embark on a ride of approximately three hours up the Tambopata River, in a covered, outboard motor-powered boat.

Forest Type The Explorer's Inn exists in a zone between Tropical Moist and Sub-Tropical Moist

Explorer's Inn Bungalow

Forest. There is a variety of floristically very different vegetation types including swamp forest, bamboo forest, and forests on alluvial, clay, and sandy clay soils.

Facilities The Explorer's Inn and its facilities exist in a clearing of 2-3 hectares at the edge of the forest, about 100 meters in from the Tambopata River. These facilities are located within the Tambopata Wildlife Reserve, a 5,500ha ecological reserve with the status of 'special protected area' that has been set aside by the Peruvian government. . . . At one side of the lodge, accessible to visitors, was a library featuring many books on flora and fauna, tropical biology, and conservation. Files of photographs of local plants and animals taken by scientists who have worked at the Explorer's Inn were also available. . . .

All meals were taken in the lodge unless a boxed lunch or breakfast was specifically requested. . . . Food was simple and adequate. . . .

. . . Rooms for tourists at the Explorer's Inn were situated in seven bungalow buildings located on either side of the lodge. Bungalows were elevated approximately a meter off the ground, had

thatched roofs, and a wide covered veranda in front with chairs and tables. . . . Rooms were screened and no mosquito nets were provided (nor did biting insects in the room appear to be a problem). . . .

A bathroom with sink and shower were also present in each room. Both sink and shower used filtered water, originally pumped up from the river. Visitors were told that this water is acceptable for brushing one's teeth, but that it should not be swallowed or used for drinking water. . . .

Trail System There was an excellent network of approximately 30km of trails on the Tambopata Wildlife Reserve that led throughout a variety of habitats. . . .

Costs . . . based on a price list I obtained at the Explorer's Inn during January 1989, a 'jungle adventure' package of 3 days/2 nights for a group of 1-4 people cost $150 per person in the high season (April 15-December 14) and $135 per person in low season (December 15-April 14). This included land and river transportation from and to the Puerto Maldonado airport and room and board at the Explorer's Inn. . . .

Comments World record numbers of birds and of several kinds of invertebrates including butterflies, have been identified from the Tambopata Wildlife Reserve. . . . One of the most appealing features of the Tambopata Wildlife Reserve is the well marked and mapped trail system. Laminated copies of trail maps allow visitors to easily use the trail network with little fear of getting lost.
—Rainforests

Explorer's Inn Lodge Building

People of the Tropical Rain Forest

Visualize a tropical rain forest and one of the last things you're likely to imagine is people. Yet it is people — both in the tropics and in cities far away — who are building roads, logging trees and making forests disappear. By explaining how people live in these forests worldwide, this book makes the enormous problems of rain-forest preservation comprehensible. It's one of the great environmental challenges of our age, right up there with nuclear annihilation and acid rain.

From the Yanomami in Brazil to the recent transmigrant settlers in Indonesia, this book examines forest dwellers old and new. Over twenty scholars contribute essays, and the color photographs, from a Smithsonian exhibit, are first-rate.
—Richard Nilsen

People of the Tropical Rain Forest
Julie Sloan Denslow and Christine Padoch, Editors
1988; 231 pp.; **$24.95**
($26.95 postpaid) from: University of California Press, Attn.: Order Dept. 2120 Berkeley Way Berkeley, CA 94720 (800) 822-6657 ✳WEA

•

The few remaining Amazonian, Bornean, or African natives who walk softy through the forest and receive from it all their life's necessities and return to it all they have produced are a vanishing minority among today's rain-forest peoples. Many more forest folk participate in markets — local, national, or international. They fell large trees with chain-

saws; they plant crops that originated on the other side of the globe; their dreams reflect the lives of people who never saw a rain forest; and they worship gods who only walked in deserts. Nevertheless, they too are people of the rain forest; they make a living from its resources and what they do determines its fate.

•

Of all the many facets of the tropical rain forest perhaps the most difficult to grasp and the most threatened by deforestation is the diversity of its species. With only 6 percent of the world's land area the

An Iban tribesman sharpening his chainsaw during a logging operation in Sabah, Malaysia. Like badges that travelers collect, the tattoos on his back testify to his many journeys, most of them probably to logging camps.

Upon arrival, new settlers , like this family in the Brazilian state of Rondonia, put up temporary shelter using local materials. Many settlers come from distant regions such as southern Brazil and are second or third generation immigrants from Germany or Italy.

tropical moist forests are thought to house almost half its species. Although Costa Rica is smaller than West Virginia, it supports more than 12,000 species of vascular plants, 150 species of reptiles and amphibians, 237 species of mammals, 850 species of birds, and 543 species of butterflies in 3 families alone. That is more species of birds than in the United States and Canada combined. Madagascar has more than 2,000 tree species in comparison with only about 400 in all of temperate North America. Peninsular Malaysia has 7,900 plant species compared to Great Britain with 1,430 in twice the area. The Amazon and its tributaries hold more than 2,000 species of fish. E.O. Wilson counted 43 species in 23 genera of ants in a single tree in Peru's Tambopata Reserve, about equal to the entire ant fauna of the British Isles.

The Simple Act of Planting a Tree

*This is as much a book about organizational and motivational skills and fundraising as it is about tree planting. The subject is urban forestry, and the folks at TreePeople in Los Angeles have been at it since the early '70s. Their most notable achievement was planting a million trees in LA in time for the '84 Olympic Games. Trees in cities don't make it without people to protect them, so urban forests are really a living embodiment of community spirit. This book replaces their earlier book, **Planter's Guide to the Urban Forest**, and is filled with those niggly details most folks overlook when they write how-to books. The degree of organizational transparency this book documents makes it worthwhile for anyone involved with volunteer groups. — Richard Nilsen*

The Simple Act of Planting a Tree, TreePeople with Andy and Katie Lipkis; 1990; 240 pp. **$12.95** ($14.70 postpaid) from: Jeremy Tarcher 5858 Wilshire Blvd., Suite 200 Los Angeles, CA 90036 ✱WEA

•

Tree planting isn't free. In our experience, it costs $100-$300 to plant a street tree; the larger figure includes concrete cutting and well covers. It typically costs even more when it's done by local government or private contractors.

The ancient marriage of oil and wine; olive trees and vines grow together on the terraced hillsides of the island of Samos in the Aegean, punctuated with black spires of cypress.

Hugh Johnson's Encyclopedia of Trees

If the quest is for one volume on trees, this is the choice. Ace popularizer Hugh Johnson is a great organizer with a wonderfully personal writing style. Well captioned color photographs are included and there are 65 pages of A-Z tree species encyclopedia as well. An out of print classic that deserves to be reissued. —Richard Nilsen

Hugh Johnson's Encyclopedia of Trees Hugh Johnson; 1984 336 pp.; **Out of Print** Gallery Books New York, NY

Global Warming/Global Warning: Plant the Right Tree

By Marylee Guinon

In an effort to reduce greenhouse gases and compensate for global warming, it is likely that billions of seedling trees will be planted during the next few years. The dedicated people doing the planting hope the trees will thrive into maturity and act as carbon sponges to fix atmospheric carbon dioxide. Often non-native species are planted. These can naturalize and spread as escaped exotics, displacing native species and even driving some natives into extinction. But even when the correct native species are planted, the local biodiversity can still be lost or destroyed if no one is paying attention to the genetic source of the seedling tree stock.

Genetics conservation is the protection and preservation of the genetic raw materials of adaptation and evolution that species and ecosystems depend upon for long-term survival. Unlike humans, plants cannot modify or move from their environments as they contend with hardships like droughts, freezes, and even ice ages. Plants are able to survive on specific sites because they accumulate the large amounts of genes their ancestors evolved over millennia for life in those places. Many individual tree species are known to contain *several times* the genetic variation of our own human species. These huge pools of genes are like a bag of survival tricks, that can be called upon if needed during lifetimes that often last centuries.

Tree planters need to be aware that within a given species, each stand of trees contains a unique diversity of genes appropriate to that site, and that it is only this pool of genes that are likely to survive there through future hardships — such as global warming — over the lifetime of the trees and the lifetime of the species. Tree planting that ignores genetics conservation hurts two ways — it can lessen the variations that exist within trees on a site, and it can contaminate a local gene pool with ill-adapted introductions from somewhere else. The differences are hidden away in the genes; non-local seedlings and their offspring are indistinguishable to the eye from the local inhabitants.

In extreme cases, tens of thousands of seeds are collected from just a few parent trees. This can seriously reduce genetic variation and result in inbreeding and widespread mortality in the future. Conscientious tree planting requires more start-up preparation and expense, but the benefits will be realized over the long term, perhaps centuries.

Before undertaking a large-scale planting, it is worth preparing genetic conservation guidelines to insure that the planting stock is compatible with ecology and genetically appropriate to the site. A few private consultants can prepare these guidelines for public or private projects. Your local Cooperative Extension Office may be able to refer you to plant geneticists who do this work, or to agencies familiar with such guidelines.

Editor's note: Ms. Guinon is a private consultant specializing in genetic conservation. She can be contacted by writing to Sycamore Associates, 910 Mountain View Drive, Lafayette, CA 94549
—*Richard Nilsen*

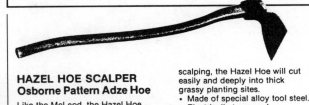

HAZEL HOE SCALPER Osborne Pattern Adze Hoe

Like the McLeod, the Hazel Hoe is another double duty tool for use during both fire season and planting season. Designed for heavy grubbing, trenching, and scalping, the Hazel Hoe will cut easily and deeply into thick grassy planting sites.
• Made of special alloy tool steel.
• Electrically tempered.
• Blade width — 6¼".
• Blade length — 5¾".
• Handle length — 36".
• Sh. weight: 5 lbs.

CAT. #	ITEM DESCRIPTION	UNIT PRICE
SFF1029	Hazel Hoe Scalper Complete w/Handle	$ 31.05

Native Seed Foundation

One of the real nitty-gritty issues in restoration work is genetic diversity within individual species. A rose ain't a rose ain't a rose, and neither is a salmon or mountain hemlock tree. These fine-grained distinctions are overlooked when, say, Yellowstone burns up and gets reseeded from airplanes hauling in seed grown two states away. Expediency and integrity are always a couple states apart anyway, so it is a real delight to find a small seed company trying to do something about this problem.

The Native Seed Foundation collects and sells seed of species native to the Pacific and Intermountain Northwest, and for their tree species at least, they tell you which national forest (or Canadian provincial park) the seed came from. Wholesale or retail, by the pound or by the ounce, here you can buy pinyon pine seed from Dixie National Forest in Utah, sub-alpine fir from Kootenai N.F. in Montana, or Douglas fir seed from five different locations. Additionally, they sell seed for over 30 native shrubs, and are also on the look-out for independent seed collectors they can buy from. —Richard Nilsen
[Suggested by Jack Monschkel]

Native Seed Foundation; Brochure **free** from: Star Route, Dept. W, Moyie Springs, ID 83845 (208) 267-7938

Global ReLeaf

The venerable American Forestry Association has caught up with the times with a national tree-planting program tied to the threat of global warming and called Global ReLeaf. They have several handbooks available, all designed to assist community tree-planting groups. One of their goals is to help get 100 million new trees growing on private land in U.S. cities by 1992.
—*Richard Nilsen*

Global ReLeaf

Titles offered: *Tree Care Handbook, Save Our Urban Trees, Gypsy Moth Handbook, Forest Effects of Air Pollution, Global ReLeaf Brochures*

Information **free** from: The American Forestry Association P. O. Box 2000, Washington, DC 20013 (202) 667-3300

TILE SPADE PLANTING SHOVEL When the contract specification says a 14" blade is required, our Tile Spade Planting Shovel is just the ticket!
• Blade length — 14"; width — 5½".
• Full blade backspine reinforcement.
• Available with or without fiberglassed, reinforced D-grip handle.
• Padded footplates.
• An excellent inspection shovel.
• Sh. Weight: 6 lbs.

International Reforestation Suppliers

This is a good source for seedling-protection tubes. No chainsaws, although there is a saw-blade-on-a-rod gizmo for harvesting Christmas trees that's bound to find its way into some bad slasher movie. Besides forestry gear, if you need to set up a weather station, fight a fire, read a map, or measure just about anything, this is a good place to find the tools.
—*Richard Nilsen*
[Suggested by Jack Monschke]

International Reforestation Suppliers Catalog **free** from: International Reforestation Suppliers, P.O. Box 5547, Eugene, OR 97405 (800) 321-1037 [in OR 345-0597]

Prairie Propagation Handbook • Prairie Restoration for the Beginner • How To Manage Small Prairie Fires

The people of the American Plains are giving up their lingering flatland inferiority complexes and falling in love — again — with their prairies. No damn mountains anywhere, but there are bluffs, coulees, and the terrain of the driftless areas the glaciers missed. No ocean, but enough springs, ponds, and muscular rivers (not to mention the Great Lakes) to make an arid Westerner think twice about the expression "green with envy." And enough ecological complexity that it is only within the last thirty years that the white man has begun to figure out just how a prairie works.

Most got turned into corn and soybeans. If more had been preserved, you wouldn't see the amount of effort being marshalled today to restore the little that remains. It's a kind of bio-regional homecoming, a collective act of reinhabitation — instead of wishing you were somewhere else, look at what used to be growing under your feet, and get it growing there again.

Here are three cheap, simple pamphlets to help. **Prairie Propagation Handbook** *describes tech-*

—Prairie Restoration for the Beginner

niques and has a monster plant listing, alphabetically by scientific name. **Prairie Restoration for the Beginner** *has a question and answer format, plus a listing of where the remnant prairies are, by state and Canadian province. And* **How To Manage Small Prairie Fires** *explains how to provide that essential ingredient — without which a prairie turns into a woodlands or a Eurasian weed-patch — without losing your eyebrows or the neighbor's goodwill. — Richard Nilsen*

[Suggested by Steve Packard]

•

The most obvious effects of a burn are easily seen. Fire rejuvenates a prairie; more plants flower, produce seed, grow taller, and are generally more robust than the previous year. Specifically, fire lengthens the growing season for most native prairie plants and shortens it for the Eurasian "weeds." Fire increases available nutrients through indirect stimulation of microbial activity in the soil, and by releasing a small amount of nutrients from the ash. Fire also controls invasion of shrubs and trees. *—How to Manage Small Prairie Fires*

•

Ecologists often advise the use of local seed and plant strains (closest ecotypes) to avoid possible loss or hybridizing of native ecotypes that have developed over many centuries and may have significant characteristics not yet understood. Also, there is the fear that the more vigorous southern strains may actually crowd out the local forbs and grasses, reducing the number and varieties in an abnormal manner. *—Prairie Propagation handbook*

How to Manage Small Prairie Fires, Wayne R. Pauly; 1985; 30 pp. $3 postpaid from: Friends of Dane County Park, 4318 Robertson Road, Madison, WI 53714 (608) 246-3896

Prairie Restoration for the Beginner, Staff of Prairie Seed Source; 1988; 32 pp. $3.95 ($5.05 postpaid)

Prairie Propagation handbook, Harold W. Rock; 1981; 74 pp. $3.95 ($5.05 postpaid)

Both from: Wehr Nature Center 9701 W. College Ave. Franklin, WI 53132

The Land Institute

The Land Institute is "Devoted to sustainable agriculture and good stewardship of the Earth." Most of their efforts are directed towards the development of cash crops that mimic natural prairie grasses, a polyculture of perennials that do not require annual plowing with its consequent loss of soil quality and quantity. Rather a perennial polyculture themselves, founders Wes and Dana Jackson have led Land experiments for fourteen years now, slowly edging the yields up to commercially useful levels. They work themselves and their crew hard — in agriculture you only get one chance per year (a reason farmers tend to be slow to accept untried ideas). Wes also keeps busy writing books (p. 45) and informing the heathen public by means of convincing addresses delivered in his inimitable, dynamic style. Despite necessarily slow progress, The Land Institute attracts wide support and interesting interns. You know in your heart that what they're trying to do is vital and ultimately, necessary.

Membership includes a subscription to **The Land Report** *where villains are discomfited, philosophy is churned, and progress is celebrated. —JB*

The Land Institute $15/year (membership includes 3 issues of The Land Report) from: The Land Institute 2440 E. Water Well Road, Salina, KS 67401

Grasslands

For an overview of the continent's grasslands — California, intermountain, desert, tallgrass, mixed, and shortgrass — get Audubon's **Grasslands**. *—Peter Warshall*

Grasslands, Lauren Brown; 1985; 606 pp.; **$16.95** ($18.95 postpaid) from: Random House, 400 Hahn Rd., Westminster, MD 21157 (800) 733-3000 ✱WEA

Black-tailed Prairie Dog

Where the Sky Began

To truly experience the prairie Midwest is to tap into a unique spirit of land and people and to feel that for a moment your soul has been touched, leaving you transformed. In **Where the Sky Began** *John Madson gives a detailed description of every aspect of the prairie Midwest: early exploration and settlement, geological influences, biological and botanical components, meteorological effects, soil classification, personal and social characteristics of early settlers as well as present day inhabitants (complete with personal anecdotes), and even a careful description of how to grow one's own backyard "prairie." The outstanding and important thing is that through all of his scientific, historical, and sociological information he allows the soul of the prairie to shine through.*
—Susan E. Sattler

•

I could never take Druids seriously. They're not in the same class as Cossacks, Zulus, Masai, Mongols, Comanches, Sioux, the highland clans of

treeless moors, and trail drovers tearing up Front Street. Grasslanders, all. There was a vein of wild exultation in such men. It wasn't just the high-protein diet, nor even that some of those men were mounted — although the horse people were among the wildest of all. I have a hunch that it was the mood of the land, stimulating its people with openness, hyperventilating them with freedom in a world of open skylines and few secrets. Such grasslanders never seemed to harbor the nasty little superstitions that flourish in fetid jungles and dank forests. Their superstitions were taller, their sagas and legends more airy and broad, and running through their cultures was a level conviction that they were the elite.

Where the Sky Began John Madson; 1982; 321 pp. **$8.95** ($11.95 postpaid) from: Sierra Club Books, 730 Polk Street, San Francisco, CA 94109; (415) 923-5500 ✱WEA

NEW JERSEY TEA

TURK'S-CAP

LUPINE

Steve Packard suggests: for a first hand prairie experience, contact your local Nature Conservancy (see review on page 111).

Prairie/Plains Journal

A true grassroots adventure, this newsletter provides insights into ongoing restoration efforts on the native prairie, riverine, and other unique native habitats of the Nebraska landscape. Artistry, botany, and history are exquisitely combined to produce a delightful creation — a bonding of nature and humans through restoration activities. —Dave Egan

Prairie/Plains Journal $10/year (2 issues) from: Prairie/Plains Resource Institute 1307 L Street Aurora, NE 68818 (402) 694-5535

See also . . . Backyard Safari, page 118.

And **The Missouri Prairie Journal**, accessed on page 33, a wonderful regional journal filled with nice graphics and good writing on prairie biology, history, preservation, and restoration.

✳WEA — Available from Whole Earth Access, see p. 2.

Streaming Wisdom

Watershed Consciousness in the 20th Century

By Peter Warshall

IN OUR TOWNS AND CITIES, two of the essential sources of life — water to drink and soil to grow food — remain hidden from our eyes. The hills and valleys are coated with asphalt, ancient streams are buried beneath housing, and soil is filler between gas, water and electric piping. Watershed consciousness is, in part, an invitation to peel off (not discard) the layer of industrial and technological activity that hides us from the water and soils of our communities. It is an invitation to reveal *where* you live and *how* your body's plumbing and, in many ways, community heart, are connected to Nature's pathways.

A watershed is a gatherer — a living place that draws the sun and the rain together. Its surface of soils, rocks, and plantlife acts as a "commons" for this intermingling of sun and water. Physically, a watershed takes many shapes. It is drawn emblematically in the shape of a teardrop or a cupped leaf or a garden trowel to depict the oblong dish-shape of the valley with its elevated hillslopes which gather runoff toward a central stream. But most watersheds do not faithfully copy the emblematic drawings. Uplifting or faulting or downwarping or layering give them a beautiful individuality. Human influences may distort or, as in city watersheds and strip-mining, completely destroy the original lay of the land. The bedrock texture of each watershed — its granite or shale, sand or limestone — holds (in a sense, cherishes) each watershed's fragile skin of soil. After the sun/water gathering has been accomplished, the watershed lets go: its unused water heading downstream or sky-up; its unabsorbed energy turning to heat or reflecting back through the atmosphere. This seasonal and daily passage of solar fire, water's flow, and the earth's metabolic breathing is as unique, in each watershed, as each human on the planet.

For humans, the watershed (and its big cousin, the river basin) is a hydraulic commons — an aquatic contract that has no escape clause. From the forested headwaters to the agricultural midstream valleys to the commercial and industrial centers at the river's mouth, good and bad news travels by way of water. Did my toilet flushing give downstream swimmers a gastrointestinal disease? Did the headwaters clearcut kill the salmon industry at the river's mouth? Did my city's need for water drain off a river and close upriver farmland that fed me fresh vegetables? Did a toxic waste dump leak into the groundwater table and poison people in the next county? Watershed consciousness is, in part, a promotional campaign to advertise the mutual concerns and needs that bind upstream and downstream, instream and offstream peoples together.

This journey is right out your window — among the hills and valleys that surround you. It is the first excursion of thought into the place you live. It is not inner geography — the continuing attempt to feel better by mapping the mysterious meanderings of our hearts and minds — nor is it whole Earth geography — the struggle to gain perspective of our place on the planet. It focuses on where your water comes from when you turn on the faucet; where it goes when you flush; what soils produce your food; who shares your water supply, including the fish and other nonhuman creatures. The watershed way is a middle way, singing a local song, somewhere close by, between Mind and Planet.

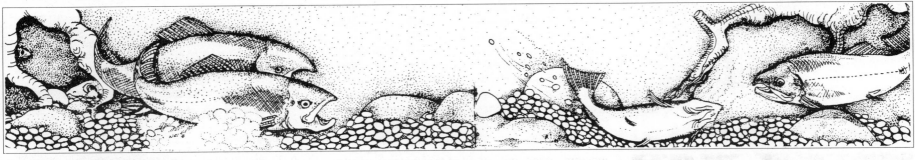

Adopt-A-Stream

The more people, the fewer fish, is how it usually goes. People tend to abuse streams — often inadvertently — with a comprehensive menu of pollutants. Free-running streams are dammed, channeled, and piped. Extensive building and pavement speed rain runoff to the point where fish eggs are washed away.

In 1981, Tom Murdoch decided to see if he could improve the situation. As an official of Snohomish County, Washington, he began a modest program of support for community groups and schools that were interested in watershed stewardship. He called it Adopt-A-Stream. To date, 31 schools and 24 community groups have joined Adopt-A-Stream programs of stream enhancement. Teacher workshops have trained more than 200 teachers in the Adopt-A-Stream principles. They, in turn, have brought Adopt-A-Stream programs to something like 20,000 students.

In 1985, Adopt-A-Stream left its government parent and became the Adopt-A-Stream Foundation. It's an international affair, including states and countries of the Pacific Rim. Already, there's a lively exchange of ideas (and students) between Washington State and the Japanese Come Back Salmon group. It seems certain that Adopt-A-Stream programs will spread across the U. S.

To hasten that process, the foundation has published a handbook, **Adopting A Stream**. *Though specifically aimed at Pacific Northwest readership, the principles will work just fine in most of the U.S. and anywhere else streams need enhancing. It starts with the basics of stream ecology and the effects of human activity, so well written and illustrated that the chapters could be used directly as a lesson plan. Then comes the real meat of the book: how to go about adopting a stream. The instructions are there, detailed right down to suggestions as to how media coverage should be arranged. Inspiring examples follow. I am particularly impressed with the effectiveness of grade-school kids — some classes have brought salmon back to streams that have been barren 25 years! The last few pages present a glossary, an extensive, up-to-date bibliography, and a list of useful names, addresses, and services.*

Adopting A Stream *is not only a great handbook, it is a model of what a handbook can be. It is a call to action. —JB*

Storm drain stencils remind citizens to protect streams.

Adopting A Stream
Steve Yates; 1988;
116 pp.; **$9.95** ($12.95 postpaid) from:
University of Washington Press
P. O. Box 50096
Seattle, WA 98145-5096
(800) 441-4115 ✳WEA

●

We tend to devalue urban streams because many of them have lost their pristine beauty, and stretches may even seem lifeless. But all of them once ran clear, and many supported healthy fish populations. City creeks offer great potential for clean-up projects, water quality improvements, or restoration of salmon runs. Few school or neighborhood adopt-a-stream projects are more satisfying than rejuvenating a damaged urban stream.

●

"Over the past eight years I've run 1200 to 1400 kids through the program," Bayes relates, "and of course that gets some of the parents involved, too. The number of fish we add to the stream is no big deal, but the educational value to the students and to the community is immense. I think the most rewarding thing of all is having ex-students calling up six or seven years later from another town, inquiring about a stream problem there and what to do about it. It's good to see the stream ethic spread." . . .

Part of F.I.S.H.'s public awareness campaign has been informing people about the impacts of dumping antifreeze and used motor oil down storm drains. Bothell High students also joined Woodinville High School students to create "Sally Sockeye" and "Cathy Coho" — two salmon costumes — to wear when explaining salmon life cycles to elementary school students. "Sally and Cathy" have also appeared at city and county council hearings to ask "Why aren't land use regulations that are intended to protect streams and watersheds being enforced?" Schultz agrees with other adopt-a-stream "parents" that "if you don't raise the awareness of the community and the interest of government agencies, planting fish is all for naught."

Cathy Coho

●

One valuable experience is to drive (or bicycle) around the stream's immediate watershed, stopping at access points, especially upstream of the stream section you plan to adopt. This tour will give you a feel for the land uses affecting the stream, the condition of the riparian zones, and the number of landowners or user groups affected by your projects.

Sally Sockeye

Cadillac Desert

*A book about dams and canals might seem rather tame fare, even if the water that is controlled makes life in the western desert third of America possible. Marc Reisner has taken seven years of exhaustive research and a passionate environmentalist perspective and has written a popular history of western water projects that reads like good adventure fiction. He has interviewed virtually all of the players still living, including the significant coup of gaining access to former Bureau of Reclamation Commissioner Floyd Dominy's recollections and personal files. Each chapter easily stands alone, so if you want just the story of how Los Angeles got its water from the Owens Valley, or why the Teton Dam collapsed, it's easy to get. The last time a book brought me this close to the workings of unbridled bureaucracies, political power and money was reading Robert Caro's biography of Robert Moses, **The Power Broker**. The immense size of these water projects keeps Reisner hustling for superlatives, but in the end the wild west meets the era of limits, even if it is happening a drop at a time.*

—Richard Nilsen

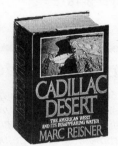

Cadillac Desert (The American West and its Disappearing Water) Marc Reisner; 1986; 582 pp.; **$9.95** ($11.95 postpaid) from: Penguin USA, 120 Woodbine St. Bergenfield, NJ 07621 (800) 526-0275 ✴WEA

George Gillette, chairman of the Ft. Berthold Indian Tribe Business Council, weeps as he watches Secretary of the Interior J.A. Krug sign a contract whereby the tribe sells 155,000 acres of its reservation's best land in North Dakota to the government for the Garrison Dam and Reservoir project on May 20, 1948.

•

This whole hydrologic ballet, this acrobatic rise and fall of megatonnages of water performed on a stage twice the length of Pennsylvania, is orchestrated by a silent choreographer in the Water Resources building in Sacramento: a Univac Series 904 computer punched and fed floppy disks by a team of programmers. At the south end of the valley, the aqueduct arrives at its moment of truth. The Sierra escarpment curves westward and the Coast Range bends eastward and they mate, producing a bastard offspring called the Transverse, or Tehachapi, Range. The Tehachapis stand between the water and Los Angeles, which sits in the ultramontane basin beyond.

The water is carried across the Tehachapis in five separate stages. The final, cyclopean one, which occurs at the A. D. Edmonston Pumping Plant, raises the water 1,926 feet — the Eiffel Tower atop the Empire State — in a single lift. To some engineers, the Edmonston pumps are the ultimate triumph, the most splendid snub nature has ever received: a sizable river of water running uphill. At their peak capacity, if it is ever reached, the Edmonston pumps will require six billion kilowatt-hours of electricity every year, the output of an eleven-hundred-megawatt power plant. Moving water in California requires more electrical energy than is used by several states.

Ground Water and the Rural Homeowner

City dwellers moving to the country make new acquaintances, and one of the first will be their well. Altho trial and error will educate a new well owner, this little pamphlet can assist the learning curve. It discloses first principles of water movement, aquifers and wells. Should any of these matters be in your future this primer will introduce the basics. A worthwhile bibliography of more advanced reading is also included.

—Dick Fugett

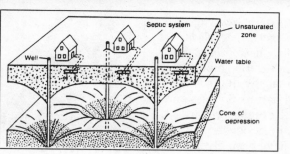

Ground Water and the Rural Homeowner, Roger M. Waller 1988; 37 pp.; **free** from: U.S. Geological Survey, Federal Center, Box 25425, Denver CO 80225; (303) 236-7476

Overtapped Oasis

*For all who read Marc Reisner's earlier book on western water history, **Cadillac Desert**, and wondered what now, Reisner has written **Overtapped Oasis**. Cadillac Desert left us with a bleak portrait of the results of this century's manhandling of water: dams filling with silt, dwindling underground aquifers, and fields crusted over with salt. Now Reisner holds out some hope for water-hungry westerners' continued survival and growth — efficiency and water marketing.*

Farmers use 80 to 90 percent of water in the western states, but not all of that water is used well. If farmers changed their inefficient ways, enough water could be freed up to slake the thirsts of the millions of expected new and immigrant Californians, for example. But thanks to government subsidies farmers often profit by using as much water as they can get. Reisner teams up with water law specialist Sarah Bates and examines how federal and state laws support this kind of overuse and what changes are needed to promote conservation instead. The solution they propose sounds bizarre — changing water laws to allow more farmers to profit from saving and selling excess water. Can a little unfettered capitalism really rescue us from our impending environmental crisis? Reisner and Bates make a strong case for it. —Mary James

Overtapped Oasis (Reform or Revolution for Western Water), Marc Reisner & Sarah Bates; 1989; 208 pp. **$17.95** ($19.95 postpaid) from: Island Press, Star Route 1, Box 38, Covelo CA 95428; (800) 828-1302 ✴WEA

•

THE REALM OF THE POSSIBLE

We focus on agricultural water efficiency simply because irrigation accounts for 80 to 90 percent of consumptive use in the West. Let no one doubt that we strongly support urban water conservation programs, however. According to some experts, simply metering the city of Denver could obviate the need for the $800 million-plus Two Forks Dam; inclining block rates would result in even greater savings. In semiarid and arid regions, we do not see how unmetered homes or flat water rates (as they exist in Fresno, where homeowners pay a fixed monthly fee whether they use 40 or 40,000 gallons per day) can be justified any longer.

•

Another reason that wells "go dry" is the lowering of the water table by increased pumpage in the immediate area. Housing developments with small lots and individual wells have been built in many rural areas. If the aquifer is low yielding so that pumping creates a large drawdown, a cone of depression will develop around each well. Thus, several domestic wells close together can create a steady lowering of the water table if pumpage exceeds the natural recharge to the system (unless the withdrawn water is returned to the aquifer through septic systems). A third major reason that rural wells "go dry" is the installation of larger capacity wells for municipal, industrial, or agricultural purposes adjacent to residential areas. The increased withdrawals may cause large widespread cones of depression that intersect one another and cause general water-level declines that affect nearby domestic wells.

The Poisoned Well

The flyleaf says "If legal advice or other expert assistance is required, the services of a competent professional person should be sought." Keep that boilerplate warning in mind while reading this guidebook; "if you find this, you should do this" is the editorial style throughout. Summary chapters on groundwater geology, health, testing, and mapping fill the first hundred pages; the bulk of the volume covers federal and state laws and administrative procedures, the process of presenting complaints under them, and methods of grassroots action which often can work quickly while legal proceedings are grinding slowly along. Each chapter includes extensive references to publications and to the relevant laws and rules.

It's a good guidebook. Better read it before you call your lawyer, or while you're calling your neighbors. —Hank Roberts

The Poisoned Well (New Strategies for Groundwater Protection); Eric P. Jorgensen Editor, Sierra Club Legal Defense Fund; 1989; 420 pp. **$19.95** ($21.95 postpaid) from: Island Press, Star Route 1 Box 38, Covelo, CA 95428 (800) 828-1302 ✴WEA

•

Important Early Steps in the Permit Process

As a general rule, the permit process begins with an application from the facility owner to the regulatory agency. The basic steps that follow are the preparation of a draft permit, public comment, and final agency decision on the permit. To be most effective in the process, you should not wait until the formal public comment period to begin working with the agency. By the time a draft permit is written by the agency, many preliminary decisions will have been made that could be difficult to reverse.

By looking for clues in local news stories and other community sources, you may be able to identify planned new facilities with potential impact on groundwater quality even before an application for a permit is submitted. Another approach is to develop a relationship with staff at the agency who can notify you when an applicant first contacts the agency. You can also request the agency to notify you that a permit application has been received (most agencies have a mailing list for this purpose).

ᴇᴀᴄʜ ʙɪᴏʀᴇɢɪᴏɴ has its own: *cienaga, tanque, branch, creek, swamp, marsh, bog, glade, slough, swale, wallow, bottoms, bayou, oxbow, pool, pond, brook, run, kill.* Wetlands define bioregion personality, create the intimacy with the local lore and the local pacing of nature. Sources and springs used to be held in the highest regard . . . a few hot springs still remain associated with healing and a few springs have been given a second lease on life by the bottled water business. But water is so precious to commodity production (irrigated crops, cattle forage, land-filling and channelization for real estate, cooling power plants, etc.) that wetlands are our number one endangered ecological and cultural region. In the United States, there are fewer free-flowing rivers of any length than living condors. River-life, duck hunting, trout fishing, swimming, boating . . . many of the areas Americans use for escape are disappearing, just as the desire for open water floods our hearts. —Peter Warshall

National Wetlands Newsletter

For those interested in the legal and policy aspects of wetland restoration, this newsletter is definitely worth reviewing. Wetland mitigation, 404 permitting, "no net loss," and other wetland issues are discussed in guest columns. Standard features include updates on federal legislative action, pertinent legal suits, as well as to-the-point book reviews and a detailed events calendar. I always look forward to this engaging publication.

—Dave Egan

National Wetlands News-letter, Nicole Veilleux, Editor; **$48**/year (6 issues) from: Environmental Law Institute, 16 P Street NW, Suite 200, Washington, DC 20036; (202) 328-5150

●

The Coalition for the Conservation of Aquatic Habitat — otherwise known as FISH — is a rather unlikely alliance. . . . After agreeing that they had been unable to wield enough force individually to effect the preservation of fisheries habitat, the coalition's members decided that "it would be more fun to

Great Blue Heron

Wetlands

Audubon's Wetlands is the best of Audubon survey guides written by one of the finest ecologists to immerse himself in the subject. —Peter Warshall

Wetlands
William A. Niering
1985; 638 pp.; **$16.95**
($18.95 postpaid) from:
Random House
400 Hahn Road
Westminster, MD 21157
(800) 733-3000 ✳WEA
●

Wetlands evoke powerful emotions. To some they are dark, mysterious, forbidding places, to be avoided at all costs. . . . Perhaps one of the most memorable descriptions of a wetland occurs in Sir Arthur Conan Doyle's "*The Hound of the Baskervilles*," in which he describes the Great Grimpen Mire, where the villain meets his horrible fate:

> "Rank weeds and lush, slimy water plants send an odour of decay and a heavy miasmatic vapor into our faces, while a false step plunged us more than once thigh-deep into the dark, quivering mire, which shook for yards in soft undulations around our feet."

This is surely a masterful description of a bog, one of North America's most fascinating wetlands.

fight over more fish to harvest than less fish." And thus, the FISH Coalition was born.

●

United States v. Key West Towers, No. 87-10034-Civ-King, 20 ELR _____ (S.D. Fla. Aug. 10, 1989). Following a jury verdict in July of 1988 that found the defendant liable for filling wetlands adjacent to U.S. waters and therefore within the Army Corps of Engineers' jurisdiction under §404 of the Federal Water Pollution Control Act, the court ordered the defendant to restore the site to its original condition and either pay a $250,000 civil penalty or deed the 1.9-acre pond and the 50-foot buffer zone to a charitable organization that will appropriately maintain the wetlands in perpetuity. [See *National Wetlands Newsletter* "In the Courts," Vol. 11, No. 1.]

Adopting a Wetland

Adopting a Stream (p. 22) has spawned, so to speak, the next book in what's beginning to look like an adopt-the-entire-watershed series. It's a guide to learning what a wetland is, who lives in it, and how to take care of them. It's intended for the Pacific Northwest, but the methods and general approach will work anywhere. The community action part so well delineated in Adopting a Stream is not repeated here. You'll need it, so buy both books. —JB

Adopting A Wetland, Steve Yates 1989; 38 pp.; **$5** ($7 postpaid) from: The Adopt-A Stream Foundation P.O. Box 5558 Everett, WA 98206

WET MEADOW
1. Horsetail, 2. Buttercup, 3. Marsh speedwell, 4. Bulrush, 5. Sedges, 6. Reed canarygrass, 7. Horsetail, 8. Skunk cabbage, 9. Bur-reed, 10. Yellow monkey flower, 11. Spike rush, 12. Soft rush, 13. Dock

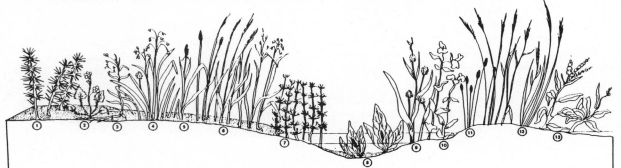

Izaak Walton League of America

An old conservation group with a distinct midwestern twang. Rooted morality. Never upstarts. Founded in 1922 by people interested in good fishing, they are hard, persevering workers who maintain, protect, and restore soil, forests, water and air. A wholesome 50,000 members. Publishers Outdoor America and has an endowment fund to purchase unique natural areas. —Peter Warshall

These days the League is especially active in the prevention of poaching. They also are on the front lines of the fight to prevent Disneyfication of National Parks. Typical of these good folks. —JB

Izaak Walton League of America; $20/year (membership includes 4 issues of **Outdoor America** and Splash, a quarterly newsletter) from: 1401 Wilson Blvd., Level B Arlington, VA 22209; (703) 528-1818

Ducks Unlimited

This 500,000-member organization has been responsible for the preservation of more waterbird breeding grounds (especially marshlands) than any government or other group. Working internationally (ducks haven't learned about Canadian, U.S., and Mexican boundaries), Ducks Unlimited restores, manages, and purchases wetlands throughout North American waterfowl flyways.

—Peter Warshall

Their magazine is both intelligent and beautiful.
—Don Ryan

Ducks Unlimited
$20/year membership (includes subscription to bi-monthly magazine, **Ducks Unlimited**) from: One Waterfowl Way Long Grove, IL 60047 (708) 438-4300

Trout Unlimited

TU bill themselves as "The Action Organization" with good cause: for 30 years their 65,000 members (distributed among 400 chapters) have been a major force in the fight for clean water. While fishing, rather than environmentalism, is their focus, they've long realized the importance of pollution control, cleaning up streams, and sound watershed management. TU has not always enjoyed good relations with certain environmental organizations whose purist members deplore "killing fish." But a look at the record shows TU to be indisputably at the forefront of effective action, both in the field and in legislatures. TU members receive a great (mouthwatering) magazine. What's good for fish is usually good for all of us. —JB

Trout Unlimited
$20/year (membership includes 4 issues of **Trout** magazine); Contact your local chapter or Trout Unlimited 501 Church Street, NE #103, Vienna, VA 22180 (703) 281-1100

THE DESERT is a bioregion defined by its lacks: no blizzards, no fog, no tornadoes, no regular rainfall. What it's got is solar heat. The light is intense. The rare clouds become instantly sacred. Rain is loved like nowhere else. The visual arts flourish: Pueblo pottery, Navajo weaving, outdoor ritual, Georgia O'Keefe. A common pride in survival connects humans, sidewinders, roadrunners and cacti. This is the most diverse cultural region (not counting cities). Native peoples still speak their languages and practice their blessings. A regional sense of spirit has been slowly fused together from Native American, Spanish, and Anglo-European influences. Mormons, followers of a religion native to the U.S., flex much moral and financial muscle. Sunbelt cities eat up the desert and suck the once lush rivers dry. It was all foretold by Hopi prophets and John Wesley Powell and fueled by a web of powerlines; there is no turning back.

—Peter Warshall

Biotic Communities of the American Southwest • Desert Plants

With intimacy and care, **Biotic Communities** reveals what makes the Southwest so intriguing. It lists the unique plants and animals; contrasts them to neighboring biotic communities; tells the story of their recent evolution; points out changes wrought by Anglo-European settlement; explains how climate nurtures the prosperity of each community of the Southwest mosaic; connects Mexico to the United States across irrelevant political borders; is clearly laid-out and illustrated; and on and on and on.

I carry **Biotic Communities** in my truck like friends carry the AAA road guides. What once looked like endless, dreary desert now has me yelling: "Stop! Look at that!" I pull over and read the section on Sinaloan thornscrub or Chihuahuan desert scrub. In short, this is a paragon of bioregional nitty-gritty. If you inhabit the Southwest, it is as important as your phone book.

Desert Plants, which published **Biotic Communities** as a special supplement, is a quarterly journal on indigenous and adaptable plants of arid regions. The high quality of its work can be seen in issues with titles like "The Annual Saguaro Harvest and Crop Cycle of the Papago with Reference to Ecology and Symbolism" and "The Desert Tepary as a Food Source." Informative and thorough. For desert rats like myself, this journal is as wonderful as a year with late rains.

—Peter Warshall

Biotic Communities of the American Southwest, David E. Brown, Editor; 1982; 342 pp.; **$20** postpaid

Desert Plants
Frank S. Crosswhite Editor; **$20**/year (4 issues). Both from: Boyce Thompson Southwestern Arboretum, P.O. Box AB Superior, AZ 85273 (602) 689-2723

Cross-sectional profile of a canyon floor, with an elevational gradient from higher terrraces (A), to intermediate flood plains (C), and to streamside (D) where beavers browse. The secondary channel is at (B). Such a profile is often, but erroneously, interpreted as "succession."

Upper bajada/transition

Deserts

Audubon's **Deserts** is a broad natural history of the four major North American deserts: the cold Great Basin, the lush Sonoran, the winter-rain Mojave, and the summer-rain Chihuahuan.
—Peter Warshall

Deserts
James A. MacMahon
1985; 638 pp.; **$15.95**
($17.95 postpaid) from:
Random House
400 Hahn Rd.
Westminster, MD 21157
(800) 733-3000 **✳WEA**

Desert Solitaire

The desert perceived on its own terms by one very skilled. How to perceive, how to fight (for your survival or the desert's), how to die well when life requires it. —Stewart Brand

Desert Solitaire (A Season in the Wilderness), Edward Abbey 1968, 1988; 8th ed.; 303 pp. **$5.95** ($7.95 postpaid) from: Random House, Inc. 400 Hahn Rd. Westminster, MD 21157 (800) 733-3000 **✳WEA**

•

The wind will not stop. Gusts of sand swirl before me, stinging my face. But there is still too much to see and marvel at, the world very much alive in the bright light and wind, exultant with the fever of spring, the delight of morning. Strolling on, it seems to me that the strangeness and wonder of existence are emphasized here, in the desert, by the comparative sparsity of the flora and fauna: life not crowded upon life as in other places but scattered abroad in spareness and simplicity, with a generous gift of space for each herb and bush and tree, each stem of grass, so that the living organism stands out bold and brave and vivid against the lifeless sand and barren rock. The extreme clarity of the desert light is equaled by the extreme individuation of desert life-forms. Love flowers best in openness and freedom.

I stood on the top of the pile and stretched upward, straining my arms to their utmost limit and groped with fingers and fingernails for a hold on something firm. There was nothing. I crept back down. I began to cry. It was easy. I didn't have to be brave. . . .

The Desert Smells Like Rain

Gary Nabhan tells how the Papago Indians lived with the desert, farming when it rained, collecting wild plants, spinning myths of animals, and breeding a diversity of dry-climate plants that let them live more healthfully than many of their descendants do now. Here Gary shows that the desert — wet or dry — is a place where people can thrive if they seek stewardship, not conquest.
—Art Kleiner

The Desert Smells Like Rain (A Naturalist in Papago Indian Country), Gary Paul Nabhan; 1987; 192 pp. **$8.95** ($10.45 postpaid) from: North Point Press 850 Talbot Ave. Berkeley, CA 94706 (415) 527-6260 **✳WEA**

One of the few crops domesticated north of Mexico, Devil's Claw is used as a black basketry fiber.

•

My first lesson about Coyote's plants left a bad taste in my mouth, to say the least. I had brought some wild desert gourds out to a village with me, curious to find if the Papago used them in any way. An elderly woman looked at the little gourds in the bed of my pickup.

"What you got there? Oh, that's what they call **a:d**! Long time ago they used to go out, and when those fruit got ripe and turned yellow, they would eat it just like a sweet apple."

Before she had a chance to finish her story, I grabbed one tender, yellow gourd and took a bite into it. She yelled "DON'T" but it was too late — that taste was so terrifically bitter that my tongue muscles went into shock. I spat the pulp out and ran for water.

When I returned to where the woman was, she was grinning.

"It *used* to taste just like an apple, they say. Then Coyote came along and he *shit* on it. I guess ever since then it has had that taste that is in your mouth right now. . . ."

Both wild plants such as acorns and gourds and cultivated plants such as tepary beans and Devil's Claw are used by the Papago.

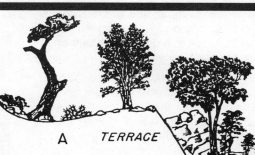

A TERRACE

FLOOD PLAIN C

B D

*S*oil is the stage from which all things — good, beautiful, vicious, creative, dull, outrageous and evil — emerge. A teaspoon of living earth contains five million bacteria, twenty million fungi, one million protozoa, and two hundred thousand algae. Amoebas slide over sand grains hunting bacteria. Bacteria swim through microrivers scarfing nutrients. Viruses attack bacteria. Nematode worms, like soil hyenas, devour almost anything. There are about 9,500 kinds of soil in the United States and no one has ever tried to create sanctuaries for any of them.

—Peter Warshall

Soil and Civilization

*Edward Hyams writes the first and best "watershed history" of ancient and present civilizations. Rather than focusing on the genius of Pericles or the naval talents of Themistocles, he focuses on the ultimate, long-term strength of Greece or any nation: its soil. He elegantly chronicles, for instance, how oak forest cutting led to topsoil erosion creating a subsoil economy (olives and vineyards) which made Athens dependent on naval trade to get topsoil crops (wheat). Includes the Euphrates and America's dustbowl. If one book on history should be read by everyone, I would choose **Soil and Civilization**.*

—Peter Warshall

Soil and Civilization
Edward Hyams
1976; 312 pp.; **$24.95**
($28.85 postpaid) from:
State Mutual Books
521 Fifth Avenue
New York, NY 10017
(212) 682-5844 **✱WEA**

•

The Egyptians were not obliged to discover manuring before settling, not obliged to advance from soil-parasitism to soil-making in order to found cities. The Nile replaced every year what the Egyptians took out of it.

Many advantages of the Egyptian and of Mesopotamian environment have been put forward to explain the precocious rise of their urban civilizations, while the peoples of other regions were still held back in the simpler ways of Neolithic culture. But the attribute of the Nile valley, which it shared with the Euphrates-Tigris delta, and which assured to the Egyptian and Mesopotamian peoples their long lead in the progress towards civilization, was surely the one which enabled them to settle down and exploit the soils of their countries as soon as they had learnt to till them, and without having to find a way of re-making the soil every year.

•

The men of European culture and with European techniques who exploited the grass soils of the region which has since become known as the Dust Bowl, naturally applied to those soils the methods they knew and understood and which had answered so well in Europe for centuries. It seemed to them that they were in a peasant's paradise, for the soils were rich in plant foods, and had the appearance and texture of the best agricultural soils. But North-west European rainfall is hardly anywhere less than 20 inches a year and in most parts nearer 40 inches. The soils of the Middle West had a mean rainfall of nearer 10 inches a year, and it was their grass cover alone which enabled them to maintain their stability during thousands of years of such arid conditions. Every drop of water was absorbed and held in the vast sponge of the grass-roots. But once ploughed the soil had no means of retaining water. In years of

The Nature and Properties of Soils

A college text on soil science. The writing is clear, there is a glossary of terms, and the section headings make it easy to find the information you want quickly. More facts than most people need, but well worth consulting on specific subjects.

—Richard Nilsen

The Nature and Properties of Soils
Nyle C. Brady; 1989
10th ed.; 750 pp.; **$56**
Macmillan Publishing Company; Order through your local bookstore **✱WEA**

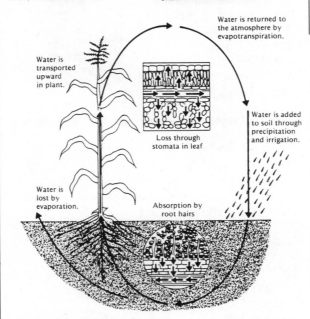

Water is returned to the atmosphere by evapotranspiration.

Water is transported upward in plant.

Loss through stomata in leaf

Water is added to soil through precipitation and irrigation.

Water is lost by evaporation.

Absorption by root hairs

In recent years scientists have come to realize that a common set of basic principles governs relationships among water, soil, plants, and the atmosphere. This continuum is best illustrated by following water as it is added to soils through precipitation or irrigation, as it behaves in soils, is lost directly to the atmosphere from soils, or is absorbed by plants, transported upward, and subsequently evaporated into the atmosphere. Water behavior in all cases is subject to the same basic physical and chemical laws.

subnormal rainfall, the crops simply perished: in other years they might flourish by virtue of unremitting cultivation which conserved some water about the roots by means of a dust-mulch. Such cultivation, in arid conditions, helps to destroy the granular texture of the soil. If two or three inches of top-soil are reduced — nowadays it is done with the disk-harrow — to a fine dust, the soil immediately below that dust remains damp, the dust forming a kind of natural "capillary tubes" which are the products of soil porosity, and by way of which soil water is drawn to the surface. Such a method is only safe where manuring with organic material is consistent and ample, and where some kind of crop rotation avoids the withdrawal from soil of a particular group of elements year after year.

But in Oklahoma not only were artificial fertilizers made available to the farmer a decade or so after the settlement of the state, but monoculture very rapidly became the common-place of the region, a monoculture which was perfectly in accord with the American trend towards a thorough industrial specialization in all walks of life.

Local Soils

Every citizen should be able to say: "I live on a sandy-loam that is about ten feet deep and covers half my community." Soil Conservation Maps are step one but are not detailed enough for some projects (like house-to-house septic tank assessment or gardening problems). Scales vary from one inch equals 1,320 feet to one inch equals one mile. Maps are available (for free, usually) from your local Soil Conservation Service (see telephone book) or write to the SCS in Washington, DC. —Peter Warshall

Soil Conservation Maps; Call your local Soil Conservation Service or write to: Soil Conservation Service, Department of Agriculture, Public Information Division, P.O. Box 2890, Washington, DC 20013

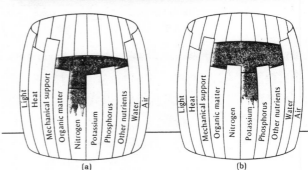

(a)   (b)

The level of water in each barrel above represents the level of crop production. (a) Nitrogen is represented as being the factor that is most limiting. Even though the other elements are present in more adequate amounts, crop production can be no higher than that allowed by the nitrogen. (b) When nitrogen is added, the level of crop production is raised until it is controlled by the next most limiting factor, in this case potassium.

World Soils

This introduction to the soils of the world is complete with a brief course in soil science (pedology). A knowledge of what kind of soils are where, and why they are there, is critical for geographers, land use planners, and food-raisers. —JB

World Soils, E. M. Bridges
1978; 128 pp.; **$11.95**
(postpaid) from:
Cambridge University Press, 110 Midland Avenue
Port Chester, NY 10573
(800) 872-7423 [in NY (800) 227-0247] **✱WEA**

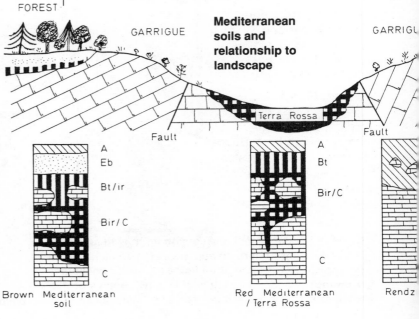

FOREST

GARRIGUE   GARRIGU

Mediterranean soils and relationship to landscape

Terra Rossa

Fault   Fault

A
Eb
Bt/ir
Bir/C
C

A
Bt
Bir/C
C

Brown Mediterranean soil

Red Mediterranean / Terra Rossa

Rendz

Soil and Water Conservation Society of America

*Over one million acres of prime farmland disappear in urban development each year. In the Great Plains and the Pacific Northwest, 85% of the farms lose five tons/acre of topsoil yearly. The Soil and Water Conservation Society of America provides a meeting ground for all the specialized interests who are interested in preserving the ultimate strength of this nation: its soil. They publish a technical but, for my interest, totally absorbing magazine — **The Journal of Soil and Water Conservation.** It's a mature group, organized in 1945.* —Peter Warshall

Soil and Water Conservation Society, besides having a great seed directory (see Sources of Native Seeds and Plants, p. 42) also has an excellent publications list with books and monographs available on soil erosion, soil conservation, sustainable agriculture, and water conservation.
—Susan Erkel Ryan

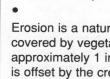

A well-designed storm drain in Fairfax, Virginia, has a semi-fixed liner to drain away erosive storm water. —*Journal of Soil and Water Conservation*

●

Landscape Medicine

When perception of the landscape as a living organism is combined with concepts of health, traditional land management becomes, as Frederick Steiner suggests, the practice of landscape medicine. This practice parallels in many ways the process a medical doctor follows in diagnosing and treating human illness. It suggests an approach that examines the landscape from the point of view of maintaining or enhancing the landscape's health — its ecological well-being. It views the landscape in a holistic sense, with all life integrally linked; it does not separate biological functions from physical functions, nor human well-being from that of the landscape.

Journal of Soil and Water Conservation
Max Schnepf, Editor
$30/year (six issues)
Publications list free

Both from: Soil and Water Conservation Society
7515 N.E. Ankeny Road
Ankeny, IA 50021-9764
(515) 289-2331

Soil Erosion

No moralizing. No righteous insinuations that farmers or corporations are out to starve future generations by mining the nation's soils. Instead, the political nitty-gritty: how terribly difficult it is to harmonize cash-flow problems (farm debt, land prices, fluctuating markets, federal subsidies, equipment purchases) and soil conservation practices. Learn how "targeting" erosion-control funds to the worst situations can slip into pork-barrel funding; how cross-compliance policies (e.g., the feds insure crops against weather disasters in exchange for farmers following good erosion-control guidelines) lose control in times of high crop demand; how punishing farmers for sloppy land use practices has never worked; how incentives for farmers who rent must be different from those for farmers who own.

This book competently fills a vacant niche, the niche of America's most important politics — saving its topsoil.
—Peter Warshall

●

Erosion not only robs farmland of its fertility, it also seriously pollutes the nation's waterways. . . . Ironically, most Americans believe our soil erosion problem was resolved during the 1930s when severe droughts and dust storms swept across the prairies and midwestern soil accumulated on windowsills of the Capitol in Washington, D.C. . . . If Americans do not take seriously the accumulating evidence about the extent and consequences of erosion, the country's agricultural future may be undermined, perhaps not this decade or next, but sometime early in the twenty-first century.

●

Erosion is a natural process. When lands are covered by vegetation, the rate of erosion is slow, approximately 1 inch every 100 to 250 years, and is offset by the creation of new soil. But on lands devoid of vegetation. . . erosion rates increase by magnitudes.

Soil Erosion, Sandra S. Batie
1983; 136 pp., **$8.50** ($10.50 postpaid) from: The Conservation Foundation, P. O. Box 4866, Hampden Station
Baltimore, MD 21211
(301) 338-6951 ✱WEA

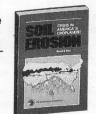

Dixon Land Imprinters

Desertification is a creeping planetary blight. Once land is deforested, over-grazed, or otherwise denuded of most or all vegetation, the soil surface rapidly loses its porosity and becomes smooth and hard. Rainfall runs off, rather than soaking in for use by plants, causing severe flooding and erosion. To revegetate an area you have to repair the damaged soil surface before you can expect your plantings and seedlings to take hold well or at all.

The imprinters developed by Dr. Robert Dixon mechanically roughen and shape the soil surfaces to make it no longer smooth and hard. Water pools and soaks in for seeds and plantings to use. Flooding and erosion are sharply reduced or even eliminated. Vegetation can get a good foothold and then biologically maintain and enhance the porous and roughened soil surface initially provided by the imprinter. Imprinters have been in use in the U. S. Southwest for over ten years, with good results that I have personally verified. They are increasingly turning up in the Third World now.

Imprinters come in various sizes, from one best pulled by a D4 Cat down to hand- or foot-operated models. Imprinters can be bought, or you can roll your own homemade model with a little help from the Imprinting Foundation run by Dixon.
—James Kalin

Dixon can custom design imprinters for specific revegetation projects for large or small acreage. Last May they made an imprinter for use on the notorious Staten Island landfill.
—Susan Erkel Ryan

Dixon Land Imprinters construction plans **$2** (specify foot-or hand-operated) from: The Imprinting Foundation
1231 East Big Rock Rd.
Tucson, AZ 85718
(602) 297-6165

Imprinter operating near Tombstone, Arizona, to revegetate land on the western fringe of the Chihuahan Desert, severely overgrazed by Spanish cattle between 1850 and 1900. This is a prototypic rolling imprinter invented in 1976. Many other types have been developed since then.

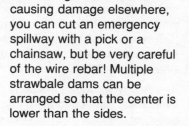

Groundwork

Too much of coastal California has been washing into the sea for a good chunk of this century. What logging didn't set loose the cows did. This handsome handbook is the product of one of America's more than 3,000 resource conservation districts. With a locally elected board, but no power to make or enforce laws, RDCs function as the glue between governmental bureaucracies and private landowners in cooperative efforts to conserve soil and water. Superb line drawings of techniques and a succinct text make this pamphlet one to emulate.
—Richard Nilsen [Suggested by Judith Goldsmith]

Groundwork
Liza Prunuske; 1987
60 pp.; **$1.25** postpaid
from: Marin County Resource Conservation District, P.O. Box 219
Point Reyes Station, CA 94956
(415) 663-1231

●

Willows are an effective and inexpensive way to armor active headcuts and gully banks.

Be sure to plant the willows right-side up. One almost foolproof method is to point the planting end of the sprig with an axe right after it is cut from the tree.

Willows spread easily — usually an advantage; but in some cases when an open channel is needed to carry stormflows, this can be a nuisance.

●

Strawbales are an inexpensive and easy-to-install form of check dam for use in mild, shallow gullies. They perform best in gullies with relatively stable sides and some existing grass cover. Since the bales deteriorate in two to three years, it is essential that

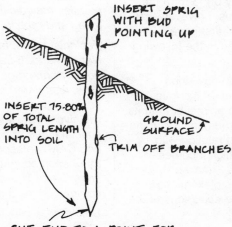

INSERT SPRIG WITH BUD POINTING UP

INSERT 75-80% OF TOTAL SPRIG LENGTH INTO SOIL

GROUND SURFACE

TRIM OFF BRANCHES

CUT END TO A POINT FOR EASIER INSTALLATION

Willow sprig installation.

vegetation be well established on the deposited sediment within that time. Bales should be keyed into the bank and secured with two pieces of rebar per bale. Multiple bales can be used in a row across the gully floor.

Generally, single strawbale checkdams are constructed without spillways. If you find runoff overflowing the gully channel during a rainstorm and causing damage elsewhere, you can cut an emergency spillway with a pick or a chainsaw, but be very careful of the wire rebar! Multiple strawbale dams can be arranged so that the center is lower than the sides.

If cattle have access to strawbale checkdams, they may eat the checkdams down to two lone pieces of rebar. Wrapping the bales in chicken wire before installing them usually discourages such voracity.

✱WEA — Available from Whole Earth Access, see p. 2.

"*Ecology*" has come to mean just about anything. Doom-gloom to the end-of-the-worlders. Mystical harmony to the religio-eco-freaks. Grants to the college crowd. The word comes from Greek: "Oikos" and "Logos." "Oikos" means house, or dwelling-place. "Logos" primarily means discourse, or "word, thought or speech." To the early Greeks, "Logos" was the moving and regulating principle in things (associated with fire-energy), as well as the part of human nature that was able to see this ordering energy at work.

Ecology, at its root and origin, means domestic chatter; talking about where-you-live; feeling out the household rules; remaining open and perceptive to the moving and regulating principle of your watershed and/or planet home. —Peter Warshall

Concepts of Ecology

There is a crusade called Ecology. And also a science called Ecology. And they're not as distinct as they think they are.

This book is about the science, unhindered by rhetoric. Its subject is energy flow, cycles, populations, ecological communities, and man's place in the system. The emphasis is on theory and observation rather than math. Areas that are still poorly understood get due attention. I wish this book had been around when I studied ecology.
—Stewart Brand

Concepts of Ecology
Edward J. Kormondy
1984; 288 pp.; **$26.40**
($28.90 postpaid) from:
Prentice-Hall
200 Old Tappan Rd.
Old Tappan, NJ 07675
(800) 922-0579 ✱WEA

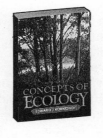

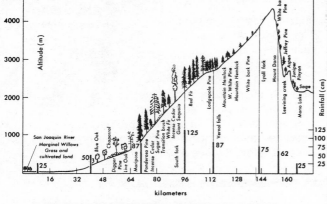

Profile of the central Sierra Nevada showing altitudinal distribution of principal forest types.

●

Ecology's roots extend to the origins of humanity itself. Our ancestors had to have been students of the environment, else our species would have been extinguished. . . . Hanns Reiter appears to have been the first to combine the Greek words *oikos* (=house) and *logos* (=study of) to form the term ecology. There is consensus, however, that (German biologist Ernst) Haeckel first gave substance to the term in 1866 and in the following statement in 1870:

By ecology we mean the body of knowledge concerning the economy of nature — the investigation of the total relations of the animal both to its inorganic and to its organic environment; including above all, its friendly and inimical relation with those animals and plants with which it comes directly or indirectly into contact — in a word, ecology is the study of all the complex interrelations referred to by Darwin as the conditions of the struggle for existence.

Ecology

The science of ecology has suffered from success. It can mean many things in the popular mind and seems to have emerged all at once as a full blown discipline around 1970. One of the best things this college text does is to take pains to trace the evolution of ecology as a branch of science and explain the significant changes it has undergone since the early '70s. Colinvaux writes clearly and is sparing with the jargon and math unless absolutely necessary. He even offers several routes through his book for short-course browsers.
—Richard Nilsen

Ecology
Paul Colinvaux
1986; 725 pp.
$48.95 postpaid from:
John Wiley & Sons, Inc.
1 Wiley Dr., Somerset,
NJ 08875-1272
(201) 469-4400 ✱WEA

●

The Clementsian view led to attractive systems for classifying plant communities. In every climatic region there was a single climax plant community, the CLIMAX FORMATION. . . . All other communities found in the region were related to the climax formation as various stages of its development. Essential to this point of view is the idea that a community is a SUPERORGANISM, an entity of many species that has EMERGENT PROPERTIES of its own. Realizing that his *superorganism* drew some of its properties from animals as well as plants, Clements coined the word BIOME to replace the earlier *climax formation* for his ultimate community unit. . . .

Clements' work is still important because it lies at the root of many of the political or social movements that take their names from ecology in the present day. Whenever activists accuse their political or exploiter adversaries of "ecocide" they invoke Clements' teachings. They borrow from him the idea that the ecosystem of the climax is an organism, saying that therefore it can be killed.

The modern view is that succession is an inevitable consequence of the coexistence of plants with different strategies. . . . Plants, like all products of natural selection, are individualists. This essential truth was argued strongly even in Clements' day, most notably by Gleason. But the final triumph of Gleason's *individualistic hypothesis of succession* came only with the concept of species strategies in the 1960s.

Ecological Engineering

Ecology is the subject of a rousing debate going on right now between theoreticians, engineers, and experimenters. Perhaps debate isn't the proper word; there is little direct communication between the camps. Scholars want to do more studies; the experimenters want to explore without having to endure sneers, or, all too often, peer review. Engineers are caught in the middle. Few have enjoyed formal training in ecological matters, yet their job is to DO something that satisfies that most implacable settler of arguments: it has to work. This utterly professional book is remarkably comprehensive, though a bit behind the cutting edge, as any academic tome must be. (Periodicals take up the slack.) The critical, inextricably imbedded politics and sociology are not discussed. This unfortunate omission can give ecologically illiterate readers the impression that a technical fix is always possible and desirable — an impression that is at the root of many current problems. Nonetheless, the very recognition of Ecological Engineering as a discipline is a welcome sign that ecologists and engineers are finally talking. It's a start. —JB

Ecological Engineering
Jørgensen Mitsch; 1989
472 pp.; **$54.95** ($57.95
postpaid) from: John Wiley
& Sons, Inc., 1 Wiley Dr.
Somerset, NJ 08875-1272
(201) 469-4400 ✱WEA

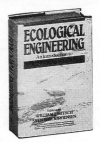

●

If the mechanisms of higher-level reinforcement provide goals that the mechanisms at lower levels must conform to to be reinforced, they are teleological mechanisms. Those who were taught that teleology was a sin do not allow themselves to think of mechanistic performance goals for survival in self-organization. This becomes a mental obstacle to understanding what controls ecosystems or how ecological engineering works. Understanding ecosystems and their management requires recognition of the control by higher levels of the components of a smaller level. Ecosystems cannot be understood by studies at one level alone (i.e., population ecology) because control comes from the next level.

Why Big Fierce Animals Are Rare

Ecology is having a kind of personality crisis at the moment . . . feeling bewildered . . . searching for new harmonies amid the raucousness of Nature's wild ways. It is a healthy time. Some even question if there is really a "system" in ecosystem. Life is certainly viewed as more complex than simple parallel, melodic lines — like a Bach canon — of foxes and rabbits.

Ecologists must face the new metaphors of music: Nature as a 16-track multi-mix; African polyrhythms; raga modes or natural dissonance. New, less deterministic harmonies of community ecology await human expression. The new music will give great weight to the invisible, for example, special types of plant biotechnology like C3, C4 and CAM metabolism; to a karmic biogeochemistry of each community's soils and to the ability of some bacteria and pigeons to orient to their community by magnetism.

*Until then, Colinvaux's **Why Big Fierce Animals***

Why Big Fierce Animals Are Rare, Paul Colinvaux
1978; 256 pp.; **$8.95** postpaid from: Princeton
University Press,
3175 Princeton Pike
Lawrenceville, NJ 08648
(609) 896-2111 ✱WEA

***Are Rare** is the only literate book to confront fashionable math and information theory with naturalist news.* —Peter Warshall

●

The grand pattern of life was clearly and directly a consequence of the second law of thermodynamics. We can now understand why there are not fiercer dragons on the earth than there are; it is because the energy supply will not stretch to the support of super-dragons. Great white sharks or killer whales in the sea, and lions and tigers on the land, are apparently the most formidable animals the contemporary earth can support.

BioDiversity

*"BioDiversity": the fantastic multitude of different forms of life on planet Earth. Just one group of animals alone, the insects, may account for an inconceivable 50 million species, according to the latest estimates of entomologist Terry Erwin, a contributor to this book. Unfortunately, what has taken evolution over three billion years to produce may take the human species only a few generations to wipe out: Erwin estimates that human activity may eliminate 20 to 30 million species in the next generation alone! This wholesale obliteration of species has profound consequences for all humans, not just "nature lovers." As ecologist Paul Ehrlich, another of **BioDiversity**'s authors, points out, the complex ecosystems formed by the Earth's plants, animals, and microorganisms supply the mixture of gases that makes the atmosphere livable, prevent habitable land from turning into desert, insure the pollination of our crops, and maintain a balance of predators and prey that keeps humans from being overrun by pests. Perhaps most important of all, the assemblage of species with which we share the planet represents a vast untapped genetic library, teeming with undiscovered pharmaceuticals and other beneficial substances.*

*Ehrlich and Erwin are only two of over fifty contributors to this book, the product of a National Forum cosponsored by the National Academy of Sciences and the Smithsonian Institution. A superb lineup of biologists graphically outlines the terrifying enormity of the current extinction crisis — which dwarfs all of the natural extinctions of the past — and makes suggestions about how it can be reversed. Their essays are complemented by contributions from pharmacologists, economists, environmentalists, poets, and philosophers. (Included are a number familiar to **Whole Earth Catalog** readers: Ehrlich, Ocean Arks Institute founder John Todd, James "Gaia Hypothesis" Lovelock, beat poet Michael McClure.)*

What emerges is pretty grim, but not hopeless. Ehrlich predicts that unless human cultures are transformed by a "quasi-religious . . . appreciation of diversity for its own sake," most of the Earth's surface will soon become desert, and "civilization will disappear some time before the end of the next century — not with a bang but a whimper." This book amply demonstrates that if Ehrlich's apocalyptic vision comes to pass, it won't be because the human species wasn't smart enough to see it coming. The question to ask now is: Are we smart enough to do anything about it? —Ted Schultz

BioDiversity
E.O. Wilson, Editor
1988; 521 pp.; **$19.50**
($21.50 postpaid) from:
National Academy Press
2101 Constitution Ave.
Washington, DC 20418
(800) 624-6242 ✱WEA

•

I will go further: the magnitude and control of biological diversity is not just a central problem of evolutionary biology; it is one of the key problems of science as a whole. At present, there is no way of knowing whether there are 5, 10, or 30 million species on Earth. There is no theory that can predict what this number might turn out to be. With reference to conservation and practical applications, it also matters why a certain subset of species exists in each region of the Earth, and what is happening to each one year by year. Unless an effort is made to understand all of diversity, we will fall far short of understanding life in these important respects, and due to the accelerating extinction of species, much of our opportunity will slip away forever. —E.O. Wilson

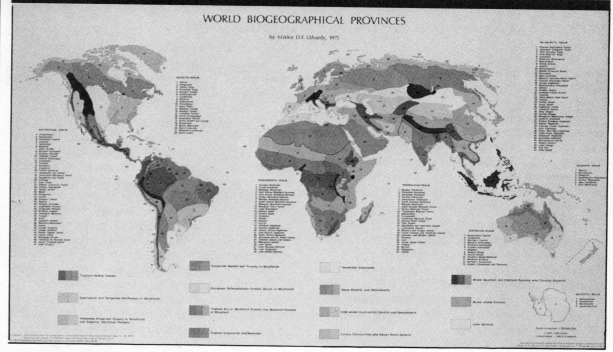

World Biogeographical Provinces

This map is the gem of 15 years of thought and work on the Whole Earth Catalog. It is the map of how the Earth itself has simultaneously produced variety and parallels during its long evolution . . . how water, soils, plants, animals, and locations near or far from the oceans create provinces of similar like. Besides its beauty, it's being used to insure that every biogeographic region of the planet will have at least one representative ecological community preserved. It is a meditative map.

By scanning similar provinces I understand why Australian eucalyptus do so well in California; why the "Mediterranean" regions have similar heritages and can look to each other for advice on wine, sunlight in art, fire, grasses, and erosion management. —Peter Warshall

World Biogeographical Provinces Map
Miklos D. F. Udvardy, S. Brand, T. Oberlander
1975, 1976, 1978; **$5** postpaid from:
Whole Earth Access, 2950 7th Street
Berkeley, CA 94710; (415) 428-1600

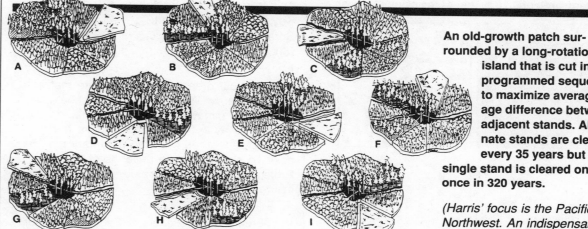

An old-growth patch surrounded by a long-rotation island that is cut in a programmed sequence to maximize average age difference between adjacent stands. Alternate stands are clearcut every 35 years but any single stand is cleared only once in 320 years.

(Harris' focus is the Pacific Northwest. An indispensable book for the Oregonian bioregion.) —Peter Warshall

The Fragmented Forest

No land is an island isolated in itself. But each piece of intact land, so-called virgin land, is a lovely locale matrixed in a jigsaw puzzle of humanized habitats. This reality has only recently been addressed. The best forester thinking of "habitat islands" is Larry Harris. This is a book crucial to all conservationists. In my travels in Africa, I dialog with this book. I check out the size and scatter of remaining habitat islands. I note the distances between "good habitat" and ignore political borders. I try to describe the linkages (the drainageways, river crossings, mountain passes, valleys) which might, by acting as safe-passage corridors, increase a herd of elephants' effective home range. I lecture on the need for these corridors and try to reduce the dangers of migration or attempt to soften the contrast between rich habitat and farmland with middle-use buffer zones.

*As global warmth and Sahelian drought set in, many animals and plants will try to move away from the changing heat flux. In their way stand cities or mono-crops or reservoirs. This too is the reality of the latter half of the twentieth century. If you can't move and it's too hot, you become extinct. The **Fragmented Forest** is by now a classic. You can argue about habitat size and minimal viable populations but you can't argue with its messages.*

•

All factors considered, an ideal old-growth area would occur on a moist site containing surface water and a stream. It would contain a topographic bench and a riparian strip dominated by hardwood species. This same riparian strip would connect it with at least two other stands. The site would be at a low elevation with a north or east aspect, but would ideally extend over a ridge top so that the ridge system could be used as a dispersal route and so some sunny, south-facing area would be included. The site would be as far removed from traffic and attendant risks such as wild crown fire as possible. It would be nearly surrounded by replacement stands that can serve as a buffer area and by at least two stands in early stages of growth to provide the full spectrum of successional stages in close proximity.

The Fragmented Forest
Larry D. Harris; 1984; 211 pp.
$11.95 ($13.70 postpaid) from:
University of Chicago Press
11030 S. Langley Avenue
Chicago, IL 60628
(312) 568-1550 ✱WEA

Where Have All the Birds Gone?

The biosphere is knit together by species that migrate long distances, like fish and birds. This book synthesizes recent research about where birds spend the winter, in Central America, after summering in the US and Canada, and shows how changes in both their northern and southern habitats may now threaten their survival. It makes a strong case for international cooperation in identifying and protecting preserves for species that don't recognize the political boundaries humans draw.

Terborgh combines the enthusiasm of an amateur birdwatcher with the analytical skills of a scientist. Birders will enjoy learning how the pieces of the migration puzzle fit together. They may also be proud to see how much their recreational record-keeping has contributed to our understanding of the links between ecologies.
— Robert Horvitz

Where Have All the Birds Gone?, John Terborgh; 1989 207 pp.; **$14.95** ($16.20 postpaid) from: Princeton University Press, 41 William St. Princeton, NJ 08540 (609) 896-1344 ✳WEA

Changes in wooded area of Cadiz Township, Green County, WI, during the period of European settlement. Within the span of one human lifetime, the total area in forest was reduced by more than 90 % and broken into over 60 fragments having an average area of 0.16 % that of the original forest.

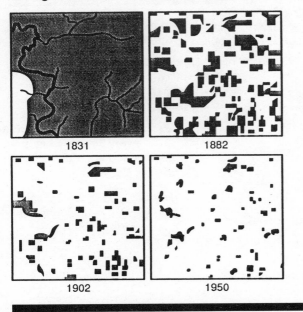

1831   1882

1902   1950

World Wildlife Fund

WWF is one of the world's major conservation organizations, with 800,000 members and a $31 million annual budget. With that sort of heft, they should be effective, and they are. Besides well-known programs that have led to the banning of much international traffic in wildlife species and products, WWF supports the protection of individual species and their habitats, and the scientific investigations that make that protection effective. They sponsor multinational programs that develop citizen appreciation of the importance of protecting their local wildlife. They train wildlife professionals (you, perhaps?). Wildlife populations are monitored, and endangered species lists are published. And of course, WWF lobbies vigorously. I am frankly amazed at the breadth of their efforts — just listing their work would fill this page. —JB

World Wildlife Fund; Information **free** from: 1250 Twenty-Fourth Street, NW, Washington, DC 20037; (202) 293-4800

Mama Poc

We generally review "here's-what's-being-done-about-it" action rather than the "what's-wrong" outrage and warnings so adequately covered by other publications. We do read the what's-wrong literature though, paying particular attention to that illuminating an unfortunate process. Here, we read the first-person account of an American woman who took on the difficult task of organizing a movement to save an endangered Guatemalan grebe — the Poc. She goes through the usual painful learning curve of the displaced naïve American meddler, finally embedding herself in the culture well enough to enlist local support (and to develop a heartbreaking love life). For awhile, things go well. A Poc refuge is built, the Poc population grows. But ultimately, she fails not only to save the Pocs, but to preserve their lake. Her failure stems from the usual (but in this case especially cruel) combination of natural disaster, development pressure, political dishonesty and military exigency. Though she misses no opportunity for dramatic storytelling, she does not spare herself blame. Her story makes it clear that such efforts are most likely doomed unless done at a scale that can encompass the complex interactions of cause and effect. The lesson is taught from the heart. —JB

Mama Poc (An Ecologist's Account of the Extinction of a Species), Anne La Bastille 1990; 313 pp.; **$19.95** postpaid from: National Book Co. Keystone Industrial Park Scranton, PA 18512 (800) 233-4830 ✳WEA

•

There, to our great surprise, we were met with stares of horror. We tied up our three boats and hurried to the mayor's office. Children and women scurried away in fright. No one spoke to us. Finally, we learned from the Secretary that the color I'd chosen for the uniforms of Operation Protection Poc was the same as that worn by insurgent guerrillas!

•

In February I sent a cable to Edgar, asking for information. Nothing came back.

Late in May I received a letter from Pedro with a clipping from the newspaper. On May 7, 1982, Edgar had been killed by unknown assailants on his farm at night. His buildings were burned down. The World Wildlife Fund boat had disappeared.

Preserving Communities & Corridors

A handful of well-chosen examples take the place of pedantry in showing the basic principles of wildlife preservation in a time of reduced habitat. It's a lot more complicated than you might think. The terms 'migration' and 'range' take on a more exact and insistent meaning here. No Bambi-eyes stuff; scientists track a radio-equipped bear as it riskily traverses 200 miles of human-infested Florida, teaching us a lot more about what bears really do and need. (It even stopped to covertly watch fireworks! Luckier than many of its colleagues, it managed to dodge the cars.) The book makes it clear what the problems are, and what will probably work best to help our wilder companions survive our proximity. Rich and realistic. —JB

Preserving Communities & Corridors, Gay Mackintosh, Editor; 1989 96 pp.; **$10** postpaid from: Defenders of Wildlife 1244 Nineteenth Street NW, Washington, DC 20036; (202) 659-9510

•

A Growing Constituency

Perhaps the greatest potential source of support for funding the Fish and Wildlife Conservation Act is the wildlife-watching American public — so far essentially silent on this issue. Nongame wildlife-related activities are of great interest to Americans. A 1980 survey by the Fish and Wildlife Service and the Bureau of the Census found that 83 million adults engaged in watching, photographing, or feeding birds or other wildlife in 1980, and 93 million participated in some form of non-consumptive wildlife activity that year (U.S. Fish and Wildlife Service 1982). By 1985, when the national survey of fishing, hunting, and wildlife-associated recreation was conducted again, this constituency had expanded dramatically: 110 million Americans (more than half of all adults) actively participated in nonconsumptive wildlife-related activities, and 74 percent were classified as "nonconsumptive participants" (U.S. Fish and Wildlife Service 1987b). These numbers continue to grow. Birdwatching, in fact, is currently ranked as one of this country's most popular outdoor recreational activities.

Although the wildlife-viewing constituency is not particularly vocal or well organized, it represents the great majority of Americans, who enjoy wildlife in nonconsumptive ways and who believe it is the responsibility of the government to prevent species from being exterminated.

Endangered Species UPDATE

*In response to federal legislation, the U.S. Fish and Wildlife Service has developed thousands of recovery and/or reintroduction plans for endangered plant and animal species. They are discussed in the Service's **Endangered Species Technical Bulletin.** Budget cuts in the Reagan years limited distribution, so the **Bulletin's** contents are now reprinted in **Endangered Species UPDATE** along with longer articles, opinion and book reviews. The total package provides an interesting look at one form of restoration — the restocking of individual species into their original environment.*
—Dave Egan

Endangered Species UPDATE, Suzanne Jones, Editor; **$23**/year (10 issues) from: School of Natural Resources, University of Michigan Ann Arbor, MI 48109-1115; (313) 763-3243

Native Seeds/SEARCH

Native Seeds/SEARCH is a nonprofit rescue mission for the food plants of native peoples in southwestern North America. The turf extends roughly north/south from Durango, Colorado, to Durango, Mexico, and west/east from Las Vegas, Nevada, to Las Vegas, New Mexico.

The rescued plant might be a bean grown by Tarahumara Indians in the Copper Canyon in Mexico or Hopi corn from Northern Arizona. Species of native American food plants got scarce and began disappearing with the advent of mechanized irrigation in the 1920s. The ethnobotany involved in searching out the survivors is as remarkable as the fact that so many varieties (200 for sale in the catalog) are still clinging to mostly marginal existences.

Plants and people that survive in the desert have to be resilient and with these seeds that often means high food value, drought tolerance, and resistance to insects and disease.

The Native Seed people ask that you save seeds from what you grow for future gardens and for friends. Proceeds go toward propagating more varieties. For those interested in the work there is a newsletter, **The Seedhead News.** *—Richard Nilsen*

Native Seeds/SEARCH Catalog **$1**, Membership **$10**/yr. (includes the quarterly **Seedhead News**) from: Native Seeds/SEARCH 2509 North Campbell Ave. #325, Tucson, AZ 85719 (602) 327-9123

Enduring Seeds

In his third book, ethnobotanist Gary Nabhan continues his exploration of American Indian farmers and their crops. (The preceding books are **The Desert Smells Like Rain**, *reviewed on p. 25, and* **Gathering the Desert**. *Nabhan collects seeds from native American food crops and distributes them to Indians and others willing to grow and thus preserve these often rare and endangered varieties. He is also a good writer, and this time travels far beyond the Sonoran desert bioregion. This collection of essays is filled with good stories of interesting people in out-of-the-way places. It is history with roots in the soils of the present. —Richard Nilsen*

Enduring Seeds Gary Paul Nabhan 1989; 225 pp.; **$18.95** ($20.45 postpaid) from: North Point Press 850 Talbot Avenue Berkeley, CA 94706 (415) 527-6260 ✱WEA

•

Modern agriculture has let temporary cheap petrochemicals and water substitute for the natural intelligence — the stored genetic and ecological information — in self-adjusting biological communities.

•

For centuries, local seed-saving was the norm. Ethnobotanist Janis Alcorn has described how traditional farmers follow unwritten "scripts," learned by hand and mouth from their elders, that keep agricultural practices relatively consistent from generation to generation. Most land-based cultures have such scripts that guide plant selection and seed-saving. Each individual farmer might edit this script to fit his or her peculiar farming conditions, but the general scheme is passed on to the farmer's descendants. Thus, the crop traits emerging through natural selection in a given locality are retained or elaborated by recurrent cultural selection.

The Garden Seed Inventory • Seed Savers Exchange

The **Inventory** *is a piece of cataloging heroics: an alphabetical listing of each and every variety of nonhybrid vegetable seed for sale by seed houses in the U.S. and Canada. That's 5,785 varieties from 239 wholesale and retail seed companies. So if you're a gardener used to buying your favorite chili pepper seed from the same source for years — only this year it's NOT THERE — you look that variety up and find out who sells it. If you're a northern gardener faced with a short growing season, you scan the column that lists days to maturity for each variety of a kind of vegetable, and come up with whatever is quickest and best for your situation.*

***Seed Savers Exchange** is the kind of good-works nonprofit outfit that people ought to leave money to in their wills. Run on a shoestring by Kent Whealy, it is the place where gardeners raising unique or endangered vegetables swap seeds. Many of the varieties have been passed down within families for generations. Here seeds are passed from the old to the young via the mailman. If you raise vegetables, consider joining in and adopting a variety or two.*
—Richard Nilsen

The Garden Seed Inventory, Kent Whealy, Editor; 1985; 422 pp. **$17.50** postpaid

Seed Savers Exchange Yearbook; 3 issues/yr. **$15-25** Membership (yearbook included) Informational brochure **$1**. All from: Seed Savers Exchange, Route 3, Box 239 Decorah, IA 52101

The Journal of Wild Culture

What happens when a bunch of rogue ecologists and whacked-out artists have a head-on collision? **The Journal of Wild Culture**, *that's what.*

You won't find a lot of statistics in **The Journal**. *They are less interested in the exact number of snail darters in Lower East Baby Fat than they are in emerging philosophies that link human activities to the planet as a whole.* **The Journal** *also takes frequent detours through the imaginations of artists and writers who offer up such tidbits as spurious new insect and animal species (like the ink-eating Print Grub, blamed for numerous magazine typos), thoughts on the loss of goddess culture, a William Burroughs-type cut-up short story, and ways of showing proper reverence for your recipe ingredients.*

Cultural Survival

Homogenization is consuming even the most isolated indigenous cultures on the planet. Can the languages of threatened cultures be saved? Can indigenous people share game parks where white men come to play? Is the drug trade crucial to some tribal peoples' cultural survival? Does "education" really mean loss of identity?

***Cultural Survival** is an organization of concerned anthropologists and other citizens trying to preserve threatened cultures and explore ways in which native peoples can accommodate to the twentieth century without too great a loss of their own uniqueness. Their magazine,* **Cultural Survival Quarterly**, *provides thorough coverage of their efforts. —Peter Warshall*

Cultural Survival Quarterly, Jason Clay, Ph.D., Editor; **$25**/year (4 issues) from: Cultural Survival, Inc. 11 Divinity Avenue Cambridge, MA 02138 (617) 495-2562

Divided Twins: Alaska and Siberia

A Russian poet and an American photographer teamed up to produce this appeal for political sanity. Since there isn't room here for a complete poem, and we can't show the shockingly pure color of the photos, I'll let the poet tell you what he had in mind. Maybe it's because I lived in Alaska for three years, but this really got to me as few coffee-table books do.

"In order to come together, people must see each other even through walls erected by politics, and understand that beauty is not the exclusive property of politics but the common property of all the inhabitants of the earth. Nature is a potential means of mutual understanding."

In Russian and English. —JB

Divided Twins (Alaska and Siberia) Yevgeny Yevtushenko 1988; 224 pp.; **$40** ($42 postpaid) from: Viking Penguin, P.O. Box 120, Bergenfield NJ 07621-0120 (800) 331-4624 ✱WEA

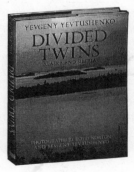

Siberian babushkas.

If, like some of us, you have occasionally thought of the ecological movement as a bunch of dour, no-fun sprout-munchers, **The Journal of Wild Culture** *will cure you once and for all.*
—Richard Kadrey

The Journal of Wild Culture, Whitney Smith, Editor; **$15**/year (4 issues) from: The Society for the Preservation of Wild Culture 158 Crawford Street Toronto, Ontario Canada M6J 2V4 (416) 588-8266

WORKING AT ENVIRONMENTAL RESTORATION helps get priorities straight. If you have to step around a homeless person on the way to the mailbox with a check supporting Third World peoples, you are overlooking a basic contradiction. If there are no trees on your block, or pollution is killing the trees there now, then focusing on rainforest depletion in the Amazon basin is a misplaced concern. And if lack of habitat has eliminated the frogs or songbirds from your neighborhood, then dolphins or grizzlies should not be the first species you try to help. There is urgent work for us all, and it begins in our own backyards.

Some argue that local environmental good works are diversionary, that the most urgent need is for broad changes in national policy. It's true that the situation cries out for strong leadership. Consider one glaring example: we began the last decade with a millenarian deconstructionist for Secretary of the Interior, and have ended it with that office occupied by a spent political hack. How do we change that? By first educating enough people about what a healthy environment needs — beginning with their own communities.

This country is about freedom and justice, but it began over particular local grievances. Will the process of building a popular groundswell of informed demand for changes in our environmental laws be any different? Doing environmental restoration work gives you intimate understanding of what a healthy environment should look like, and new eyes that will begin to see the rest of the world a little differently. —*Richard Nilsen*

Society for Ecological Restoration & Management

This organization serves a new profession — environmental restorationists — although membership in the Society is open to anyone interested in the subject. One of the healthy things about restoration work is that it involves diverse professional specialties in a generalist pursuit. This is also part of the challenge for a new discipline, since anyone can call himself a practitioner of environmental restoration. SER is where the philosophy and the politics of restoration are getting thrashed out. —*Richard Nilsen*

Society for Ecological Restoration
Membership information from: University of Wisconsin Arboretum, 1207 Seminole Highway Madison, WI 53711; (608) 263-7889

The Earth Manual

Just like the man says:

"Between well-trimmed suburban lawns and the vast regions of mountain wilderness, there are millions of patches of land that are semi-wild. They may be wood lots, small forests, parks, a farm's 'back forty,' or even an unattended corner of a big back yard — land touched by civilization but far from conquered. This book is about how to take care of such land: how to stop its erosion, heal its scars, cure its injured trees, increase its wildlife, restock it with shrubs and wild flowers, and otherwise work with (rather than against) the wildness of the land."

A book of gentle advice and easily-absorbed wisdom. Great bibliography. —*Peter Warshall*

For beginners, it has the best exploration of small-scale restoration techniques. —*Richard Nilsen*

The Earth Manual
(How To Work On Wild Land Without Taming It) Malcolm Margolin; 1985; 237 pp.; **$12.95** postpaid from: Heyday Books P.O. Box 9145, Berkeley CA 94709 ✱WEA

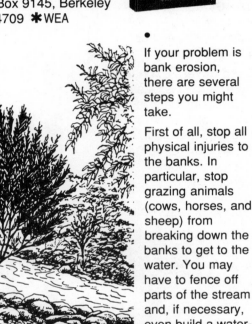

rock deflector

If your problem is bank erosion, there are several steps you might take.

First of all, stop all physical injuries to the banks. In particular, stop grazing animals (cows, horses, and sheep) from breaking down the banks to get to the water. You may have to fence off parts of the stream and, if necessary, even build a watering trough away from the stream's edge.

Next, you can build deflectors. Deflectors are basically piles of stone placed upstream from an eroding bank to absorb the force of the water.

Contour trenches are simply ditches that you dig along a hillside, following a contour and running perpendicular to the flow of water. They catch water and allow it to sink into the ground before it can get a running start down the hill. Contour trenches are particularly valuable on hardened soil — like old logging roads — where water penetration is painfully slow.

To make contour trenches, first gather all your friends and issue them picks, mattocks, and shovels. When the moaning and groaning stop, begin digging several short trenches five or six inches deep and no more than about two or three feet apart. Keep this project short! Digging ditches on a hard-packed, heavily eroded slope is nobody's idea of great fun.

Restoration & Management Notes

This "bulletin board" of environmental restoration does a nice job of serving both a profession and a movement. It's the best single source for restoration news. Because this is a new field full of pioneering spirit, the writing is usually straightforward, and the dreaded and stultifying peer-reviewed prose found in so many scientific trade journals is missing. There are longer articles, plus abstracts from diverse small publications and conference proceedings. To the casual observer two things are readily apparent — there is a lot of restoration work going on, and it is beginning to happen all over the world. —*Richard Nilsen*

Restoration & Management Notes, William R. Jordan III, Editor; **$15**/year (2 issues) from: University of Wisconsin Arboretum, 1207 Seminole Highway, Madison, WI 53711 (608) 263-7889

Among other things, [Disneyland] creates tangible fantasy and apparent reality in ways that are pleasing to most of its visitors. But it is not reality. Let us further be clear that the fantasy of a "Disneyland" is better than the reality of another suburban parking lot. Similarly, if a truly native ecosystem cannot be restored, then restoration of something biologically viable and sustainable is far preferable to the complete loss of that ecosystem.

Exactly what are the factors that distinguish a "Disneyland" from a restored native ecosystem? One set of factors that has so far been treated only superficially is the genetics of restoration. The genetic nature of introduced stock can profoundly influence the behavior of the individuals, which in turn may affect the dynamics of the entire community and disrupt or alter the course of co-evolution within the community. All of these effects are of great concern to the restorationist.

What the restorationist creates is rarely, if ever, a finished product. Rather it is a beginning — often an early stage in succession. And if the restoration is to mean anything at all in the long run, attention must be paid to its likely course of development in the future. Thus, the question becomes not just what exists at any particular time, but what processes have been set in motion, what dynamics prevail? In short, how successfully has the project been *aimed*?

Volunteer Chevron Corp. retirees pair off and plant valley oak seed at the Nature Conservancy's Cosumnes River, California, site.

A Survey of Publications Covering Restoration
by Dave Egan

Environmental restoration news is scattered far and wide, often in tiny newsletters, or magazines that cover it occasionally. Dave Egan scans these publications and writes up abstracts of what's interesting for **Restoration & Management Notes** *(see review p. 32) where he is assistant editor. Here are his choices of the best publications. Like the subjects they cover, many of them are fragile — tiny budgets, no advertising revenues, few subscribers — and worthy of your support.*
—Richard Nilsen

American Midland Naturalist

One of the best experimental science journals available to the restoration community. Its articles are well researched and written, not overly laden with technical jargon or unruly statistical data. Recent examples include: "A 12-year study of vegetation and mammal succession on a reconstructed tallgrass prairie in Iowa," "A 20-year study of the effect of prescribed burning on Andropogon scoparius in Connecticut," "Response of Hamamelis virginiana to canopy gaps." Definitely worth trying to obtain either as a subscriber or through your local college library.

American Midland Naturalist, Robert P. McIntosh, Editor; **$50**/year (4 issues) from: American Midland Naturalist, University of Notre Dame Notre Dame, IN 46556

BioScience

While fairly technical in its approach and subject material, this journal still provides restorationists with some interesting reading, particularly in the areas of genetics and biological diversity. Articles from recent issues include: "Blueprint for conserving plant diversity," "Shredders and riparian vegetation," and "Integrated conservation strategy for Hawaiian forest birds."

BioScience, Julie Ann Miller, Editor; **$42**/year (11 issues) from: AIBS, 730 11th Street NW Washington, DC 20001-4584; (202) 628-1500

California Waterfront Age

As the title suggests, this journal focuses on the California coastline, although the information is applicable to other states as well. Recently funded dune, beach, and littoral wetland restoration projects are featured. By placing restoration within the context of a multiple-use resource, **CWA** *provides a pragmatic look at the balancing act between human use and resource management. Recent articles include: "Restoration standards: how to guarantee environmental protection," "Watershed restoration: an idea whose time has come — again," "How public access affects wetlands," and "Stream restoration: the healing touch."*

California Waterfront Age, Rasa Gustaitis, Editor; **free** (4 issues/year) from: California Waterfront Age, State Coastal Conservancy 1330 Broadway, Suite 1100, Oakland, CA 94612 (415) 464-1015

Conservation Biology

This relatively new, smart-looking journal carries very cogent articles about the international preservation and conservation of animal species, especially those which are threatened or endangered. Habitat and ecosystem restoration are discussed as a strategy for accomplishing this larger goal. Recent issues have had some restoration-oriented articles, including: "Restoring island ecosystems: the potential of parasites to control introduced mammals," "Vegetation dynamics (succession and climax) in relation to plant community management," and "Consequences and costs of conservation corridors."

[Suggested by Dave Foreman]

Conservation Biology; David Ehrenfeld, Editor **$32.50**/year (4 issues; includes membership) from: Blackwell Scientific Publications, Inc. 3 Cambridge Center, Suite 208, Cambridge, MA 02142; (617) 225-0401

Fremontia

This journal, like most native-plant society publications, seeks to educate the public on the need to appreciate and preserve their region's native plant populations. An intelligent, horticulture/genetics bent surfaces not only in its articles about rare-plant propagation, but also in probes regarding the long-range effects of restorative plantings amongst native plant populations. Good information on exotic species control is typically available, as well. Recent articles include: "Restoration: Disneyland or a native ecosystem?" and "Can native flora survive prescribed burns?." Interesting reading no matter what your bioregion, and one of the best examples of what an organization might do to encourage others to value their local landscape and native flora.

Fremontia, Phyllis M. Faber, Editor; **$18**/year (4 issues) from: California Native Plant Society 909 12th Street, Suite 116, Sacramento, CA 95814; (916) 477-2677

Natural Areas Journal

This publication provides reports from natural areas about rare species management and monitoring as part of the overall goal of ecosystem preservation. Although it is not **NAJ**'s *major emphasis, restoration has recently received more attention (and thus more journal space) as an important tool for the land manager. It is well written, with a good bibliography of recent publications about restoration and management. Articles from previous issues include: "Structure and composition of low elevation old-growth forests in research natural areas of southeast Alaska," "Managing prairie remnants for insect diversity," and "Design of a long-term ecological monitoring program for Channel Islands National Park, California."*

Natural Areas Journal, Greg F. Iffrig, Editor **$25**/year (4 issues) from: Natural Areas Association, 320 S. 3rd Street, Rockford, IL 61104; (815) 964-6666

Park Science

While the National Park Service is the recipient of criticism from various circles, it nevertheless maintains a solid commitment to scientific, restoration-oriented activities. Their in-house newsletter, **Park Science,** *documents those activities along with myriad other NPS projects. Previous issues have included articles entitled "Non-native mountain goat management undertaken at Olympia National Park," "Endangered species restoration at Gulf Islands Seashore," and "Galapagos botanical management provides perspective for Hawaii."*

Park Science, Jean Mathews, Editor; **free** (4 issues/year) from: Park Science, 4150 Southwest Fairhaven Drive, Corvallis, OR 97333

Wildflower

This journal is very easy to read, yet contains insightful horticultural information for both lay and professional audiences. Its articles are about native wildflowers, their propagation and use in home landscaping as well as in revegetation projects. While the intent is national in focus, many pieces deal with vegetation native to the southern and southwestern United States. Articles from a recent issue include: "Task force recommends: wildflower policy for Minnesota," "Wild sunflowers: heritage and resource," and "Desert botanical garden research: owl-clover and commercial mixes."

Wildflower, John E. Averett, Editor; **$25**/year (2 issues) from: National Wildflower Research Center, 2600 FM 973 North, Austin, TX 78725 (512) 929-3600

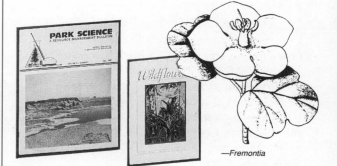

—Fremontia

Other Journals

Other interesting journals and newsletters also cross my desk which are more local or specialized in nature. If they are located in your vicinity or deal with a topic in which you have an interest, I urge you to contact them. The local newsletters can be especially helpful for putting you in touch with restorationists in your area.

Plant Conservation; **$35**/year (4 issues) from: The Center For Plant Conservation, 125 The Arborway, Jamaica Plain, MA 02130 (617) 524-6988

Creek Currents; **$15**/year (4 issues) from: Newsletter of the Urban Creeks Council 2530 San Pablo Avenue, Berkeley, CA 94702 (415) 540-6669

Missouri Prairie Journal; **$20**/year (4 issues) from: The Missouri Prairie Foundation P.O. Box 200, Columbia, MO 65205

The Palmetto; **$20**/year (4 issues) from: Florida Native Plant Society, 2020 Red Gate Road, Orlando, FL 32818; (407) 299-1472

Wetlands Research Update; **free** (2 issues) from: United States Environmental Protection Agency Corvallis Environmental Research Laboratory 200 Southwest 35th Street, Corvallis, OR 97333

*Aquatic biologist Bill McLarney is a founder of
both the New Alchemy Institute (see p. 83) and the
Costa Rican ecodevelopment group ANAI (formerly,
Asociación de los Nuevos Alquimistas). —JB*

ANAI: Restoring a Balance of People and Nature

by Bill McLarney

THOUGH we may not have foreseen it, those of us who pioneered the "Alternatives Movement" in the seventies would come to a crossroads. One road led to bureaucracy — joining or evolving into a "big" organization capable of moving large amounts of money and people. The gratifications of this road are obvious. Less obvious is the apparently ineluctable law that large do-gooder organizations must spend a high percentage of their budgets on non-essential trim.

The bumpy road less taken, which should be posted "fanatics only," leads to a high level of economic efficiency within a deliberately limited area. If the high road may be likened to the R and D department of a large industry, the fanatics' road is like the inventor in the garage, hoping first that the gadget will work, second that it will be used, and finally that it will help him make a decent living.

ANAI has reached the second objective. Not only do our ideas — some of them, anyway — work, other people and organizations are beginning to borrow and adapt them, and we find ourselves being cited as among the few who are actually implementing "sustainable development."

Our agroforestry project, which has assisted some 1,500 farmers in Costa Rica's canton of Talamanca to plant some 2 million crop trees, is being emulated in other parts of Costa Rica, and in Honduras and Belize. Though none of us were trained as organizers, the fact that farmers in 25 communities have worked together voluntarily one day a week for over three years has brought students of community organization knocking on our door. Our land-titling project, already successful in accomplishing its stated goals, is beginning to be studied as one of the first efforts to link peasant land tenure and wildlands conservation. While sustainable development is all the rage these days, it is being realized that Talamanca is one of the few places where such seemingly disparate elements as a wildlife refuge and a marketing cooperative are being fused into a coherent whole, based on an idealistic vision of the future and a lot of hard work in the present.

None of this would have happened without the kind of fanaticism that perversely finds more pleasure rattling down the bumpy road with a toolkit behind the seat than in cruising the four-lane with an AAA card in one's pocket. I unblushingly credit myself as the first fanatic. The proper way to found an organization is to rent an office, hire some administrative help and then set up field projects. ANAI began with a swampy "farm" purchased for 471 dollars and a wild-cane shack with no floor.

Our paid staff at last count numbered 25, plus assorted volunteers and occasional consultants. Some were recruited by me, others are "once or twice removed," via Alberto or someone else. They comprise a diverse lot of Ticos, Gringos, Nicaraguans, Hondurans. . . . One or two are waiting to vote for the first time, while Matute is in his late sixties. In terms of formal education we range from Matute, who never made it to first grade, to yours truly Dr. McLarney. But without exception the crew (including a couple of non-imbibers) are "good drinking company" — people I would choose to spend time with even if we weren't working together.

ANAI's success comes in large part from living with the campesinos of Talamanca. After one eats a certain amount of rice and beans and drinks the requisite amount of guaro, irreplaceable friendships with wonderful people are formed. But if one is honest, one realizes that some of these people really are as lazy as the stereotypical Mexican under the hat. Some are incurably stupid. Some of the most apparently generous individuals turn out to be motivated solely by plans to rip off the "rich" Gringo. In short, they're just like us. But all of them, the thieves and the jerks as surely as the salt of the earth, have children who are scraping by in a deteriorating environment on criminally low incomes and likely receiving an "education" which will prepare them to unwittingly make things worse for *their* children. All the children deserve better.

A man who knows how to keep things in proper perspective, Bill McLarney shows the amateurs how the pros spend lunch hour. He advises,"Never trust a man who owns more than one necktie."

It is possible to simultaneously be awed by some campesino's knowledge of a hundred species of forest trees and appalled to learn that in his mind the only realistic options for forest management are "cut it all down at once" or "cut it all down little by little." One of the questions that should follow this sort of experience is "What can I do to help?" Or, more specifically, "What do I know that they don't know? What door can I help open?" If you can't come up with a convincing answer, admit it, you're a tourist.

It comes down to walking a tightrope between excess humility and paternalism, a viewpoint corroborated by Thomas F. Carroll and Helga Baitenmann of George Washington University. In an evaluation of our work done for the Inter-American Foundation, they wrote that "It may not be enough to help groups of struggling poor people to do what they already know and want. . . . The ANAI case shows that people at the grassroots level often do not 'know how' to maximize their opportunities because they cannot always know what options they have." Part of our job is to point out and cautiously recommend some of the options of which we are aware.

An example comes from our agroforestry projects. Its start found the campesinos of Talamanca reeling from the loss of cacao, their only cash crop, to a disease. When we began organizing community nurseries in Talamanca we envisioned alternatives to cacao — new options in the expanding tropical fruit market. The Talamancans had never heard of an arazá or a mangosteen. How then could they imagine who might buy such fruits? They wanted disease-resistant varieties of cacao and better management techniques.

The nurseries ended up planting both cacao and "the Gringos' crazy fruits." One result is that

Making soil at a community nursery in Talamanca.

Talamanca is back in the cacao business. *But* management costs are much higher than before, and the world price is dropping. And now we are hearing of farmers selling arazá for the equivalent of 65 cents a fruit, or fresh-squeezed arazá juice at 40 cents a glass. Or we hear of a farmer who took a chance and sent four boxes of biribá fruit to San José, where it sold out quickly at a similar price. And where did you say I could get some seed of that new fruit you've imported from Australia?

What it is all evolving toward is an integrated development plan for Talamanca, which we hope will embody lessons and ideas for other places with similar needs. But I think it's important to note that that was not the original goal, even though from the beginning it has been clear that there was an ultimate need for such a plan. Good plans grow from experience, and ANAI's first goal was to experience the place, the people, the problems. Then to identify one project that might do some good if it succeeded and not too much damage if it failed. One project built the confidence — within and outside ANAI — that led to another project. The projects began to make linkages which suggested a "plan," which now involves multiple government and local agencies and thousands of campesinos — and changes every day.

A few funding organizations realize that while adversity may build character, we survivors have character to spare. But there is still plenty of opportunity for others to gain a reputation for sagacity by making the same statement of faith as ANAI's $25 and $100 donors who give what they can knowing we won't quit until the job is done. With more general support and less time invested in writing and repackaging proposals, we could stretch dollars further and be even more efficient in what Carroll and Baitenmann identify as "a task that international centers cannot themselves do and that few national agencies achieve."

Where to write

ANAI gratefully accepts donations, and sometimes takes on resilient, Spanish-speaking volunteers. Write ANAI Incorporated, 1176 Bryson City Road, Franklin, NC 28734.

Man of the Trees

Richard St. Barbe Baker was a man ahead of his time, so far ahead in fact that nearly a decade after his death, the reforestation concepts he was preaching sixty years ago are just beginning to enter the popular consciousness. He traveled the globe teaching people the importance of planting trees, and his description of forests as the lungs of the earth anticipated in a conceptual way the Gaia Theory debated today. It's fair to call him a pioneer of environmental restoration.

*The book **Man of the Trees** is short selections of St. Barbe Baker's writing, taken from seven of his many books. The video by the same name is a documentary of his life, and includes a great sequence with him hugging a big tree as he explains that he does this daily as a way of gathering energy and charging up his batteries. Who knows, in another sixty years maybe we'll understand that too. —Richard Nilsen*

●

For hundreds of miles we had been passing through a graveyard of dying races. That solitary tree we had recorded indicated the extent and speed at which the Saharan octopus has spread itself. It was hard to believe that when Livingstone was exploring Nyasaland, this area was part of the great rain forests of Nigeria. In other areas, flourishing farms have disappeared within the memory of man, and later during this expedition I was to trudge through sand wastes which had been my forest haunts when I had been in Africa thirty years ago. Here one could actually see all the process of degradation, from high forest through the stages of orchard-bush and savannah to drifting sand.

Man of the Trees Video (VHS); **$23** postpaid: catalog **free** from: Music for Little People, P. O. Box 1460, Redway, CA 95560; (800) 346-4445

Man of the Trees
Karen Gridley, Editor
1989; 115 pp.; **$12.50** ($13.50 postpaid) from: Ecology Action
5798 Ridgewood Road
Willits, CA 95490 ✳WEA

Wildlife Habitat Enhancement Council

Corporations control lots of land, and often have little idea what's happening on it (think of the miles of power-line right-of-ways stretching across the landscape). This two-year-old organization is a cooperative venture between some very large U.S. corporations and some very mainline conservation groups. The goals appear to be restoring landholdings to environmental usefulness, making the public happy, and polishing tarnished images a bit. Let's see, that's win, win, win. If you live next to some BIG neighbors, these folks might be able to help you meet them. —Richard Nilsen

Wildlife Habitat Enhancement Council
Membership **$100**;1010 Wayne Avenue/Suite 210, Silver Spring, MD 20910; (301) 588-8994

●

Case Study: Delaware, Maryland and Virginia. **Company:** Delmarva Power & Light, Vienna Power Plant. **Habitat:** The Nanticoke River, a Chesapeake Bay tributary. **Project:** Delmarva Power constructed a $50,000 brooding pond on its Vienna Power Plant grounds to help save the dwindling striped bass population in the Chesapeake Bay and its tributaries. Since 1985, Delmarva Power has released more than 40,000 striped bass fingerlings or rockfish into the Nanticoke River in Maryland.

The Man Who Planted Trees

Jean Giono's short story about a treeplanting hermit in the south of France is a parable of restoration. The oaks and beeches sown by this one man over forty years transform an entire region which had been degraded by deforestation. The animated film of this inspiring story is not just good, it's excellent — winning an Oscar in 1987. Frederic Back's drawing is soft, shimmering, and uses a point of view that's constantly in motion.

Case Studies in Environmental Hope

Yes, the postage does cost more than the book, but this "accentuate the positive" collection of eighteen case studies in environmental progress from Western Australia is the kind of effort that every bio-region on the planet should be publishing. Buy one and use it as a model.
　　　　　　　　　　　　　—Richard Nilsen
　　　　　　　[Suggested by Stephen Hodgkin]

Case Studies in Environmental Hope, Peter Newman, Simon Neville, and Louise Duxbury, Editors; **$6*** ($13.50 postpaid) from: E.P.A. Support Services 2nd Floor, 1 Mount Street Perth, WA 6000, Australia

* Prices quoted are in Australian dollars. The cheapest way to buy this book is to get Australian currency at an exchange and send cash: a bank check adds a lot to the cost.

Environmental Restoration

In 1988, John Berger and his organization Restoring the Earth sponsored a landmark conference in Berkeley, California, that helped put environmental restoration on the map. This book, a collection of the technical papers from the conference, demonstrates the amazing diversity of restoration projects and of the people and groups doing them. Restoration ecology is giving amateur and professional earth workers a common place to hang their hats. —Richard Nilsen

Environmental Restoration, John J. Berger Editor; 1990; 298 pp. **$19.95** ($21.95 postpaid) from: Island Press P.O. Box 7, Covelo, CA 95428; (800) 828-1302 ✳WEA

●

Woodland restorations vary in composition and structure depending on their purposes. . . . Pest species, in this context, are plants that interfere with such restoration goals. The plants may be native or nonnative, and the same species may

Christopher Plummer narrates. The video version is packaged with two other animated shorts by Back; one of them, Crac!, also won an Oscar in 1982. —Richard Nilsen
　　　　　　　　　[Suggested by Tom Waller]

This story has also been made into a wonderful book with striking wood engravings by Michael McCurdy. The hardback version in particular is a treasure both for its subject matter and its high quality of production. —Susan Erkel Ryan

The Man Who Planted Trees Video (VHS) **$33.45** postpaid from: CBC Home Video P.O. Box 6440/Station A, Montreal, QC H3C 3L4, Canada; (514) 597-4040

The Man Who Planted Trees
Jean Giono; 1985; 51 pp.; **$6.95** (paperback); **$13.50** (hardcover) ($8.95 & $16 postpaid) from: Chelsea Green Publishing Co. P.O. Box 130, Route 113 Post Mills, VT 05058 (800) 445-6638 [in VT (802) 878-0315] ✳WEA

Rolly Carrol of Westralian Sands, and his tree tubes.

●

Following sandmining, the deep sands are left in an almost unconsolidated form, and are very difficult to rehabilitate. Rolly reasoned that if a plant had very deep roots and very few leaves, it would stand a greater chance of survival than normal seedling stock. He developed a method using split PVC tubing, and now produces plants which can be planted all year round, even in paspalum or kikuyu grasses, and have a very good chance of out-competing the weeds and flourishing.

operate as a pest in one situation but not in another. . . . These effects are reinforced by microclimate changes brought about by the presence of pest species. In woodlands, such changes can include increased shade, reduced moisture availability, and changes in soil fertility. For example, in the Midwest, Eurasian species often have a longer growing season than American species. Woodland spring ephemerals

Harvesting a wild seed assortment with a Grin Reaper.

require high sun levels to bloom and produce food. Such levels typically occur under the leafless April and May canopies of native trees and shrubs. These herbs are weakened when their habitat is invaded by Eurasian species which produce solid canopies as early as April in parts of the Midwest.

The Restoration of Nonsuch

By David Wingate

In 1951, the world scientific community was stunned by the announcement that the cahow — a bird whose name had become synonymous with extinction because it was thought to have become extinct in the 1600s, around the same time as the dodo — had just been rediscovered. The cahow is a member of the petrel family, in the order which contains albatrosses and shearwaters. It ranges widely in the North Atlantic to the western edge of the Gulf Stream, where it feeds on squid and fish, but it breeds only on the 20 square miles of oceanic islands of Bermuda, located at 32° N and 64° W in the western reaches of the Sargasso Sea, 580 miles east of Cape Hatteras.

As the conservation program launched to save this extraordinary bird from extinction has gradually succeeded against all odds, expanding into the restoration of an entire terrestrial ecosystem on 15-acre Nonsuch Island, the name "cahow" has ultimately attained wider significance as a symbol of hope for conservationists around the world.

Metropolitan Pembroke Parish, modern-day Bermuda.

The history of man on Bermuda provides a stark contrast to the story of the cahow. Settled as a British colony on the strategic sea lanes between the old and new world, the island has become so successful economically that it is now threatened with environmental self-destruction. Bermuda is now the most densely populated, isolated geographic and political unit in the world.

In telling the story of man and the cahow on Bermuda together, from pre-colonial time until the present, I want to try to convey in a chronological perspective what it is like to be involved with a very long-time restoration project — the patience required, the drudgery, the occasional agonizing setback, and, finally, those exhilarating breakthroughs that make it all seem worthwhile.

Our story begins more than 400 years ago when Bermuda was first discovered by Portuguese and Spanish navigators exploring the New World. In those days the treasure-laden galleons from the Spanish Main used to sail north from the West Indies to catch the westerly winds for their return home. Many came to grief in sudden, violent storms on Bermuda's uncharted reefs. As darkness overtook the stranded survivors they were terrified by the hordes of nocturnal seabirds coming and going to and from their nesting grounds each night.

It was in circumstances similar to those of the Spanish that the British first landed on Bermuda. In 1609, a fleet sailing to relieve the Virginia Colony was dispersed by a hurricane near Bermuda and the flagship, the Sea Venture, was shipwrecked on its shores.

In the clear surrounding waters the fish were so tame they could be caught by hand. The land itself was covered in dense forest, and two trees in particular were especially common. The Bermuda cedar provided valuable timber for ships and the palmetto provided leaves for thatching the huts and making ropes and basketware. Both trees provided edible berries for food.

It was a land devoid of mammals. Indeed, the only four-footed land creature to reach Bermuda before man arrived was a small lizard of the skink family. An abundance of sea turtles hauled themselves up on the beaches to bask in the sun or lay their eggs. But by far the most dominant element of the fauna was the birds, because these had no difficulties in colonizing the island across the ocean.

There were landbirds of several species, so tame that they readily landed on the settlers' shoulders. We do not know all the species involved because many were soon to be exterminated by the impact of human settlement. Seabirds were even more abundant, because they were adapted to exploiting the food supply from a vast area of surrounding ocean. By day, tropicbirds or longtails, as we have come to know them, were conspicuous.

These diurnally active seabirds were eclipsed at night by nocturnally active shearwaters and petrels in even larger numbers. One of these, which came to be known as the cahow, outnumbered all of the others put together. The cahow was a ground-nesting, soil-burrowing seabird, and it nested both along the coast and inland, under the forest canopy. Cahows are also some of the fastest and most efficient flyers in the world, and it was this extraordinary ability that enabled them to reach beyond the relatively sterile waters of the Sargasso Sea to feed in the rich upwellings of the Gulf Stream more than 400 miles away.

As on other oceanic islands, the fauna of Bermuda proved exceptionally vulnerable because it had evolved in the absence of man and other mammal predators and showed no fear or defences against them when they eventually arrived.

Legislation was passed in order to save the sea turtles as early as 1620. Seabirds were destroyed not only by man himself, but by a plague of rats which reached the islands accidentally in 1614 and by the cats and dogs which were brought in to control the rats. In less than thirty years the abundant cahow was reduced to the verge of extinction and only its fossil bones — which remain in caves and manmade excavations even today — attest to its former abundance.

By 1684 it was all over. The Bermuda Company, formed to exploit the islands' virgin resources, disbanded and those settlers who remained were ultimately forced to go it alone, and to learn a new way of life in order to live in balance with the land. Thus evolved a race of true Bermudians who disdained to work the land, but like the cahows turned their attention back to the sea as a source of survival.

The middle and late 19th century was a time of great cultural infusion and contact between Bermuda and the outside world. Many of the officers of the British naval garrisons had an interest in the natural sciences and their explorations provided the first detailed scientific descriptions of

Nonsuch Island.

Bermuda's geology and natural history, beginning about 1840. Among other things their curiosity inspired them to look into the almost legendary accounts of the cahow bird by the early settlers. Their investigations were concentrated on the remote Castle Harbour Islands, where local fishermen continued to report nocturnally active seabirds which were indiscriminately referred to as pimlico or cahows. These islands were investigated by a number of naturalists between 1840 and 1900, but the only nocturnal seabird they ever succeeded in finding was the pimlico, or Audubon's shearwater. This led some to conclude that "cahow" was a synonym for the shearwater, but others, like the famous naturalist Addison E. Verrill, concluded that the cahow must have been a species of auk!

The confusion lingered on into the early 1900s, when new evidence clarifying the identity of the bird was discovered in the form of abundant fossil bone deposits in Bermuda limestone caves. By 1915 these bones had been examined by the avian paleontologist R. W. Shufeldt at Carnegie Museum, who identified them as a species of gadfly petrel, quite distinct from the bones of Audubon's shearwater which also occurred, though in lesser numbers, in the same caves. It was the sheer abundance of these bones together with the pronounced hooked bill that led Shufeldt to conclude that they must represent the legendary hook-billed cahows of the early settlement days.

Then an amazing fact came to light. In 1906 Louis Mowbray, a Bermudian naturalist, had actually collected a living gadfly petrel from a crevice on one of the Castle Harbour Islands. The specimen had been preserved and sent to the American Museum of Natural History. Its bones were now compared with the fossils and found to be identical! Thus was the type specimen of the Bermuda petrel — *Pterodroma cahow* — described in 1916.

It may seem incredible now that no one followed up on this revelation at the time, until we remember that this was during the Great War, when an entire generation of European and American men were wiped out in the muddy trenches of Europe. It was also before the age of conservation when the emphasis was still on collecting and cataloging of species in the world's museums, rather than studying the living organisms in their actual environment.

Thirty years were to pass before another specimen of the cahow turned up: this time a fledgling which was killed when it flew against St. David's lighthouse in June 1935. The specimen was taken to Dr. William Beebe, who was based on Bermuda doing fish studies with the New York Zoological Society at the time. Beebe was an ardent naturalist and prolific writer who was one of the first to popularize natural history subjects for the general public. He would have liked nothing better than to claim the rediscovery of a bird that had been presumed extinct. Nevertheless, he continued to be confused between the cahow and the shearwater and his photographs confirm that the shearwater was once again the only species whose nests were found. It was Dr. Robert Cushman Murphy, Curator of Birds at the American Museum of Natural History and a world authority on seabirds, who eventually provided the identification of this second known cahow specimen.

When World War II broke out, Bermuda's strategic location resulted in an airport. The airport greatly facilitated the process of new plant and animal introductions, especially those species (such as insects) with a short life span, which had previously had difficulty surviving the transit time to the islands. In the mid-1940s two small scale insects were accidentally imported to Bermuda on ornamental junipers from California. The Bermuda cedar (actually a juniper) had evolved in isolation from such pests and had no natural resistance to these scales. There were no parasites or predators to keep them under control. In the space of only three years, between 1948 and 1952, more than 96 percent of those trees which had formed a virtual monoculture on the island, were destroyed. It was a harsh reminder, once again, of the eco-

The beginnings of restoration: native palmettos planted amid the dead cedars, 1964.

logical fragility that is so characteristic of oceanic island fauna and flora.

Due to the cedar forest decimation, for the first time in their history Bermudians began to think seriously about the need for conservation. No event could have been more timely to focus this concern, or to give hope that all need not be lost, than the rediscovery in 1951 of the cahow by Dr. Robert Cushman Murphy and Louis S. Mowbray.

It seemed inconceivable that the cahow, the most vulnerable species of all, which had declined to oblivion within the first few years of Bermuda's settlement, could possibly have survived up to and beyond such recent traumatic events as the bulldozing of the airport — which destroyed more than half of its original nesting islands — and the loss of the cedar. Nevertheless, a third cahow was found washed up dead on the beach of Cooper's Island in 1945 and provided the inspiration for a last-ditch search expedition.

I was only a schoolboy at the time, but my budding interest in birds secured me an invitation to join

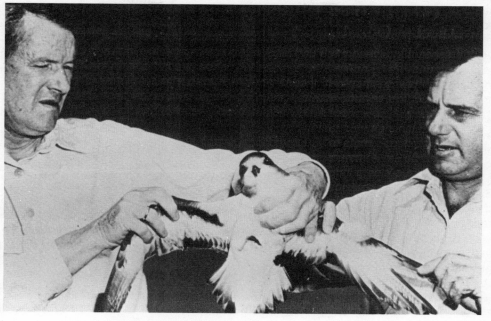

"By Gad, the cahow!", 1951.

the expedition on the day of rediscovery and I will never forget the elation on Dr. Murphy's face when he and Mowbray succeeded in noosing a bird out of its deep nesting crevice, held it up to the light, and exclaimed, "By Gad, the cahow!"

Incredibly it had survived for over three and a half centuries on a few inconsequential offshore islets, totalling no more than three acres in area, which the mammal predators had been unable to colonize. The government immediately declared these islands sanctuaries in 1951 and a conservation programme was launched to try to help the bird.

To replace the dead cedar forest, a massive reforestation programme was begun at about the same time. The emphasis was on fast-growing exotic species like the Australian casuarina tree and a variety of more colourful ornamentals such as the poinciana. Concentrated on roadsides and government-owned lands at first, it eventually led to the establishment of parks and formal gardens for the recreational benefit of the general public.

The decade of the 1960s saw such a rape of the environment for new real estate subdivisions that the government was forced to act by imposing stringent new planning regulations. But even though a planning department was established in 1965 and a succession of development plans with different categories of zoning have been set into law, the fact remains that between 300 and 600 new housing units are still being added to the diminutive and finite landscape each year.

The most frightening aspect of this trend is that it involves the entire island and is wreaking havoc with that resource of natural beauty, peace and tranquility — the Bermuda Image — which is the fundamental selling point of our tourist-dominated economy. Bermuda is turning into a city without a countryside. Open spaces survive only as a few isolated green islands, completely surrounded by suburbia.

The task at hand is urgent and complex but the miracle of Bermuda is that despite such intense development and abuse so many fragile features of our unique natural heritage survive in small pockets here and there. We haven't lost a species since 1900.

Of all the nature reserves which have been established on Bermuda since the 1960s none has attracted more attention internationally than the Castle Harbour Island group where the rediscovery of the cahow in 1951 has inspired an ambitious restoration effort to create a Living Museum of precolonial Bermuda on 15-acre Nonsuch Island.

Nonsuch Island differs from most other nature reserves in that it is a product of restoration rather

than protection. When first established in 1961 it was essentially a desert island, having formerly been used as a yellow fever quarantine hospital and later as a reformatory. Its once-magnificent cedar forest had been entirely destroyed by the cedar scale epidemic; wind, salt spray and free-roaming goats had reduced the remaining vegetation to a dense grass cover. The bird life had disappeared with the forest.

Nevertheless, its potential for restoration as a reserve for endangered native flora and fauna was enormous. In the first place its isolation from Bermuda's mainland meant that many of the introduced exotic species had not yet reached the island and could be prevented from doing so by quarantine measures. The second feature of Nonsuch which made it so ideal as a reserve for endangered flora and fauna was its diverse topography, which made it possible to restore samples of all the major habitats of precolonial Bermuda except the wetlands.

The cahow conservation programme was launched immediately after the discovery of the breeding islets in 1951. It soon became apparent why the cahow had escaped detection for so long. The bird is an extremely elusive and difficult subject to study. No one has ever photographed one on the open ocean, where the cahow spends most of its life. Returning from the ocean to breed only on the darkest and stormiest nights of winter, when its isolated and wave-swept nesting islets are least accessible to boats, it nests only in the deepest crevices of the rocky cliffs. It is impossible to see the nesting birds without the aid of a bright flashlight and a mirror attached to a pole. Cahows seldom leave any sign of their coming and going at nest entrances; even when they do, rain and salt spray soon obliterate the evidence.

It took ten years just to discover the entire nesting population of 18 pairs. By that time research had revealed that the major factor limiting the cahow was not rat predation, as previously suspected, but nest-site competition with the still common white-tailed tropicbird or longtail, whose breeding niche has always been the natural crevices and holes of Bermuda's coastal cliffs. In the absence of sufficient soil for digging their own burrows, two-thirds of the surviving cahows were trying to nest in coastal cliffs. This might not have mattered except that the breeding seasons of the two species overlapped. The winter-breeding cahows lay their single egg in January and are already leaving their newly hatched chick unattended in daytime when the larger and more aggressive tropicbirds return to breed in early March. These birds would simply peck the cahow

White-tailed tropicbird.

chick to death, push it to one side and take over the nest for their own purposes. The adults of the two species rarely met, because by the time the tropicbirds laid and began staying overnight to incubate, the nocturnal cahows had abandoned their failed nest for the year. Both species are long-lived and faithful to the same nestsite, so the pattern would repeat itself year after year. It is incredible that the cahow could have survived for so long when two-thirds of the breeding pairs were being subjected to this loss every year.

The first major emphasis of the conservation programme, therefore, apart from rat control, was to solve this problem of nestsite competition. This was eventually achieved with a simple device called a baffler, which took advantage of the size difference between the two species. By fitting a board with a fixed-dimension, elliptical hole in the entrance to each crevice, the larger tropicbird could be excluded — just as starlings can be excluded from bluebird nestboxes. When this program was fully implemented by 1961, it effectively trebled the reproductive success and laid the foundation for recovery. No chicks have been lost to tropicbirds since that time.

To accommodate the anticipated increase, I began constructing nesting burrows artificially on the vegetated tops of the nesting islets, where the tropicbirds were less likely to find them. This "government housing scheme," as I dubbed it, has gradually expanded until now more than half of the cahows depend on these artificial nest sites. They really had no choice because new pairs will colonize only close to pre-established pairs and there simply are no other suitable natural crevices on these islands.

Cahow government housing.

The most obvious island to accommodate an expansion of cahows was Nonsuch because of its close proximity to the existing cahow islets and its isolation from the rest of Bermuda, making its management as a predator-free reserve feasible by quarantine. We finally persuaded the government to add Nonsuch to the Sanctuary system by declaration in 1961. The following year one of the vacant and derelict quarantine hospital buildings was restored into a house, so I could move onto the island as a warden. I was newly married at the time and needed a place to live. Despite the

Restoration plantings slowly begin to resemble a forest, 1975.

hardship of island living — there was no electricity or telephone when I first moved out — I could hardly have dreamed of a greater paradise. I already knew that the cahow was unlikely to increase fast enough to spread back onto Nonsuch in my lifetime, because of its extremely low reproductive potential. Each pair produces only one egg a year, and only about half of these are fledged successfully. In addition, it takes eight to ten years before those fledglings reach breeding age, and during this time natural mortality reduces their number even further. By 1965 there were new and ominous signs that the breeding success was declining even further. After long and tedious international research the cause was eventually identified as the breakdown product of DDT poison in the environment.

The cahow, feeding at the end of the foodchain, obtained just enough poison to cause eggshell thinning by enzymatic imbalances. The thin-shelled eggs were vulnerable to breakage in the nest, reducing breeding success from 60 percent to as low as 35 percent by 1967. The worst aspect of this problem was that it was international in scope and totally beyond my personal control.

The progress of the cahow breeding program was agonizingly slow; with the added menace of DDT, my efforts became a numbed routine. I needed a distraction, something with more hope of success, to justify Nonsuch Island's continued existence as a nature reserve. This is when it occurred to me to take advantage of its unique isolation and topography, and make it a living museum for all of Bermuda's terrestrial flora and fauna.

The restoration of Nonsuch Island began as a spare-time diversion, but it quickly became my main project. Between 1963 and 1972 I planted more than 8,000 trees and woody shrubs on Nonsuch Island, representing the full range of Bermuda's native forest species. Progress was painfully slow at first, because with no windbreaks severe winter gales and salt spray burned the little palmetto palms, olivewoods and other native trees right back to grass level. I began to fear that I would never even see the fruits of this labour in my lifetime. I was really doing something for the future, just hoping that the next generation would still believe in it.

In an effort to speed things up, I began using castor pomace fertilizer, and in 1967 I decided to plant the periphery of the island with a windbreak forest of casuarinas, the fast-growing, non-native, evergreen tree which was used extensively on mainland Bermuda for reforestation purposes after the loss of the cedars. The castor pomace fertilizer turned out to be an ideal high-protein food for the soil-burrowing, native land-crab, which began to multiply rapidly, causing soil erosion problems.

The windbreak of casuarinas around the periphery of the island made it possible for the native forest to grow a little faster, and once it began to knit together into a thicket, the winter gales rode over the top. When that happened, the forest really began to take off, and I began to get some habitat diversity — microhabitats — and I could begin to seed in

David Wingate captains a boatload of native plants to Nonsuch.

some of the more fragile understory species.

Throughout this period I had been unable to include the endemic Bermuda cedar in my reforestation, because the scale insects were still abundant and seeding trees were barely viable. However, approximately 4 percent of the mainland forest had managed to survive the scale, and by 1970 it had become apparent that natural selection, combined with effective biological control methods implemented by the government, were beginning to turn the tide. I finally undertook my first mass-planting of 600 Bermuda cedars on Nonsuch in 1972. Although death rates were high, approximately 200 ultimately survived and emerged above the other slow-growing native trees to dominate the canopy in several parts of the island.

By the early seventies, I had an emerging native forest, and it was now possible to begin thinking about restoring the native fauna which had lived in that forest. My first attempt at faunal introduction involved the Bermuda race of the white-eyed vireo. I netted several of the vireos on the main island and released them on Nonsuch. They settled so successfully into the recreated environment that they now exhibit a population density twice that on Bermuda's mainland. They even seem to be reverting to their original fearlessness, as described by the early settlers.

Constructing the artificial freshwater pond, 1975.

In 1975 my dream of artificially creating wetland habitats on Nonsuch was finally realized. A small freshwater pond was created by slightly deepening a depression between two hills, laying down an impermeable plastic liner and covering it with soil. The liner formed a hanging water table, which trapped rainfall to produce a four-foot-deep pond. Within little over a year I had established a community that was indistinguishable from a natural marsh. The saltmarsh pond was created in a very low-lying area immediately behind the South beach dune by simply excavating to below the water table level. In this area a pond resulted from natural seepage without the need for a liner.

Freshwater pond two years old, 1977.

The ponds were a prerequisite for my next project in restoration, which was the reestablishment of a species that had been totally exterminated from Bermuda. The early settlers had described herons and egrets of several species, so tame that they could be clubbed down out of the trees. It wasn't long before they were completely exterminated. Although their nearest relations — migrant herons from North America — continue to be common as transients and winterers, they had never reestablished nesting colonies. For several years I had noticed that one of these species, the crustacean-eating yellow-crowned night heron, would eat my fertilizer-feeding landcrabs during stopovers on Nonsuch. It occurred to me that if I could induce night herons to breed on Bermuda, they might serve as a valuable biological control for these crabs, which are generally regarded as a pest on lawns and golf courses.

The fossil discovery of a night heron skeleton in a Bermuda sinkhole at about this time confirmed the wisdom of my choice. The endemic Bermuda night heron had clearly been derived from the yellow-crown, but had evolved shorter legs and a heavier bill, adaptations specific to feeding on the heavily armoured terrestrial crabs.

Night heron nestlings imported from Florida.

With Bermuda government funding and support as a landcrab biological control measure, I was able to obtain nestlings from a large rookery in Tampa Bay, Florida. From 1976 to 1978, a total of 44 yellow-crown nestlings were shipped to Nonsuch and reared in an abandoned building. Although hand-rearing of this species had never been attempted before, it proved to be the easiest and most successful of my restoration projects. Night herons feed their chicks by regurgitation into the nest rather than feeding each chick directly. This meant that I merely had to place the chopped-up crabs onto a food tray. Whenever the chicks were hungry they would gather around this tray like barnyard chickens. As soon as they were old enough to fly, I permitted them to escape from the building to learn to hunt on their own, but they continued to return to the food tray until they were proficient.

As I had hoped, these herons did not leave Bermuda, although they wandered extensively in the landcrab-infested areas beyond Nonsuch Island. At first I was disappointed that they did not nest on Nonsuch Island. They made good use of its ponds, often bringing their fledglings over to bathe and roost there as soon as they could fly. Then in 1985 I discovered that a small nesting colony had established in coastal buttonwood bushes on the isolated South Point of Nonsuch. As the native forest continued to grow, it gradually became more favourable for them. After a quarter-century, the palmettos, olivewoods and cedars were at last attaining maturity and beginning to self-seed. Everything was knitting together. My elation could hardly be contained when in 1987 I found night herons nesting throughout the island's forest, just as they must have done in precolonial time. They continued to feed almost entirely on landcrabs, reducing the Nonsuch population to manageable levels again and doing such an effective job on the golf courses on Bermuda's mainland that the managers were soon able to stop the use of poison baits for crab control.

Although the project suffered a setback in 1988 as a result of illegal harvesting of most of the breeding stock, my discovery of more than 300 additional juveniles that had been produced outside the reserve gives hope that the species will establish successfully.

As the project has matured, the island has become ever more diverse and interesting and its value as an aid in teaching about Bermuda's heritage has increased. By confining visitors to a system of grassy trailways and making use of blinds, it is possible to show all of Bermuda's terrestrial habitats in microcosm without disturbing the wildlife.

The Living Museum continues to provide new insights, too. On September 25, 1987, Bermuda experienced its first hurricane in 25 years and the most severe winds and sea flooding in almost a century. In the 35 years since the loss of the native Bermuda cedars, an entirely new flora had developed on the main island through deliberate and natural reforestation. It was characterized by fast-growing and tall tree species, more than 95 percent of them non-native. This forest had never been tested by a major hurricane and the result, when it finally happened, was unmitigated disaster.

In less than three hours, Hurricane Emily destroyed more than 30 percent of the trees, mainly by uprooting and breakage. Ornamental parks and gardens dominated by the tall-growing casuarinas were especially hard hit, with 70 percent blowdown in some areas. Utility wires were devastated, leaving most of the island without electricity for two weeks. The vulnerability of this new non-native forest to wind damage had been predicted and forewarned against for several years, as local conservationists tried to encourage residents to make more use of native species in their gardens. But the warnings went unheeded until Emily. It only needed the benefit of a field trip to Nonsuch after that to put the point over forcefully, because its smaller-statured native forest survived virtually unscathed. The demand for native tree species for planting gardens and roadsides has since soared.

Emily began to provide some real character to the maturing forest by enhancing the wind-sheared and gnarled appearance of the trees, and by partly uprooting some palmettos, which will now record a pronounced bend in their trunks as they continue to grow. And there was a further lesson. I had often pondered how the cahows could have exca-

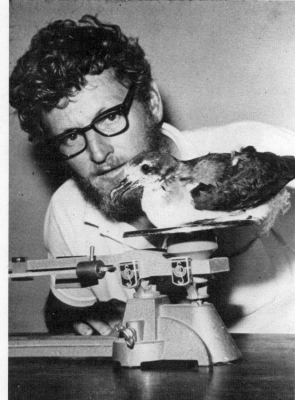

David Wingate and orphaned cahow chick, 1973.

vated their burrows into the root-matted soil under Bermuda's precolonial forest, because the soil on Nonsuch had remained hard-packed despite the shallow burrowing efforts of the landcrabs. But in a few moments of extreme violence, Emily had slightly uprooted a number of trees, lifting the root mats to create ready-made underground cavities ideal as nesting places.

This brings me back full circle to the cahow itself, that incredible symbol of survival and hope, which inspired the Living Museum project in the first place. Out on the offshore islets, the cahows' fortunes had begun to turn around. This resulted in part from the baffler-induced increase in productivity of the early 1960s which was beginning to be reflected eight to ten years later, as those extra chicks returned to breed. The battle to ban the use of DDT in the U. S. and Canada had finally been won and the breeding success of the affected species was gradually beginning to improve.

In the eighties the cahows experienced a further surge of population increase. By 1987, the population had doubled to 42 pairs. It was even resilient enough by then to absorb the loss of five sub-adult birds, killed by a vagrant snowy owl from the Arctic.

Throughout the sixties and seventies I would often walk down to the South Point on Nonsuch Island at the end of a hard day's work, hoping just once to be lucky enough to see or hear a cahow from there, without having to take a boat to the smaller islets. It finally happened one stormy night about 1982 and I have never been disappointed since. Indeed, I can now on occasion sit in comfort on the porch of the Nonsuch warden's residence and listen to the eerie calls of cahows out over the bay. I still don't know whether my dream of seeing them colonize under the island's restored native forest will be realized in my lifetime, but I might have good reason for cautious optimism — were it not for what is happening to the rest of my homeland on the other side of the harbour.

Editor's note: Endangered species require human champions if their survival is to be assured. If you would like to help fund an endowment to guarantee the cahow's future, send contributions to:

Cahow Account, Bermuda Audubon Society, P. O. Box HM 1328, Hamilton, Bermuda

Fences are an integral part of many restoration, preservation and land-stewarding efforts; seems like you're always fencing somebody or something in or out. Moreover, the situation tends to change, requiring fences to be removed (preferably without damaging the parts) about as often as built. Either way, we are talking labor-intensive at its most labor intensive. Here are a few helpful ways to ease the pain. —JB

Building Fences

You can save yourself money and grief if you choose the appropriate fence type wisely, and install it using procedures proven by more than a century of farm experience. I recommend that you resist the temptation to use shortcuts. Do it by the book. This one covers the most commonly used fence varieties and materials, gates, and the tools involved. It's all presented in an easily used, unambiguous manner — just what you'd expect from a publication emanating from a Vocational Instruction outfit.

Building Fences
J. Howard Turner
Editor; 1974; 96 pp.
$5.50 postpaid from:
AAVIM
120 Driftmier Center
Athens, GA 30602
✳WEA

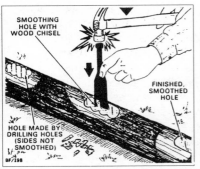

Chisel out hole to accommodate rail. Smooth uneven sides with wood chisel or wood rasp. Corner posts will have two holes drilled at 90 degrees to each other at each rail position. Do not drill all the way through the post. End posts are not drilled all the way through.

Fence Post Pounder

Anyone who has attempted to drive steel fence posts with a sledgehammer knows what it feels like to nurse a thoroughly bruised hand (even the experts miss the post now and then). A pounder slips over the post so it can't miss. This not only saves your hand, the work goes a whole bunch faster. I prefer a pounder of medium weight and equipped with handles. That may sound nitpicky, but any advantage you can get will be welcome after a few dozen posts are behind you; using one of these all day is just plain S&M.

$15-$20 check your local hardware store.

Kevin Kelly

Last-A-Lifetime Post Hole Digger

Liz Fial

Lifetime, eh? Well, this tool might just help you live out your allotted years, because it sinks nice, round holes more easily than any other people-powered device. The secret is in the height or, rather, the lack of it. It's just right for leaning your entire weight upon — something not possible with conventional designs. The handlebars encourage authoritative twisting through hard spots and past villainous stones. It'll accept abuse too: it's all humongous thick steel except for the not-quite-soft-enough handgrips. A handy adjustment gives hole diameters from 5" to 7" diameter, making the thing useful for transplanting chores. This is the one to get, even for the hired hand.

Last-A-Lifetime Post Hole Digger, $60 postpaid. Brochure free from: Seymour Manufacturing Co., 500 N. Broadway, Seymour, IN 47274 (800) 457-1909; in IN (812) 522-2900

Wire Gripper • One-Man Stretcher

This cam-action gripper transforms a come-along or even a small block

Liz Fial

& tackle into a fence-tightener. A pair of them will enable you to bring the loose ends of broken fencing close enough to splice. Note that it is possible to get the blood blister of a lifetime if you happen to feed this thing any part of your anatomy; stand clear and wear extra-thick barbed-wire proof leather gloves. Goggles are a good idea too, in the event something lets go suddenly and goes zzzzzzzssssssssshhhhh.

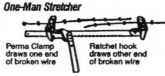

One-Man Stretcher

Perma Clamp draws one end of broken wire   Ratchet hook draws other end of broken wire

If you do lots of wire fencing, you might consider a purpose-built fence tightener such as this one made by Durbin-Durco. It's lighter than many come-alongs, and is easier to manipulate, especially if you are a crew of one. Like the Handyman Jack (see right) this device is a wonderful example of good old American rural hardware of a sort seldom seen these days. It works just fine.

Wire Gripper Information **free** from: Maasdam Pow'r-Pull, Inc., P.O. Box 6130, Burbank, CA 91510; (213) 845-8769

One-Man Stretcher Information **free** from: Durbin-Durco, P.O. Box 8396, St. Louis, MO 63132; (314) 993-4750

Miscellany

*A fencer will also find use for small bolt-cutters (18" is handy — buy good quality only, or cuss notched cutter jaws, **$45-80),** a 6-foot digging bar with flat chisel tip at one end and a tamper at the other (about **$25),** and a simple carpenter belt to hold tools, staples, water and lunch. Check your local hardware store.*

Handyman Jack

If you think fence-building is an onerous task, I invite you to try fence-removing. The wire succumbs without a whimper to small bolt cutters or a fencing tool. But the posts . . . ah, the posts. Three-hundred-and-fifty of them suckers per mile. Be they wood or steel, they don't wanna be uprooted, and they'll fight you every inch of the way, screaming. Flatlanders yank them with a tractor-mounted hydraulic rig made for that purpose. Unfortunately, many unwanted fences festoon terrain that will not permit tractor operation or the land-scarring therefrom.

I've taken out many miles of fence posts with the simple arrangement shown here. You'll need a Handyman or similar big farm jack. And you'll need about a yard of good-quality welded-link chain made of 1/4" steel. Make up the chain into a loop, using a 3/8" bolt 3" long, equipped with a washer at each end to keep it from pulling though the links. The nut will have to be jammed, or fiended with a punch to keep it from leaving under stress. Under jacking force, the chain will grip any post by wedging action.

Liz Fial

To yank a steel post, repeatedly loop the chain over the post until you have an unseemly wad just loose enough to slide down to ground level. Pull a bit of slack from the bottom of the tangle and slip it over the jack nose. The jack should be nuzzling the post.

For wood posts, drop one chain loop over the post and let it fall to the ground. Twist the chain choke-tight, using the bolt as a handle. Slip the bolt and a bit of slack over the jack nose.

Jack away, taking care not to pinch your free hand between the post and the jack as they lean together under pressure. It may help to rock the jack a bit, using it as a lever. The post will come out, usually undamaged, or it will break off underground (not surprising, as the jack can muster 7000 lbs. of moxie). A crew of two can jack about three posts every ten minutes, including the walk. The extra person greatly speeds the procedure by helping to steady everything as the jacking proceeds, then sprinting ahead to ready the next post. Works great!

Handyman Jack
$42-$49, Information **free** from: Harrah Mfg. Co. Drawer 228, Bloomfield, IN 47424-0228

Fencing Tool

This all-purpose tool hammers in and extracts staples from wood fence posts. It cuts and twists wire. It installs and removes clips. It saves you carrying a whole beltload of separate tools.

Fencing Tool (Utility Pliers), 10 1/2" length, 7/32" wire cap. **$16.50** ($18.98 postpaid) from: A.M. Leonard, Inc., P.O. Box 816, Piqua, OH 45356-0816; (800) 543-8955; in OH (513) 773-2694

Weed Wrench

Here is a new tool designed for restoration ecology work in the Marin County, California, section of the Golden Gate National Recreation Area. In the endless contest between native plants and escaped exotic species, the broom family is a major problem. It's fast-growing, shallow-rooted and self-seeds with a vengeance. For the park rangers and volunteers attempting to remove acres of the stuff, the Weed Wrench was invented. Pincher jaws clasp plants up to 2 1/2 inches in diameter at ground level, and the long handle levers out the roots. It has also been used with success on gorse and young acacias and eucalyptuses. Consider it a major back-saver. —Richard Nilsen

The Weed Wrench comes in three sizes: Light, up to 1.5 inch stem, 42 inches, 12 pounds; Medium, up to 2 inch stem, 51 inches, 18 pounds; Heavy (shown here), up to 2.5 inch stem, 60 inches, 25 pounds.

Weed Wrench; **$90-$140** f.o.b.; brochures **free** from: New Tribe, 3435 Army Street #330 San Francisco, CA 94110; (415) 647-0430

These same folks also manufacture the SaddlePack (a daypack that distributes the weight of your load around your torso, actually supporting your back instead of straining it) and the Treeboat hammock modular sleeping system. —S.E. Ryan

A.M. Leonard

For the serious gardener, or plant propagator, Leonard's has the most complete line of pruning shears, grafting and budding knives, nursery hoes, planting tools, watering accessories and marking equipment available by mail order. Most horticulture supply companies demand professional credentials before they will sell to you — Leonard's doesn't. Prices are retail, but if you order more than one of most items, there are discounts. Leonard has been around a long time, and most of the products have withstood the test of their professional users over time. —Paul Hawken

A.M. Leonard; Catalog **$1** from: A.M. Leonard, Inc., 6665 Spiker Road, P.O. Box 816, Piqua, OH 45356; (800) 543-8955, in OH (513) 773-2694

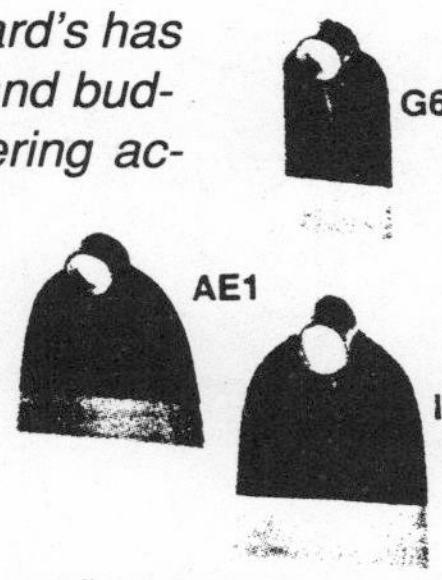

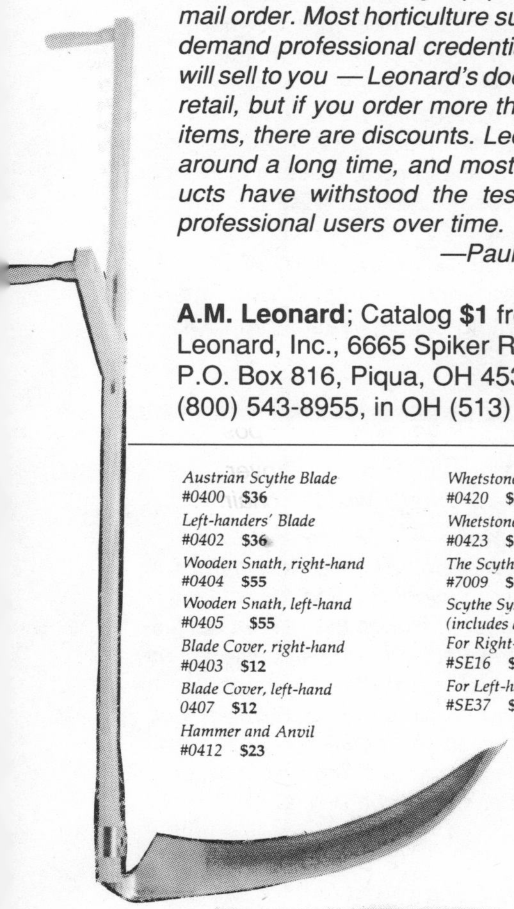

Austrian Scythe Blade #0400 **$36**	*Whetstone* #0420 **$3.75**	
Left-handers' Blade #0402 **$36**	*Whetstone Sheath* #0423 **$3.50**	
Wooden Snath, right-hand #0404 **$55**	*The Scythe Book* #7009 **$6.95**	
Wooden Snath, left-hand #0405 **$55**	*Scythe System Set (includes all of the above)*	
Blade Cover, right-hand #0403 **$12**	*For Right-handed Use* #SE16 **$125**	
Blade Cover, left-hand 0407 **$12**	*For Left-handed Use* #SE37 **$125**	
Hammer and Anvil #0412 **$23**		

6FEL-HEAVY DUTY FELCO Blades are shorter, narrow, tapered design resulting in more powerful cutting stroke. Narrow grip for smaller Hands. Blades easy to replace. Ea. .... NET **$28.50** *$SAVE MORE; 3 $26.00; 6 $24.50*

5FEL-FELCO MEDIUM WEIGHT 9" all steel construction of high resistance. easy-to-change replaceable cutting blades; quality pruner economically priced; coated handles. Ea. .... NET **$16.30** *$SAVE MORE: 3 $15.20; 6 $14.10*

GRUBBING / GRADING HOES
G6-GRUBBING HOE heavy duty one piece 41/2" x 81/2" forged blade. Tapered cutting edge for exceptional balance. 54" handle. Wt. 4 lbs. .... NET ea. **$21.00**
XG6-GRUB HOE head only ..... NET ea. **$14.60**

OAT-ALUMA-BOSS-Aluminum Tags for inexpensive permanent all-weather labeling. Each side takes an impression, with no show-through. Complete with 9" non-rust aluminum ties. Packed 500 Tags with wires per box, 25 boxes per carton* 12,500 labels)

OAT-3" x 7/8" Standard size. Per box. **$23.60**

OAT-4-4" x 13/4" extra large size. Per box. .... **$56.90** *2000-5000 Less 10%; 5000 Less 20%; *Per Carton Less 33⅓%*

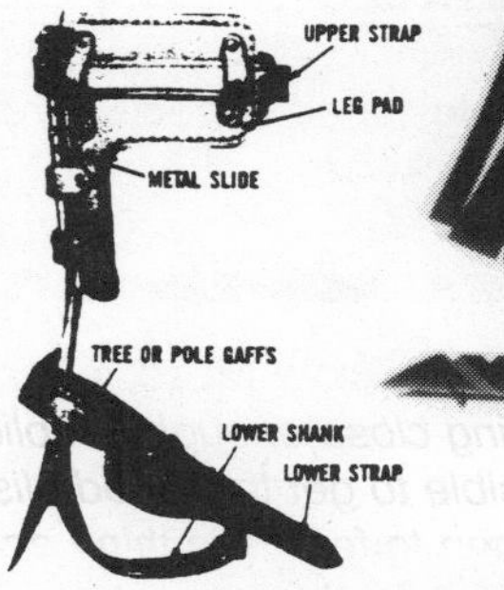

Buckingham permanent gaff, adjustable tree climbers with 31/2 "gaff, measured on the underside. Leg irons are medium weight. Straps and pads of top quality leather.
1400-CLIMBING SPURS 31/2" gaff for rough bark.(Spurs only). Wt. 4.6 lbs. **$84.67**

Wood Rim Riddles

Riddles are sieves that have a dozen uses. This traditional riddle, made near Derbyshire in the Peak district of England, is excellent for sifting soil, removing rocks, screening potting soil, winnowing beans or seeds. Made from timber elm or English beech, depending on availability. ¼" mesh. 16" diameter.
#4850 **$21**

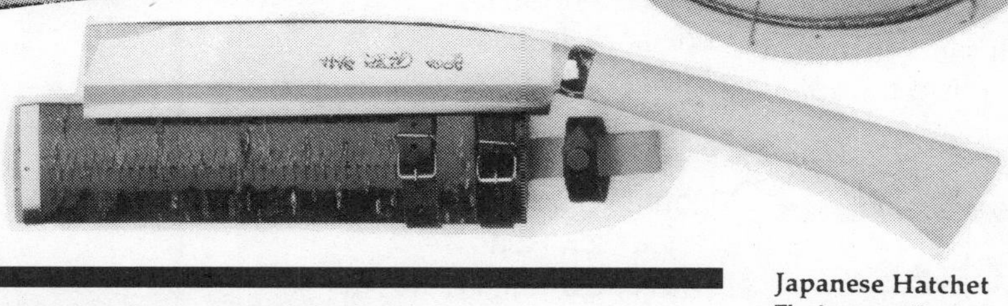

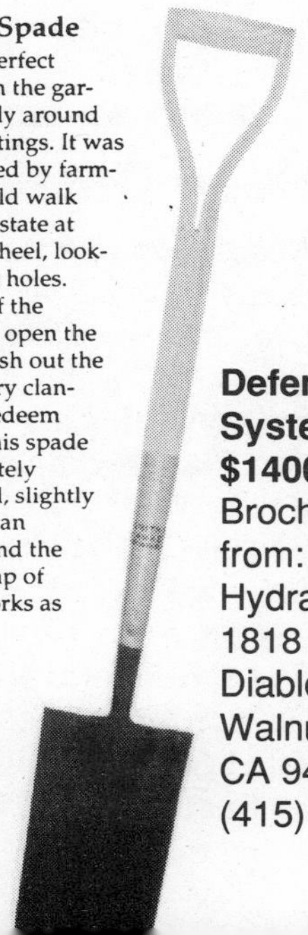

Poacher's Spade

This tool is perfect for digging in the garden, especially around existing plantings. It was originally used by farmers who would walk the squire's estate at dusk, dog at heel, looking for rabbit holes. A swift cut of the spade would open the warren to flush out the game. All very clandestine. To redeem it, we offer this spade as an exquisitely balanced tool, slightly dished, with an ash handle and the Bulldog stamp of quality. It works as well in the garden as it ever did in the field. Head: 5½" by 10½". Length: 36". 3 lbs., 1oz.
#5514 **$45**

Smith & Hawken

Smith & Hawken's reputation is based on good service and their super-duty garden implements. My own experience matches that of most folks who own these tools: the forks and spades are damn near unbreakable, even under severe abuse such as busting caliche. The high quality and good design make the tools satisfying to handle and use, a rare experience these days. (Smith & Hawken also have a catalog of fancy garden accessories.) —JB

Smith & Hawken; Tool Catalog **free** from: Smith & Hawken, 25 Corte Madera, Mill Valley, CA 94941; (415) 383-2000

Japanese Hatchet

The Japanese Hatchet resembles a cleaver more than our own traditional hatchet. This particular one borders on art. It is made of laminated steel, the blade is highly polished and it comes in a cherry bark case which can strap handily onto your belt. Great for chopping, kindling, limbing, trimming and shaping. Each of these is handmade by a single craftsman. Certainly, one of the most beautiful tools we have ever carried. Overall length: 16½". Blade length: 8½". Weight: 1¼" lbs.
#2730 **$69**

Wildfire Across America • Dragon Assassin Kit

Do you live, as I do, in fear of a wildfire destroying your homestead? The possibility of disaster is ironically increased for us land stewards who attend the ecological need for occasional range fires; controlled burning of grass and underbrush before it accumulates to dangerous levels can go wrong. This book gives the information you need to defend your turf: how to landscape and detail your house fire-retardant, and how to fight fire until the official firefighters get there. This information isn't always easy to find because in these lawsuit-ridden days, many fire districts demand that you leave instead of defending your own home. Of course, there are times when flight is the best move. But there are also times when a skilled, resolute stand can save your place, or at least hold the line until help arrives. If you live in a vulnerable place (and this can be right in town) you need to know this stuff. —JB

After you learn what to do in Wildfire Across America this tool kit will help you slay the beast. Safe, comfortable, effective, these three tools attach to a common handle and do the work of twelve traditional fire tools in any wildfire ecosystem in the world. —Susan Erkel Ryan

Wildfire Across America Trooper Tom Lugtenaar 1988; 120 pp.; **$14.95** ($17.45 postpaid) **＊WEA**

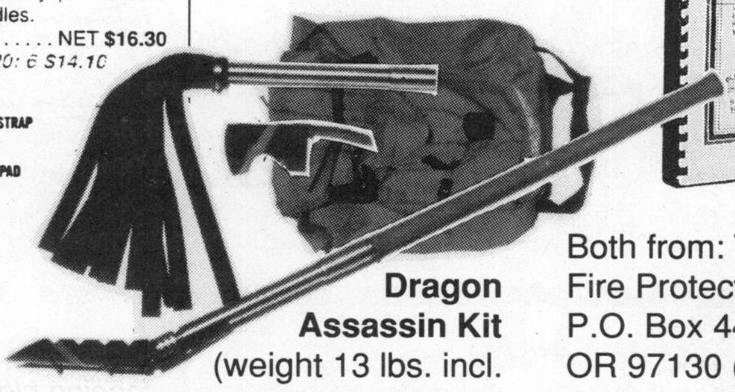

Dragon Assassin Kit (weight 13 lbs. incl. pack) **$175** plus shipping

Both from: Trooper Tom's Fire Protection Company, P.O. Box 44, Manzanita, OR 97130 (503) 368-7099

Defender Foam Systems

If fire does come your way, you'll need some means of keeping it from getting a bite on your buildings and close-in landscaping. A professional firefighting foam called Silvex makes this nerve-wracking and physically demanding task a lot easier and more likely to succeed. It's now available to civilians as an additive to just plain water, as might be found in your swimming pool, stock pond or even (in CA) a hot tub. The Defender Foam System utilizes a small, hand-carryable gasoline-engined pump that sucks water from whatever source, and mixes it with the Silvex foam concentrate. The mix discharges vigorously through a one-person hose with which you spray your house and landscaping, rendering it damply resistent to ignition for up to six hours. A salvo of Silvex is much superior to plain water for smothering active flames, too. It's non-toxic. A rig much like this Defender model saved many structures in the infamous Yellowstone Park fire. —JB

Defender Foam Systems; **$1400-$1900** Brochure **free** from: Brushfire Hydrant Co. 1818 B Mount Diablo Blvd., Walnut Creek, CA 94596; (415) 932-5080

The New Organic Grower

Here's a current newspaper article on the success of Czechoslovakian collective farms, and their post-Communist future:

"Many farm experts say it will be difficult to return to the age-old practice of private farming, because the knowledge passed from generation to generation on how to run a private farm has largely been lost. . . . 'People no longer have an idea of everything that is required to do private farming,' said Zdenek Janousek, a dairy technician. 'They are used to being told what to do.' " (New York Times, 4/16/90)

And here is author Eliot Coleman, writing about how he got started as an American organic market gardener twenty years ago: "The major obstacle I had to overcome . . . was a lack of models. There were almost no commercially successful organic small farmers from whom I could get inspiration and with whom I could share ideas. My prototype of the economically viable five-acre farm didn't even exist. I began with the assumption that if it could be done once it could be done again."

What Coleman has learned since is in this book, and he is no longer a lonely farmer. Small-scale commercial market gardeners are sprouting up everywhere, and most of them will profit from a look here, because Coleman's credo — "small, manageable, and efficient" — is aimed at saving growers time and effort. He is extremely practical, and also a serious scholar of the art of growing vegetables; the book even includes an annotated bibliography. For home gardeners interested in knowing why as well as what, this well-illustrated book provides a real education. —Richard Nilsen

•

The New Organic Grower, Eliot Coleman 1989; 269 pp.; **$19.95** ($22.45 postpaid) from: Chelsea Green Pub Co., P.O. Box 130, Route 113, Post Mills VT 05058; (800) 445-6638 [in VT (802) 878-0315] **✱WEA**

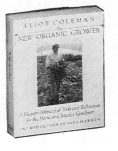

Soil blocks provide the modular advantages of plug trays without the problems and expense of a plug system. Blocks free the grower from the mountains of plastic containers that have become so ubiquitous of late in horticultural operations. European growers sell bedding plants in blocks to customers, who transport them in their own containers. There is no plastic pot expense to the grower, the customer, or the environment. Soil blocks constitute the best system I have yet found for growing seedlings.

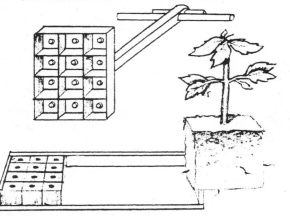

Despite our modern motorized prejudices, hand tools, when designed correctly, are preferable for many operations. Good hand tools and techniques are not a step backwards.

How to Grow More Vegetables

John Jeavons did not invent the biodynamic/ French intensive method of gardening, but he clearly qualifies as its chief popularizer, and this book boils the technique down to its simplest terms. It is organic gardening using hand labor, raised beds, close spacing between plants to eliminate weeds and conserve soil moisture, and heavy feeding and composting. It can produce very large yields in very small spaces, and is therefore applicable to many diverse situations. —Richard Nilsen

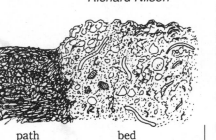

Soil in path is subject to compaction, soil in bed remains loose.

path   bed

The biodynamic/French intensive method raised bed. A balance between nature's natural stratification and man's shepherding landslide loosening.

How To Grow More Vegetables John Jeavons 1982; 159 pp. **$11.95** ($12.95 postpaid) from: Ten Speed Press P.O. Box 7123, Berkeley, CA 94707 **✱WEA**

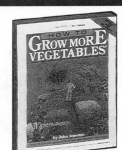

•

A good growing bed will be 4 to 12 inches higher than the original surface of the soil. A good soil contains 50% air space. (In fact, adequate air is one of the missing ingredients in most soil preparation processes.) The increased air space allows for an increase in the diffusion of oxygen (which the roots and microbes depend on) into the soil, and the diffusion of carbon dioxide (which the leaves depend on) out of the soil. This increased "breathing" ability of a double-dug bed is a key to improved plant health.

Seed Catalog Directories

Keeping up with the fast-changing seed business is easier with a list of the players. Here are two good ones. —Richard Nilsen

Sources of Native Seeds and Plants; Catalog **$3** from: Soil & Water Conservation Society, 7515 Northeast Ankeny Road, Ankeny, IA 50021

SOIL AND WATER CONSERVATION SOCIETY

Seed, Bulb and Nursery Suppliers List Catalog **$1** from: Organic Gardening Magazine Attn.: Seed, Bulb & Nursery Suppliers List 33 East Minor St., Emmaus, PA 18098

USDA Plant Hardiness Zone Map

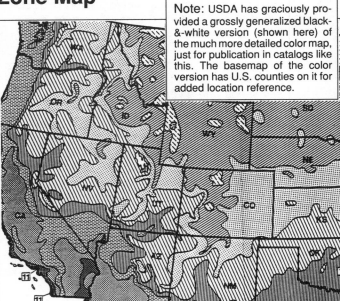

Note: USDA has graciously provided a grossly generalized black-&-white version (shown here) of the much more detailed color map, just for publication in catalogs like this. The basemap of the color version has U.S. counties on it for added location reference.

This four-foot-square color map shows the average annual minimum temperature for twenty climate zones, twice the number of the map it replaces. It covers all 50 American states, plus Canada and Mexico. Any map is a poor substitute for a person with detailed local knowledge about what will grow where, and more precise maps may exist elsewhere for your locality. For instance, anyone in the 11 western states should rely on the vastly more detailed 24 zone maps in the **Sunset New Western Garden Book.** But to see the whole collection of wiggly lines in one place, this is a fine map at a good price. — Richard Nilsen

USDA Plant Hardiness Zone Map; $6.50 postpaid from: Superintendent of Documents Government Printing Office, Washington, DC 20402; (202) 783-3230

HortIdeas

Magazine publishers are well aware of the growing interest in things green — a visit to any good newsstand will reveal numerous glossy gardening magazines. One you might not find there that's worth knowing about is **HortIdeas.** *It's an unillustrated, monthly newsletter that describes itself as "filling the gap between watered-down popular gardening magazines and esoteric research journals." It provides an excellent filter on academic horticultural research and is a fertile source for new gardening ideas. —Richard Nilsen*

HortIdeas Gregory and Patricia Y. Williams, Publishers **$15**/year (12 issues) from: HortIdeas Route 1, Box 302 Black Lick Road Gravel Switch, KY 40328

•

Yardlong Beans: Over 5 Pounds Per Square Yard

Looking for a crop capable of producing lots of protein per unit area? The yardlong bean (also known as the asparagus bean, *Vigna unguiculata* subspecies *sesquipedalis*) appears to have great potential. In Dutch greenhouse trials with three cultivars (planted in early July and harvested during September and October), yields ranged between five and six pounds per square yard. That's around 60 pounds of beans from a 5' x 20' bed in less than four months! Reference: Abstract 9095, *Horticultural Abstracts* 59 (11), November 1989, 1044.

Drip Irrigation

Anything that saves a person time and money is bound to be popular; drip irrigation does both. Plastic tubing delivers water to each plant in a slow, steady drip. Timers can further control how often you irrigate. The small army of drip irrigation manufacturers and products can be confusing. A solution is to shop at a store where you know and trust the salespeople. Or shop by mail order with the Urban Farmer. They specialize in drip irrigation and carefully select what they sell from more than 40 manufacturers. Their catalog lists components and also explains the basics of design and installation. —Richard Nilsen

The Urban Farmer Store's Drip Irrigation Catalog $1 from:
Urban Farmer, 2833 Vicente Street
San Francisco, CA 94116; (800) 666-DRIP
[in San Francisco (415) 661-2204]

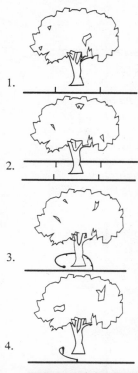

1.

2.

3.

4.

There are four common ways to set up emitters in an orchard: **1)** run laterals down the row of trees with emitters placed on the lateral at the base of each tree: **2)** run two laterals along the row about 3' on either side of the trees to encourage more balanced root growth: **3)** "tee off" each lateral with a loop around each tree to water the entire circumference of the root zone: **4)** in locations with sandy soil mini-sprinklers are often used. One mini-sprinkler on a stand can cover the entire root-zone of a tree. Remember to design the system for the flow that will be required when the trees are fully mature.

Gardening by Mail

Take one reference librarian with green thumbs, add one Kaypro computer and two years of work and — lucky for us — comes this amazing book. More than 2,000 mail order sources are ingeniously listed. Separate alphabetical lists of seed companies and nurseries are followed by a plant index, so that if you are looking for, say, Siberian Iris, you go to that heading and there are all the sources that sell them. Then comes a geographical index of the same sources, providing traveling gardeners with a ready-made tour guide. This

Hidden Springs Nursery – Edible Landscaping
Route 14, Box 159
Cookeville, TN 38501
(615) 268-9889
Hector Black

Offers plants for **edible landscaping and low maintenance fruits for** sustainable agriculture. Antique apples, apricots, figs, grapes, mayhaws, hardy kiwis, medlars and quinces, pears, plums, jujube, goumi and several nitrogen-fixing shrubs for reclamation. (1978)
▯ Catalog: $.50, CAN/OV, SS:10-4, $15m
⌂ Nursery: March-December, by appointment only
▼ Garden: March-December, by appointment only

Attracting Backyard Wildlife

This Canadian book, useful anywhere, gives careful consideration to little critters and little details. There is plenty of information on birds and small animals, but nice coverage of lizards and insects too. And for all, there are excellent diagrams of building housing and feeding stations. —Richard Nilsen

Attracting Backyard Wildlife
Bill Merilees; 1989; 159 pp.
$10.95 ($13.95 postpaid)
from: Voyageur Press
123 N. 2nd Street
Stillwater, MN 55082
(612) 430-2210 ✳WEA

Two ideas for improving backyards for toads are providing day-time retreats and hiding places, and a low power light source to attract night insects. Toad holes can be constructed in many imaginative ways, with soft sandy soil at the bottom being the key.

Gardening By Mail
Barbara Barton; 1990
381 pp.; **$16.95** postpaid from: Houghton Mifflin, Wayside Road
Burlington, MA 01803
(800) 225-3362 ✳WEA

same detailed attention is also given to garden supply companies, societies, libraries, magazines, and even one hundred gardening books.
—*Richard Nilsen*

400 – 500 cm
(12 – 15 FT)

100 cm
(3 FT)

ROCKERY OR ROCK WALL.

BAT LIGHT

ROCK ROOF TO PREVENT BURROW FROM COLLAPSING

CAVITY.

LIGHT SHADE

CONCRETE DRAIN PIPE.

TOAD LIGHT

SOFT SAND IN BOTTOM OF CAVITY.

A toad light may be a light designed to illuminate a foot path. If the light is placed near a border between a garden or rockery and a lawn area, toads will have some cover while waiting for their meal to arrive.

Worms Eat My Garbage

Before climbing onto a new bandwagon, especially one that involves as much trudging and toting as recycling does, it's a good idea to ask yourself, "Is anybody already doing this a simpler way?"

Take composting. You have smelly organic kitchen garbage, and you want great fertilizer for your garden. What else besides composting with your muscles can accomplish this transformation?

Worms can. Their castings are prized fertilizer, and they will live in an old box by the back door (or in the basement during a freezing winter when compost heaps stop working). This book tells you how. — *Richard Nilsen*

Worms Eat My Garbage
(How to set up and maintain a worm composting system)
Mary Appelhof; 1982; 100 pp.
$7.95 ($8.95 postpaid) from:
Flower Press
10332 Shaver Road
Kalamazoo, MI 49002 ✳WEA

What kind of garbage and what do I do with it?

Any vegetable waste that you generate during food preparation can be used. . . . Spoiled food from the refrigerator, such as baked beans, moldy cottage cheese, and leftover casserole also can go into the worm bin. Coffee grounds are very good in a worm bin, enhancing the texture of the final vermicompost. Tea leaves, and even tea bags and coffee filters are suitable. Egg shells can go in as they are, and I have found as many as 50 worms curled up in one egg shell. Usually, I dry them separately, then pulverize them with a rolling pin so they don't look quite so obvious when I finally put vermicompost in my garden.

Landscaping for Wildlife
Carrol L. Henderson; 1987
144 pp.; **$8.95** ($10.95 postpaid) from:
Minnesota Bookstore
Documents Division
117 University Avenue
St. Paul, MN 55155
(612) 297-3000 ✳WEA

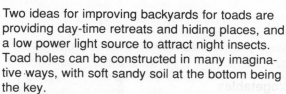

Container garden for butterflies, bees, moths, and hummingbirds for use on a balcony, patio or deck in full sun to partial shade.

One of the greatest opportunities that exists for homeowners to help wildlife is within the boundaries of their own yards! In most yards that have been landscaped in the past, wildlife benefits were accidental or incidental. Only the most adaptable species like robins, house sparrows and European starlings thrived in such habitats. More than 100 wildlife species, however, may use a well-planned backyard habitat at one time or another.

Landscaping for Wildlife

The Minnesota Department of Natural Resources has produced an outstanding how-to wildlife-landscaping book. It also covers Wisconsin, Iowa, Michigan, and northern Illinois, Indiana and Ohio. People who live elsewhere should consider buying the book anyway. It's cheap. There are enough glorious color animal pictures to make it a great bedtime book for small children. And there is also a mountain of detail made comprehensible and accessible, plus directions and plans for back yards, farmsteads or whole woodlands. This book is good enough to be used even as a lever — show it to the Natural Resources department where you live and then ask politely why your state doesn't have a book like this.
—*Richard Nilsen*

In extreme circumstances where snags are lacking, you can create snags in a woodlot by girdling several diseased or deformed trees. The

best trees for creation of snags are oak, sugar maple, basswood, ash and elm. Girdling involves cutting a ring around the trunk through the bark and well into the sapwood so that the cambium layer between the bark and wood is completely severed.

Aʟᴛʜᴏᴜɢʜ megafarms will continue to be an important part of the food production business, I don't think the future belongs to them at all, despite the predictions of wishful-thinking agribusiness interests. The real action is going to occur in comparatively small-scale food production systems now sprouting up everywhere, and in those which have handily survived the economic crunch of the eighties. In short, there is no better time than right now for dedicated young people, determined to own and operate their own businesses, to make it in agriculture. —Gene Logsdon

"The Future: More Farmers Not Fewer," *Whole Earth Review*, Spring 1989.

The Farming Game

The Unsettling of America

Our land is more undone by our agriculture than by any other mischief. Farmer, poet, essayist Wendell Berry speaks to the matter with plain speech — it rasps the brain, leaves a memory of the thought. Don't say it is no longer possible to do our farming right. Berry is. —Stewart Brand

The Unsettling of America
(Culture & Agriculture) Wendell Berry; 1986; 228 pp.; **$7.95** ($10.95 postpaid) from: Sierra Club Books, 730 Polk St. San Francisco, CA 94109 (415) 923-5500 ✱WEA

●

A part of the health of a farm is the farmer's wish to remain there. His long-term good intention toward the place is signified by the presence of trees. A family is married to a farm more by their planting and protecting of trees than by their memories or their knowledge, for the trees stand for their fidelity and kindness to what they do not know. The most revealing sign of the ill health of industrial agriculture — its greed, its short-term ambitions — is its inclination to see trees as obstructions and to strip the land bare of them.

●

Social fashion, delusion, and propaganda have combined to persuade the public that our agriculture is for the best of reasons the envy of the Modern World. American citizens are now ready to believe without question that it is entirely good, a grand accomplishment, that each American farmer now "feeds himself and 56 others." They are willing to hear that "96 percent of American manpower is freed from food production" — without asking what it might have been "freed" *for*, or how many as a consequence have been "freed" from employment of any kind.

The Farming Game

*Farms and farmers have been disappearing in large numbers in America since the 1950s. **The Farming Game** explains the arithmetic that has greased this economic slide, and also suggests strategies for people interested in surviving this trend and farming in the future. Bryan Jones has a style reminiscent of Will Rogers — an ear for ironic humor, political savvy, and a simmering contempt for bureaucratic institutions (big banks, government, universities). His lectures on profit and advice on diversification are the perfect antidote for romantic agrarian notions. This is a book that any beginner will need and anyone with experience will nod at knowingly. —Richard Nilsen*

●

I have never owned any sheep. To make a living you'd have to have a couple of thousand of 'em and that's a lot of baa-baas.
—B.J. Tupper

Owning sheep is not one of your major status symbols in this country. In the rural community it is regarded as considerably less than that. It is a very similar situation to that of the successful surgeon who complains that his garbage man makes more money than he does but does not then rush out and buy a garbage truck. The sheep business, like the garbage business, has some odious connotations. Sheep are regarded as stupid, smelly, and quite likely to die for no reason. Sheep men reinforce the prejudice by wearing oil-caked hats and driving ancient pickup trucks. Indeed, within the sheep industry the folks with the cruddiest, sloppiest hats and the most rust-encrusted pickups are regarded as very superior fellows. Red 1952 Chevy pickups with wood stock racks and spotlights are the vehicles of choice, although there are some die-hard Studebaker drivers out there who are downright snobbish.

Altars of Unhewn Stone

Wes Jackson continues his radical prescriptions for America's agricultural future with this collection of essays. His scientific credentials and practical farming experience, combined with his humor, humility and a God-fearing respect for man's correct relationship to the natural environment, make him unique among agricultural writers. Following the contours of his arguments, you are led in directions far from the mainstream. Here is a man who looks at the last fifty-odd years of our agricultural program and concludes, "Where we were then [1935] was a better takeoff point for where we need to be than where we are now. There was more resilience in the culture at large because more people were on the land." —Richard Nilsen

●

There is more to be discovered than invented, and the future of the human species on this planet will depend more on discovery than on invention. Long ago, Charles Lindbergh said, "The future of the human race will depend on combining the clever-

Altars of Unhewn Stone
Wes Jackson; 1987; 158 pp. **$9.95** ($11.45 postpaid) from: North Point Press, 850 Talbot Avenue, Berkeley, CA 94706 (415) 527-6260 ✱WEA

ness of science with the wisdom of nature." But through domestication we have removed our major crops so far from their original context that most farmers (and I suspect, most agricultural researchers) regard both crops and livestock as more the property of humans than relatives of wild things. Yet all of these creatures evolved in ecosystems that had little to do with humans. None of these ecosystems was of our design. Somewhere in the midst of this thinking and research the scripture in Exodus 20:25, from which the title of this book came, took on a deeper meaning for us. Right after Moses had delivered the Ten Commandments, he received instructions to build an altar of unhewn stone "for if thou lift up thy tool upon it, thou has polluted it."

The Farming Game
Bryan Jones; 1986
221 pp.; **$19.95** ($21.95 postpaid) from: University of Nebraska Press 901 North 17th St. Lincoln, NE 68588 (402) 472-3584 ✱WEA

●

With all their personal freedom, farmers may be the most financially exploited class in the nation. Governments kowtow to consumers by holding down farm prices, local governments tax farmlands at ruinous rates, and eastern elitists are continually conspiring to drive a few hundred thousand people from the farm to cheapen up the labor market. Nonetheless, the sheer size of the parasitic industries that farmers support (farm equipment, banking, chemical, fertilizer, land-grant universities, and transportation) attest to the tremendous wealth generated by farmers every year.

The New Farm

This magazine is "dedicated to putting people, profit and biological permanence back into farming by giving farmers the information they need to take charge of their farms and their futures." It is run by a non-profit organization and is the best single source for economically sound alternative techniques for commercial farmers. —Richard Nilsen

The New Farm
George DeVault Editor
$15/year
(7 issues)
The New Farm Box 14 Emmaus, PA 18099-0014

●

If you're doing all you can to keep livestock costs low and you still have trouble making ends meet, consider diversifying into rare breeds or so-called "exotic" animals. It's a good way to help preserve the genetic diversity of livestock and tap profitable niche markets at the same time.

. . . The Tamworth hog would be a good candidate for organic pork production because of its hardiness and extra lean meat, suggests Carolyn Christman, program coordinator of the American Minor Breeds Conservancy. Plus, it can be raised outdoors on forage, she notes.

Scotch Highland cattle offer the same opportunities. As the name implies, they developed under the extremely harsh conditions of the remote Highlands of Scotland. They require little in the way of shelter, grain or feed supplements to maintain good condition, and they even seem to enjoy cold weather and snow. . . .

Because Scotch Highland cattle are insulated by their long hair, they have little outside waste fat — a prime selling point to today's cholesterol-conscious shoppers.

●

There's a kind of interactive diversity that goes on in nature. For example, during the '88 drought, we found cactus growing in our native prairie pastures. I don't know where it came from. But it was there, waiting for the right conditions. I don't know anything as diverse and stable as a prairie. We need to look at how we can manage our farms to mimic that stability. —Fred Kirschenmann, who farms 3000 acres near Windsor, North Dakota.

Meeting the Expectations of the Land

The title of this collection of essays about sustainable agriculture conveys an apt reversal. A line from Robert Frost might help: "The land was ours before we were the land's." The ideas here are visionary in that they look both forward and backward in time, but lest you think the book advocates a retreat to agricultural animism, it is worth emphasizing that these ideas are also very practical. You won't find them in use on most American farms today because the emphasis has been on productivity and profits.

Profits? Even if your news from the farm comes only from the TV, you know you can forget about "profits" in farming. And productivity? Sure, that's there, but it is the same kind you find in a coal mine. When the coal is gone you shut it down and move on. When the topsoil is gone, or the soil is salted out from irrigation, where do you go?

You go to a kind of agriculture that can sustain; not only the land, but also the life on it and in it, as well as the people who work it and those who depend on them for food. This book is full of clues to how that kind of agriculture will work, by people like Gene Logsdon, John Todd, and Gary Snyder.
—Richard Nilsen

Meeting the Expectations of the Land (Essays in Sustainable Agriculture and Stewardship) Wes Jackson, Wendell Berry & Bruce Colman, Editors; 1984 250 pp.; **$12.50** ($14 postpaid) from: North Point Press 850 Talbot Ave., Berkeley CA 94706; (415) 527-6260 ✳WEA

Family Farming

By most accounts the family farm is all but finished. The food system of the future will be dominated by relatively few superfarms owned by multinational conglomerates. This is clearly the trend, but why? To the acolytes of agri-business the answer is "progress," i.e. that inevitable march toward large-scale, computerized efficiency. In **Family Farming**, Marty Strange argues convincingly to the contrary. According to Strange the decline of family-owned and -operated farms does not lie in their inefficiency, but in the public policies governing tax codes, land ownership, farm benefit and subsidy programs, and research priorities at land-grant universities. Peak efficiency in agriculture occurs at a relatively small scale: between $45,000 and $133,000 of gross sales. The very large farms, that have diligently farmed the tax code, are less resilient, less flexible, and operate with far less margin for error. They have also contributed substantially to the decline of rural environments and communities. The largest part of **Family Farming** is a detailed analysis of the economic and policy factors behind the evolution of U.S. Agriculture.

Strange proposes to reconcile farm policy with traditional rural values. This requires public policies that reward good farming, not land speculation and carelessness. His suggestions include: an end to subsidies for capital investment; better production controls; a national land policy; regulation of input industries and commodity markets; and careful guidelines for agricultural research and technology. Sensible stuff.

Family Farming is the best analysis I've seen of American agriculture. It is clear-headed, informative, practical, and well-written. Strange has taken much of the mystery out of a complex subject. This is an honest book that acknowledges the mistakes and shortcomings of family farms while

---

I once asked an Amish farmer who had only twenty-six acres why he didn't acquire a bit more land. He looked around at his ten fine cows, his sons hoeing the corn with him, his spring water running continuously by gravity through house and barn, his few fat hogs, his sturdy buildings, his good wife heaping the table with food, his fine flock of hens, his plot of tobacco and acre of strawberries, his handmade hickory chairs (which he sold for all the extra cash he really needed), and he said, "Well, I'm just not smart enough to farm any more than this *well*." I have a hunch no one could. —Gene Logsdon

Good farming is farming that presrves the earth and its network of life. Obviously, agriculture involves the rearranging of nature to bring it more into line with human desires, but it does not require exploiting, mining, or destroying the natural world. The need for agriculture also does not absolve us from the moral duty and the common-sense advice to farm in an ecologically rational way. Good farming protects the land, even when it uses it. It does not knock down shelterbelts to squeeze a few more dollars from a field. It does not poison the animal creation wholesale to get rid of coyotes and bobcats. It does not drain entire rivers dry, causing irreversible damage to estuaries and aquatic ecosystems, in an uncontrolled urge to irrigate the desert. It does not tolerate the yearly loss of 200 tons of topsoil per acre from farms in the Palouse hills of eastern Washington. Those are the ways of violence. American agriculture of late, pushed by market forces and armed with unprecedented technology, has increasingly become a violent enterprise. —Donald Worster

---

arguing for their preservation. For those interested in sustainable agriculture, this is a plausible view of how we get from here to there. —David Orr

A Faustian bargain has been made between the use of the technology and the impersonal market. The bargain is this: In return for the splendid increase in production made possible by this technology, the producer must accept less money for each unit sold, and share the rewards of increased output with those who produce the technologies.

Agriculture can't live up to a public standard of moral purity that is higher than that expected of the rest of our society. If farmers are expected to steward natural resources even when doing so is not in their immediate self-interest, the rest of us must be willing to sacrifice the immediate benefits of cheap food for the long-range benefits of a sustainable food system. If we expect farmers to conserve resources without providing sufficient economic reward for doing so, we only shift an impossible burden onto their shoulders. Farmers should not have the right to exploit land, but cannot resist the market forces that encourage them to do so without the support of the rest of us. The market alone should not determine the use of resources, and it alone should not determine the economic fate of farmers, either. Public funds must be committed to support conservation.

Family Farming (A New Economic Vision) Marty Strange; 1988; 311 pp. **$8.95** ($10.95 postpaid) from: University of Nebraska Press 901 North 17th Street, 327 Nebraska Hall, Lincoln, NE 68588-0520; (402) 472-3584 ✳WEA

---

agAccess

It takes considerable hubris to bill youself as The Agricultural Information Source, but that's just what agAccess has grown to be. The 850 books in their catalog cover virtually every aspect of agriculture and related matters such as irrigation. Each is reviewed by an expert on the subject. Eco-righteousness is stressed. If a book isn't in their catalog, it's probably in their enormous data base. They can get you any ag book in print — eco-righteous or not — and will look for out-of-print ones too. They also deal ag-related software. For an appropriate stipend, they'll research a subject for you and get you together with consultants. Even the government comes to them for information. But perhaps the best part of this most useful and well-organized service is the agAccess bookstore in Davis, CA. There you can meet the congenial crew and the always-interesting customers while you peruse the tasty offerings. Bet you don't leave empty-handed even if you aren't a farmer; agAccess is a wonderful example of a business truly attuned to what people need. --JB

agAccess Catalog **free** from: agAccess P.O. Box 2008 Davis, CA 95617 (916) 756-7177

Promising Fruits of the Philippines
Roberto E. Coronel 1983

This fascinating book describes the durian and 36 other noteworthy tropical fruits that have potential to contribute substantially to a tropical country's economy. Everything known about such provocatively named fruits as balimbing, tiessa and singuelas is contained in this unique pomology resource. 508pp, soft. **UPH001 $36.00**

Spanish in the Field:
Practical Spanish for Ranchers, Farmers or Vintners
Clough, Comegys, & Saddler. 1983

Organized by agricultural topic- weather, soil, tools, machinery, chemicals, grapes, cotton, orchards, row crops, grains, etc.- these excellent California Spanish lessons will be immensely helpful to those whose Spanish is limited, and will quickly make it possible for non-speakers to communicate. The labelled drawings are great for quick consultations. The book comes alone, or with a handy 3,000 word pocket dictionary containing well detailed vocabulary lists, and a set of four cassette tapes to speed up the learning process and aid pronunciation. Highly recommended. 248 pages, softcover.

PAN003 - book only - **$19.95** **PAN004** - book, dictionary, & four tapes - **$49.95**

Farm Supplies

There are lots of good mail-order sources for farm and garden supplies. Here are four of our favorites.
—Susan Erkel Ryan

Gardener Supply (Innovative Gardening Solutions) Catalog & Gardening Bulletin **free** from: 128 Intervale Road Burlington, VT 05401 (802) 863-1700

Harmony Farm Supply Catalog **$2** (refundable with purchase) from: P.O. Box 460 Graton, CA 95444 (707) 823-9125

The Necessary Trading Company Catalog **$2** (refundable with purchase) from: P.O. Box 305 New Castle, VA 24127 (800) 447-5354

Peaceful Valley Farm Supply Catalog **$2** (refundable with purchase) from: P.O. Box 2209 Grass Valley, CA 95945 (916) 272-4769

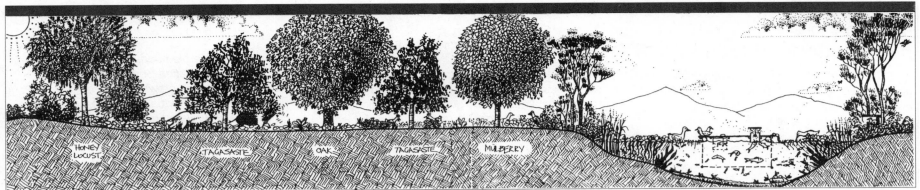

HONEY LOCUST | TAGASASTE | OAK | TAGASASTE | MULBERRY

PERMACULTURE [permanent agriculture] is the conscious design and maintenance of agriculturally productive ecosystems which have the diversity, stability, and resilience of natural ecosystems. It is the harmonious integration of landscape and people providing their food, energy, shelter, and other material and non-material needs in a sustainable way. Without permanent agriculture there is no possibility of a stable social order.

—Bill Mollison, *Permaculture*

An evolved system provides forage, firewood, aquatic and animal products. Larger foragers (sheep, pigs) can be grown seasonally. The system provides its own mulch and fertilizers. The mature system requires management rather than energy input, and has a variety of marketable yields (including information).

Permaculture

Bill Mollison has taught permaculture design courses all over the world, so it's no surprise his book is organized as a training manual for use by an individual or groups. Topics covered include affordable housing, clean water and air, decent neighborhoods, landscape restoration, sustainable agriculture, ethical investments, economic development, unpolluted food and sane organizations. The chapter on patterns in nature — detailing what he calls "pattern understanding" — is a sparkling

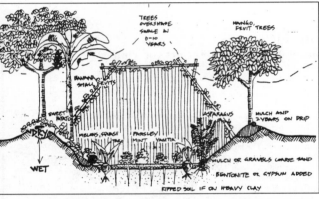

A developed swale, with humus and mulch, will provide water at root level for established trees.

Permaculture Periodicals

These folks are expanding the work begun in Australia by Bill Mollison. It was he who coined the term permaculture for a kind of ecosystem design that recognizes that sustainable land use is only possible within the context of sustainable and humane culture. Whether in a backyard or an entire watershed the goal is the same: to produce food and energy in ways that mimic the conserving stability and resiliency of natural ecosystems. There is a great emphasis on tree crops here, but fundamentally permaculture is asking many of the same basic design questions being raised at the Land Institute (see p. 21). —Richard Nilsen

The Permaculture Activist, Guy Baldwin, Editor; **$13**/year (four issues) from: The Permaculture Activist Subscription Dept. P.O. Box 101 Davis, CA 95617

Robin Newsletter Dan Hemenway, Editor; **$15**/year (1-4 issues sporadically) from: Yankee Permaculture, P.O. Box 16683, Wichita, KS 67216

Permaculture (A Practical Guide for a Sustainable Future) 1990 2nd Ed.; 576 pp. **$34.95** ($37.95 postpaid) from: agAccess P.O. Box 2008 Davis, CA 95617 (916) 756-7177 ✳WEA

gem of a read (with beautiful illustrations) unlike anything I've seen anywhere else. **Permaculture** *is so full of information that if information had mass, the book would surely be a black hole — yet a generous dose of sketches and color photos, lucid prose and lively anecdotes make it easy reading in spite of its size and technical depth. An extraordinary book. —James Kalin*

This is that book everybody was looking for 20 years ago. The one that explains how to grow food, fix broken land and devise a better society — anywhere you happen to live. Couldn't find it then because the only folks doing decentralized, ecologically sustainable agricultural systems in those days were scattered around the Third World, and they didn't publish. Well, here it is — a treasure-house of keen observation, responsive design, patience and hope. —Richard Nilsen

•

Mollisonian Permaculture Principles:

1. Work with nature, rather than against the natural elements, forces, pressures, processes, agencies, and evolutions, so that we assist rather than impede natural developments.

Forest Farming

The essential tree library includes **Forest Farming***. After this book has been read, there is nothing to do but start working, experimenting, and writing your own local manual. A visionary integration of farming, animal husbandry, and horticulture with tree crops — fruit, nuts, oil, fodder. This is not a book on woodlots for maintaining firewood. Foreword by E. F. Schumacher. —Peter Warshall*

Forest Farming J. Sholto Douglas & Robert A. Hart; 1984; 207 pp. **$13.50** ($16.30 postpaid) from: ITDG/NA 777 UN Plaza, Suite 9A New York, NY 10017 (212) 972-9877 ✳WEA

•

One of the great advantages of making tree-planting the spearhead of desert reclamation is that trees, especially of drought-resistant species,

2. The problem is the solution; everything works both ways. It is only how we see things that makes them advantageous or not (if the wind blows cold, let us use both its strength and its coolness to advantage). A corollary of this principle is that everything is a positive resource; it is just up to us to work out how we may use it as such.

3. Make the least change for the greatest possible effect.

4. The yield of a system is theoretically unlimited. The only limit on the number of uses of a resource possible within a system is in the limit of the information and the imagination of the designer.

5. Everything gardens, or has an effect on its environment.

The One-Straw Revolution

By changing one of the grasses in his rice fields to another variety, Fukuoka started a process that brought his part of the ecosystem into a natural balance. On his farm he gets yields comparable to traditional farms' but without plowing; he lets nature do the work. He simply plants and harvests — pretty revolutionary. The book describes his method. —Rosemary Menninger

An out-of-print classic worth looking for at your library. —Susan Erkel Ryan

The One-Straw Revolution, Masanobu Fukuoka; **Out of Print**, Rodale Press

•

are less dependent on water than annual crops; and this reduces the need for expensive irrigation schemes, which often involve the construction of large dams drowning thousands of acres of land and lead to alkalisation problems. Trees seek out their own water supplies, sending their roots sometimes hundreds of feet into the subsoil, and creating their own local irrigation systems, which benefit their shallow-rooting neighbours as well as themselves, and which, being underground, are not subject to evaporation, whereas, especially in tropical climates, at least half the water trapped behind a big dam may be evaporated.

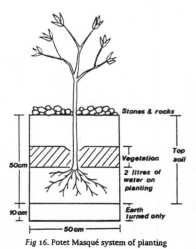

Stones & rocks
Vegetation
Top soil
2 litres of water on planting
Earth turned only
50cm
10cm
50cm

Fig 16. Potet Masqué system of planting

Pests of the Garden & Small Farm: A Grower's Guide to Using Less Pesticide

It has been a long wait, but here is the first dose of Integrated Pest Management (IPM) aimed at home gardeners and organic growers. The University of California's IPM Project has been cranking out a whole series of books explaining how to use less synthetic pesticides by working with nature, not against it — the bottom line of IPM — on specific agricultural crops since 1978. It made good sense to first offer these practical alternatives to the farmers spraying thousands of acres of cotton, alfalfa and tomatoes, but for most people, the major exposure to pesticides occurs in their own gardens. "Each year in California, home gardeners use about one pound of pesticide for every man, woman, and child in the state," says author Flint.

This richly illustrated book is filled with all the details about what you can do instead — for insects, plant diseases, nematodes and weeds. It's worth buying just to have good pictures of so many little critters finally gathered all in one place. It is keyed to California, but most of the species discussed occur throughout North America, and the techniques (like soil solarization — cooking weed seeds and fungi to death in the soil under plastic sheets) will work anywhere. We have been making do with a small handful of books on these subjects for long enough. Now you need to own only one. —Richard Nilsen

Pests of the Garden & Small Farm (A Grower's Guide to Using Less Pesticide), Mary Louise Flint, PhD; 1990; 276 pp. **$25** postpaid from: ANR Publications 6701 San Pablo Ave. Oakland, CA 94608 (415) 642-2431 **＊WEA**

•

Most biological control occurs naturally without assistance from the grower or gardener. Often its importance is not appreciated until a broad spectrum pesticide which kills certain natural enemies as well as targeted pests is applied and a new pest — suddenly released from biological control — becomes a serious problem. This type of phenomenon known as secondary pest outbreak occasionally occurs in gardens. One example might be the sudden outbreak of aphid, scale, mite or whitefly populations throughout a garden soon after a large tree has been sprayed with a broad spectrum insecticide such as carbaryl: not only are the pest insects in the tree destroyed, but also the insect parasites and other natural enemies in, beneath, and adjacent to the tree canopy.

Life cycle of a *Trichogramma* **wasp. The tiny** *Trichogramma* **wasp attacks eggs of caterpillars. Larval and pupal stages take place entirely within the egg of the host and the life cycle may take only a week. Each female wasp attacks many host eggs.**

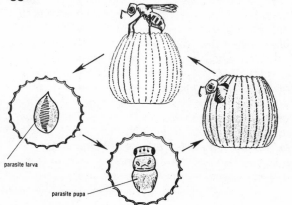

parasite larva

parasite pupa

Common Sense Pest Control Quarterly • The IPM Practitioner

Integrated pest management isn't just for farmers and gardeners. It works on cockroaches, rats, and clothes moths too. Plenty of techniques are known, and getting them to people who can use them are what these two magazines are all about. The **Quarterly** *is for a general audience and the* **Practitioner** *is read by professional pest managers interested in offering alternatives to chemical poisons. A wide variety of pests receive state-of-the-art coverage — mosquitoes, head lice, poison ivy, and lawn pests.*

The Bio-Integral Resource Center has also forged a link with scientists in China, with two important goals in mind. The first is to access the wealth of non-chemical pest control techniques Chinese farmers have evolved over thousands of years of practicing sustainable agriculture — this is the only U.S. group scanning the Chinese literature and printing abstracts. The second is to help Chinese policy makers head off a wholesale adoption of western chemical control techniques by offering them workable large-scale alternatives. It is nice to know that even though the two governments currently are at odds, the science marches on.
—Richard Nilsen

Bio-Integral Resource Center; **$25**/year membership (includes one journal of your choice) **$45**/year dual membership (includes both journals) Sheila Daar, Helga Olkowski, William Olkowski, Editors **Common Sense Pest Control Quarterly** (four issues a year) **The IPM Practitioner** (ten issues a year)

All from: BIRC P.O. Box 7414 Berkeley, CA 94707 (415) 524-2567

•

Effective barriers must be considered in an IPM context because barriers do more than just keep slugs and snails out — barriers also lock resident pest populations in. . . . It has been found most effective to build the copper or screen barrier first, then handpick and trap within it *after* it has been constructed. We hunt the pests on alternate nights for several weeks during the rainy season or after sprinkling the garden in the evening.

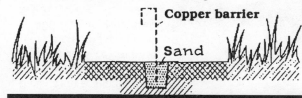

Copper barrier

Sand

Insecticidal Soap

Soaps are made of fatty acids from plants and animals.

There are hundreds of these fatty acids, and while most will get dirt off your hands, a select few will also kill insect pests yet not harm people, beneficial insects, or the plants themselves. Safer Agro-Chem has built an innovative line of products around these special soaps — the one for use against fruit and vegetable pests is safe to use right up to the day of harvest. Others kill moss and algae, powdery mildew, and fleas on pets.
—Richard Nilsen

Introduction to Integrated Pest Management

Integrated pest management (IPM) has come into its own in the last 20 years as the shortcomings of reliance on synthetic chemical pesticides have become glaringly apparent — the bugs become immune to the sprays, which are oil based and expensive; natural checks and balances get wiped out, groundwater becomes contaminated, birds die, and people eat foods laced with carcinogens. This is an easy-reading introduction to a system based on looking at pests in their total environmental setting via careful monitoring in the field and use of computer-built predictive mathematical models of insect behavior. Compared to using only chemical pesticides, IPM is gentle on the earth and frequently cheaper. —Richard Nilsen

Introduction to Integrated Pest Management, Mary Louise Flint and Robert van den Bosch; 1981; 240 pp. **$27.50** ($29.50 postpaid) from: Plenum Press, 233 Spring St. New York, NY 10013 (800) 221-9369 **＊WEA**

•

Grape growers in California have learned that blackberry bushes have their beneficial aspects, especially in the control of an important insect pest — the grape leafhopper. Insecticides have often failed to provide effective control of the leafhopper, or their use has aggravated other pest problems such as spider mites. Entomologists had known that a tiny natural enemy, the parasitic wasp *Anagrus epos*, which lays its eggs in the eggs of the grape leafhopper, kept the pest under control in some vineyards — but not in others. Nobody knew why.

The riddle was solved when it was realized that the wasp spent its winters parasitizing a different insect on a different plant host. Since the leaves fall off grapevines in the winter and the grape leafhopper retreats to the edge of the vineyard and becomes inactive, the nonhibernating parasitic wasp has no shelter, food or means of survival in this environment. Nearby blackberry bushes, however, keep their leaves during winter and host their own leafhopper species all year round. Thus, the weedy blackberry patches were providing a winter home for this important natural enemy of the key grape pest.

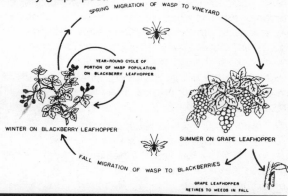

SPRING MIGRATION OF WASP TO VINEYARD

YEAR-ROUND CYCLE OF PORTION OF WASP POPULATION ON BLACKBERRY LEAFHOPPER

WINTER ON BLACKBERRY LEAFHOPPER

SUMMER ON GRAPE LEAFHOPPER

FALL MIGRATION OF WASP TO BLACKBERRIES

GRAPE LEAFHOPPER RETIRES TO WEEDS IN FALL

Insecticidal Soap, Information **free** from: Safer, Inc., 189 Wells Ave., Newton, MA 02159 (800) 544-4453, or at your local garden supply.

Designing and Maintaining Your Edible Landscape Naturally

Edible landscaping is a new term for an old idea. It is a reaction to the lawns and shrubs that make many suburban yards look so boring. Its goal is to integrate food plants into the landscape: specifically to liberate fruits and vegetables from rectangular prisons often hidden out at the back of the lot. Bring those salad herbs up and put them right outside the kitchen door where they will be tended and used. And put the peaches (dwarf) under a south-facing eave of the roof where they can enjoy maximum frost protection and warmth.

What used to be common sense was lost when people stopped growing any of their own food and ran out of time even to be in their gardens, let alone work them. That is changing, and these books suggest that vegetable gardening can also be aesthetic.

Robert Kourik has produced a classic homemade

An example of how your five-year plan might look.

Designing and Maintaining Your Edible Landscape Naturally
Robert Kourik; 1986
400 pp.; **$16.95** ($19.95 postpaid) from: Edible Landscape, P.O. Box 1841, Santa Rosa, CA 95402 ✳WEA

book in the best sense of the term. His mind works referentially and fortunately by publishing his own book he didn't have to meet up with a linear-minded editor eager to streamline his work. The book is massive, detailed, and totally indexed. It is full of charts and graphs that allow the kind of comparing and decision-making that landscape designing is all about. There is extensive information on selecting fruit tree varieties and appropriate rootstocks.

Best of all, he is not dogmatic. If there are two schools of thought, say till versus no-till gardening, he will explain the advantages and disadvantages of each in different situations. Like all gardening books, this one is written with a sense of place in mind (Northern California), but Kourik is aware that your garden, right down to its microclimates, is unique. —Richard Nilsen

•

The amount of effort needed to sustain a landscape or garden is, perhaps, the single most important design consideration. Planting happens quickly, at the peak of the gardener's enthusiasm. Maintenance usually ends up being crammed into busy, everyday life.

The Complete Book of Edible Landscaping

Somewhere in the 1970s friends of mine began to dig up their front lawns and plant vegetables. Neither those vegetables nor this book signal the end of ornamental horticulture, but they do represent a useful alternative to the lawn and the shrubby sameness of suburbia. Titles with the "the complete book of" in them make me leery. In this case the phrase is deserved, for in addition to garden planning, construction, and maintenance, there is an exhaustive alphabetical treatment of 120 edible species that tells everything from where they grow to how to cook them. The art described here is in combining utility with beauty to produce a garden that looks good enough to eat.
—Richard Nilsen

The Complete Book of Edible Landscaping
Rosalind Creasy
1982; 379 pp.; **$19.95** ($22.95 postpaid) from:
Sierra Club Books
730 Polk Street
San Francisco, CA 94109
(415) 923-5500 ✳WEA

•

Preserving and Preparing

Raw or Boiled Bamboo Shoots: For all types of bamboo peel the outer layer to expose the white flesh. Cut small-diameter shoots into rings one node at a time, cut large shoots into slices. If the shoots are sweet they are edible raw in salads or with dips as an appetizer. However, most shoots are bitter until parboiled for 15 to 20 minutes. Change the water after the first 10 minutes, and drain shoots when you are done parboiling them. To serve immediately, cook until tender, or preserve for later use. The raw shoots deteriorate very quickly, so process or serve them on the day they are harvested.

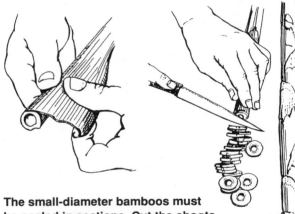

The small-diameter bamboos must be peeled in sections. Cut the shoots into sections and discard the woody joints.

Cooking From the Garden

I'm not in the habit of reading or reviewing cookbooks, so the notion of turning pages and salivating is a bit new, but this book did that for me. It is actually several books rolled into one. The price and full-page color photography make it suitable for the food-as-art coffee table — along with all the other pretty-food cuisine books that make me hunger for a Sloppy Joe. (Pretty or not, dinky portions scare me.) The information on gardening techniques, and what varieties gardeners around America are growing, make this a fascinating gardening book. And the recipes, which come from all over the world and which use vegetables but are by no means only vegetarian — well, that's where the drooling comes in.

This enormous book is really a state-of-the-art survey of America's gardens and kitchens. The link between the two is not new but very old, and by artfully re-establishing it, Rosalind Creasy is providing that awareness so essential before the public can demand and get food that is not only tastier, but safer to eat.

The book is filled with profiles of people from both ends of the food spectrum — market gardeners, specialty growers, seed dealers, and chefs — and Creasy is always asking not just "what are you growing or using?", but "how do you cook it?" The recipes come pouring in from everywhere, because every gardener is a cook and, by implication, every cook should be a gardener, or at least care more about where the ingredients come from. Creasy's first book, **The Complete Book of Edible Landscap-**

ing (reviewed on this page), put vegetables outside the kitchen door, and even into the front yard; this book puts them in the soil, the kitchen, and the imagination. —Richard Nilsen

•

Potage is the French word for soup, and in a gardening context a *potager* is a garden containing whatever is necessary for soup at any time throughout the year. Traditionally, the *potager* garden is planned in little three- or four-foot-square or rectangular plots, which rotate with the seasons, along with a nursery area for young seedlings. . . .

As Georgeanne put it, "This garden fits into your life; it doesn't dominate it. Once the garden area is prepared, an average of twenty minutes a day is required to keep it up. For instance, a typical day might include harvesting a handful of snap beans and a few herbs, cleaning up the spent chard plants in one of the small beds, and seeding that bed with beans."

Cooking From the Garden, Rosalind Creasy; 1988; 547 pp. **$35** ($38 postpaid) from: Sierra Club Books 730 Polk Street, San Francisco, CA 94109 (415) 923-5500 ✳WEA

A Guide to Urban Wildlife Management

Urban wildlife, eh — you mean rats, pigeons, starlings and maybe a bunch of cockroaches, right? Or do you mean canaries and goldfish, hee hee? Well, I've seen raccoons in downtown San Francisco, and a friend of mine in Berkeley boasts of a neighborhood fox. In many cities, hawks and owls head a veritable birdbookload of feathered friends. And what about the butterflies in the parks? Citizens of enlightened cities can fish in local streams and lakes. This guide shows you how to attract and keep wildlife in settings commonly thought of as unsuitable or even inappropriate. The authors are realistic about animals-as-nuisance. Their advice will reduce the effects of humans-as-nuisance; an urban area friendly to wildlife is much more pleasant and healthy for us, too. —JB

Arizona Solar Oasis

It's a glaring August noon in a desert city's downtown. Pedestrians sit chatting in the shade of taut fabric canopies and verdant gardens. Fountains sway gently in the cool breeze. I ain't been nibblin' locoweed — sometime in 1991, Phoenix will boast a whole city block with that description. Designed by ERL, the same outfit that is doing much of the work on Biosphere II (p. 6), the Oasis not only celebrates water, it collects the precious stuff. The canopies capture and store 1,500,000 gallons of rain runoff annually. From storage, it feeds the fountains and gardens, contributing to the heat-reducing microclimate. Most of the cooling comes from the innovative towers. Air

Heavier air, cooled by evaporation in wetted mesh at top of prototype tower, falls down tower bore, drawing in more. No fans needed. Air exits tower base as much as 25 degrees F cooler.

cooled by evaporation near the top falls to street level where it is contained by sunken patios and plantings. No fans; the cooled, falling air draws more in at the top in a more efficient version of the ancient cooling structures described by Hassan Fathy (see review this page). In addition to being pleasant and a boon for business, the Oasis actually conserves scarce water. Will it work? Yes. A smaller proof-of-concept version performed very nicely, and attracted thousands of visitors, too. —JB

The Arizona Solar Oasis Project; Information **free** from: Environmental Research Laboratory, 2601 E. Airport Drive, Tucson International Airport, Tucson, AZ 85706 (602) 741-1990

Natural Energy and Vernacular Architecture

Egyptian architect Hassan Fathy created a stir in 1973 with his heretical **Architecture for the Poor** *(University of Chicago Press) in which he showed that common people in hot-arid climates had intuitively developed an architecture that was superior to modern fashion. This book takes the theme much farther as he explains the scientific basis for the energy efficiency of the traditional styles, and how they can be used today to great mechanical, energetic and cultural advantage. This is one of the world's few master architects talking: skilled, urgent, frustrated, yet still hopeful. I've rarely seen the complexities of the modern-vs.-traditional argument so well presented. —JB*

•

By increasing the size of the *malqaf* and suspend-

Natural Energy and Vernacular Architecture
Hassan Fathy; 1986; 172 pp.
$10.95 ($12.70 postpaid) from: University of Chicago Press, 11030 South Langley Ave., Chicago, IL 60628 (312) 568-1550 ✳WEA

ing wetted matting in its interior, the airflow rate can be increased while providing effective cooling. People in Iraq hang wet mats outside their windows to cool the wind flowing into the room by evaporation. The matting can be replaced by panels of wet charcoal held between sheets of chicken wire. Evaporation can be further accelerated by employing the Bernoulli effect or Venturi action with baffles of charcoal panels placed inside the *malqaf*, as shown. The wind blowing down through the *malqaf* will decrease the air pressure below the baffle, which increases airflow and thus accelerates evaporation. Metal trays holding wet charcoal can be advantageously used as baffles. Air can be directed over a *salsabil*, a fountain or a basin of still water, to increase air humidity.

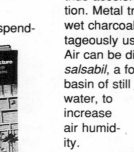

Simple *salsa bil*

fountain

Shading Our Cities

If you are an urban resident involved with trees or wanting to be, this is a useful and comprehensive book. Over forty contributors cover everything from keeping city trees healthy to strategies for community involvement with urban forest. Resources like books, periodicals and helpful organizations are also included. —Richard Nilsen

Shading Our Cities
Gary Moll and Sara Ebenreck, Editors; 1989 333 pp.; **$19.95** ($21.95 postpaid) from: Island Press, Box 7, Covelo, CA 95428 (800) 828-1302 ✳WEA

•

One of the earliest and certainly one of the most inspiring greenways is in Denver, Colorado. The city was, like many others, built alongside a river — in this case the South Platte. As the city grew, the river became a dividing line between the rich and poor sides of town, and a sewer for both. So things stood for a century on a river once described as too thick to drink, too thin to plow. Then in 1965 a devastating flood swept through Denver, sending the Platte over its banks and foul water throughout the city. The cost of damage was a third of a billion dollars. Everybody said something should be done. In 1973, another flood hit. An engineering report was prepared: the price tag for fixing up the river would be $630 million.

At that point, Denver had $1.9 million to use on the river. What to do? The answer was to call in Joe Shoemaker, hard-nosed Republican state legislator, a lawyer and ex-navy man, who, as he says of himself, doesn't take any crap from anybody. His idea was, instead of trying to pass a $630 million bond for flood control, which would probably be impossible anyway, why not set up a foundation and "return the river to the people" — not as a riprapped channel, but as a greenway.

And so it is today. Joe Shoemaker and a cadre of devoted young colleagues (now including his own son, also a state legislator) created the Platte River Greenway from one end of the city to the other (and nowadays, beyond) by assembling a foundation board of directors made up of powerful figures who might have been enemies, by resolutely avoiding the accession of any government trappings whatsoever ("to have no power is to have all power," says Shoemaker), and by piecing together from scores of public and private sources some $15 million to do the job. The result is a greenway that provides 450 acres of riverside parks, forty miles of interconnected hiking and biking routes, and a river that brings the city together rather than dividing it.

Concrete-lined ditches result in rapid runoff from the community on the right and have little value to fish and wildlife. In developing the community on the left, the natural stream and marsh were preserved. Water is retained between rains and excellent habitat is provided.

A Guide to Urban Wildlife Management
Daniel L. Leedy and Lowell W. Adams 1984; 42 pp.
$3 postpaid from: National Institute for Urban Wildlife, 10921 Trotting Ridge Way Columbia, MD 21044; (301) 596-3311

Grouping urban trees into blocks rather than rows provides room for root growth, as well as beauty and focus in a courtyard.

Max's Pot has been quietly successful for about 15 years now, working to improve the economy and environmental quality of specific regions by making efficient use of their local materials and human skills. There isn't any "Max"; the outfit was co-founded, and continues to be co-directed by Pliny Fisk III, who recently sent a few words our way. —JB

The Center for Maximum Potential Building Systems
("Max's Pot")

Dear J.,

I thought I'd just write an open-ended letter and ramble on for a while about the principal objectives of our work and about our current projects.

I've been spouting off to folks that the 70's focused on renewable energy <u>production</u>, the 80's on <u>conservation,</u> and that the 1990's have got to focus on <u>integration</u>. I will go as far as to say that integration is a totally different tactic than conservation and in the long run saves far more resources including but not limited to energy. It can be looked at from the scale of the house or the community. For example, the energy for cooking, hot water, and refrigeration are in the same ballpark. By taking the heat off your fridge you increase its efficiency by about 25-35% and your cooking comes out the other end virtually free. Now I'm talking about <u>over</u> 100% improvement within two combined sectors of household energy use.

I could go on. In our work with sustainable cities, by breaking down the bureaucratic and technical walls between energy, materials, food, water, waste water, solid waste, etc. new integration levels occur on many levels.
We have written numerous

pa-
pers in
house if
anyone is in-
terested.

Another area is
the issue of planning.
For years we at Max's Pot have been planning our buildings, complexes, and technologies as if they were tiny fractals of a Biom-Metric™ global pattern of information sharing between regions with similar resources. We identify how much of a particular indigenous resource exists, what people we have to work with there, what regionally based businesses are supported, what skills, vocational programs, etc. Ideally we hope that regional ecology and regional economic development can become acomplementary programs. Businesses as individual processes in nature becoming metabolic units, one connected to the other in continuous necklaces.

Net energy is another important matter. Basically, it's a comparison of the energy cost in, compared to the energy out, of whatever process one can dream of. Recently I gave a workshop with some of Howard Odum's associates. One of the more disturbing results gleaned from their research was how bad the net energy of solar hardware is, for the most part, as currently approached. Almost everyone has known for years that a typical flat plate solar water heater is merely a conservation measure when comparing the energy cost to produce it and the energy out. At this time petroleum is one to six, one unit of energy in to 6 out, nuclear (disregarding the energy associated with toxic waste handling) is approximately 1:2.5, a large scale centralized photovoltaic facility is (let's just say it without causing too much commotion) is less than 1. Ethanol production in a large centralized facility is a little over 1. It all depends on where you set your energetic modeling boundaries, and Odum's boundaries are usually larger than most analyses that I have seen. The conclusion could mean several things: a) we have a lot more work to do; b) our assumptions about how we think of dispersed forms of energy being used and/or processed in complex centralized facilities has got to change; or c) we are in deeper trouble than we thought about basic life style standards and no one, not even Odum's people, are using their method to come up with viable alternative structural scenarios for human life on earth. So, folks, think NET ENERGY!

Our current work ranges from the Demonstration Farm in conjunction with the Texas Department of Agriculture, to planning, housing and infrastucture development in Nicaragua and Grenada, regional housing and community design for Transcendental Meditation communities, resource and ecological planning and housing development for American Indian nations, and architectural design for private clients.

Two current projects on college campuses stand out as major catalysts for change in their regions: one, the farm in Laredo located on the campus of Laredo Junior College and two, a multi-million dollar student union in Montana. Both these projects essentially reevaluate the whole connection that a campus has to its community and to its region as well as what it teaches.

Sincerely,
Pliny Fisk III

The Laredo Blueprint Demonstration Farm combines ancient and modern methods for farming the arid lands that comprise 45% of the Earth's land surface. An integrated approach increases crop yields, improves and protects soil, and maximizes rainwater capture and retention. Solar energy is used to dry crops, make electricity, purify and heat water, heat and cool living and work spaces, and process solid wastes. The building utilizes local agricultural materials and ma-chinery for its construction. It will beused to train farmers on similar land worldwide. It's being built with local labor too.

For more information and a list of publications contact:
The Center for Maximum Potential Building Systems, 8604 F.M. 969, Austin, TX 78724; (512) 928-4786

Figure labels (isometric drawing)

RIO GRANDE RIVER
SEDIMENTATION POND
WIND-GROW COMPOSTING
SLUDGE THICKENING
MAIN OFFICE
MAINTENANCE SHED
DRYING SHED
POROUS PAVING ENTRANCE ROAD
WEEKEND FARMERS MARKET
TRUCK LOADING DOCK
PACKING SHED
VERTICAL GROW GREENHOUSE / SOLAR HEATER
SOLAR REFRIGERATION
BIOFUELS PRODUCTION
AGROFORESTRY AREA
FISH TANK
FISH INSECTUARY
COMPOST SEPARATION UNIT
10 KW ELECTRIC WIND GENERATION
FARM INSECTUARY

Underground Buildings

Twenty-six years ago, architect Malcolm Wells designed his first "underground" (they're certainly not caves) building. His early ones were the first well-publicized structures of their kind. Building underground has many advantages besides good thermal performance. As he says in the intro: " Rather than stand in contrast to Nature, underground architecture lies in her arms." He envisions whole towns with little evidence of structure showing amongst the natural vegetation and geology. A worthy goal, I'd say. This sketchbook is a chronicle of how an idea gets developed, patiently, with years of dedication and meticulous, adventuresome thought. Only twenty of his more than four-hundred underground designs have actually been built, so few that he refers to the book, with characteristic modesty, as a "catalog of failure". But the many drawings and photographs of the twenty and their unbuilt kin are convincing proof that the concept offers a way of actually building those fabled "sustainable communities." —JB

Underground Buildings, Malcolm Wells; 1990; 200 pp. **$14.95** postpaid from: 673 Satucket Road Brewster, MA 02631 (508) 896-6850

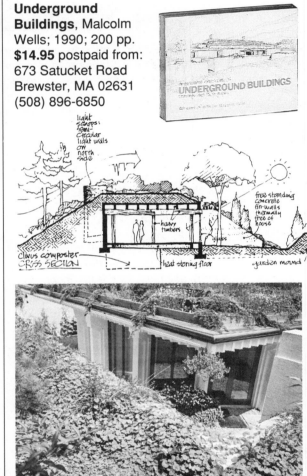

My first underground building, the office at Cherry Hill, New Jersey. 1970

Nothing adorns a building quite as beautifully as do masses of plants. If they feel uncomfortable with the way they were arranged they will rearrange themselves so naturally that the result is always far better than any human artist could achieve.

Do I see seagulls flying below an underground house? How I wish I could! These people put another damned Cape Cod cottage on that beautiful site.

Tiny Houses

Remember how silly a VW Beetle looked next to a Caddy about twenty years ago? Things have changed in the auto business, but a similar logic switch has yet to occur in the building business, where huge is still considered desirable, if not affordable. This nifty book sets you up for a big attitude change; the houses shown exhibit such variety and imagination that it's hard not to be charmed. Here's George Bernard Shaw's writing studio, mounted on a turntable so it can follow the sun. Here's Thoreau's cabin. Here's a two-person shelter-cart designed for the urban homeless, and the layout for the refugee shacks mass-produced for 1906 San Francisco earthquake victims. All the tiny houses are presented with text, photos and diagrams depicting layout and structure. I haven't been so stirred up by a book in years. Highly recommended. —JB

Tiny Houses (or How to Get Away From it All)
Lester Walker
1987; 220 pp.; **$22.50**
($25.45 postpaid) from:
The Overlook Press
RR1, Box 496
Woodstock, NY 12498

•

1950s Ranch House
12' x 9' 108 square feet.
This classy little pink house with white trim sits just north of the Rappahannock River Bridge in a small development of tiny houses near Whitestone, Virginia. A 1960s Cadillac, completely dwarfing the house, is usually parked in the driveway.

Even though the house is tiny, it manages to exhibit most of the characteristics of a 1950s

ranch house. On the exterior, first one sees the Cadillac, then the picture window, then the charcoal gray pyramidal roof and the pink clapboard siding, and on the interior, the drapes and the over-stuffed furniture aimed at the TV. In fact, the lack of a dining table indicates that many TV dinners are probably consumed on the ever popular TV trays.

Building With Junk and Other Good Stuff

Loompanics Unlimited is infamous for publishing the outrageous stuff of anarchy and fringe — claiming (as do we) that it's your right to know about anything you choose, whether offensive to others or not. **Building With Junk** won't be offensive except maybe to banks and developers, but it has that Loompanics spirit encouraging individual action and sass. The author is a master scrounger (recycler, in ecospeak) and imaginative make-do person, yet is aware of energy matters as well as unhealthy materials and building practices. His writing makes you feel like you're hatching a plot with your Uncle Jim; nothing illegal, mind you, but he's certainly out to circumvent and exploit The System. The advice is detailed, true, and full of wit. Before you give up on that unaffordable dream house, better give this a read. —JB

•

Laminated safety glass, which is two pieces of

Building With Junk And Other Good Stuff
Jim Broadstreet; 1990
155 pp.; **$17.95** ($20.95 postpaid) from:
Loompanics Unlimited
P.O. Box 1197
Port Townsend
WA 98368 ✻WEA

glass stuck onto either side of a film of plastic, is all over the place, including auto salvage yards. Again, it is hard to cut. Sometimes curved pieces are available from older model cars and trucks, cheap because there is little call for it. It might seem pretty far-out and far-fetched, but a good craftsman with routers, etc., or someone with a lot of time, patience, determination and a chisel can do some pretty astounding things with windshields and curved glass pieces for protruding windows, furniture bases, light fixtures, etc.

Adobe and Rammed Earth Buildings

We liked **Adobe-Build It Yourself**, an earlier book by the same author. This book covers some of the same ground (so to speak), then gets into a much more detailed discussion of the engineering principles that must be attended to if adobe is to withstand weather and quake, not to mention the beady gaze of the building inspector. While not usually thought of as appropriate for, say, Michigan, properly designed and built adobe and rammed earth ("pise'") can be used almost anywhere there is suitable soil, the code permits, and the climate isn't downright liquid. Recent environmental concerns have brought renewed interest in the energy and resource-efficiency potential of building with local materials. This is some of what you need to know. Bear in mind that in nearly all common types of construction, including adobe, walls represent only about 20% of building costs.

You can keep up with the latest in building with earth by subscribing to **Earth & Sun** (formerly **Adobe Today**). —JB

Window sill section.

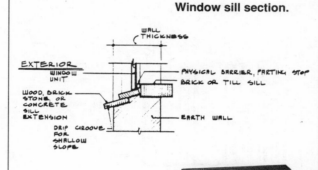

Earth & Sun, Gaylord Bird, Editor; **$40**/year (five issues) from:
Solar Earthbuilder International, P.O. Box 16119, Las Cruces, NM 88004-6119
(505) 524-1416

Adobe and Rammed Earth Buildings, Paul Graham McHenry, Jr. 1989; 217 pp.; **$24.95** ($26.95 postpaid) from: University of Arizona Press, 1230 North Park Avenue #102, Tucson AZ 85719; (602) 621-1441 ✻WEA

Finnish Fireplaces

The etymologically distinct definitions of the words hearth and heart come together when describing a place that is the center of a culture. Forced-air furnaces and electric radiant heaters hardly serve the same function, although other wood-burning stoves and even kerosene heaters may provide at least some succor in times of great stress and late-winter glumphs.

Northern peoples with long and intact material cultures, especially the Finns, have evolved a clean-burning masonry heater which, by its bulk and radiant attractiveness, truly can become the heart of a home. I imagine these massive fire-places to be a sleeping beneficient Grendel, curled up on the hearth and oh-so-eager to protect the household.

This book is intended to teach design of these heaters, their function, construction, and installa-tion to owner-builders and to masons. It serves them well. —Don Ryan

Finnish Fireplaces
(Heart of the Home)
Albert Barden; 1988
102 pp.; **$25** postpaid
from: Maine Wood
Heat Co., Inc.
RFD 1, Box 640
Norridgewock, ME 04957
(207) 696-5442

The Journal of Light Construction

You want to know the difference between hype and what's real, ask the person who actually builds — in this case, traditional architecture. Savvy articles discuss the solving of technical problems arising from recent interest in energy efficiency, new materials, and the latest tech-niques. A feeling of pride in doing things right pervades the writing and the lively and occasion-ally acrimonious letters column where controver-sies get settled by folks who have learned the hard way. The advertising —always an indicator of where technology is really at — will keep your hardware and software current. Good writing and lots of pictures make the experience of the pros easily available to build-it-yourselfers. I've not seen this sort of thing done better in my 20 years of reporting. —JB

The Journal of Light Construction (Eastern, Midwest, & Western Editions) **$27.50**/year (12 issues) from:
The Journal of Light Construction Sub-scription Service
P.O. Box 686, Holmes PA 19043-9969
(800) 345-8112

Energy Saver's Catalog

This juicy catalog features a good selection of hardware needed for solar heating. It's where you order products made of Sun-Lite® — the best fiberglass-reinforced plastic glazing. It can be had

Sun-Lite® Tanks offer TWO unique features: (1) they admit light; (2) when filled with water, you can see inside.

Diameter of Tank (Nominal)	12"	12"	18"	18"	58"
Height	4'	4'	8'	10'	5'
Volume	23.5 gallons	47 gallons	66 gallons	132 gallons	725 gallons
Wall Thickness	.040"	.040"	.040"	.040"	.060"
Material	Sun-Lite	Sun-Lite	Sun-Lite	Sun-Lite	Sun-Lite
Weight Empty	8 lbs	12 lbs	16 lbs	19 lbs	52 lbs
Weight of contained water	204 lbs.	404 lbs.	567 lbs.	1122 lbs.	6162 lbs.
	$49.95*	$79.95*	$89.95*	$119.95*	$349.95**

Sun-Lite® Tanks are being used successfully — worldwide — in many diversified applications in aquaculture. For example, growing micro-algae, fingerlings, rotifers, marine phytoplankton, shrimp, and lobsters.

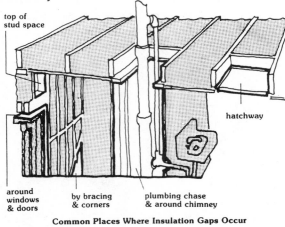

Solar Card

Is the neighbor's tree gonna shade your solar hot water heater in February? Will your proposed garden get enough sun for tomatoes? You can find out easily by viewing your surroundings through the lines printed on a Solar Card. It's a bit awkward to use but it's cheap and it works. Tell them your city and state when ordering. —JB

Solar Card; $12.95 ($15.85 post-paid) from: Design Works, Inc., 11 Hitching Post Road Amherst, MA 01002; (413) 549-4763

---

in rolls, or in prefabricated panels ready to install. The roll stock can be used to make solar heated water tanks for thermal storage and aquaculture. It works well for greenhouses. Note that this catalog, like most others, doesn't criticize or otherwise comment on suitability of items shown. It pays to read up on prospective purchases, and to discuss them with folks who have some experience. —JB

Energy Saver's Catalog; $2 from: Solar Components Corp., 121 Valley Street, Manchester, NH 03103; (603) 668-8186

Massachusetts Audubon Society: Energy Booklet Series

Yeah, these folks do nature books, and nice ones, too. But, realizing that wasteful energy practices directly threaten wildlife, they also publish an excellent series of booklets — primers, really — intended to help you make your house a model of efficiency. —JB

top of stud space

hatchway

around windows & doors

by bracing & corners

plumbing chase & around chimney

Common Places Where Insulation Gaps Occur

•

#019-How to Weatherize Your Home or Apartment

#020-All About Insulation

#021-Oil and Gas Heating Systems

#022-Saving with Home Appliances

#023-Solar Ideas for Your Home or Apartment

#024-Financing Energy Improvements

#025-An Introduction to Superinsulation

#026-Heating with Wood and Coal

#028-A Contractor's Guide to Finding and Sealing Air Leaks

Massachusetts Audubon Society Energy Booklet Series (9 different booklets) **$3** each; any four **$11** (order #095); set of nine **$22.50** (order #027) postpaid from: Education Resources Office Massachusetts Audubon Society, South Great Road Lincoln, MA 01773

SOLAR IDEAS

NCAT

"En-Cat" (National Center for Appropriate Technology) publishes the findings of their research as inexpensive booklets (most less than $5). The subject matter is aimed at ordinary folks who wish to know more about subjects common to the appropriate tech field: solar water heaters, composting toilets, biogas, weatherizing a moblile home . . . lots more. Their publications tend to summarize the baffling amount of information available elsewhere — a very useful service. —JB

NCAT Information **free** from: NCAT, P.O. Box 3838 Butte, MT 59702; (406) 494-4572

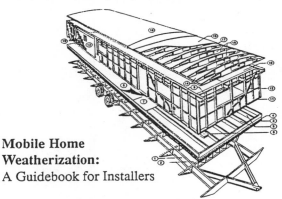

Mobile Home Weatherization: A Guidebook for Installers

NATAS

The National Appropriate Technology Assistance Service is operated by NCAT, but does business in a different way; when you need technical assistance or advice on energy matters (including recycling), you write them or call their 800 number. Your question will be answered within two or three weeks by an NCAT staff expert in the field. They will still respond to virtually any request as long as it "will help to implement a renewable energy or energy conservation project." No mention is made of what scale — they'll even advise individual homeowners. It's nice to see our government doing something right. —JB

NATAS, P.O. Box 2525, Butte, MT 59702 (800) 428-2525 [in MT (800) 428-1718]

CAREIRS

The Conservation and Renewable Energy Inquiry and Referral Service is yet another government source of information on energy matters. In response to your question, they'll likely send you one of their free fact sheets. If that's not enough, they'll get you together with the appropriate government agency (probably NATAS). —JB

Conservation and Renewable Energy Inquiry and Referral Service; Information **free** from: CAREIRS, P.O. Box 8900, Silver Spring, MD 20907; (800) 523-2929

Builders Booksource

Oh boy, a bookstore just for people who build things. The catalog is very comprehensive, covering every aspect of building with at least one good book, and usually with several — each with a review. The store carries many more titles than are in the catalog (lucky Bay Area residents can visit). If you have special needs, ask them for a reference. Bet they have it. —JB

Builders Booksource; Catalog **free** from: Builders Booksource, 1817 4th Street, Berkeley, CA 94710; (800) 843-2028 [In CA (415) 845-6874]

Rehab Right: How to Realize the Full Value of Your Home, Helaine Prentice, Ten Speed, $9.95(pb). Originally developed for Oakland residents, *Rehab Right* has gained a national reputation. This book offers guidance for the person who won't settle for the quick fix and who wants help in thinking through the sensible restoration of just about any house built since the late 19th century. This revised edition covers codes, permits, and financing, and presents a full array of repair solutions to fit various architectural styles. Highly recommended.

ears

A mail order bookstore specializing in solar and alternative energy books, mostly oldies-but-goodies from the '70s when things were seething. Good selection. —JB

HOMEGROWN SUNDWELLINGS, by Peter Van Dresser This book is an outgrowth of two years of research and experimentation by a team of architects, engineers, physicists, designers, and builders with the intent of developing low-cost, low-technology, solar heated dwellings, suitable for construction by owner-builders us-

ears Catalog **$1** from: Environmental Action Resource Service, Box 514, La Veta, CO 81055

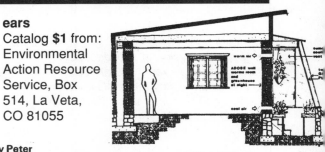

ing native materials. Four demonstration cottages were built and have been monitored for performance by the Los Alamos Scientific Laboratory. Solar heating methods include direct gain, trombe wall, and heating via an attached greenhouse. **#538** - 133 pgs, 5x8 paperbound ©1977 $7.95

Zomeworks

It's easy to spot Zomeworks products: They tend to fulfill basic needs such as providing hot water, or keeping PV panels aimed directly at the sun. The clever designs — many original inventions — are honed down to an elegant, ultimate simplicity. They're made well out of good stuff. They work. Zomeworks founder and chief designer Steve Baer says this is only to be expected from a group that has been entirely supported by innovating, producing and selling quality hardware, rather than depending on the government tit. To survive for twenty-one years in a developing marketplace, you have to be good. A recently added division, Solo Power, deals photovoltaic systems. —JB

Zomeworks; Information **free** from: Zomeworks Corp., P.O. Box 25805 Albuquerque, NM 87125; (505) 242-5354

SUNFALL™ Awning shown in "up" position left and "down" position right.

•

The Sunfall™ Automatic Awning, ideal for use on East and West facing windows, is a rectangular frame of square steel tube with a canvas, fiberglass, or metal skin, fixed on brackets to pivot 1/3 of its width out from the top edge of the window. It tracks perpendicular to the sun when the sun tries to enter the window below it. During the night and cloudy weather, the awning rises to its up position.

Sizes: 6 to 15 feet in length, 3 to 8 feet in width.

Copper Cricket

One of the few reliable (they claim not one has failed) and practical solar hot water heaters, the Copper Cricket has no pumps or recalcitrant electric valves and electronic controls. It simply cannot freeze. It'll furnish 45%-95% of a home's hot water — depending of course on climate and season — and might do even better in a conservation-minded household. The relatively high price actually works out pretty well as an investment. This is the way things should have been done all along. —JB

Copper Cricket About **$2700** installed from: Geo Trading Company 2220 W. 27th Ave. Eugene, OR 97405 (503) 343-6071

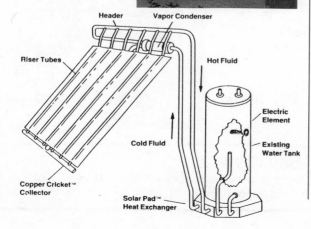

The Solar Ice Breaker™ melts a hole in ice, but does not add heat to the stock tank. It works by moving heat already at the bottom of the tank to the ice on top. The stream of bubbles rising from the bottom of the tank carries warm (about 40°F) water from the bottom to melt the ice at the top.

Super Insulated Houses and Air-To-Air Heat Exchangers

Superinsulation has turned out to be the most economical and least complicated way to build or remodel for energy efficiency. But as with all conceptually simple solutions, "All you gotta do is superinsulate" has turned out to be not so simple in practice. It soon became painfully apparent that tightly sealed superinsulated buildings had indoor air pollution problems. Burnt toast was no longer a trivial matter. Radon, never a trivial matter, became a drastic problem that scared some critics into suggesting that energy-saving buildings were a dangerous idea.

Air-to-air heat exchangers have solved the indoor pollution problem by continuously changing the air without losing much of the heat. (The fresh incoming stream is charged with heat extracted from the outgoing dirty flow.) Again, this simple idea has not been entirely problem-free, but it generally works pretty well. Mr. Shurcliff, long a respected and often critical commentator on energy matters, here sorts out insulation techniques and a selection of heat exchangers. He discusses the exchangers by brand name. He specifically addresses radon problems and what to do about them. Typical of his writing, the advice is usefully up-to-date, and is accompanied by diagrams and succinct lessons in the principles so you can buy wisely when he isn't around. Especially fine. —JB

Sunwings

Add a greenhouse to your househouse. Done well, you'll gain lots of solar heat in winter (and too much in summer if you aren't careful to design it correctly) plus veggies and nice flowers all year. Statistics show that most add-on sunspaces are used more for living than serious gardening, which isn't surprising; even on a cool cloudy day, a well-executed sunspace will heat up to an enticingly comfy temperature. Our grandparents called them sunporches, and spent a lot of time in them. Statistics also show that poor design is common. I have heard many horror stories featuring damp-ruined structure in the main house, increased heating bills, and roasted shingles. Do it right, be it prefab kit or homebuilt: read this book first. —JB

Sunwings (The Harrowsmith Guide to Solar Addition Architecture) Merilyn Mohr 1985; 151 pp. **$14.95** ($15.85 postpaid) from: Firefly Books 250 Sparks Ave. Willowdale, Ontario M2H 2S4 Canada (416) 499-8412
***WEA**

Super Insulated Houses and Air-To-Air Heat Exchangers

William A. Shurcliff; 1988 144 pp.; **$19.95** ($22.95 postpaid) from: Brick House Publishing, P.O. Box 2134, Acton, MA 01720; (508) 635-9800
***WEA**

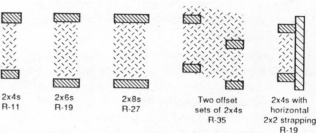

| 2x4s R-11 | 2x6s R-19 | 2x8s R-27 | Two offset sets of 2x4s R-35 | 2x4s with horizontal 2x2 strapping R-19 |

Horizontal cross sections of portions of exterior walls, with fiberglass insulation, showing several ways of achieving high R values.

•

A rotary exchanger, which is one class of reversing flow exchanger, employs a slowly rotating wheel, or rotor, that receives two adjacent airstreams of opposite direction. The rotor is massive and contains thousands of tiny passages parallel to the axis (and parallel to the airflows).

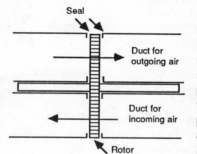

Each sector of the rotor passes across one airstream and then the other; it accepts heat from one and gives up heat to the other. The heat-exchange surface is so large that the efficiency of sensible-heat recovery is 70 to 90%, typically. Because 80 to 90% of the frontal area of the rotor is open, the pneumatic resistance is low and low-power blowers may be used.

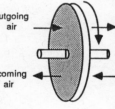

SOLARIUM SUNWING: Instead of maximizing solar heat gain or sunlight, solarium design concentrates on human comfort, combining the principles of energy efficiency with passive solar collection.

> ## See Also . . .
> Page 82 for another look at greenhouse living.

Power Play

Take a hefty portion of often unrealistic idealism, add a desire or need to live in remote places, stir in lots of effort and Good Old American Ingenuity, garnish with a dollop of courage, and let season about twenty years. Done right, you get a comfortable, practical home that's independent of the commercial power company. The energy-autonomous house can now be equipped right off the shelves of firms such as Real Goods (p. 58).

It's important to remember that even with the best hardware, life in the boonies will not be as technologically carefree as it is in town. There is certain to be a need for service, maintenance, trouble-shooting and repair — often at inconvenient times. You're it.

And please remember that all this nice equipment can make it all too easy to put a house where a house should not be put. Despite the charm and energy-efficiency of your power-independent home, you may well be acting as a *developer* of the worst sort in a previously unsullied area. This is especially true of any roads or driveways you make; roads are *the* number one invitation to land-abuse. Watch it. —JB

Home Power

Extinction is the usual fate of small publications that serve amateurs developing a field ahead of the big-time corps. **Home Power** *survives because it's needed more than ever by the increasing I'll-do-this-myself-thanks crowd, and because it's too nifty to die. It has that '70s funky look and feel: straightforward, down-home, authoritative, reporting doings and controversies at the cutting edge. I especially like their Things That Work column where staffmembers mercilessly test devices and schemes under real-life conditions. There seems to be no unseemly connection to advertisers who used to pay for the whole mag. Now you have to subscribe at a paltry fee, but it's still a great bargain; you can't find this sort of essential information anywhere else.* —JB

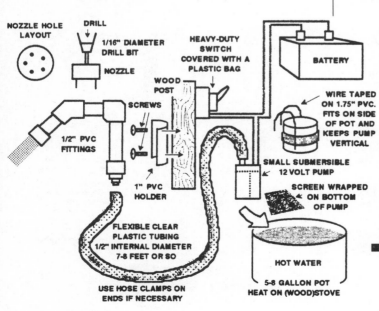

Home Power
$6/year (6 issues)
from:
Home Power
Magazine
P.O. Box 130
Hornbrook, CA
96044-0130
(916) 475-3179

The New Solar Electric Home

This updated version of one of our favorite photovoltaic books is what I most often recommend to beginners. It's a bit of history, the basic principles (though not at lab-scientist level), and the basics of sizing your photovoltaic system to fit your needs and budget. Many of the tricks of the trade are revealed so you won't have to repeat the mistakes made by your adventurous predecessors. The book is especially adept at subtly adjusting your attitude to the realities of PV — something that most other books ignore. —JB
[Seconded by Christopher Freitas]

The New Solar Electric Home (The Photovoltaics How-To Handbook) Joel Davidson; 1987; 408 pp. **$18.95** ($20.95 postpaid) from: AATEC Publications P. O. Box 7119, Ann Arbor MI 48107; (313) 995-1470

SOLVIVA WINTER GARDEN

The Solviva Winter Garden, an extraordinary 400 square foot solar-heated and -electrified bioshelter built by Anna Edey on Martha's Vineyard, provides a nurturing environment for the year-round production of dozens of varieties of vegetables and herbs, eggs from 100 chickens, and fleece from 50 Angora rabbits. A 175-watt 12-volt PV array powers directly, or via a battery bank, two de-stratification fans, two pressurization fans (which keep the outer two of the structure's four thin polyester glazings taut during windy conditions), a circulating pump for solar water heating which is used to pre-heat irrigation water, and supplementary winter lighting for evening chores and to maintain egg production during shorter daylight hours.

Joel Davidson's Pettigrew, AR, cabin. This small PV system uses only four 33-watt solar modules and a 420 amp hour battery bank located in the crawlspace to power lights, tv, stereo, radio, fans, computer, appliances, and tools.

●

Bebop Jazz Power Shower

The only thing I dislike about HP is the fact that I don't have a copy of your first issue. Keep up the good work. As a bebop jazz guitarist I'm pretty obscure up here in Ish River country (Puget Sound), but maybe they'll remember me for the 12 volt power shower — xeroxes included. Feel free to recopy, pass around, whatever. After pots of water on the head, solar shower bags, this setup *really works* . It only has a couple of problems, both because it's outside off the front porch: The lines will freeze in cold weather if you're not careful, and it gets a little chilly when the wind blows hard on colder days. —Chuck Easton

Fridges

It's economically and technically ridiculous to power a conventional, inefficient refrigerator with an independent home power system (except maybe a strong hydro rig) — the constant demand of the fridge requires an excessive number of batteries. There are two options: a super-efficient electric fridge such as the elegantly engineered **Sun Frost**, *or a model that burns propane or kerosene. The Swiss* **Sibir** *is the best-known of those, but it has recently been joined by a revived domestic* **Servel**, *famous in the '50s. There is also a selection of propane models made for recreational vehicles, though most of those are not really designed for continuous household use. (Nonetheless, I used one for 13 years with few problems.) Gas fridges are silent, long-lasting, and surprisingly fuel-efficient. They're an especially good choice if you use propane for cooking. All these machines are relatively expensive, but not nearly as expensive as the alternative of buying a much larger power system.* —JB

Sun Frost
$1295-$2395
Information **free**
from: Sun Frost
P.O. Box 1101
Arcata, CA 95521
(707) 822-9095

Sun Frost

ENERGY CONSUMPTION	
SUN FROST RF-12	
Most Efficient Competitor	
Typical Domestic Refrigerator	

Sibir $995-$1099
Information **free** from:Lehman Hardware and Appliances
4779 Kidron Rd
P.O. Box 41-Q
Kidron
OH 44636
(216) 857-5441

Sibir

Servel
$1025
Information **free** from:
Real Goods
966 Mazzoni Street, Ukiah CA 95482
(707) 468-9214

Servel

See Also . . .
For a superior book on Micro-Hydro Electric Systems see p. 93.

PV Suppliers

*At the risk of offending the many PV suppliers around the country, I list only these three because they are representative of the way the industry has developed. (For a long list of PV dealers, see PV Network News on this page.) Twenty years ago, PV was rare, utilized industrially by a few radio stations and oil rigs, and by a small number of lonely experimenters. Some of the brave experimenters became dealers. The few remaining small dealers tend to be specialized. One such is **Kirkby Solar Electric**, experts in photovoltaic systems for recreational vehicles and boats. (They authored the **RVers' Guide to Solar Battery Charging**, reviewed on this page.) In contrast, another small venerable firm specializing in water pumps, **Flowlight Solar Power**, Windy Dankoff prop., is now connected with **Photocomm**, a corporation that has eaten or become "intimately connected" with many smaller companies, and is now the biggest PV outlet. Though controversial, this move has tended to bring PV to the professional level that customers, building inspectors and mortgage lenders understand — a sign of a recognized industry that is here to stay. The colorful **Photocomm** catalog is also a basic education in PV. —JB*

Kirkby Solar Electric; Catalog **$2** from:
P.O. Box 12455, Scottsdale, AZ 85267
(602) 433-8520

Flowlight Solar Power
Catalog & Handbook **$6** from: P.O. Box 548
Santa Cruz, NM 87567; (505) 753-9699

Photocomm, Inc.
Energy Systems Catalog **$5.95** from:
Catalog Division, P.O. Box 649, North San Juan
CA 95960; (800) 544-6466 or (916) 292-3754

•

THE SOLAR ELECTRIC RULE OF THUMB

Whether or not you choose to install a solar system, we encourage you to calculate your energy requirements. It will show you how to better manage your situation. But, based on the thousands of systems we've been involved with, the average RVer, one without unusual needs, generally finds that one panel and one 105AH battery (or equivalent) per person provides an adequate system. A third panel then provides insurance during bad weather and enough power to charge portable batteries and handle unexpected requirements. Frequently, in this situation, panels may be left flat — even in the Winter. Also, if using a regulator like POWER GUARD™ with a trickle charge output, excess power can be automatically directed to maintain the vehicle starter battery as well. —*Kirkby Solar Electric*

PV Network News

This quarterly newsletter continues to serve as a clearinghouse for PV know how developed by folks using PV in their daily lives. The product reviews and field-proven tips are often way ahead of more formal publications not so intimately connected with reality. Once a year you get the peerless Resource Issue listing PV books, catalogs, newspapers, magazines, and dealers. It alone is worth the price of the subscription. —JB

PV Network News, Paul Wilkins, Editor
$15/year (4 issues)

Resource Issue
(without subscription) **$6** from:
PV Network News, 2302 Cedros Circle
Santa Fe, NM 87505; (505) 473-1067

Hoky Carpet Sweeper

Next time you're in a restaurant or hotel lobby notice the silent ministering of the lowly carpet sweeper: quiet enough to be masked by the flutter of the napery and unobtrusive enough to disappear on a crowded floor.

The Hoky carpet sweeper is not "old-fashioned" but rather, timeless; sweeps effectively on carpets or hard surfaces, and picks up even the difficult stuff: dropped pins, pet hair, sand.

The commercial model Hoky is durably all-steel and small enough to both clean around all those things under your desk and hang up for storage in the corner of the closet. Nothing hokey about a Hoky if you're off the grid or just tired of the tangle and that damn racket. Clean up your ecological niche! — Don Ryan

Hoky Carpet Sweeper; **$36.95-59.95**
Information **free** from: Hoky International
Dept. WE, 707 Wilshire Blvd. Suite 3680
Los Angeles, CA 90017; (800) 446-4659

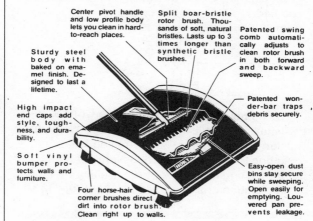

RVers' Guide to Solar Battery Charging

RVers' Guide to Solar Battery Charging is a finely detailed guide to installing PV systems in your motorhome, trailer, boat, or cabin. I've lived PV-powered for six years now and can vouch that this book is what you need to know. Wish I'd had it in 1980 when I equipped our Airstream trailer. —JB

RVers' Guide to Solar Battery Charging
Noel and Barbara Kirkby
1986; 200 pp.; **$12.95**
($14.95 postpaid) from:
AATEC Publications
P. O. Box 7119
Ann Arbor, MI 48107
(313) 995-1470

•

The Sun Frost refrigerator/freezer, very popular with homeowners, has now been discovered by RVers because of innovations which achieve exceptionally low power consumption. The Sun Frost is superinsulated with 3-4 inches of polyurethane foam. A top-mounted, hermetically sealed compressor runs cool and prevents heat from entering the cabinet. A high level of efficiency is developed in a "low differential" evaporator coil. . . . Its superinsulation allows 24-hour shut-off without spoilage.

Technically, this unit could run on the output of only two standard PV panels; however, this would not allow any reserve for bad weather. We allow three panels full output just for refrigeration.

•

Contrary to popular belief that solar cells use the heat of the sun to make electricity, it is the wave or photo energy of sunlight that is converted to power. Solar cells, then work anywhere the sun shines — not just where it's hot. Like a pump, the panel moves electrons through wires back into the battery and causes the recharge. That is all it does. Many RVers use solar panels as their sole means of battery recharging for powering lights, TV, and water pumps. Others replace their fuel generators with solar panels to supply extra energy for 120VAC inverter-supplied equipment. For others, solar trickle chargers maintain their batteries while the RV is in storage. In each case, the solar panels act only to recharge the battery.

Wind

Our previous Catalogs listed wind generators. The few homestead-size machines still made are useful and economical only where wind is plentiful and steady. (It is important to carefully "prospect" the site before purchasing a windpower set; a mistake of as little as one mile-per-hour in estimating the average windspeed can halve your take.) Experience has shown that few wind machines can develop sufficient output at the low wind speeds (under 9 mph average) common in most locations. Even fewer have proven to be reliable over the long haul — not surprising when you consider that the thing must withstand a terrible beating from the weather. If wind is your only hope, look for a reconditioned Jacobs machine from the '30s through the 50s. They are virtually the only ones with a good rep. Under most conditions, PV is a better deal. —JB

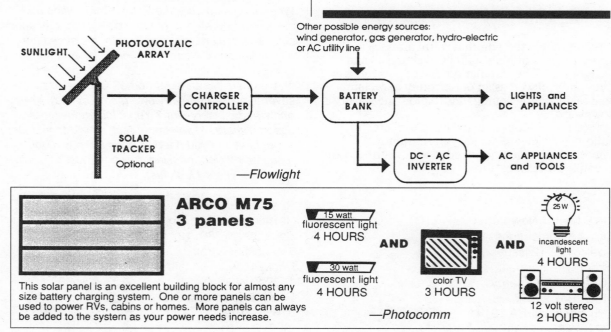

—*Flowlight*

ARCO M75 3 panels

This solar panel is an excellent building block for almost any size battery charging system. One or more panels can be used to power RVs, cabins or homes. More panels can always be added to the system as your power needs increase.

15 watt fluorescent light 4 HOURS

30 watt fluorescent light 4 HOURS

AND

color TV 3 HOURS

AND

incandescent light 4 HOURS

12 volt stereo 2 HOURS

—*Photocomm*

Resource Conservation Technology

One of the most important things I've learned about energy efficient housebuilding is how important just plain old good building practices are. A foot of insulation in the walls won't keep the heat in if there are gaps around its edges, triple-glazed windows won't be worth the money you spent unless the appropriate weatherstripping is carefully installed, and if you insulate your water heater but forget the pipes downstream you're just wasting what you gained as you keep your crawl-space nice and warm. Equally as important as building practices, though, are building materials.

But building materials are changing. Once you get past the basic stuff: nails, studs, and plates, even beyond drywall screws and hurricane ties and house-wrap, you run into a domain of synthetics and alloys and something called Ethylene Propylene Diene Monomer. These are products originally developed for the new era of factory-built houses — especially those being made in efficiency-conscious northern Europe and Japan.

Are materials engineered for the controlled conditions of the factory floor applicable out on your building site? Emphatically yes! The producers of these new materials have developed products for window and door sealing, for gap bridging at sills and rough openings, and liners and coatings and caulks enough to tempt me to start another house, just to get it right. Great! you say, but where can I get these things and how do I use them? Well, you get them right here — along with sun-control awnings and skylight blinds, ultra-low-flush toilets in 3(!) price ranges, drainage management products like nylon mesh matting and filter fabric, and pond lining, and custom-made, seamless EPDM rubber roofing (proven great for earth-sheltered houses). And they show you right in the catalog how to install them. Quantities available range from home-owner-scale to contractor-size lots and although not directly comparable to poorer substitutes found in your local hardware store, you're likely to find better stuff, cheaper, here. —Don Ryan

BG34

BG36

BG38

"P" gaskets solve a variety of structural and non-structural sealing problems. All feature wide stapling flanges for easy installation in any weather, even when the lumber is wet or dirty. The hollow center assures effortless compression over a wide range of movement.

Applications include joints in log and heavy timber construction, joints between manufactured wall or roof panels such as stress-skin panels, and joints between sections of manufactured homes ("marriage walls"). Small P gaskets can also be used to make inexpensive yet reliable seals around attic access doors.

We stock three sizes: BG34 for gaps up to 3/8", BG36 for gaps up to 5/8", and BG38 for gaps up to 7/8". Larger sizes are available on special order.

ICE

The Interfaith Coalition on Energy has been helping to reduce energy costs in religious buildings for ten years now. Theirs is a tough assignment; most church leaders know very little about energy matters. Indeed, many seem to behave as if they accept gross inefficiency as God-given — perhaps as another trial to be borne. The good folks at ICE know better. With a God-helps-those-who-help-themselves attitude, they have labored to make church buildings more affordable to keep, freeing scarce funds for higher purposes. In addition to publishing the ICE Melter Newsletter, they conduct workshops, purvey technical advice, and administer energy audits. It's all marked with a commendable honesty tempered by the naive mistakes of their early days. I am particularly impressed by their ability to say no to eco-popular ideas that make no economic sense — always a mark of professional expertise. ICE is Philadelphia-based, but their ideas will work fine elsewhere. Your church could probably benefit from their work. —JB

The Most Energy-Efficient Appliances

The most energy-efficient appliances will certainly save resources, and reduce pollution, but you have to have the conscience of a saint to pay the dealer extra for that. (Ever notice how it always costs extra to save energy, money, or anything else?) Let's face it, most folks will not fork out the extra bucks unless they can expect to save money too.

This annually produced guide lists only the top handful of each type of appliance — why show the pigs? Performance figures are given, along with a brief explanation of what they mean. The booklet concludes with an easily-used chart that helps you calculate lifecycle costs (cost, plus the cost of running it for its expected lifespan, including a fudge factor for interest that you would have made on the money if you had bought a cheaper model). Lord love a duck, it turns out that an appliance with respectable performance and (relatively) low energy use often turns out to be cheaper in the long run despite its higher initial cost. The guide only covers the big gobblers: furnaces, fridges, air conditioners, and the like. If a big-ticket appliance purchase looms, this booklet and Consumer Reports (p. 65) is your homework. —JB

The Most Energy-Efficient Appliances; 1989-90 Edition American Council for an Energy-Efficient Economy 1988; 28 pp.; **$3** postpaid from: American Council for an Energy-Efficient Economy 1001 Connecticut Ave, NW, Suite 535 Washington, DC 20036

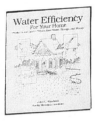

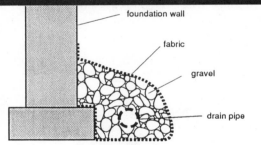

foundation wall

fabric

gravel

drain pipe

Using polypropylene liner protection fabric as filter fabric to keep soil from clogging foundation drain.

Resource Conservation Techonolgy, Inc.; Information **free** from: 2633 North Calvert Street, Baltimore, MD 21218; (301) 366-1146

Ceiling Fans

It is commonly thought that warm air rises to the upper reaches of high ceilings in churches and synagogues. The installation of a ceiling fan is frequently viewed as an opportunity to reclaim lost heat by installing ceiling fans to blow the warm air downward.

In fact, the air does not stratify as expected in buildings which are heated intermittently. Therefore, fans are not needed to redistribute and equalize air temperature.

ICE Melter Newsletter Free (contributions welcome) 12 issues/year from: The Interfaith Coalition on Energy P.O. Box 26577 Philadelphia, PA 19141 (215) 635-1122

Water Efficiency For Your Home

Turns out the tiresome eco-naggers are right after all: every drop counts. It wouldn't matter so much if there weren't so many of us using the stuff. As it is, millions of water users can (and usually do) waste a LOT of water, mostly a little at a time. Building codes are set assuming an appalling level of waste. Municipal water-saving programs commonly specify 40 gallons per person per day! We can do better; to prove it can be done, I have lived well for years on 40 gallons a week, including a daily shower and one load of laundry. Remember that water saving also saves pumping electricity somewhere, water heating fuel, sewage treatment, purification procedures, and the resource depletion, pollution, and money involved. This booklet tells what to do and how much it will help. You can get the associated hardware items, low-flow shower heads and the like, from most of the suppliers on pages 54-61. —JB

Water Efficiency for Your Home, John C. Woodwell; 1989; 10 pp. **$5** postpaid from: Rocky Mountain Institute, 1739 Snowmass Creek Road Snowmass, CO 81654-9199

Home Energy

Home Energy attends to the efficiency of appliances (even waterbeds), home and apartment energy-use analysis, and a host of detailing that is hard to find anywhere else. These folks used to call themselves Energy Auditor and Retrofitter, and they still have plenty to say on that subject. A useful service for newcomers to the game as well as grizzled veterans wishing to keep up on the latest news. —JB

Home Energy Alan Meier, Executive Editor; **$45**/year (six issues) from: Home Energy 2124 Kittredge St., #95 Berkeley, CA 94704 (415) 524-5405

Resource-Efficient Housing Guide

When someone calls the Whole Earth office and asks could we steer them to a college that teaches solar architecture, we look it up in this exceptionally useful book. Need the address of your state's Energy Office? It's in here too. What about a book on weatherizing an older home? Choose from several, all with brief reviews (some by me). Water purity and conservation? Yup. House design for desert climates? Um-Hm. In fact, where to find just about anything you need or need to know about resource-efficient housing is in here, just as you'd hope. It's where I look first. —JB

Resource-Efficent Housing Guide, Robert Sardinsky; 1989; 127 pp. **$15** postpaid from: Rocky Mountain Institute 1739 Snowmass Creek Road, Snowmass, CO 81654-9199 (303) 927-3128

Rocky Mountain Institute

I'll eliminate the middleman and let these folks introduce themselves:

"Rocky Mountain Institute is a nonprofit research and educational foundation with a vision across boundaries.

"Seeking ideas which transcend ideology, and harnessing the problem-solving power of free-market economics, our goal is to foster the efficient and sustainable use of resources as a path to global security.

"Rocky Mountain Institute believes that people can solve complex problems through collective action and their own common sense, and that understanding interconnections between resource issues can often solve many problems at once.

"We focus our work in five areas — Agriculture, Economic Renewal, Energy, Security, and Water — and carry on international outreach and technical-exchange programs."

It all started when Amory Lovins stirred up the Big Power folks in 1976 with a paper called The Road Not Taken, *and then a 1977 book called* Soft Energy Paths. *His principal argument was, and still is, that energy conservation makes a lot more sense than increasing energy production. He proposed a strategy of "plugging the leaks" by increasing the efficiency of energy-using hardware. He called the saved energy "negawatts." Necessary power would be derived from renewable sources, which eventually would replace fossil-fueled and nuclear power plants. The advantages are many: oil imports could be eliminated, as could offshore and Alaska Wildlife Refuge drilling; nuclear proliferation would be stopped; acid rain and greenhouse gases greatly reduced. Billions less dollars would be directed to utility bills and pollution cleanup, freeing it for economically beneficial uses. With less dependence on imported energy and huge, centralized power plants, national security would be enhanced. There's more; the list is long.*

Of course, such talk invited vigorous attack. But Amory's arguments were backed by numbers — the same numbers and analytical methods used by his detractors who had not been paying attention to changes in technology, economics, and public environmental concern. Moreover, Amory did not assault the opposition as an enemy to be beaten; he regarded them as unenlightened (and occasionally stupid), in need of education. In the confrontational '70s, this uncommonly businesslike stance, aided by a dynamic speaking style, helped him reach the influential people who most needed to understand his message.

Obviously this was more than one person could handle. In 1982, Amory and his wife, Hunter, founded the Rocky Mountain Institute and commenced work on their home/headquarters, itself a demonstration of energy efficiency. A crew of researchers and volunteers assembled to advance the work on many fronts. They have been remarkably successful. RMI advises major power companies, assorted corporations, managers of cities large and small, and the federal government at the highest levels, including the military. Amory regularly consults with foreign governments — true citizen diplomacy — and has been actively working with the Russians to reduce international political tensions as well as their internal problems with energy, the environment, and economics.

Institute Director Hunter Lovins, Amory, and many of the researchers spend a lot of time on the road giving lectures and workshops all over the world.

At home, the RMI folks keep busy. Their publications list fills three typewritten pages (which you can send for — see below). At any given moment, several books and papers are in the works, money is being raised, new projects are being planned, dignitaries are being entertained, friends greeted, phone questions answered. Daily visitors throng the building, adding to the quiet tumult as they take the self-guided tour. Yet despite the urgency and seriousness, a good spirit is in evidence. There is music and laughter as well as the sound of computers humming. When the sun hits its solar panel, a fan above the garden begins to flup-flup-

flup as it chews the banana leaf that has once again grown into its path overnight. A rather odd dog, Nanuq the Beastoid, wanders about. Even a visitor can feel the rightness of all this — that it's a good way to do things.

And so it is. RMI is an inspiring example of good scholarship, tough discipline, and high spirits (and of course talented people) making a real difference. In less than ten years, this modest group has become the world's most effective force encouraging the intelligent use of our resources. They're working for all of us. Make use of what they've learned, and support 'em when you can.
—JB

Fun Energy Facts To Know And Tell At Cocktail Parties

These quickies are also stunning at town meetings, for torturing parents who have missed the message, and for impressing anachronistic teachers. If challenged, you can defend yourself with hard numbers from other RMI offerings. Reform the heathen! —JB

•

2 Just lighting (and, in the process, heating) American food stores, recooling the people inside, and — lest we forget — cooling the food keeps about 28 huge power plants busy full-time. The cost of all that electricity shows up on your food bill as part of the high cost of food that doesn't get back to the farmer.

7 Replacing all U.S. light vehicles with 60-mpg models would save over five million barrels of oil per day, which is more than we import.

9 About 80 to 90 percent of the money you spend for energy leaves your local economy. In a typical town, that amounts to approximately 10 percent of the local payroll each year.

30 Nuclear power presently delivers about half as much of the nation's energy as wood. Wood, by the way, has never been a significantly subsidized energy source.

RMI Publications List

The impressive list of RMI publications includes books, reports, reprints of articles by and about RMI, plus T-shirts and the like. It's free. —JB

Energy Casebook

This is what you need to convince the powers-that-be, or perhaps even yourself, that this stuff works. It's an inspiring collection of real-live implementation of RMI strategies and the consequent results. (The Publications list offers a Business Opportunities Casebook too). —JB

Competitek

This is a professional-level service intended to serve corporate, institutional and government planners requiring the latest information on electrical efficiency strategy and equipment. It's offered by subscription at three levels of involvement — $9000 to $24,000. There are now more than 100 subscribers in 20 countries. Perhaps your town or company could use some advice? —JB

RMI headquarters building is home to founders Amory and Hunter Lovins, office for 17 researchers, and controlled-climate space for a year-round, semi-tropical garden (complete with iguana). The 4000 sq. ft. structure consumes only 10% of the electricity and 50% of the water expected for a building of its size and use. Heat, hot water, and clothes-drying is solar. Electricity soon will be too. Energy savings alone will pay for the entire "eco-palace" in 40 years or less. (See RMI publications list for Visitor's Guide and hardware sourcelist.)

Rocky Mountain Institute; $10/year (includes quarterly newsletter)

Visitor's Guide (Descriptive/Tour Guide plus a where-to-get-it list of technologies); 1988; 22 pp. **$5** postpaid

RMI Publications List; free

Fun Energy Facts to Know and Tell at Cocktail Parties, Amory Lovins & John Klusmire; 1986; 3 pp.; **$2** postpaid

Energy Casebook, William D. Browning & L. Hunter Lovins; 1989; 64 pp.; **$20** postpaid

Competitek; for more information contact Ted Flanigan at RMI (303) 927-3851

All from:
Rocky Mountain Institute
1739 Snowmass Creek Road
Snowmass, CO 81654-9199

RMI Videos

There are two nifty RMI videos available. Lovins on the Soft Path *is a dramatic introduction to the Lovins' work, featuring the irrefutable logic and wicked wit of both Hunter and Amory. When I used this in a college environmental studies class, many students asked to take the tape home for another look. For teachers not yet familiar with the subject, a study guide is available from RMI's publications list. Convincing and deadly.*

The other film is from CBS-TV 60 Minutes: A Visit With Hunter and Amory Lovins. *It's a bit better than what you'd expect from mainline tubies. —JB*

Lovins on the Soft Path
$75 Rent; **$295** Purchase VHS, **$650** 16mm

A Visit with Hunter & Amory Lovins
$30 Rent; **$95** Purchase

Both films from: Bullfrog Films, Oley, PA 19547 (800) 543-3764. (Bullfrog Films review p. 119.)

Real Goods

It has been a true pleasure to watch Real Goods grow from a funky counterculture supply store to a thoroughly professional enterprise grossing about two million a year (and still growing vigorously). Real Goods is now the country's leading purveyor of "alternative energy" hardware. Their diverse stock includes such things as solar-powered deepwell pump sets and hand-powered washing machines. The wide selection of goods appears to be a bit less wide than it used to be, and some items carried by competitors are not offered. Reason: unlike most of the competition, Real Goods insists that the goods have been proven to work reliably — often by staff members who actually live with the stuff as part of their normal day-to-day routine. Customers are encouraged to report deficiencies, and to suggest improvements or better products. Inept performers are dropped. The Sourcebook thus evolves, getting better as it goes.

This latest Sourcebook (with foreword by RMI's Amory Lovins, p. 57) continues a tradition of being more than a mere catalog; it's also a veritable alternative technology (AT) textbook explaining theory and practice so you can choose products intelligently. Most items are acompanied by experienced comments in addition to specifications and the manufacturer's description. If that isn't enough, Real Goods offers a consulting service. This edition features a comprehensive discussion of low-energy lighting by Robert Sardinsky, founder of Rising Sun (see p. 60) with particular attention being paid to the DC lighting needed for a home powered by photovoltaic

panels or other so-called alternative energy. (I don't consider the sun to be "alternative," since our lives depend entirely upon it.)

Sourcebook buyers also receive quarterly supplements offering new items, special sales, and — most important — vigorous reader/user commentary. Gee, this is beginning to sound like I'm on their payroll! I'm not, but I do appreciate a business that's doing a difficult job well. I, and many of my friends, have had good advice and dependable service from Real Goods for many years.

And check the Sourcebook cover: it's a one-megawatt photovoltaic power plant in the front yard of the now-closed Rancho Seco nuclear facility. Yes indeed. —JB

Real Goods Alternative Energy Sourcebook 1990; **$10** postpaid (deductible from your first $100 order)

Real Goods News; **$20** postpaid (three issues plus annual update of AE Sourcebook)

both from:
Real Goods
966 Mazzoni
Street, Ukiah
CA 95482
(800) 762-
7325 [in CA
(707) 468-
9214]

Sun-Mar Composting Toilets

We have now supplied over 300 Sun-Mar toilets (formerly Bowli's) to our customers, and we are pleased to report that these toilets have exceeded our expectations and the manufacturer's specifications. We're convinced that this is the best small composting toilet system on the market. The old problem of resistance from doubting building inspectors has mostly been eliminated with the recent NSF approval.

The Non-Electric is our most popular selling unit. It's perfect for many of our customers living off the power line and not wanting to be dependent on their inverters. The tremendous aeration and mixing action of the Bio-Drum, coupled with the help of a 4" vent pipe and the heat from the compost creates a "chimney" effect which draws air through the system similar to a wood stove. The N.E. is designed for one to three people in residential use and four to six people in cottage use (Sun-Mar rates usage **very** conservatively). It is 23" wide, 28" high, and 32" long. Because the N.E. lacks a heater like the larger models, it has a small evaporation capacity. It therefore requires a small drain connected to a small 1' x 1' drain pit for occasional overloads: 8 ft of 3/4" pipe is included for this purpose.

N.E. **$1,049**
FOB Buffalo, NY

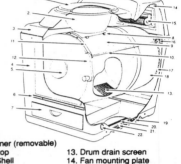

1. Seat
2. Bowl liner (removable)
3. Tiolet top
4. Main Shell
5. Drum bearing
6. Step support
7. Compost drawer
8. Drum door hinges
9. Drum door
10. Crank shaft
11. Drum locker
12. Crank handle
13. Drum drain screen
14. Fan mounting plate
15. Fan 30 Watts with speed control
16. Crank sprocket
17. Drum sprocket (moulded into drum)
18. Drum
19. Insulation base
20. Heating element 250 Watts
21. Insulation
22. Vent hole

Pacific Yurts

Because of the incredible success of our Shelter Systems Portable Shelters, we've decided to take one step further in introducing **Pacific Yurts.** *These portable, yet semi-permanent structures meet all of our criteria for quality.*

The yurts are extremely easy to install. The 30' yurt takes two people less than a day to erect, and the 12' model only a few hours. Materials are of the finest quality available, including a center ring of cross-laminated kiln-dried fir, select fir rafters, galvanized steel tension cable, electronically bonded vinyl-laminated polyester top cover, and large clear vinyl windows. All top covers come with a five-year pro-rata warranty. Many custom options are available like windows, deck, solar skylight arc, and fabric colors.

Size (diameter)	Sq. ft.	Center height	weight	Price
12'	115	8'0"	350#	**$1,995**
14'	155	8'9"	450#	**$2,595**
16'	200	9'3"	550#	**$2,995**
20'	314	10'0"	700#	**$3,895**
24'	452	11'6"	900#	**$4,395**
30'	706	13'	1,200#	**$5,895**

Prevailer Gel Cell Batteries

Prevailer gel cells, made by Sonnenschein, are truly 100% maintenance free. Prevailer batteries can be **charged** and discharged more frequently than any other battery because the lead-acid electrolyte is totally gelled. Gel cells are leakproof, sealed for life and can operate in any position (even upside down) with an extremely low self-discharge rate. These batteries can be taken down to a 100% depth of discharge and can sit totally discharged for 30 days with absolutely no damage. They are really the only batteries to use in extreme cold environments as they are rated at. To compare gel cell capacities with standard lead-acid batteries, multiply the amphour rating by 1.5. To summarize some of the advantages of gel cells (to justify their high cost!) over standard lead-acid batteries:

• They don't require acid checks or watering
• They can withstand shock and vibration better
• They can be stored up to 2 years without recharging
• They tolerate extreme cold and extreme heat
• There is no gassing or emission of corrosive acid fumes

All Prevailer batteries come with a 5-year warranty and can be shipped via standard UPS (if 70 lb or less). There are numerous Prevailer gel cells available at voltages from 2V to 12V and capacities available from 1 to 110 amphr, but we'll only list the two most popular here as an introduction. Send SASE for more information.

A212/85G Gel Cell 85 amphour(12V) **$241**
Ship wt. 68#
A212/110A Gel Cell 110 Amphour(12V) **$325**
Ship wt. 82#

Burkhardt & Harris Turbines

We refer repeatedly to Burkhardt & Harris as if the companies were interchangeable. In reality Don Harris is Harris Hydroelectric and John Takes is Burkhardt Turbines. Both companies use virtually the same components, have the same prices, and the same warranty. Both are well-proven reliable systems.

When calculated on a cost-per-watt basis, the average hydro-electric generator costs as little as ONE-TENTH as much as a solar (photovoltaic) system of equivalent power. Solar only generates power when the sun is shining; hydro generates power 24 hours a day.

The generating component of the Burkhardt & Harris turbines is an automotive alternator (Delco or Autolite, depending on system requirements) equipped with custom wound coils appropriate for each installation. The rugged turbine wheel is a one-piece Harris casting made of tough silicon bronze. There are hundreds of these wheels in service with NO failures to date.

1 nozzle **$595**
2 nozzle **$695**
4 nozzle **$850**
8 nozzle **$1,050**

REGULATOR

TURBINE   BATTERY

DC-AC INVERTER

Real Goods helped design and provided all materials for this unique project in North Carolina. The main structure is a "Bio-dome" (see p. 83) for which Real Goods supplied 156 Sovonics 20 watt PV modules. Two five-HP Sterling generators provide the back-up power. Six Trace 48 volt 2200 watt inverters with stacking interfaces were provided for the AC power.

Survivor 06 - Hand Water Purifier

The new Survivor 06 is a hand operated water purifier that will convert sea water, brackish water, or contaminated water into fresh and pure drinking water. It will produce one cup every thirteen minutes at 30 strokes per minute, or six gallons per day. This is the only manually-operated desalinator in the world. It uses no batteries, generators, or alternators. It combines reverse osmosis technology with energy recovery technology. A pre-filter removes larger particles and debris. The unit measures 5" high x 8" long x 2-1/2" wide. It will suck to a maximum suction height of ten feet. It will work under a temperature range of 33 to 120 degrees farenheit.

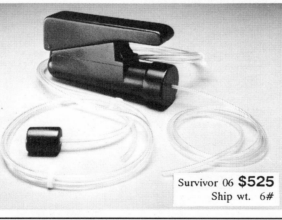

Survivor 06 **$525**
Ship wt. 6#

Econo-Sub Deep Well Submersible

The Econo-Sub (also known as the SolarJack SDS-3A-24) is a low power deep well submersible pump, capable of lifts up to 230 feet using less than 100 watts of 12 or 24-volt DC power, and able to deliver a flow rate from 30 to 100 gallons per hour. It installs easily by hand and is a real breakthrough in deep-well solar pumping. It is made of all stainless steel and solid brass parts with absolutely no nylon or plastic. This pump is strong! During testing water was brought up from 100' in the well with a 20 watt solar module! The Installation kit (below) is highly recommended.

SDS-3A-24 Econo-Sub **$795**
Ship wt. 26#

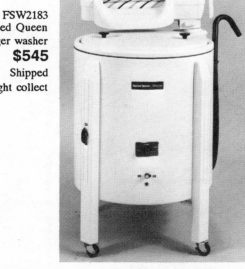

FSW2183
Speed Queen
wringer washer
$545
Shipped
freight collect

Speed Queen Wringer Washer

The Speed Queen is the best 110V washing machine we've found, and is a great choice for low-voltage homesteads because it has no spin cycle. It uses far less water, far less electricity, and gets clothes much cleaner than energy-guzzling standard washing machines. The Speed Queen has an 18-gallon stainless steel tub and a 1/3 hp motor that uses 800 watts. The Speed Queen comes on four easy-rolling casters. The wringer swings and locks in eight positions. Pressure from the 2-1/4" rollers is self-adjusting for efficient wringing.

Holly Hydro Heater

The Wood (Coal)/Solar Connection

The Holly Hydro Heater's concept is very simple; trap some of the excess heat given off by your wood or coal burner and channel it to an area where it will do the most good. You can use this "captured" heat to substantially reduce your domestic hot water heating bills every time you use your wood or coal stove. You can also tie the Holly Hydro Heater into your solar hot water system, creating the wood (coal)/solar connection. This supplies you with sun-heated hot water on sunny days, and wood or coal-heated water on cloudy days. With the proper Holly Installation Package, you can help heat your hot tub, sometimes even supply a back-up for hydronic heating systems.

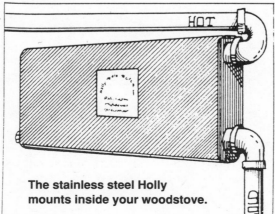

The stainless steel Holly mounts inside your woodstove.

There are certain situations where you should always use the largest Holly that will fit your stove. For solar back-up where there is at least 200 gallons of storage, for hydronic heating applications, for backing up a boiler system, and for heating hot tubs, these applications generally require all the hot water they can get. In all other instances, think about storage before picking your Holly.

Model no.	Size	Ship wt.	Price
SS-12	12"	16 #	$150
SS-14	14"	11 #	$170
SS-18	18"	13 #	$220
SS-24	24"	16 #	$275
Stanley Cookstove model			$165
Vermont Castings model			$265

All units are stainless steel.

Rising Sun

Just One Bulb...

Would you put money into a scheme that pays an average 34% return on investment? What if that investment also had a powerful, positive environmental effect? Sounds too good to be true, but that's what happens when you buy and use low-energy lighting. Even a single lamp — just one, the one you buy to start retrofitting your home or business or church — will eliminate the need for mining and burning about 350 lbs. of coal, and the consequent emission of about 1000 lbs. of carbon dioxide, a "greenhouse gas" thought to be the principal cause of global warming. Your lamp will also keep about 20 lbs. of acid-rain-causing sulphur dioxide out of our atmosphere. Low-energy lamps run cool too, reducing the need for air conditioning in larger buildings. And a typical low-energy lamp lasts ten to thirteen times longer than a regular incandescent, important for hard-to-reach locations and for businesses where bulb-changing labor costs are significant. Icing on the cake: many people prefer the quality of light from the low energy lamps. Not bad for one little bulb!

Disadvantages? There are a few. First is the price. The return on investment may be high, but so is the capital outlay. In some locations this problem is being met by subsidy or even give-aways by power companies with management intelligent enough to realize that reduced demand means no risky outlays for new power plants. For a substantial number of lamps, you can work out lease/purchase, shared savings or other plans designed to ease the pain. Just plain folks may find it easier to spread costs by buying one lamp a month. (That's what I do.) Remember, these lamps are truly an investment, and a better one than you'd likely find anywhere else.

Another drawback is that most of the low-energy lamps start slowly and flickery when cold (say, 40° F.) and may not start at all below 30° F. This might prove to be a winter problem in homes, garages, churches, and shops with wide temperature swings due to wood heat or occasional use. I've had no intolerable problems down to 30°.

These lamps are not economical for quick on-and-off duty such as in a closet. Their fatter bases will not fit all fixtures, shades, and reflectors. The added weight of certain bulbs will cause some spring-arm lamps to droop. In short, the field is still new; you should be prepared for a bit of experimentation.

One last point: These lamps are fluorescent, and many people (including me) just don't like fluorescents. But these lamps don't hum or flicker, and the light has a warm feel to it. I suggest trying before deciding. Turns out that I actually prefer mine to conventional incandescents. In fact, this Ecolog has been edited by light from an

Rising Sun Sampler Catalog; $5 postpaid from: Rising Sun Enterprises, Inc., P.O. Box 586, Old Snowmass, CO 81654; (303) 927-8051

(Right) Passive infrared wall switch saves energy otherwise spent lighting unoccupied spaces.

(Below) The "real cost" of lighting: this sample worksheet compares the life-cycle cost of operating a long lived, energy-efficient compact fluorescent lamp to a standard incandescent lamp — "light bulb" — of comparable light output. As the sample calculations below illustrate, the compact fluorescent lamp offers substantial economic savings both by operating 75% more energy efficiently (using 55 less watts) than the incandescent and lasting more than 13 times as long.

- Simply replaces existing light switches
- large 800 sq. ft. of coverage
- Built-in light level sensor
- Adjustable Sensitivity & Time Delay
- Advanced transformer/latching relay design
- Proven 30% to 60% savings
- Three-year warranty; UL Listed

The Watt Watcher WI-120 and WI-277 automatic wall switches simply replace existing wall switches and turn lighting systems on only when offices, conference rooms, copy rooms or utility rooms are actually occupied. Lighting systems are automatically turned off after the controlled area is left unoccupied for a user-specified length of time. When the area is used again, the lights are automatically turned on. Savings of 30% to 60% are common.

REFLECT-A-STAR. These unique 9- and 13-watt quad compact fluorescent reflector lamps replace 50-75 watt incandescent reflector floods. The product is engineered to provide many years of high performance and is available in two wattages and 2 reflector sizes. Choose one that fits your fixture.

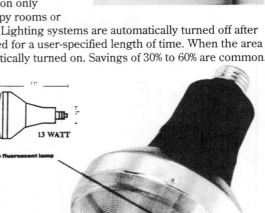

13 WATT

Replaceable fluorescent lamp

	COMPACT FLUORESCENT OPTION		INCANDESCENT OPTION	
	20-WATT (INTEGRAL ONE-PIECE) "DULUX EL" COMPACT FLUORESCENT LAMP RATED LIFE: 10,000 HOURS LAMP COST: $25.95		75-WATT STANDARD "A" LAMP INCANDESCENT LAMP RATED LIFE: 750 HOURS LAMP COST: $0.75	
20 watts	(1) What is the rated wattage of the lamp --"light bulb" (including ballast draw for the compact fluorescent)?		75 watts	
10,000 hours	(2) What is the rated life of the lamp?		750 hours	
1	(3) How many lamps will have to be installed to produce light for as many hours as the single compact fluorescent lamp?		13.33	
	[Divide the rated life of the compact fluorescent option by the rated life of the incandescent option and place answer in blank at right]			
200 kWh	(4) How much energy does each option consume over the life of the compact fluorescent lamp?		750 kWh	
	[Multiply (1) x (2) x (3) to get watt-hours, and divide the result by 1,000 to convert to kilowatt-hours]			
0.074 $/kWh	(5) What does your utility company charge you for electricity per kilowatt-hour? (The national average is $0.074/kWh.)		0.074 $/kWh	
$ 14.80	(6) How much will it cost you to operate each option over the life of the compact fluorescent lamp?		$ 55.50	
	[Multiply (4) x (5)]			
$ 25.95	(7) What will it cost you to purchase the lamps for each option over the life of a single compact fluorescent lamp?		$ 9.99	
	[cost per lamp x (3)]			
$ NA	(8) What will it cost you to install the lamp(s) for each option?		$ NA	
	[If you pay someone to maintain your lighting system, multiply their hourly wage ( ) x the amount of time it will take them to replace the lightbulb x (3)]			
$ NA	(9) How much will it cost you to get rid of the unwanted heat produced by each option over its lifetime?		$ NA	
	[If you use an air conditioner or fan to cool your home or business for part of the year, multiply (6) x .055 cooling penalty for residences or (6) x .14 cooling penalty for commercial facilities.]			
$ 40.75	(10) What will it cost you to buy, operate, and maintain each option over the lifetime of a single compact fluorescent lamp?		$ 65.49	

[Add (6) + (7) + (8) + (9)]

11) How much money have you saved by investing in a single compact fluorescent lamp?

[Subtract (10) left column from (10) right column.]

$ 24.74

ALPINE BANK of BASALT
SUMMARY OF LIGHTING RETROFIT COST AND SAVINGS
"THE BOTTOM LINE"

RETROFIT NUMBER	ANNUAL O+M EXPENSE	POTENTIAL ANNUAL O+M SAVINGS	TOTAL COST OF PROPOSED RETROFIT	RETURN ON INVESTMT	PAYBACK ON INVESTMT	FIXTURE COUNT
1	$364.50	$349.08	$118.38	295%	0.3 YR	6
2	$149.50	$143.22	$133.92	107%	0.9 YR	2
3	$57.75	$55.75	$58.00	104%	1 YR	1
4	$46.76	$37.07	$55.88	66%	1.5 YR	1
5	$52.96	$46.68	$66.60	70%	1.4 YR	2
6	$96.25	$53.75	$96.95	56%	1.8 YR	5
7	$1,370.46	$787.02	$3,178.11	25%	4.0 YR	39
8	$491.20	$431.36	$1,336.00	32%	3.1 YR	32
9	$125.25	$97.51	$472.80	20%	4.9 YR	6
10	$187.87	$146.27	$718.20	20%	4.9 YR	9
TOTALS		$2147.71	$6234.84	34%	2.9 YR	

*1 - Average Return on Investment = 34%
*2 - Average Payback on Investment = 2.9 years
*3 - Reduction in electric lighting base load demand = 8829 watts.
    Original base load demand = 12,248 watts
    After retrofit = 4,419 watts
*4 - kWh of electricity saved = 22,952 kWh/yr
    Original annual kWh consumption = 34,690 kWh/yr
    After retrofit = 11,738 kWh/yr
*5 - Burning of 22,953 lbs of coal avoided
*6 - Emissions of 91,812 lbs of carbon dixiode (CO_2) from burning of
    coal avoided (prime culprit of global warming/greenhouse effect)
*7 - Emissions of 597 lbs of sulfur dioxide (SO_2)
    from burning of coal avoided (prime culprit of acid rain)

The Asymmetria uses the new, energy-efficient lighting technology of the compact fluorescent tube. This mighty little fluorescent operates on only 13-watts, yet produces light output comparable to a 75-watt incandescent bulb. No need to worry about bulb changes with a life expectancy of 10,000 hours (5 to 7 years of normal use). An added benefit of this new fluorescent technology is the soft, warm, natural color of the light which flatters skin tones and enhances your viewing pleasure.

The sleek design of the Asymmetria was created to compliment modern decor and office settings. The slender lamp head remains unobtrusive in compact work stations, around computer screens, and on the smaller modern drawing boards.

Asymmetria desklamp with clamp-on base   **$57.95**
Asymmetria desklamp with weighted base   **$60.95**

Much of this Ecolog was read and typed by the light of my 13 watt Asymmetria. I like it a lot. —JB

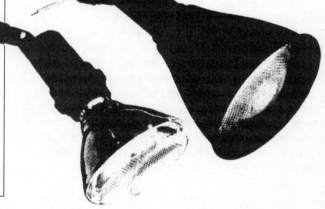

This 7-watt PL* compact fluorescent floodlight delivers approximately the same amount of light as a 75-watt incandescent floodlight. It can often replace higher wattage floodlights in applications where not as much light is needed. A glare shield option is available.

TOTAL POWER CONSUMPTION: 10 watts
DIMENSIONS: approx. 9" L X 6" W
INSTALLATION: 1/2" male swivel mount connection fits 1/2" female opening in any standard junction box cover.

PRICE: $35.95

With glare shield $41.95
Spare PL*7 lamp $4.95

Asymmetria (this page) and not just because it's the politically correct thing to do.

It is edifying to note the large-scale implications of the potential savings afforded by these lamps. The bank statement on this page shows what you can typically expect from a relamping program in a commercial building. Similar savings can be expected in any building where lights are left on for long periods, making relamping of particular interest to schools, churches, and municipal buildings on a tight budget. Of course, any business can expect added profits from a relamping program. Studies have shown that merely relamping required fire exit signs can save about $40 per year per sign.

This was the proposal. The actual performance of this contract came very close to predictions. The bank and its employees are highly pleased.

The real paydirt comes on a national scale: Lighting, and the air conditioning necessary to remove the waste heat from conventional inefficient lighting, eats about one-fourth of all electricity used in this country, and one-half of the coal used by utilities. The potential is there to save $30 billion a year in electric bills. The electricity from more than 100 nukes and inefficient coal-fired power plants would not be needed. Other than using your car less, these lamps represent the easiest, most cost-efficient and painless way for you to really make a difference. —JB

Dave Scruby, Alpine Bank, with compact fluorescent bulb. Christian Scheder, Robert Sardinsky, and Chris Myers of Rising Sun Enterprises juggle replaced incandescents.

In many ways, Rising Sun Enterprises is a typical business of the sort that media hacks dub New Age. Its CEO and crew are young, bushytailed and noticeably idealistic. They live and work hard, far from the maddening crowds (unless you count those on the ski runs of nearby Aspen), just down the street from Rocky Mountain Institute (see p. 57) whose energy statistics they use and whose policies they help implement. Their products are not yet considered mainstream — most will not be

found at your neighborhood True Value Hardware. Yet. Yet most of their products, like the lamps shown here, a line of DC lamps for those living off-grid, plus other energy and water-saving items, are manufactured by big-name outfits like Panasonic and Phillips. The business is expanding quickly; indeed, they have a tiger by the tail. What founder Robert "Sardo" Sardinski, 32, started eight years ago as a modest source for environmentally respectable goods has become the nation's leading expert source for the lamps and consulting services pertaining thereto. It's more of a New Era business, I think, a model of what can be done by folks in tune not only to market opportunity but to social and environmental imperatives as well. May they live to be a hundred. —JB

✱WEA — Available from Whole Earth Access, see p. 2.

The Natural House Book

No paranoia-inducing diatribes from this author, and no smug admonitions to strive for an impossible level of environmental correctness in your home. Instead, we get an encouraging look at the basic principles of design and materials choice that will help you make a naturally joyful and healthy home. The author makes it clear that the use of "natural materials" does not necessarily mean better health or reduced environmental impact — a point often missed. This book glows with wonderful examples (from all over the world) of things done imaginatively and well. There's nothing to make you feel guilty or remiss, you are enticed into wanting to make your house better, and to do it in a way that fits your style. It isn't all structure; for instance, the physiological effects of light, color, and space are enthusiastically stirred into the brew. There's even a discussion of Feng-Shui — geomancy. Lots of good ideas. Lots of inspiration. Lots of reasons to buy the book — it's the best I've seen on the subject. —JB

**The Natural House
Book**, David Pearson
1989; 287 pp.; **$17.95**
($20.95 postpaid) from:
Simon & Schuster, Inc.
200 Old Tappan Road
Old Tappan, NJ 07675
(201) 767-5937 ✱WEA

●

Aroma as part of design

It is an interesting fact that when interior design or architectural magazines describe a home, colour, form, space, and texture are all frequently mentioned — but smell hardly ever. It is as if this was of no consequence, or that all interiors are expected to be odourless and sterile. But unfortunately many modern interiors have a decidedly unpleasant smell, which gives warning of an accumulation of pollutants, stale air, condensation, and cooking odours. The design of a home, in order to be complete, must embrace aroma, too.

Daylight floods this airy Swedish living room. The light, reflective surfaces and bright splashes of colour enliven the atmosphere and lift the spirits. Bright sunlight and daylight produce an atmosphere of optimism, which is especially important in climates where there are too many grey cloudy days and depressingly long, dark winters.

Healthy House Catalog

This is where to find out where to get the materials, design services, hardware, and all the other knowledge and stuffs you need to build or rebuild your home in a way that will render it less threatening to your health. Like all good catalogs, this one helps you gain the knowledge necessary for wise choices; the first section is titled Understanding Indoor Pollution. Alas, it would have been impossible for the editors to check each of the 500 entries for veracity and usefulness or even environmental merit (or lack thereof). That's probably the government's job, and probably it won't get done. So it's up to us. This catalog will help you get real about what's available and what you can afford. A useful service, well executed. —JB

Healthy House Catalog; 1990; 208 pp.; **$19.95**
($22.95 postpaid) from: Environmental Health
Watch and the Housing Resource Center
4115 Bridge Avenue, Cleveland, OH 44113
(800) 222-9348

Formaldehyde monitoring made simple

★ ★ **PF-1 passive detector excellent
for screening homes, offices, modular
buildings, hospitals, schools, etc.**

- Gives time-weighted average over 7-day sampling period—avoids misleading spot measurements.
- Able to detect levels as low as 0.01 ppm over full sampling period.
- Field proven—more than 300,000 measurements made to date.
- Easily installed by user—no need for you to get involved.
- Low cost—kit includes two monitors, analysis and report.

AIR ⌂ QUALITY RESEARCH

901 Grayson Street, Berkeley, CA 94710
(415) 644-2097

But Not a Drop to Drink!

I first picked up this book to get information regarding my own home water situation. I soon discovered this book is much more than a good information guide for personal water systems. Coffel's comprehensive and painstaking research offers a broad view of the water situation for the whole country. He focuses instead on the job of cleaning up the mess, beginning with one's own water.

Where does your water come from? What is the watershed that supplies it? What uses has the watershed been put to? These questions, and more, will guide your search in identifying the contaminants in your water, and what you can do about removing them.

The author completes his survey of water cleanup with a look at bottled waters, the pros and cons of various water-purification systems, as well as ideas and examples of successful community-wide cleanups and alternative ways of treating city waste water. Particularly intriguing is the description of "circular" water management which allows sewage to break down naturally and be filtered by the soil as water drains back down into the aquifer.

Coffel has four Resource appendices to assist you in locating water information, toxic waste sites, and quality water in your area. —Richard Ditzler

●

People buy bottled water primarily to protect their health. Unfortunately, many of the same contaminants found in drinking water also show up in

Bau-Biologie™

In a typically German manner, the Bau-Biologie folks analyze the problems of our built environment, and then present a system as a guide for doing better. To some, their suggestions will seem extreme; for instance, are you really going to worry about radioactivity in wallboard? Should you? What can be done about it? What do you use instead? How should you think about such things? Bau-Biologie (rough translation: building biology, but it's more comprehensive than that) has been active in Germany for more than 20 years. Now they're here, with seminars and correspondence courses. They're a tad too New Age for some tastes; and just what's needed for others' — that seems to be their reputation in Europe, too. If you're unfamiliar with healthy building concepts, you may find their courses save you a lot of snooping and sifting. —JB

Bau-Biologie; Information &
book list **free**

Bau-Biologie Correspondence Course; **$750** (course
length 1 year approx.)
Course consists of 22 course
packs (equivalent to 800 pages)

Both from:
International Institute for Bau-Biologie and
Ecolgy, P.O. Box 387, Clearwater, FL 34615
(813) 461-4371

●

Some of the Topics Covered in This Course:

* Environmental situation

* Bau-Biologie and building culture

* Ecology and building site

* Location and geo-biology

* Climate in residential areas

* Biologically-sound building materials

* Construction and building methods

* Heating and thermal insulation

* Furnishing and interior design

* Architectural acoustics and noise control

* Light and illumination/electro-climate

* Color and coloring products

* Mental/emotional and physiological aspects of living

* Rural habitation and town building

* House inspection

bottled water. Heavy metals, solvents, trihalomethanes, pesticides, and even traces of radioactive materials have been found. So switching to bottled water can offer little more than a change of poisons, if caution isn't used.

●

The plastic containers that hold many bulk products can give water a "plastic taste." Those made of polyethylene, the cloudy plastic used in gallon milk jugs, are worst, because the material degrades more quickly than other plastics. As it breaks down, some of its components are absorbed into the water.

But Not a Drop to Drink
(The Lifesaving Guide to
Good Water), Steve Coffel
1989; 323 pp.; **$19.95**
($21.95 postpaid) from:
Macmillan and Co.
Front and Brown Streets
Riverside, NJ 08075
(800) 257-8247 ✱WEA

The Healthy Home

Like a cop giving you a few words about your driving habits, this book is nothing but the facts. They're what you need to know to have a safe and healthy home. This unsmiling book covers just about everything — you can use it to give your place a comprehensive health audit (which my humble home flunks in a discouraging number of departments). What to do about the problems is discussed too, mostly from a straight, conventional viewpoint. Think of it as a fad-free home health & safety review book. —JB

The Healthy Home
Linda Mason Hunter; 1989
320 pp.; **$21.95** (Postpaid
price depends on destination)
Rodale Press
33 East Minor St.
Emmaus, PA 18098
(215) 967-5171 ✳WEA

A ceiling light is not a good choice to illuminate a countertop, because it throws a shadow over the work area. A better choice is a light under the cabinet.

●

Purify the air. Chemical filter systems can be used to reduce contaminants in the air. However, these may be costly and they require constant monitoring. A cheaper alternative is to buy some houseplants. Research by the U.S. National Aeronautics and Space Administration (NASA) has shown that the leaves of philodendrons, spider plants, and other common houseplants absorb formaldehyde. Dr. Bill Wolverton, senior research scientist at NASA, told *Practical Homeowner* magazine (September 1987) that about 15 to 20 such plants should completely remove the formaldehyde from an 1,800-square-foot house.

●

Unexpected sounds: . . . In the quiet of night, the creak of a door can be enormously disturbing. Even the barely audible click of an electric blanket thermostat was once likened by Consumers Union to the "stomping of a robin on a lawn."

Livos Non-Toxic Home Products • Auro Natural Plant Chemistry

These rival vendors probably will wince when they see themselves bunched together here — it has been my experience that their salespeople tend to engage in a bit of mutual sniping. Fact is that they both make paints, pigments, wood preservatives, adhesives, waxes and even kid's art supplies. Both claim to use only natural, non-toxic materials such as lemon oil and natural earth pigments. (Note that this does not mean you can drink the stuff.) Auro tells you exactly what is in each product, and how to dispose of any leftovers — Livos doesn't. Colors tend to the earthy. Smells tend to be nice. Assiduous use of these products eliminates many of the sources of chemical sensitivity in a home. Paint performance seems to be acceptable, though under severe conditions (as

on a boat, for instance) not always up to the standards of heavy-duty products redolent with foul substances. For most uses at home or office, they do very well — I've heard few complaints, and would not hesitate to use either brand. —JB

Livos Non-Toxic Home Products
Catalog **free** from: 1365 Rufina Circle, Suite WE
Santa Fe, NM 87501; (505) 438-3448

Auro Natural Plant Chemistry
Catalog **free** from: Sinan Company, P. O. Box 857, Davis, CA 95617-0857; (916) 753-3104

See also . . .
Water pp. 22-23, Staying Healthy pp. 64-65, and Pollution p. 86. For a performance test of home water filters, see Consumer Reports, Jan. 1990, pp. 27-43.

For Our Kids' Sake

Yeah, well, it's one thing to eat bad stuff yourself — after all most of us have probably been doing that for many years, much of the time unknowingly. But our kids . . . and now we know! This book, as I suppose it must, makes clear the unhappy problems. At least there isn't any preaching and blame-laying. More usefully, it goes way beyond the usual media-hyped scary stories, and authoritatively spells out just what pesticides are used on what edibles, what the dangers are, and what you can or can't do about it.(Will it wash off, for instance.) And then comes the Big Message: WE can and WE must DO something about all this. And the rest of the book is how to lobby, cajole, support, and otherwise take action to make things better for the kids, of course, and ourselves. Strong stuff, unusually well detailed and well presented. —JB [Suggested by Keith Jordan]

For Our Kids' Sake
(How to Protect Your
Child Against Pesticides
in Food), Ann Witte
Garland; 1989; 87 pp.
$6.95 ($9.95 postpaid)
from: Sierra Club Books
730 Polk Street
San Francisco, CA 94109
(415) 923-5500 ✳WEA

Differences in Relative Exposure
(Children vs. Women)

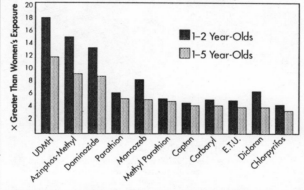

7 Ways to protect your family against pesticides in food

1. Wash all produce.

2. Peel produce when appropriate.

3. Buy certified organically-grown fruits and vegetables.

4. Buy domestically-grown produce in season.

5. Beware of perfect-looking produce.

6. Grow your own produce if possible.

7. Write to your elected officials.

Thermal Pest Eradication (TPE)

You are invited to a house roast. No, not arson for insurance; heating for pest eradication. Seems that nearly all destructive and otherwise obnoxious insects that infest buildings can be killed by simply raising the interior temperature of the building's structural components to 120° F. That's done by "bagging" the building with lightweight tarps, then fan-blowing the bag full of hot air from a portable propane furnace (after people and heat-sensitive equipment such as computers have left, of course). About 8 hours later — it takes that long for the heat to penetrate structural members — you can move back in. You'll be lonely: the termites, cockroaches, lygus bugs, powderpost beetles, etc. will be gone. Even better, there is no danger from pesticide residue, no smell, and reinfestation rates are much lower than with other pest control methods. Does it work? Yes, it does, according to many scientifically controlled tests and many houses so treated. Cost is little, if any, greater than chemical treatment.

I'll guess that this method, developed by Walter Ebeling and the late Charles F. Forbes, will soon take the place of chemical fumigation. It's a good example of modern technology (and good thinking) being used to solve a very old problem. Franchises and training are available, in case you're looking for work.

Late news: it seems that house-roasting also has the effect of baking volatile organic compounds out of the materials used in new building construction. Where this has been done, occupant complaints of illness caused by reactions to construction materials have fallen dramatically — often to zero. —JB

Thermal Pest Eradication
Information **free** from:
Isothermics, P.O. Box 18703
Anaheim, CA 92817-8703; (714) 778-1396

Blowing a house full of hot air kills virtually all obnoxious and destructive insects, including termites and cockroaches. This is the test rig where the TPE technique was proven and made practical.

From IPM Practitioner, see p. 47

The Blizzard System

Freezing the little buggers to death is another way of de-insecting your place without using noxious chemicals. The enemy is zapped with liquid nitrogen injected through a little nozzle inserted into the affected area. (If water pipes are in there, they get drained first.) Under appropriate conditions, it works well. So far, the proprietary technique is available only in the San Diego area, but national availability is planned. Might work for infestations of obnoxious relatives, too. —JB

For more information contact Tallon Termite and Pest Control (213) 422-1131.

Natural Health, Natural Medicine

In a field choking on books catering to dietary fads or else full of sectarian sermonizing, here is one about how to stay healthy that you can use and learn from. It's a doctor's bag full of calmly presented information and remedies selected from a broad spectrum of medical treatments, including herbal, oriental and western. Weil is an M.D. who trained first as a botanist (common in the 19th century; unheard of today) and he uses herbal remedies in his own practice along with synthetic drugs. He also uses his understanding of diet and nutrition in presenting strategies in individual chapters on how not to get heart attacks, strokes and cancer. And there is news here — Weil's discussion of fats has gotten me off of safflower oil after 30 years of believing I was doing the right thing by eating it.

Andrew Weil has a couple of earlier books (from 1983) worth knowing about too. **Health and Healing** *(Houghton Mifflin Co.) considers western allopathic methods in a broader context of alternatives like homeopathy and Chinese medicine.* **Chocolate to Morphine** *is a classic book on mind-active drugs. Peter Warshall called it "good enough to replace all drug-use books previously reviewed in the* **Whole Earth Catalogs***" in his review, and that is still true. If you are about to be kicking young'uns out of the nest, this is an important book for parent and teenager to read first. Unfortunately it has gone out of print, a victim perhaps of ten years of official "Just say no" drug hysteria. It deserves to be reissued.*

— Richard Nilsen

Natural Health, Natural Medicine (A Comprehensive Manual For Wellness and Self-Care) Andrew Weil, M.D. 1990; 356 pp.; **$19.95** postpaid from: Houghton Mifflin Co. Wayside Road Burlington, MA 01803 (800) 225-3362 ✳WEA

●

Heart attacks, strokes, and cancer are not simply the results of bad heredity and bad luck. They are often diseases of lifestyle, and lifestyle can be changed.

●

I do not place much stock in the advice of professional nutritionists and dietitians. . . .

Nutritional science gave us the Basic Four food groups, the concept responsible for much of our unhealthy obsession with protein (more on this in a moment). Registered dietitians are frequently witting or unwitting tools of the food industry. . . . If you are tempted to follow their recommendations, remember that dietitians are the people responsible for the food served in hospitals.

●

Never draw water from the hot water tap for drinking or cooking even if you are going to use it to make tea or boil pasta. Hot water leaches out impurities much more readily than cold and, in addition, it has sat for long periods in a heater tank, which is probably not very clean inside. Water from the hot tap is unfit for human consumption, no matter what your pipes are made of.

●

Remember that meats and other proteins become carcinogenic when they are seared black over open flames or on a charcoal grill. Do not eat charred flesh or, if you do, cut away the charred outer layers. Never breathe the smoke of burning meat or burning fat.

●

Tea tree oil, a recent Australian import, extracted from the leaves of *Melaleuca alternifolia*, a native tree of New South Wales, is the best treatment I know for fungal infections of the skin (athlete's foot, ringworm, jock itch). It will also clear up fungal infections of the toenails or fingernails, a condition notoriously resistant to treatment, even by strong systemic antibiotics. You just paint the oil on affected areas two or three times a day.

●

Allergy is misplaced immunity. Allergens like dog hair, pollen, dust, and mold cannot really hurt us, so the immune system need not react to them. Allergy is a learned response of the immune system, and anything learned can be unlearned. The goal of treatment should be to convince the immune system that it can coexist peacefully with these substances. Conventional medicine does not achieve this goal. Instead it suppresses allergic responses, perpetuating them and creating much toxicity.

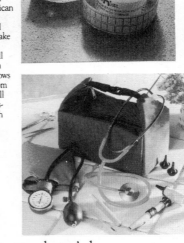

Radon detector

Radon is an odorless, colorless, and potentially harmful gas that seeps from the ground into American homes (in some states, 70% of homes contain levels considered unsafe). Some radon detectors take a "snapshot" measurement, but because radon levels rise and fall seasonally, experts recommend a long-term reading. This one allows you to choose exposure time from two weeks to one full year. You'll get a dependable reading, professional evaluation, and with each report over four pci/l an EPA action recommendation will be included.

#1087 Track Etch Radon Detector $35.00

Your very own doctor's bag

The *Medical Black Bag* is filled with medical instruments physicians use, specially selected to meet your family's home health needs. It's organized to make it easy to use and contains an earscope, hospital-quality stethoscope, blood pressure cuff, digital thermometer, surgical scissors, and surgical forceps for splinter removal. Sturdy, durable, nylon bag.

#2017 Medical Black Bag $99.00

SelfCare Catalog & Journal

A classy catalog of mostly-not-too-faddish self-care health products and publications. It's not just products. Each edition includes educational columns by respected authors such as Debra Lynn Dadd, Jeff Cox, and Whole Earth's longtime medical consultant, Tom Ferguson, M.D. Useful advice, nice stuff, good service. —JB

SelfCare Catalog & Journal; free from: SelfCare Catalog, P.O. Box 130 Mandeville, LA 70470-0130; (800) 345-3371

LAB SAFETY **OILUP™ Sorbent**
Large Spill Assortment
Pallet includes: 12, 8" x 10' booms; 10, 18" x 25" Spill Control Pillows™; and 1, 36" x 150' x 3/8" thick sorbent roll—enough to keep a large oil spill or hazardous materials incident under control. Sorbent booms, pillows and rolls can be wrung out and reused at the scene. Total weight: 105 lbs.

The Wary Canary

Miners carried canaries as early warning of foul air — the hypersensitive birds fell off the perch way before a human could detect danger. This newsletter serves the "canaries" of today —those unfortunate people who suffer Multiple Chemical Sensitivities (MCS). Despite some claims that MCS is yet another fad, the numbers are increasing. (Have you, by any chance, noticed that you "seem to be getting more allergic to things"? I certainly have.) Their need for surroundings fashioned from benign materials is one of the forces goading the rest of society towards new standards. From the same folks that publish **Environ** *(p.112). —JB*

The Wary Canary Suzanne & Ed Randegger, Editors; **$20**/year (4 to 6 issues) from: Wary Canary Press P.O. Box 2204 Fort Collins, CO 80522 (303) 224-0083

●

In his article in *Workers with MCS*, Yale professor Robert K. McLellan, MD, pointed out that court proceedings and disability hearings force people to become victims. And that gives them a stake in not getting back into the mainstream. The debilitating effects of legal wrangling should be considered when you decide to "fight for your rights."

. . . occupational health studies have found no link between food allergies and environmental poisoning even though the symptoms may sometimes be similar.

But some victims seem to enjoy punishing themselves by setting up stringent diets focusing on foods they hate. Most if not all, people have problems some times with some foods. But a relaxed approach to a truly diversified diet will minimize the problems without worrying whether or not it's Tuesday.

. . . wary canaries are not victims, they just value the health of themselves and others.

Lab Safety Supply

This company sells industrial safety equipment: masks, gloves, goggles, protective coveralls, detectors — warning and protection equipage for just about any imaginable threatening circumstance. Unlike much of the stuff in your local hardware store, these products must meet the strictest UL, OSHA and insurance company standards. Not cheap, but you know what you're getting. (Note: This is a professional outfit, so don't bother them unless you're serious.) —JB

Lab Safety Supply, General Catalog (Safety Equipment & Supplies for Today's Technologies); **free** from: Lab Safety Supply, Inc., P.O. Box 1368, Janesville, WI 53547-1368; (800) 356-0783

KleenGuard®

Total Body and All-Purpose Coveralls
Light and Cool Even During Extended Wear
Fabric breathes to keep wearer cool and comfortable, yet repels liquids and keeps particulates out. All styles feature zipper closure, triple-stitching, and elastic back and wrists. **Total body coverall** comes with attached hood and boot covers, and an elastic face closure. Please specify size: (M) (L) (XL) (XXL). **All-purpose coverall** comes with shirt collar. Also available in gray. Please specify size: (S) (M) (L) (XL).

No.	Description	Each	Dozen	Case of 24
M-8626	Total Body Coverall, White	6.75	72.90	131.25
M-8627	All-Purpose Coverall, White	4.85	52.40	94.30
M-10266	All-Purpose Coverall, Gray	5.00	54.00	97.20

Nontoxic, Natural & Earthwise • The Earthwise Consumer

Debra Lynn Dadd's **Nontoxic, Natural & Earthwise** adds the best one yet to her impressive output of how-to-live-without-toxics books. She's outdone herself this time, not only giving us a quick education in what's undesirable in conventional goods, but the remedies as well: 400 recipies for home-made nontoxic household products, plus 600 sources for store-bought versions. Her choices and recommendations, and the reasons for them, are all explained in terms even a grade-school kid can understand. Fortunately, she is not tempted by the opportunity for polemics and sinner-smiting, though I'd appreciate a bit more criticism of eco-faddish nostrums (hard to do unless you have a well-equipped laboratory). Unlike most Earth-Saving books, the advice in this one is of direct, immediate, personal benefit. She promises regular updates. My guess is that much of the updating will take place in **The Earthwise Consumer**, a skinny newsletter she already publishes, and her column that appears regularly in other publications such as the **Self Care Catalog** on this spread. Another good example of one dedicated person making a difference. —JB

Nontoxic, Natural & Earthwise, Debra Lynn Dadd; 1990; 320 pp., **$10.95** ($12.95 postpaid) **✱WEA**

The Earthwise Consumer Debra Lynn Dadd; **$20**/year (8 issues)

Both from:
The Earthwise Consumer
P. O. Box 279
Forest Knolls, CA 94933

•

One of my most frequently asked questions is "What about Amway, NeoLife, and Shaklee products?" You may notice they are conspicuously absent from these pages. There are two reasons. For many years I have been trying to get ingredients lists for the cleaning products made by these companies and I finally got a list for one of the companies. Without going into detail, the general ingredients were synthetic detergents, optical brighteners, some animal ingredients, fragrances, and artificial colors. Also, there is some question as to whether these companies test on animals. Some animal rights organizations report yes, others say no. Since there are plenty of other cleaning products available that have more natural ingredients and clearly don't test on animals, I have listed those instead.

—Nontoxic, Natural & Earthwise

See Also . . .
More healthy stuff, pages 108-109.

Ecologue

It's spelled differently than the one you're holding, but the spirit is similar, and so is much of the menu. (When editor Bruce Anderson and I discovered we'd chosen the same name for our books, we gulped once or twice, shook hands telephonically, and informed our respective publishers that we were colleagues and did not care to fight about it. To their credit, and our immense relief, they agreed.)

This encouragingly useful book concentrates on environmentally respectable products — which ones are OK, and why, and how you can decide for yourself. The selection and spotlight is different from that of conceptually similar rivals, including us (we're more network and principle-oriented) and Debra Lynn Dadd's book (more into health) on this page — there's a lot out there to cover. Unlike save-the-world books, thing catalogs, like this one, offer moves you can make right now without waiting for the rest of society to change first. Changing your buying habits can be done one product at a time. Every little bit counts. —JB

Ecologue
(The Environmental Catalogue and Consumer's Guide for a Safe Earth)
Bruce Anderson, Editor 1990; 256 pp.; **$18.95**
Prentice Hall Press
Check your local bookstore **✱WEA**

Seventh Generation

The "Squash a Can for Gaia" books infesting this Earth Day Anniversary year make good suggestions, but rarely get into specifics. Where do you get toilet paper made from recycled material? And no local store has even heard of organic babyfood, much less solar battery chargers and natural-ingredient household cleaners (that work — not all do), much less eco-chic T-shirts, interesting toys, and, well, the stuff that Seventh Generation stocks in their handsome, tempting catalog. It's trustable stuff, too — no crystals or little magnets that you tie to your car's gas line for "26% more ecologically wonderful gas mileage." The Seventh Generation folks must be doing a good job; business has been growing at a rate Wall Street types have been saying is impossible for this sort of enterprise. By the way, Easterners, they stock many of Rising Sun's (p. 60) bulbs, too. And they do wholesale; schools take note. —JB

Seventh Generation
Catalog **free** from: 10 Farrell Street
South Burlington, VT 05403; (800) 456-1177

The Body Shop

Anita Roddick has rightly won fame and fortune with a store selling body-care products made as much as possible of natural materials, and sold for health rather than beauty reasons. (If you're healthy, beauty will come naturally.) The Body Shop eschews fancy sexist advertisements, aerosols and other gross packaging, and animal testing. Ingredients are sourced from many third-world countries, with due respect maintained for the welfare of local people and their surroundings. "Trade, not Aid" is the motto. Satisfied customers abound. So do imitators, but they just don't seem to have Ms. Roddick's touch: there are now more than 400 Body Shops around the world. And now mail-order, too. —JB

The Body Shop; Catalog **$2** from:
The Body Shop, Inc., 45 Horsehill Road
Hanover Technical Center, Cedar Knolls, NJ
07927-2003; (800) 541-2535

Consumer Reports

The consumer's first line of defense is the crew at Consumers Union. Not only do they publish the authoritative (no advertising) **Consumer Reports** magazine, they sell a large assortment of books, some of which concern health matters. Quacks are revealed, fads deflated, and the proven is celebrated. They of course take some flak from stung frauds and their adherents, as well as folks taking one of the less accepted alternative paths. That doesn't mar CU's usefulness one bit. There's a Canadian version, too. —JB

Consumer Reports
$20/year (11 issues, plus Buying Guide) from:
Consumer Reports
Subscription Department
Box 53009
Boulder, CO 80321-3009

Canadian Consumer
$28/year (12 issues) from:
Candian Consumer
Box 9300
Ottawa, Ontario
K1G 3T9 Canada

To simulate real-life stroller use, we loaded test models with a 20-kilogram sandbag and took them for a lengthy "carousel" ride over obstacles such as a gravel patch and a curb-like ramp.
—Canadian Consumer

A BICYCLES

A HUMAN *on a bicycle moves more efficiently than any other vehicle or animal, including birds and fish! Bikes are not entirely pollution-free, though. Nothing is. A bicycle consumes resources and energy in its manufacture and maintenance. Its "motor," you, consumes calories and discharges a catalog of toxic waste. Bicycles also need a reasonably well-manicured riding surface, though mountain bikes reduce the necessity for expensive, energy-intensive paving.*

The bicycle's remarkable efficiency and affordability make it the best personal transportation choice where conditions permit its reasonable use. Ironically, even though our country ranks fourth worldwide in bicycles per capita, we use them mostly for recreation. On the other hand, we have the bikes. Now all we have to do is use them instead of our cars. Perhaps the rapidly growing auto-caused pollution problems will force us to. Meantime, surprisingly satisfying urban machines — the so called "city bike" clones of mountain bikes — can be had for less than $300. Their friendly riding characteristics, sturdiness and low maintenance make bicycle commuting easier than ever before. Give it a try. —JB

Bicycling Science

For 16 years this book has been the best place to learn the engineering principles of bicycle design. The information is solidly backed by extensive lab and field testing, yet is presented in a jargon-free, easily understood manner. All aspects of the bicycle are covered, including the rider and bike/ rider relationship (ergonomics). If you're considering the construction of a bike or HPV, or are just curious about your mount, this is lesson one. —JB

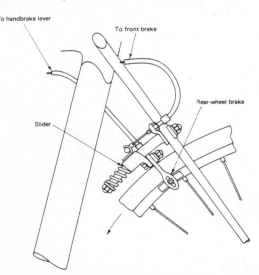

To handbrake lever
To front brake
Rear-wheel brake
Slider

Calderazzo feedback brake system. When hand-brake is operated, rear brake is carried forward on slider against spring, actuating front brake simultaneously. If bicycle starts to pitch forward, rear wheel is no longer rotated by road surface, and front brake is released.

Bicycling Science (2nd Edition)
Frank Rowland Whitt & David
Gordon Wilson; 1982; 364 pp.
$12.50 ($15 postpaid) from:
The MIT Press, Attn: Ordering
Dept., 55 Hayward Street,
Cambridge, MA 02142
(800) 356-0343 ✴WEA

Mountain ATB

Alex Moulton Bicycles

Probably the state of the art in bicycles, the AM utilizes a supple suspension to enhance roadholding and ride comfort. Small wheels permit a low center of gravity for stable load carrying, and combine with a clever take-apart feature to give compact storage. Models available for touring, racing, commuting, and off-road. You have to ride one to believe how good it is. —JB

Alex Moulton Bicycles, $1500-$4200;
Information **free** from:
Angle Lake Cyclery, 20840 Pacific Highway,
South Seattle, WA 98198-5999; (206) 878-7457

Advantages of AMMTB over traditional design.

20 inch wheels:
A. Stronger– shorter spokes, etc.
B. Less weight-net– also less rotating weight.
C. Compactness/stowability.
D. "Nimble" handling. Less effort required in actual Mountain Bike use–upper body wise–when negotiating obstacles–26" wheels much heavier, taxing your endurance.

Suspension (patented)
A. Smooth ride–NOTE: A dampening, simple suspension–no hydraulics. Not to completely isolate the individual.
B. Traction. Wheels on the ground much more of the time.
C. Wrist fatigue drastically reduced.
D. Person more relaxed because of more control.
E. Faster. For the enthusiast you can just plain go faster because the bike is not being thrown off course.

F. Suspension is adjustable.
G. Allows radial spoking of front wheel and X-3 rear without any durability side effects.
H. Less wheel maintainance. Suspension absorbs shock rather than wheels.
I. More "in saddle" time off road reducing leg fatigue.

"Space" type frame design–patented
A. The most rigid frame on the market–virtually no BB flex.
B. Combined with 20" wheels–the lowest center of gravity available.
C. Lack of "Lethal" top tube (also a unisex design).
D. Patented separating feature– simple–w/no changes in frame strength over rigid design. Fits in car trunk. A traveling "Go With" mountain bike.
E. Pump stowage inside seat post tube.

Incredible balance.
No weight penalty vs. competing non-suspended bikes.

Burley Lite Bicycle Trailers

One reason I don't use a bike trailer much is because of the time I loaded one with builder's supplies to the recommended capacity of the trailer and was just humpin' along when I had to make a hot stop halfway around a curve. No, my problems didn't arise from inadequate brakes; the resultant pirouette was initiated by the trailer hitch transferring the trailer momentum to my seatpost, high, not aligned with my direction. But this trailer hitches low, to the axle, and actually adds weight to that axle in a stop so you don't tend to do over-the-bars so easily. I've only ridden with one a short distance, but even the short ride showed clearly that this arrangement works better than the usual. Yes, you can turn the bike either way despite the asymmetry. Workmanship seems good. —JB

Institute for Transportation and Development Policy

*These folks are best known for their **Bikes Not Bombs** programs all over the world. They help local people and sometimes governments develop bicycle programs and the support necessary to keep them going. It's tough work, but this sort of thing is essential if developing countries are not to fall even further into the hopeless trap of spending huge amounts of scarce capital to make fancy auto roads for a population too poor to drive. —JB*

Institute for Transportation and Development Policy, $30/year regular member from: ITDP, P.O. Box 56538, Washington, DC 20011

Sid Shutt's Hydro-ped in operation.

Human Power

People-as-engines is the underlying theme of this lively journal put out by the International Human Powered Vehicle Association. There is an air of pioneering about it all; the people involved are trying everything imaginable in the search for more efficient transportation. Controversy abounds. Innovation abounds. Hot-blooded spirit abounds. Just what you'd expect on a frontier. —JB

Human Power David Gordon Wilson, Editor; **$20**/year (4 issues) includes membership in IHPVA and 8 issues of HPV News; All from: The International Human Powered Vehicle Association, P. O. Box 51225, Indianapolis, IN 46251-0255 (317) 876-9478

●

It seems only natural when commercial sponsors ask approaching HPV builders to lay their cards on the table. It is thus only fair when such donors claim their money's worth of the deal in return. Yet, HPV activists often risk falling into the hands of unscrupulous marketing strategists who all too often misuse clearly ecological pioneering deeds to promote polluting consumerism.

Has any recipient ever managed to ask a commercial donor to lay open his forthcoming publicity plans in return? —*HPV News*

Burley Lite Tourist Bicycle Trailer
$235 (approx.)

Burley Lite Bicycle Trailer
(child carrying model) **$250** (approx.)

Burley d'Lite Bicycle Trailer
(foldable child carrier) **$335** (approx.)

(All models are available with extra options)
Check your local bike shop

Nearest dealer information **free** from:
Burley Design Cooperative, 4080 Stewart
Road, Eugene, OR 97402; (503) 687-1644

Allsop's flexible seat suspension. Besides absorbing shock, suspensions keep the wheels on the ground in rough terrain.

Cycling Science

This welcome new quarterly presents the results of rigorous, scientific analysis and practical application of the various aspects of cycle technology. It's written by the experimenters themselves, many of them famous. Their firsthand reporting gives a sweaty, greasy-hands feel to the whole exercise. No obtuse science jargon, either; the idea is to disseminate good information to all who can make use of it, manufacturers and amateurs alike. This is a good place to get a feel for (and perhaps add to) what's coming next. —JB

Cycling Science (New Developments for the Technical Enthusiast) Chester Kyle, Editor **$19.97**/year (4 issues) from: Cycling Science P. O. Box 1510 Mount Shasta, CA 96067 (916) 938-4411

The Bicycle: Vehicle for a Small Planet

Like all Worldwatch papers (p. 8), this one is a rich, quick education on the subject. You get a little history, and a survey of the bicycle's potential for reducing pollution, congestion, and a host of other autotrauma. Tables and charts nicely show the convincing numbers. All annotated to add weight to your presentation at the city council meeting at which you had better arrive on a bike. —JB

The Bicycle: Vehicle for a Small Planet, Worldwatch Paper 90 September 1987; 62 pp.; Marcia D. Lowe; **$4** postpaid from: Worldwatch Institute 1776 Massachusetts Avenue, NW Washington, DC 20036

For longer trips, linking bicycling with mass transit through improved access to transit stations holds great potential for reducing energy use and air pollutants. According to a 1980 Chicago Area Transportation analysis, bike-and-ride is the most cost-effective way to reduce hydrocarbon and carbon monoxide emissions. Giving cyclists secure parking at transit stations would reduce hydrocarbon emissions at a public cost of $311 per ton, for example, compared with $96,415 a ton for an express park-and-ride service, $214,959 for a feeder bus service and $3,937 per ton for a commuter rail-carpool matching service. Carbon monoxide reductions would come at similar savings.

The Third Hand

Absolutely the friendliest, most knowledgeable, best-stocked source of bicycle tools anywhere. Their succulent catalog is a real challenge to your ability to resist sending for one of each item. Sigh . . . —JB

The Third Hand (Bike Tools, Books & Loose Screws); Catalog **free** from: The Third Hand, P. O. Box 212, Mt. Shasta, CA 96067 (916) 926-2600

PARK THIRD HAND

A spring-steel tool for squeezing brake pads against the rim while tightening brake cables. Fits side & centerpull brakes. Plastic-coated handle.

Item #PA-BT1 $4.00

Worksman Cycles

Getcha Good Humor vending tricycle-with-cold-box here, folks! You can also find a wide range of other heavy-duty commercial trikes and bikes — most of the ones you see on the job come from here. This company has made 'em like they used to since 1898. —JB

Worksman Cycles Catalog **$2** from: Worksman Trading Corporation, 94-15 100th Street, Ozone Park, NY 11416; (718) 322-2000

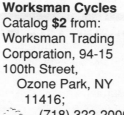

Bikecentennial

Born fourteen years ago, the non-profit recreational cycling organization Bikecentennial has become a sponsor of organized bike tours, a lobbying force, and the best source of bicycle touring maps. It's the maps that are special; they're drawn with the biker in mind as they indicate the best routes through both country and urban tanglè. —JB

Bikecentennial The Bicycle Travel Association, **$22**/year membership, Catalog **$1** (free with membership) both from: Bikecentennial, P.O. Box 8308, Missoula, MT 59807 (800) 835-2246

Rails-To-Trails Conservancy

What's the best use for abandoned railroad rights of way? As a cyclist, I say make 'em into bike trails. (Locomotives and bicycle riders have about the same idea of what constitutes a reasonable gradient.) The long thin corridors are rarely useful for parkland, highways, or real estate, but the red tape involved in using them for anything else except trains tends to paralyze innovators. The Rails-To-Trails Conservancy knows how to deal with the deadly details that must be handled before bikers and hikers can puff where the engines once did. RTC publishes success stories, a legal manual (essential!) and the comprehensive **Converting Rails-To-Trails: A Citizen's Manual**. If you have an old rail line near you, better get to work on it now — I've learned the hard way that when they take out the bridges and tunnels, trail conversions are much less likely to happen. —JB

Rails-To-Trails Conservancy, **$18**/year membership (includes subscription to RTC's quarterly newsletter)

RTC Legal Manual **$42.50** (members $32.50) postpaid

Converting Rails to Trails: A Citizen's Manual **$17** (members $12) postpaid

All from: Rails-To-Trails Conservancy, 1400 Sixteenth Street, NW, Suite 300, Washington, DC 20036 (202) 797-5400

Dahon

Why buy a little bitty bike that makes you look like a circus bear act? Theft resistance — bring it inside with you. Easy storage — keep it in the trunk of your car or in the closet. Take it with you on the bus or train. Eliminate the shuttle problem — stow it in your river raft, then ride it back to get the car. You'd be surprised how much use a folder gets, once you have it. The Dahon isn't the best or the lightest folding bike ever to hit the market, but it certainly is the best distributed. This has vanquished the opposition; Dahon is the only commonly available folding bike. It does the job pretty well, exhibiting acceptable road behavior, and with practice, easy folding-unfolding. It will fit into a suitcase-size (but lumpy) carry sack that makes it OK in places where bikes are taboo. Unless you are uncommonly proportioned, it will fit you; the seat-handlebar-pedal relationship is about the same as a conventional fullsize bike. Note that many Dahons are sold by shops that do not normally do bicycle business. If you buy from one of those (or from their catalogs), you may have to tune or even reassemble it after purchase. Bottom line: Useful. —JB

Dahon Bicycles, **$180-$380**; Information free from: Dahon California, Inc., 2949 Whipple Road, Union City, CA 94587; (415) 471-6330

By J. Baldwin

A FEW YEARS BACK, I attended a public debate between the founder of a renowned world-saving organization and the CEO of a coal mining company. The Bad Guy won the toss, took the mike and said to the large audience of obviously hostile adults, "Before we start, I'd like to know how many of you would be willing to give up your automobiles right now." A loud cheer went up, most hands waving madly in the affirmative. The miner stared maybe a full minute, waiting for the tumult to subside. Then he said quietly, with just a hint of a sneer in his voice, "I'm not about to waste an evening talking to a roomful of liars." And then he walked out.

He had our number. Though we may like to appear eco-chic, we are not about to give up cars, nor will folks in developing countries give up their dream of owning a car. There's good reason for this: cars do the best job of transporting us and our belongings from exactly where we are to exactly where we want to go, at the time, velocity and route of our choice, and with relative security from assault by weather or brigand. Cars offer rare privacy. History shows that people are quite willing to pay for the auto's advantages. No existing or proposed public transportation system can even approach them. In fact, one of Henry Ford's main reasons for developing the Model T was to give ordinary citizens — especially farmers — cheap transportation that would free them from the tyranny of mass transit (rail) rates, routes, and schedules.

When people decry the evils of automobiles, what they mostly mean is that they'd like to alleviate the deleterious effects of cars. Cars gobble resources and pollute beyond belief: a typical late-model car dumps its own weight in CO_2, a greenhouse gas, into the air each year. Cars kill people and animals in large numbers; accidents are the leading cause of death for U.S citizens under age 45. Roads — the other half of the car — eat land (often arable) and disturb water runoff patterns. There are counties where half of the land area is paved. Freeways concrete about 25 acres a mile, and require about 250,000 tons of gravel — which has to come from somewhere — to do it.

Some of the most grievous problems arise because of the overweening power of the auto industry. The average of estimates from a number of sources shows that about half of the North American workforce depends upon the auto industry directly or indirectly for its paycheck. This does not count workers using automobiles for commuting or as part of their work. This means that any social changes involving automobiles will be subject to severe political manipulation.

There are no easy answers to any of this. Indeed, I recommend that you turn a very sceptical ear to those who preface a suggested solution with the naive phrase ". . . all we have to do is . . ." or the more insistent "we must." Any simple answer, no matter how righteous, has left out something important. Here's an example: you often hear people badmouth new cars because they are complex and difficult to work on at home. (Indeed, this Ecolog doesn't list do-it-yourself books because there aren't any amateur-useful ones for new models.) Modern cars cost more to fix, too. The friendly folks at the neighborhood gas station no longer possess the specialized knowledge needed to repair local citizens' cars. Alas and woe, things used to be better. Or were they?

Such laments ignore that the old cars were simple because they had no pollution controls. Their lusty guzzling was directed by crude mechanisms. They were overweight, yet crash and handling safety were marginal. Labor costs were low, and so was the standard of living of many mechanics, who were often treated as low-skill hicks. The myth of sturdiness is simplistic too; if the old petropigs were so tough, why don't we see more of them today? That's quite a bit to leave out. True ignorance.

So there are a lot of partial answers. "Drive less" is the most obvious one; I've cut my driving 50% by commuting by computer. (I'm editing this book at home.) But it's difficult to get by with no access at all to a car because most of our nation has been built in a way that requires one.

"Buy the car you need" is another good play. Many Americans buy a car that fits their vacation needs better than their everyday needs. It's silly to do your shopping in a van whose spaciousness is used only two weeks a year. (It's usually cheaper to rent one for vacations.) If you need space often, a station wagon or one of the minivans is a good choice. Wagons are just cars with big trunks, and so cost about the same, in money and pollution per mile, as the sedans from which they are derived. But vans are not especially frugal to run or maintain. Worse, corporate villainy of the worst sort has lobbytwisted the law so that minivans (and pickups) do not have to conform to many safety standards required of cars. They don't even have to have that chintzy little third stoplight which has been proven to deter rearenders. Do carmakers believe that vans and pickups are never followed by careless drivers? Of course not, but the special logic employed by automakers decrees that if vans and pickups conformed to the safety regulations required of cars, the government would consider them to *be* the passenger cars they really are. In that case, their poor economy would reduce the average overall corporate passenger car fuel mileage standards mandated by law, ("CAFE") which most manufacturers could then not meet because of their continuing policy of selling fat, high-profit, gas-guzzler, passenger car models. Got that? By the way, the largest-selling single model of vehicle of any sort is the full-size Ford pickup, a machine with serious potential for environmental mayhem. Studies have shown that most pickups are used more for image than for hauling, making them expensive, dirty toys.

Assuming you need a new car, how do you choose one? First, make sure you really do need a new one. The cheapest way to drive, in miles per dollar, is to use an oldie-but-goodie until it quits. In addition to being cheap to buy and run, the old hog makes full use of the "embodied energy" invested in it during its manufacture. You might also keep in mind that the cost of a complete overhaul is probably less than the *interest* on a new car loan. If the old car's hunger and pollution smack unbearably of sin, consider that the pollution caused by the *making* of a new car may well be more than that caused by the *using* of an old one.

If your decision is to buy a new vehicle, you are faced with a vast but rather sad choice; no sensible "eco-car" or urban vehicle is yet available. Indeed, car companies are vigorously lobbying to reduce the standards now mandated. Obviously you are either going to have to wait, or make do once again from what's available. Take the time to investigate all the models in your desired body style and price range. Check Consumer Reports (p. 65) for their opinion on matters of economy, reliability and safety — matters difficult to ascertain from personal or magazine road tests. I would not buy any new car — especially not a small one — without air bags for both front passengers. How would you like riding beside a bag-protected driver, knowing you were not so shielded? It's not a matter of cost — the lowliest Chrysler-built car has a bag for the driver (only), the same specification as a $38,000 "highly advanced" Lexus! There

VOLVO
LCP 2000

When it became obvious that the classic "petro-pig" big cars were doomed to extinction, a few of the more alert auto companies developed prototypes of "eco-cars" as a response to future fuel crisis, and environmental, or safety regulations. These cars served both to test public opinion and to give the manufacturers and their complex system of suppliers a feel for the technology required if the need became acute. Experience is important; one of the reasons that American auto manufacturers have taken a beating from overseas competition is that until recently, management did not have the training and attitude needed to design for efficiency, or for that matter, to *be* efficient. Worse, the old guard could not be quickly replaced with new blood because no suitable people were in the educational pipeline. Americans had become such thoughtless energy wastrels that inefficiency was considered normal, if it was considered at all. Today, some companies

"Podmobile": Toyota Previa 4x4 typifies what will probably be the family car of the future, needs only airbags and a washable interior to be the champion all-purpose vehicle. Competition will challenge it soon.

is just no excuse for interiors that lack bags on both sides as standard equipment. Anti-lock brakes (ABS) should also be standard equipment on all cars, but they aren't. If the model you want doesn't have them standard or as an option, I'd just say no until they are, and I'd let the manufacturer know that.

What about optional equipment? It certainly is a pleasure to zip down the open road in cool comfort without having your ears buffeted loose, especially on long trips where fatigue can affect driver alertness. I've experimented to check claims that air conditioning eats less fuel than riding with the

windows open in a modern, aerodynamic car. Verdict: in town, air gobbles the gas. At high speeds, open windows cost more fuel. In any case, buying a white or other light-colored car will reduce the need for air conditioning: On a sunny day, the interior temperature difference between a black car and an identical white one is about 37 degrees F. Something else to consider: air conditioner service is a leading source of ozone-hole-causing CFC gases.

Automatic transmissions use more fuel than a skillfully-driven stick shift, but the difference is much less than it used to be. A good automatic will

equal a stick in town, and average about 2 miles per gallon less on the road. Check the now-trustable window sticker. Few drivers really need an automatic, but it can't be denied that a slushpump eases driving in congested traffic. Four-wheel drive is a boon if you must drive a lot in snow or other difficult conditions, but it costs significantly more to buy, maintain, and feed. It's now an option on a variety of cars (including little ones like the Subaru Justy) as well as minivans and pickups. Less ambiguously worthwhile options include multi-adjustable driver's seat, intermittent wipers, rear window wash/wipe/defrost, and full-size spare tire. I'd avoid turbo models; most have proven to be hungry for both fuel and maintenance. You don't need one for good performance, either.

If you can, I'd put off a new car purchase a year or so (plus another year to let new models work out the bugs). What's coming? Lots more minivans, many of them notably superior to the current crop. Toyota's pricey Previa represents the new generation, with ABS, fulltime four-wheel drive and, egad, respectable handling. (Though shamefully, air bags aren't even an option.) I see such "podmobiles" taking over as the standard family car. Empty truck "tin bin" versions of domestic minivans are less expensive, and lend themselves to purpose-

(continued)

still regard concern for efficiency and environment as an unwelcome and unnecessary fad. For others, it's a challenge and an accepted responsbility.

One of the better eco-cars is Volvo's LCP (for Light Component Project) 2000. Like similar efforts from Renault, Citroen, Peugeot, and Toyota, it got some mid-80s press, and then was forgotten as oil prices fell from the high levels of the "energy crisis" years. Figuring that waste is always stupid and environmentally despicable, I present the LCP 2000 as an example of what we could have right now if Volvo (and of course, their competitors) were convinced the demand was there. Let's see what this machine offers:

Statistics show that a typical car is used most often to carry less than two people through an urban area at an average speed of less than 35 miles per hour. For this duty, Volvo designed a car about the size, shape, and utility of current small hatchbacks. The only obvious difference is that the individually folding back seats face to the rear for added safety. That novel configuration allows a mid-car transverse, hollow bulkhead that protects the fuel tank, and provides unusually good resistance to the side impacts so common in urban intersection collisions. Crash protection has been very well worked out — not only as a Volvo tradition, but because a car so extraordinarily light (1555 lbs — far less than a VW Bug) must be very carefully designed if it is to protect its occupants. Safety (and comfort) is also enhanced by the usual European high standards of suspension, steering and braking. A 90s version would doubtless have airbags.

Of course the car sips rather than slurps. Volvo claims 56 miles per gallon, city, 81 mpg on long trips, and a combined figure of 65 mpg; certainly cause for applause. The best mileage occurs at 40 mph. At that common urban pace, you could expect an astounding 100 mpg! Moreover, the high-efficiency diesel will accept a diet chosen from a wide range of fuels. The press demonstration car ran on rapeseed oil! (and smelled like a pizza parlor while doing so, according to one reporter. But that's likely to be solved with a bit more development). You might think that a tiny diesel would be a noisy slug that

Volvo's LCP 2000 eco-car is much less environmentally degrading than current automobiles; gets up to 100 mpg, yet is a sassy performer.

had to be flogged down the road with the gearlever. Not so. Volvo designers realized that the public would not joyfully accept a car that wasn't refined and sassy. The machine is, in fact, something of a hotrod; its 0-to-60 mph time of 11 seconds is better than the average of the current car fleet. Top speed is about 110 mph. (Cars with escargoic top speeds are unpleasant and unsafe because they lack the power for brisk hill-climbing and passing.) An efficient CVT type automatic transmission has been developed for later versions of the car, making it even more acceptable and easy to use.

Volvo also considered environmental effects when materials were chosen. A significant portion of the car is magnesium obtained from seawater by a process far less destructive than mining. The entire car is engineered to resist deterioration by corrosion, a principal cause of premature failure. Work has been done on schemes that eliminate the need for spray painting and its inevitable pollution. The car has also been designed for easy recycling of materials and components when it finally does wear out or meets a less gentle end.

Volvo's designers have even thought of the workers who must make the thing. For instance, the roof is applied last, so that the interior can be installed without people having to struggle upside down in a contorted, physically damaging position. That reduces mistakes and labor time, increases profits, and helps keep the price down to acceptable levels. Simplified production methods also reduce the need for huge, centralized factories and their unpleasant social and environmental side effects.

Aren't there any negative aspects to all this? Well, of course there remain the usual recalcitrant problems always salient where automobiles are in use; this car just reduces a lot of them. On the other hand, if a fleet of LCP 2000s replaced a major portion of the U.S. auto fleet now in use, there would be little need to import oil, there would be a big reduction of all manner of pollution, including the sort that causes global warming and acid rain, and there would be a great savings in raw materials and the environmental degradation that accompanies their extraction. That's not bad, considering that most people, including you and me, are not going to quit driving until they are forced to by very dire circumstances indeed.

Now for the big question: when can we buy one of

Rear seats face backwards for safety, fold for 35 cu. ft. of cargo. Big lid gives easy access. A car much like this could be produced today, at normal prices.

these things? Answer: Not for awhile. Volvo insists that this machine was not built as a prototype of a production model. Its purpose was to test materials, designs, manufacturing techniques and public reaction. Yet it is obvious that an automobile very much like this one could be in production in three to five years. (It takes time to develop a complicated network of suppliers and production facilities, especially one that is not based on current practice.) It also takes money. The design and production apparatus of the Ford Taurus, for instance, took several billion dollars. A company the size of Volvo can't handle that sort of outlay without assistance, and that won't come without the assurance of vigorous demand.

Nasty remarks claiming that Volvo "refuses" to make this car are not in order. In fact, Volvo and other forward-looking firms should be applauded for developing their eco-cars and the new sense of corporate responsibility that made them possible. Now we know what we *can* have, if only we'd ask. The next move is ours. —JB

■ ■

You can let Volvo know what you think of their car by writing Bob Austin at Volvo of America Corporation, Rockleigh, New Jersey, 07647; (201) 768-7300.

Honda Wagon is frugal, fast, fun, and can be had as a 4x4. It needs airbags and antilock brakes though. Cargo room engendered by minivan shape equals much-respected '60s Volvo 122.

built interiors that exactly meet your needs. You probably won't be able to buy tin bin versions of foreign-made minivans though; they're still subject to a heavy, punitive tax imposed in 1969 specifically to hit VW after the German government hassled a boatload of American frozen chicken. To think that in a democracy, a citizen can't buy a preferred Japanese truck because of a frozen chicken quarrel in Germany 20 years ago! We live in strange times.

For people who don't need the room, there is a growing choice of sophisticated subcompacts that are capable and sleaze-free (though still rather jiggly). They too, await airbags and ABS. They're leading a trend towards specialized urban cars like the ones already seen in crowded European and Japanese cities. But buying a tiny car makes sense only if it can accommodate you and your stuff. Personally, I'd buy a size larger. A hatchback or wagon will be most useful and seem least

cramped. The Honda Civic Wagon is particularly competent, and is available as a 4x4 for you Michiganders. Cars smaller than the Honda may unacceptably compromise safety, and may also end up costing more to run than you'd hope, because of depreciation (typically your biggest expense) and high insurance premiums. Before buying any car, be sure to check insurance costs. You may find some ugly surprises.

The auto industry is in a state of flux right now as social and environmental concerns begin to affect design and to constrain use. It is unlikely that there will soon be rapid, large-scale, changes in cars or commute patterns. Little by little, the more obnoxious aspects of automobiling will be reduced. Meantime, the current auto crop is cleaner, safer and better-made than ever before. That isn't enough, but at least it's progress. ■

Rethinking the Role of the Automobile

This paper from Worldwatch (see p. 8) is your quickest education in basic auto-caused problems and the many solutions being proposed and implemented. In typical Worldwatch manner, the presentation is free of jargon, blame-laying, and political slant. (This is not to say that controversial matters are not discussed.) You need to know most of this in order to understand what must be done soon. —JB

•

A major drawback of all alcohol fuels is that some 30-40 percent of the original energy content of their potential feedstocks (biomass, coal, and natural gas) is lost in the conversion process. Numerous studies suggest that the total amount of energy inputs to obtain ethanol — including energy required to fuel farmers' vehicles, to produce fertilizer and pesticides, and to ferment and purify the alcohol — may be close to or even surpass the eventual energy output. A host of new approaches to the distillation process are under

study, such as continuous fermentation techniques, new yeasts and enzymes, and the use of solar energy. These may one day boost the efficiency of alcohol fuel production.

•

On average, a 10-percent weight reduction will yield a 6-percent fuel economy gain. Past fuel economy improvements in the United States have primarily been accomplished through lowered weights and shifts to front-wheel drive. Only 10-15 percent of the gains came from a shift to smaller cars. Fuel efficiency has thus not come at the expense of reduced car-interior space.

•

Electric vehicles essentially emit no pollutants. Their environmental acceptability, however, depends on how the electricity that powers them is generated. Nonfossil feedstocks would be most ideal. Using electricity derived from the current mix of power sources in the United States, an electric vehicle would release about the same amount of CO_2 as a gasoline-fueled car, more sulfur dioxide, but much lower amounts of other pollutants. Electric cars running on coal-produced electricity

would substantially increase the amount of CO_2 released.

•

An extensive bike-and-ride system could provide significant benefits. The average American automobile commuter can reduce his or her annual use of gasoline by some 407 gallons — equivalent to half the gasoline burned up by a typical car in the United States in a year — by switching to bike-and-ride. A 1980 Chicago Area Transportation Study found that improving bicycle access to public transit is the most cost-effective way to reduce auto emissions. Thus, transit serviceability standards need to be adopted that allow easy access to public transit.

Rethinking the Role of the Automobile, Worldwatch Paper 84, Michael Renner 1988; 70 pp.; **$4** postpaid from: Worldwatch Institute 1776 Massachusetts Ave., NW Washington, DC 20036

Urban Transit

Ah, nothing is so edifying as a bit of heresy. Why, Professor Lave even advocates the use of private cars instead of mass transit! (Under appropriate circumstances, of course.) In any case, his willingness to be politically incorrect both to the eco-chic and officialdom adds greatly to his credibility — an important point if his anti-establishment ideas are to be taken seriously by a public that has been misinformed by emotional anti-auto ranting. His main point is that years of government management of public transport systems and policy has resulted in drastic inefficiency that would be best reduced by privatization. For example, legalizing jitneys results in a system with the flexible schedule and routing necessary to serve areas of low population density — service that inevitably bankrupts the usual municipal transit authority. Vehicles can be added or subtracted as conditions change, regulated automatically by market demand. An expensive, inflexible and strike-prone mass transport system is thus made obsolete.

Urban Transit (The Private Challenge to Public Transportation), Charles A. Lave, Editor 1985; 372 pp.; **$12.95** ($14.70 postpaid) from: Pacific Institute for Public Policy Research, 177 Post St., Suite 500, San Francisco, CA 94108 (415) 989-0833 ✳WEA

Where this has been tried, it works fine, despite noisy bureaucratic predictions of disaster. Prof. Lave makes his points neatly, and answers his critics with logic, example, and humor, making the book surprisingly easy to read even if you aren't all that interested. Citizens groups and city managers need to read this; there are <u>answers</u> here, that can be implemented right now. —JB

•

. . . as in the case of the transition from animal to mechanized power, the transition from public to private transport substitutes capital for labor and in particular reduces the need for *hired* labor. This can make the automobile a relatively cost-efficient mode of transportation, especially in providing the higher quality of transportation that people tend to seek as their incomes rise. It is almost impossible for conventional public transportation at any cost to match the schedule convenience, flexibility (e.g., combining shopping or personal trips with commuting), privacy, and comfort of the automobile. —John R. Meyer

•

The most transit-dependent city in the United States, New York, now allows private firms to operate express bus services. These firms not only provide a higher quality of service than the city-operated vehicles, but do so at a profit, and without government subsidy. —Charles A. Lave

•

. . . artificially *low fares* resulted from two goals: first, to lure commuters out of their cars — which

did not work because rising incomes made commuters more sensitive to transit quality than to transit cost; second, to provide low cost transportation for the poor — though it would have been far less costly to subsidize them directly, rather than erecting a low-fare structure used by rich and poor alike. —Charles A. Lave

•

It is important to remember that transit did not lose passengers because of deficits; it lost passengers because it did not provide the kind of service they desired. —Charles A. Lave

•

Transit need not be limited to conventional buses and rail cars. The largest source of public transit rides in the United States is the ordinary taxi cab. Taxis not only carry more total passengers than standard buses or trains, they even carry more poor passengers. —Charles A. Lave

•

From the viewpoint of the transit planner, it is easier to start one new consolidated service than to rely on hundreds of vanpool operators or jitney drivers. It is hard to believe that a complex task can be accomplished via hundreds of small decisions, though this is exactly the way the energy crises were solved. In the midst of the grand government debate over which large-scale public policy actions might produce the desired result, most individuals simply got busy: They insulated their houses, bought more fuel-efficient cars and appliances, and so forth. —Charles A. Lave

Motor-Vehicle Fuel Efficiency and Global Warming

This free six-pager is a ten-minute course in car-feeding and the consequences thereof. The numbers are all here. You see what we've been doing and the effects of government policy. There's a wonderfully clear chart showing what the choices are for fuel of the future, and what they mean economically and environmentally. The act concludes with a list of suggested initiatives. With references, so you can use the info as credible ammunition. —JB

Briefing Paper: Motor-Vehicle Fuel Efficiency and Global Warming Union of Concerned Scientists; **free** from: UCS Publications, Dept. BP, 26 Church St. Cambridge, MA 02238 (617) 547-5552

Note that only 4% of petroleum is used by electric utilities. This is why pro-nuke ads claiming to reduce oil imports and consumption are misleading. —JB

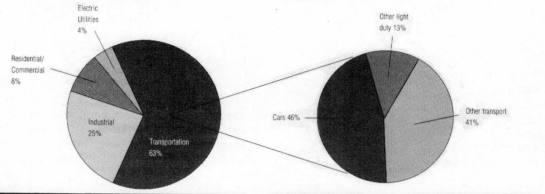

Your Driving Costs

Being true to thyself about car costs is about as appealing as your annual physical checkup: you don't really wanna know. This little pamphlet from the American Automobile Association — the ubiquitous AAA — is derived from studies by an outfit named Runzheimer International, a firm that analyzes living costs for purposes of reimbursement (you should be so lucky). The cold, hard numbers may be the best incentive to drive less. Read it and weep. —JB

Your Driving Costs; Pamphlet **free**, send **SASE** to: American Automobile Association 1000 AAA Drive, Heathrow, FL 32746 (407) 444-7000

Five Ways to Curb Traffic

Here's how six cities around the world are discouraging traffic in already congested areas:

Hong Kong

Electronic sensors on cars record highway travel and time of day. Drivers are issued a monthly bill (commuter hours are the most expensive).

Singapore

Automobiles entering downtown Singapore during rush hour are required to display a $30-a-month sticker, but cars carrying four or more passengers may pass without charge.

Gothenburg, Sweden

To encourage pedestrian traffic, the central business district has been divided into pie-shaped zones, with cars prohibited from moving directly from one zone to another. Autos move in and out only by way of a peripheral ring road.

Rome and Florence

All traffic except buses, taxis, delivery vehicles, and cars belonging to residents has been banned between 7:30 A.M. and 7:30 P.M.

Tokyo

The buyer of a standard-size vehicle must show evidence that a permanent parking space is available for the car before he can close the sale. To comply with the law, some drivers have constructed home garages with lifts to permit double-deck parking!

(Source: *Sierra* magazine, May/June 1989)

Electric Cars

On paper, electric vehicles are the best solution to urban auto-caused air pollution and noise. Unfortunately, there is a spider in the bathtub: electric cars must recharge, probably daily. Though utility companies claim that they can handle substantial numbers of electric vehicles with existing generating capacity, strong new demand would inevitably encourage the nuclear power industry. It is realistic to regard an electric vehicle as actually being fuelled by whatever fuel is consumed in the nearest generating facility. It is correct to say that an electric car is nuclear-powered, coal-powered, or even dam-powered, using the same logic as when referring to a car as diesel- or gasoline-powered. Electric car advocates don't care for this nomenclature, but its use tends to keep things clear.

Some people have suggested that electric vehicles could recharge from photovoltaic panels. Mounting the panels on the car has proven useful only for tiny, highly specialized solar race cars. Recharging from a photovoltaic array where the car parks for extended periods is the practical way things will go someday. (Such things can be done; I once rigged a small electric truck to re-charged from a windmill turning in the evening breeze.) Since cars eventually *must* run on renewable energy, and "racing improves the breed," impractical solar electric featherweights may be considered as an interesting, important gesture towards the future.

General Motors has done the best so far, with a useful city car (alarmingly dubbed "Impact") featuring brisk performance and a 120 mile range — more than acceptable to most urban drivers. As with all battery-driven vehicles, its range is noticeably reduced by extensive need to ascend hills or accelerate strongly, and by using the heating, air conditioning, and headlights a lot. Batteries must be replaced every few years for about the same price as a new engine in a conventional car. So we are not yet talking practicality for the average user, and this is what it's going to take if electrics are to make a difference. On the other hand, GM has been surprised by a strong public demand for the car even at the high price proposed.

Battery technology remains the big barrier. At present, they are expensive, bulky and very heavy. Most employ toxic substances. There are lightweight, small batteries, but they are even more expensive and potentially polluting. It has been suggested that electric cars are at their best as hybrids with a small, on-board fossil-fueled generator to recharge the batteries while parked or even while driving. It is correctly argued that a small liquid-fueled engine running at a constant speed can be made very efficient and relatively clean. The generator could also be used to power lights and air conditioner, its waste heat warming the interior in winter. It could help up steep hills. Such cars are under development

So it looks like a truly useful and affordable electric car is still a few years down the road. Its day will come, though, the advantages for urban use are just too good to pass up. To keep abreast of developments, check Electric Auto Association [**$25**/year membership (includes monthly newsletter) from: EAA, 1249 Lane Street, Belmont, CA 94002; (415) 591-6698]. If you'd like to take a crack at being the first to do it right, Michael Hackleman's **Electric Vehicles: Design and Build Your Own**, [Michael Hackleman,1977; 214 pages, $9.95 postpaid from: EARTHMIND, P.O. Box 743, Mariposa, CA 95338] will teach you the basics of electric car experimenting. —JB

GM has brought practical electric cars much closer with their high-performance Impact 2-seater sport coupe. It's about the size and weight of a Honda Civic but priced with sportscars of similar acceleration ($20-30,000). Range at 55 mph is 120 miles under average conditions — far better than rival electric cars, and certainly adequate for most urban and commuting use. Satisfying to drive, it banishes the sluggy golf-cart image often associated with electrics. It also helps GM deflect criticism of its deservedly bad reputation in environmental matters. —JB

The Car Buyer's Art

This doesn't have much to do with ecology but it's dumb to get took when you buy a car. Read this and you won't. —JB

The Car Buyer's Art Darrell Parrish; 1985; 183 pp. **$5** postpaid from: Book Express P.O. Box 1249, Bellflower, CA 90706; (213) 867-3723 ❋WEA

●

Turnover in the car selling profession is high. Because of this, a young salesman is very likely to be a new salesman, which is exactly what you want. Here's why. Being new in the business, he will lack the hardened "take 'em to the cleaners at all cost" attitude of the more experienced veteran. Along the same lines, his persuasive skills will probably not be fully developed. And finally, remember, he is keenly aware that in order to remain employed he must sell cars. In order to accomplish this and gain an initial foothold in the profession, there's a good chance he'll work his heart out for you and settle for a sale "on the books" even if the commission is small.

Pedestrian Pockets

Is there an alternative to the egregiously inappropriate 40-year-old method and pattern of suburban development? Architect/Planner Peter Calthorpe thinks so.

"The Pedestrian Pocket is a simple cluster of housing, retail space and offices within a quarter-mile walking radius of a transit system. The concept blends the convenience of the car and the opportunity to walk in an environment in which the economic engine of new growth — jobs in the service and information industry — is balanced with affordable housing and local stores. It is a planning strategy that preserves open space and reduces automobile traffic without increasing density in existing neighborhoods. By its mix, the Pedestrian Pocket allows people a choice of walking, driving, carpooling, or riding mass transit. With new light rail lines, roads dedicated to carpools and buses, and a corresponding upzoning of each of its stations, these Pockets reconnect an existing suburban fabric and its towns. The increments of growth are small, but the whole system accommodates regional expansion with minimal environmental impact: less land consumed, less traffic generated, and less pollution produced."

We've heard this sort of thing before. What makes Peter Calthorpe think his schemes will ever get built? There are several reasons for optimism: The time is ripe. Urban sprawl and its unhappy consequences are now obvious to everyone, including greedy developers and banks. The old way doesn't work; it's time to try something new. The Pedestrian Pockets concept has been very well worked out in many iterations and proposals, not only by Peter but by a coterie of other well-known architects and planners (and, inevitably, their students and imitators) who have rallied around the idea and added to it. This concentrated attention has developed things to the point of elegance. It's ready to go. And it *is* going. As you read this, a full-size Pedestrian Pocket is actually being built near Sacramento, California, a city notorious for the worst sort of land-eating, congested urban growth. It's being built by an astute conventional developer who sees the project as a challenging opportunity. The Powers That Be have given it their blessing. May all go well. —JB

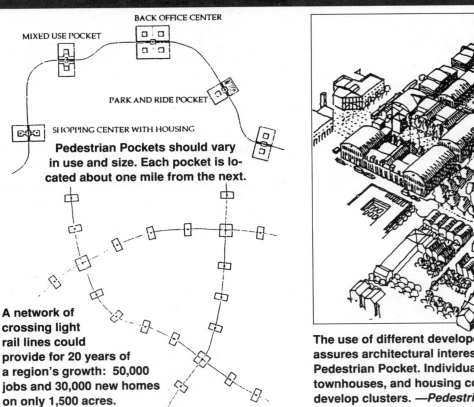

Pedestrian Pockets should vary in use and size. Each pocket is located about one mile from the next.

A network of crossing light rail lines could provide for 20 years of a region's growth: 50,000 jobs and 30,000 new homes on only 1,500 acres.

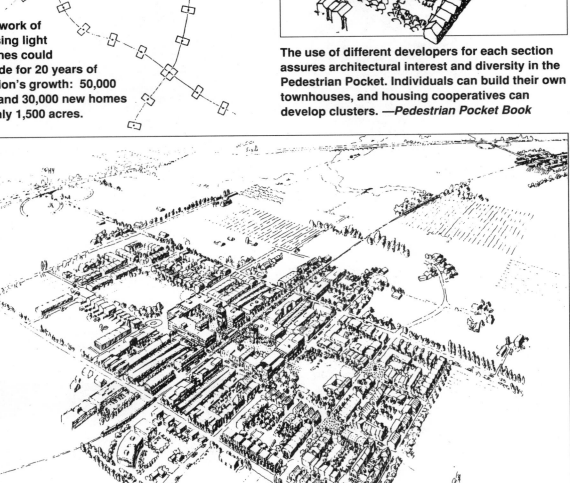

The use of different developers for each section assures architectural interest and diversity in the Pedestrian Pocket. Individuals can build their own townhouses, and housing cooperatives can develop clusters. —*Pedestrian Pocket Book*

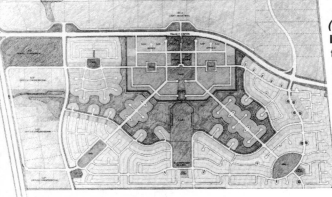

(Left) Site plan for the Laguna Creek Pedestrian Pocket near Sacramento, California: 1,858 single-family homes, 1,512 multi-family units, 73 ac. of lakes, 38 ac. of parks, town hall, elementary school, day care sites, offices and retail shops.

(Above) Balancing and clustering jobs, housing, shopping, recreation and child care, the Pedestrian Pocket uses 1/6 the land area of typical suburban development. Open space and precious agricultural land could stand along with a region's growth.

A light rail line within a comfortable walking distance of all development connects several pockets with local towns and cities to provide an alternative to freeway congestion.

(Left) The light rail station area borders ground-floor retail and neighborhood services. The office courtyard and main street intersect in a plaza with limited automobile access.

The Pedestrian Pocket Book

The Pedestrian Pocket Book gives a detailed look at the idea in several versions developed during a 1988 "charrette" by eight prominent architects and a pack of willing students at the University of Washington. (Charrette is what architects and designers call a highly focussed workshop session that often excludes sleep until the goal is attained.) It's so clear a rendition of the concept that you may find yourself mentally trying little adaptions of it to your own locale. The eight authors, are, of course, available for serious consultation and design. —JB

The Pedestrian Pocket Book
(A New Suburban Design Strategy)
Doug Kelbaugh, Editor; 1989;
68 pp.; **$9.95** ($12.45 postpaid)
from: Princeton Architectural Press
37 East Seventh Street, New York
NY 10003; (212) 995-9620

Calthorpe Associates, 246 First Street, #400
San Francisco, CA 94105; (415) 777-0181

Cohousing: A Contemporary Approach to Housing Ourselves

Like many innovative housing ideas, this one started in Denmark where there are more than a hundred cohousing projects in operation. The Danes use the word bofaellesskaber — *living communities. These are not communes or condos, though there are some similarities. People own their homes, but also share mutually owned amenities built into the project. Those might include gardens, a library, laundry, and workshops. Many have community dining — a boon for singles and seniors. (Eating together — "commensality" — is one of the best community "glues" available). Single parents find child care easily, and kids are safer because cars are banished to peripheral parking lots. There is little crime. In short, cohousing is a good way to live. Surprisingly, it can be more affordable than many less desirable alternatives.*

This beautiful and convincing book translates the concept into a form that we can put to work here. It has inspired many of the more than 40 cohousing projects being planned or built in the U.S. at this time. But there are many ways to do cohousing — "as many ways as there are people interested in living this way," asserts Virginia Thigpen, who is developing a cohousing project in Davis, California. As she tended her garden in Village Homes (see next page) which she helped build, Ms. Thigpen cautioned us to remember that the Cohousing *book is the only one available at this time, and is only one viewpoint. There is a temptation to use its ideas blindly, substituting expert opinion for personal innovation. That can lead to "buying into a lifestyle," which is rarely satisfying in the long run. She told us that in Denmark, each cohousing group is different. Though the newer ones may be structured by covenants, the older groups do not need to strive to be a community — they already are one. Experience allows flexibility without so many rules. Smaller cliques of like-minded individuals can operate within the larger cohousing scheme without disrupting it. "It takes time to evolve. It's taken 16 years to see what works for them," she said. "The important thing is that it works." My guess is that it is going to work here, too, after a bit of cuttin' & fittin'. —JB*

(Taped interview by Richard Nilsen. Our thanks to Virginia Thigpen for her time.)

•

I know I live in a community because on a Friday night it takes me 45 minutes and two beers to get from the parking lot to my front door.
                                                              —Trudeslund resident

(Above) Row houses with small front gardens line the pedestrian streets of Trudeslund, where much of the community's socializing takes place. *(Left)* Although their community was built at the same density as the single-family houses in the area, Trudeslund residents chose to cluster the 33 dwellings along two pedestrian streets, localize parking, and preserve the wooded portion of the site. *(Below left)* A child sets the table for dinner in the Trudeslund common house. *(Below)* A new 48-community cohousing development near Copenhagen. The first of four phases includes one privately financed community, three cooperatives, and one non-profit-owned rental complex.

Cohousing
Kathryn McCamant
and Charles Durrett
1989; 208 pp.
$19.95 ($21.95 postpaid)
from: Ten Speed Press
P.O. Box 7123
Berkeley, CA 94707
(800) 841-2665 ✳WEA

The CoHousing Company™

In addition to authoring the **Cohousing** *book, Kathryn McCamant and Charles Durrett have a development company dedicated to building Co-Housing communities. They give introductory slide-lectures and workshops, and maintain a national referral network of people interested in cohousing life. This last is important — it takes a determined and clever group to actually build cohousing. Once the group is together, The CoHousing Company staff assists the whole complex process of acquiring land, financing everything, getting the permits, and designing the project — all things that would be very difficult to do on your own (unless you are already a developer). —JB*

The CoHousing Company, 48 Shattuck Square, Suite 15, Berkeley, CA 94704; (415) 549-9980

Jerngarden residents have front doors facing the street, but usually enter through their backyard commons so they can visit with neighbors.

•

With a lot of imagination and two years of sweat equity, the residents of Jerngarden transformed an inner city junkyard and eight deteriorated rowhouses into an urban paradise. By combining their backyards, they created a small park in the middle of the city block.

Jerngarden residents are still active in the neighborhood organization they helped to start. Since most of them lived in the area before, they have many friends nearby who often participate in the community's parties. A community center has been built a few blocks away, and many buildings have been renovated. Some say that Jerngarden was the impetus that inspired other improvements.

Village Homes By J. Baldwin

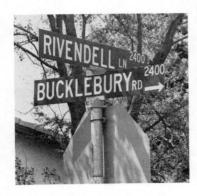

J.R.R. Tolkien street names invite the local nickname of "Hobbittown."

GENTLY CURVING bikepath/sidewalks wend past the colorful, fragrant gardens adorning the front yard of each home. Village Homes looks and feels like a park with houses. Trees abound, many festooned with ripening fruit. Neighbors chat as they garden, unconcerned for the safety of their unsupervised kids. There's no traffic roar — there are no through streets. Most cars you see are parked in carports. A few move slowly along the narrow lanes running behind the houses. The bike paths are the real streets. Kids and adults whiz by, the only sound being an occasional rumble as bike tires meet wooden bridge boards. The whole scene looks a little like a stage set. It almost feels suspicious. Are these normal people? Is this all real?

Yes, it's real, and it's even better than it looks at a glance. The Ecotopian appearance is reinforced by utility bills averaging 50% less than those of a conventional neighborhood. The small lots, gardens and porches tend to encourage neighborliness and a sense of community — the best

deterrent to crime. The tract has also been a financial success for builders, banks and homeowners. Homes usually get sold before being listed — often for 20% more than homes in ordinary neighborhoods of the same class. Originally sold for $31,000-$70,000, they're now $200,000-$300,000. (Remember, California realty prices are crazy these days.)

Community land and buildings are taken care of and insured by a strong Neighborhood Association that charges each of the 220 families monthly dues of $60. When Village Homes was opened in 1976, it was hoped that selling vegetables from the community gardens would take care of the expenses, but these days few people can afford the time for market gardening. The Association hopes to reduce the dues with revenues from apartments and offices they own. We heard few complaints about the dues; people seem to regard them as part of the price of living in such a nice place. Even kiddies and teenagers like life in the Village. Visitors resist leaving. All regard it as the way a neighborhood should be.

So why aren't there more Village Homes? The answer is complex and sadly familiar. When developer Mike Corbett built the Village, he had to fight the bureaucracy tooth and nail. Banks wouldn't lend the large sums necessary (Mike had to buy the whole tract at once in order to

Nine photos by Don Ryan

Bike paths are the real streets of Village Homes. They connect to the bike path system of the nearby city of Davis, minimizing the need for auto use. It's safer too; neighborhood kids can go from their home to any other home without crossing streets.

Alley-like cul-de-sac streets eliminate through traffic. Street parking is not allowed. Shaded, narrow pavement reduces heat gain, helping to keep summer neighborhood temperatures about 10 degrees cooler than other developments.

(Below) An early picture of part of Village Homes before trees grew to shade streets. Small lots permit neighborhood-owned and maintained gardens, community center, playgrounds, swimming pool and greenbelts. All homes face south for maximum solar advantage, with solar rights protected by law. Tight layout encourages friendly neighbor interactions. Crime is rare.

Judy Corbett

maintain the sort of control necessary for such a project). FHA turned him down. The Fire Department objected to the narrow streets. But Mike, as one of his friends put it "doesn't take no for an answer." He fought it through. (He's now the Mayor of Davis, California where Village Homes is located.)

Since then, fear of litigation has made it much harder to proceed with such projects, especially where a neighborhood association is involved. Lawsuit-resistance has taken precedent over innovation. Chickenhearted lenders will only consider conventional development; craven city governments complicate the permit process beyond the financial endurance of any who would try something new. But mostly, it's a matter of will. A Village Homes would be harder to do now, but it can still be done. Mike is busy, so it's going to have to be a very determined and skilled someone else. Meantime, Village Homes stands as an inspiring example of what a sustainable city might look like. And it's one of the very few developments *not* named for what was destroyed to make it. ■

Drainage "swales" hold rain runoff, making storm sewers unnecessary. The temporary ponds are designed to soak in before mosquitos can breed. Swales parallel bikepaths; may be graveled (above), mowed (above right), cobbled (right). This kid-oriented intersection (below) features a sandy play swale in summer; in winter it becomes a watercourse. Most swales offer appreciated "distant" views in otherwise confined landscape.

(Above) Community garden vegetables are no longer sold to help defray costs of neighborhood upkeep and insurance; folks just don't have the time anymore. They eat well, though, and most homes have their own gardens, too. Almost all the public landscaping is edible, professionally maintained, and community-accessible. The development as a whole is surrounded by a linear almond orchard which acts as a traffic-noise buffer and additional source of community income.

(Right) Most homes have solar hot water heaters, but few have air conditioners despite summer temperatures that can top 100°F. Efficient design encourages efficient use; Village Homes utility bills average about 50% of those in a conventional development.

Special thanks to Judy Corbett, Virginia Thigpen, and Richard Nilsen for information and assistance.

A Better Place To Live

This is a new edition of the story of how Village Homes came to be, by the man who made it happen. Lots of drawings and photos accompany a discussion of the philosophy and tough battles by hardworking, inspired people. You could use it as a beginner's manual for proliferating the breed. (The new edition isn't yet available as we go to press, so no samples. Sorry). —JB

A Better Place to Live, Michael Corbett (will be out in late 1990) from: agAccess, 603 4th Street, Davis CA 95616; (916) 756-7177

✱WEA — Available from Whole Earth Access, see p. 2.

How The Other Half Builds

"Existing informal sector housing, often termed slums, represents a solution rather than a problem." This is a radical concept to many theoretical low-income housing planners, but not to the author, Witold Rybczynski; he's well-known for puncturing the ineffectual arguments of self-righteous do-gooders. The basic premise is simple: In order to determine what to plan as housing for the poor, find out what they need; to find out what they need, go see what they've done without the aid of planners. You'd think this would go without saying, but planners often are blinded by class differences and elitist educations. This paper should help, and not just in less-developed areas of the world. The idea that the people can handle a lot of their own needs should be a major premise of any democratic society.

This book, which deals mostly with space utilization, is part of a series. Volume 2 examines plot planning and the process by which plots take on individual character. Volume 3 describes experiments and simulations intended to develop an urban design process that takes into account the findings of the first two books. —JB

How the Other Half Builds, Witold Rybczynski, et al., *Volume One* **$8**; *Volume Two* **$7**; *Volume Three* **$10** all postpaid from; School of Architecture Minimum Cost Housing Group, McGill University Macdonald-Harrington Building, 815 Sherbrooke Street West, Montreal Quebec H3A 2K6 Canada
✱WEA

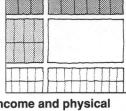

•

The priorities of the slum-dweller are frequently not those of the municipal authorities. Space takes precedence over permanence. A porch may be built before a bathroom; a work place may be more important than a private bedroom. The apparent inversion of values is especially evident in the public spaces. Whereas planned sites and services projects usually incorporate rudimentary, minimal circulation spaces, the public areas of slums are characterized by richness and diversity.

The government of India uses four income categories: Economically Weaker Sector, Low Income Group, Middle Income Group and High Income Group.

Based on these affordability criteria, it is assumed that higher income families need larger plots whereas lower income families need smaller plots. However studies of informal settlements have shown little correlation between family income and physical plot characteristics.

In designing actual housing projects, in which it is necessary to accomodate several income groups, the segregation of different income groups is taken a step further. Different income groups are seldom mixed. This separation of housing, based on income, is contrary to the settlement patterns observed in traditional housing. In informal settlements, regardless of their income level, families from the same clan or religious group live next to one another.

The Cost Cuts Manual

"Why don't the poor do something for themselves?" That timeworn anglo excuse gets two (grimy) gloves across the face in this manual of proven building rehabilitation technique. Beset by ripoff in high places, subtle racism and demoralizing bureaucratic hassles, rehab is often frustratingly ineffective in helping to furnish low-cost housing to those who need it. But there's one group that's really doing the deed: The Enterprise Foundation chaired by James Rouse, who designed the famous Columbia, MD housing experiment. The Enterprise Foundation assists groups — 69 at this writing — engaged in rehab efforts across the country. They are successful. Their strategies and tactics are presented in this manual, and you can tell that it's information hard won. It's dirty-hands all the way; no bullshit, just what works, in sufficient (illustrated) detail to invite replication. I've never seen the subject approached with anything near this combination of competence and spirit. —JB*

The Cost Cuts Manual Robert M. Santucci, Jim Thomas, Cecilia Cassidy & Peter Werwath; 1987 336; **$45** ($47 postpaid) **Cost Cuts Newsletter** Cecilia Cassidy; **free** on request (9 issues) Both from: Enterprise Foundation P. O. Box 1490 Alexandria, VA 22313

•

In Europe, people have faced almost every American social trend years before we realize it's coming.

In response to wildly escalating costs for land, material, and money, they have adopted features in their homes such as:

*Small rooms, often multi-purpose, that demand scaled down furniture.

*No unnecessary decorative trim.

*Raw floors, no carpeting, tile, or hardwood.

*Minimum number of electric outlets, no fancy fixtures.

*Few, if any, built-in kitchen cabinets.

*Often no clothes closets at all.

*Usually just one bathroom and sometimes just a shower, no tub.

Is this low-income housing? Not at all — at least not in Europe. . . .

American designers must begin to incorporate these ideas in affordable housing here.

•

Let's elevate beds to a more practical status: off the floor.

A 12-by-18-foot bedroom has more than sufficient space for a sedentary bed and its two little aisles.

That's not true in an 8-by-10-foot bedroom — the size more likely found in a low-cost house or apartment.

Two ideas create space instantly:

1. Keep one side of the bed against the wall.

2. Elevate the bed.

Idea No. 2 offers the best use of a small space, so try it whenever you can. **2**

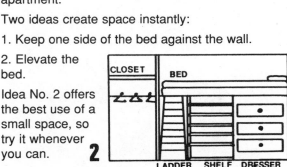

Housing America in the 1980s

Just as we enter the '90s, this remarkable study arrives to show us where we've been and where we're likely headed as we attempt to house our population. The author has managed to whip an immense mass of data into a comprehensible and useable (if not thrilling) form that makes trends visible along with their causes. Literally visible — the study results are shown superimposed on actual neighborhood maps from the more than 50 urban areas analyzed. (New York, Chicago and L.A. are included.) If you're involved in urban housing, the homeless, zoning, financing or environmental matters, the book is a real find. A bit of assiduous reading and you'll have a much better idea of what you're really talking about, because this is what's really going on whether politically correct or not. I've never seen this sort of information better presented. —JB

Housing America in the 1980s, John S. Adams; 1988; 328 pp. **$65** ($67 postpaid) from: Russell Sage Foundation /CUP Services P. O. Box 6525 Ithaca, NY 14851 (800) 666-2211

City

*A quick glance at the downtown of most cities reveals a grim decay, sometimes with a half-hearted attempt at rejuvenation that is even more depressing. There are lots of theories concerning why, and what to do about it. There is opportunity for greed and innumerable, endless studies. But what's really going on? William H. Whyte (of **Organization Man** fame) takes a look, from the street, from above the street, with hidden cameras, with notebook in hand, and comes up with what is probably the most accurate view of city life yet seen. It's a hopeful, positive view (in contrast to my own; I think that nature doesn't permit big cities in the long run). But Mr. Whyte is so witty and so obviously sharp-eyed that his view is convincing. I look at cities with new eyes, thanks to Mr. Whyte. —JB*

City (Rediscovering the Center), William H. Whyte 1988; 386 pp.; **$14.95** ($16.95 postpaid) from: Doubleday & Co./Cash Sales, P.O. Box 5071, Des Plaines, IL 60017-5071 (800) 223-6834 ext. 479
✱WEA

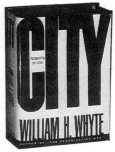

•

People are told that food vending is bad for downtown business, bad for traffic, bad for them and their health. But people do not believe this. They like eating out-of-doors. They like the choices. They like the prices. They prefer a hot dog and a soda they can afford ($1.65) to a fuller lunch they cannot. So they buy. The vendors are providing what the established order is not.

•

If you want to know what fine feature is going to go next, look at the title of the newest development. It customarily is named for that which it will destroy.

•

The days that bring out the most sitters are not the sunny, sparkling days in the seventies. They are the hot, muggy days. We must have strong tropical instincts.

Institute for Community Economics (ICE)

ICE helps local groups form community land trusts. In Dallas, Texas, 11 neighborhood groups have banded together to buy up vacant urban lots. Houses scheduled for demolition are moved onto the lots. The land trust owns the lots; individuals own the houses and lease the land. This keeps the land off of the speculative real estate market so that the only increases in price are from inflation or improvements to the houses. Result: affordable housing for low-income people. The **Handbook** *explains how to do it in your neighborhood. —Richard Nilsen*

Community Land Trust Handbook; **$10** ($12.50 postpaid) from: Institute for Community Economics 57 School St., Springfield MA 01105; (413) 774-7956

[Not the same as ICE on p. 56]

•

To most people, *private* is a very attractive word. It is strongly associated with the privacy and security of the home. However, much private land in America is not owned by people who live on it. Most land today is concentrated in the hands of a relatively small part of the population (75 percent of the privately held land in America is owned by 5 percent of the private landholders). And absentee ownership is increasingly common.

(Below) **A real estate friend of mine calls this "resegregation." Whites moved out, mostly because of black people coming in and now they're moving back. That's one way to displace people — to come in all of a sudden and say, "It's a historical area, you got to fix up this facade, you got to do this, you got to do that." And then the residents check their resources and they can't do it, so the property is condemned and someone who has money comes in and buys it and fixes it up.**

The Conservation Easement Handbook

In the world of real estate, not all easements are bad for the owner — like, say, the one allowing the electric company to cross your land with a power line. This is a detailed book for conservation-minded people about creating good easements. A joint venture between four national land-protection organizations (Trust for Public Land, Land Trust Exchange, Public Resource Foundation, and the National Trust for Historic Preservation), this book manages to be innovative, comprehensive and coherent. The scope of what's being tried in local communities across the country is heartening. Here are real win/win situations, right down to the boilerplate needed for writing an easement of your own. —Richard Nilsen

The Conservation Easement Handbook, Janet Diehl & Thomas S. Barrett; 1988; 269 pp.; **$19.95** ($22.95 postpaid) from: Land Trust Alliance 900 17th St. NW Suite 410 Washington, DC 20006 (202) 785-1410

(Right) **The sunlight, scale, and ambience of New York City's Greenacre Park are protected by the first scenic easement applied to an urban landscape. The easement, donated to the New York Landmarks Conservancy by the owner of a four-story building opposite the park, prohibits any construction that would exceed the height of the current building and prohibits the use of the site's development rights to support construction on any other site that would shadow the park or block its view.**

Building Sustainable Communities

Architects tend to see sustainability in terms of desirable amenity and plan, well integrated with nature. Economists and sociologists are more concerned with the economic basis for community. Of course, both must be heard. This book is based on seminars held by the E.F. Schumacher Society (see **Small is Beautiful***, p. 96). Some interesting principles are debated, most having to do with self-government — true Democracy. You know in your heart it's right. But you also know that The Establishment is unlikely to assist. The book is a reminder of what it is we really need to do. —JB*

Building Sustainable Communities, Ward Morehouse, Editor; 1989; 187 pp.; **$13.50** ($16.30 postpaid) from: The Bootstrap Press, 777 United Nations Plaza, Suite 9A, New York, NY 10017 (212) 972-9878 **✳WEA**

•

As working members develop the capacity to self-organize and self-administer, the managerial role becomes more one of general overseeing and planning and of following guidelines laid down by the board and by the membership as a whole. In a number of cases, however, cooperatives have started out with an unrealistic sense of their capabilities and without sufficient understanding of the need for clear job definitions and responsibilities. The tendency is often to rebel against expertise and hierarchy and to deny the validity of both. But hierarchy is legitimate so long as final authority rests not with the top figure in the hierarchy but with the whole. And expertise is necessary and does not prevent democratic management so long as it is not mystified and information needed to make basic policy decisions is disseminated throughout the organization.

The Self-Help Handbook

What's a small town to do when federal and state funds get scarce? The essential services can't very well be stopped — shut down the sewage treatment plant and the citizens would soon have to abandon the place. This handbook outlines successful strategies and tactics that have saved the day for financially strapped rural communities in New York State, but the principles should work well anywhere. The examples given also can be useful for gadflies claiming that their towns squander money; many of the suggestions here are based upon discovering amazing waste (not necessarily intentional) in the entrenched bureaucracies. When the school board cries for more money, here are some answers besides canceling the sports, music, and college prep programs. Good, sensible stuff, and about time, too. —JB

•

The presence of "spark plugs" both within the local government and technical employees (entrepreneurs). There is a lot of evidence that a successful

community enterprise — whether undertaken by a citizen group, local government, or not-for-profits — usually boils down to one key factor: a person. To a remarkable extent, when we track down successful community ventures, we find that they are not explained by the availability of money, severity of the problem, or adequacy of the plan. They are explained by a person who is able to take an idea and make it work.

•

Volunteers can be used effectively as managers as well as laborers. Some 10%-20% of project costs can be saved by keeping the management

The Self-Help Handbook
Jane W. Schautz
1985; 199 pp.
$15 ($18 postpaid) from:
The Rensselaerville Institute
Pond Hill Road
Rensselaerville, NY 12147
(518) 797-3783

local rather than employing an engineering or contracting firm to do it for you. "Outside" businesses must mark up goods and services in order to cover their overhead and profit needs. It may be that the local management must be paid, too, although probably at a reduced rate. If appropriately-qualified volunteers can be found to manage the project, so much the better.

•

Encourage women to participate at all levels of the project. The Institute is able to document that women are easily the equivalent of men whether in operating equipment, laying pipe or erecting buildings. Projects which consider women as suitable for only serving coffee and making telephone calls are depriving themselves of 50% of the work force of that community. Women will seldom volunteer for work which is beyond their physical strength, but are frequently the first to volunteer to learn a new skill — at least partly due to their lack of embarrassment in admitting they need instruction.

A New Theory of Urban Design

*This little book by the author of **A Pattern Language** is about urban design in highly specific terms, but in ways that translate neatly into other complex human endeavors. Alexander focuses on how such things as cities best develop as a whole, and his technique encourages accelerated process — doing in ten years the kind of organic growth that may have taken a Renaissance city 100-200 years. Alexander likes to distill out poetically concise rules. The key one in this book is: "Every increment of construction must be made in such a way as to heal the city." One is halfway through the book, charmed and somewhat persuaded, before it becomes apparent that this is a form of planning devoid of any plans whatever. It is a system which learns as it goes, getting by efficiently and wholesomely on general rules instead of detailed schemes. —Stewart Brand*

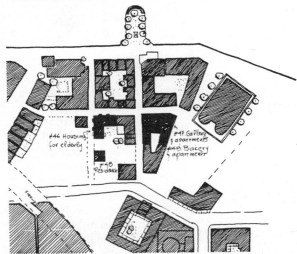

"Meanwhile, small buildings which filled out the grid continued to be built. The bakery, the housing for the elderly, the art gallery, and a small residence are among the most charming."

A New Theory of Urban Design
Christopher Alexander
1987; 251 pp.; **$39.95**
(postage varies by location)
from: Oxford University Press
2001 Evans Road
Cary, North Carolina 27513
(919) 677-0977 ✻WEA

•

In each of these growing wholes, there are certain fundamental and essential features:

First, the whole grows piecemeal, bit by bit.

Second, the whole is unpredictable. When it starts coming into being, it is not yet clear how it will continue, or where it will end, because only the interaction of the growth, with the whole's own laws, can suggest its continuation and its end.

Third, the whole is coherent. It is truly whole, not fragmented, and its parts are also whole, related like the parts of a dream to one another, in surprising and complex ways.

Fourth, the whole is full of feeling, always. This happens because the wholeness itself touches us, reaches the deepest levels in us, has the power to move us, to bring us to tears, to make us happy.

•

The principle that roads are built incrementally, to serve buildings, and fitted to the buildings after the buildings are conceived, not before, is of *immense* importance.

We insisted on this rule during the experiment, simply because present-day urban development is ruined, most often, by the hierarchy of decisions in which the road network comes first, buildings come second, and pedestrian space comes third.

The correct sequence, as we are trying to show in this system of rules, is just the opposite: pedestrian space *first,* buildings second, and roads *third.*

Sustainable Communities

"Sustainability implies that the use of energy and materials in an urban area be in balance with what the region can supply continuously through natural processes such as photosynthesis, biological decomposition and the biochemical processes that support life. The immediate implications of this principle are a vastly reduced energy budget for cities, and a smaller, more compact urban pattern interspersed with productive areas to collect energy, grow crops for food, fiber and energy, and recycle wastes."

How this concept is to be implemented is what this book is about. It isn't just talk; there are case studies and lots of eminently practical ideas here, complete with the economics. The call to action is backed philosophically by seven essays from authors such as Paul Hawken and John Todd. Solid and timely, the book is a recipe for what we can and probably must do. —JB

•

The Village Center proposal is a direct descendant of the "neighborhood school planning" dogma which dominated suburban planning a generation ago. Then, the key concept was to locate neighborhoods around a half mile walking radius of the elementary school. Today, education and other key consumer services may form the core for new pedestrian oriented energy efficient communities.

Leon Krier's drawings diagram two radical opposites: The 20th century tendency toward functional zoning made possible by the auto, and a mixed use urban quarter scaled by the pedestrian and conceived as a complete community. He challenges the modern notion of technical progress while advocating a return to the traditional form of old European cities.

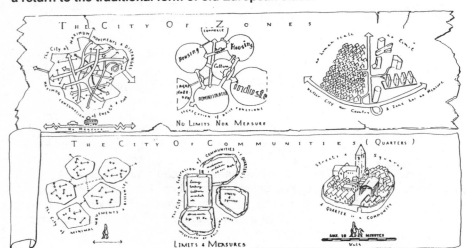

Sustainable Communities
Sim Van der Ryn and Peter Calthorpe; 1986
238 pp.; **$25** ($29.50 postpaid) from:
Sierra Club Bookstore
730 Polk Street, San Francisco, CA 94109
(415) 923-5500 ✻WEA

Redesigning the American Dream

Do you dream of living in a single-family home? You might find this eloquent argument against the idea provocative. Architect Dolores Hayden shows that the traditional home is often inappropriate for the rising number of single-parent families, families with more than one adult wage earner, and the elderly. Much better would be further development of the housing we already have by means of "mother-in-law" apartments and cleverly refurbished neighborhoods. The role (some would say plight) of women is discussed with unusual sensitivity — rare in books addressing planning — with women's needs incorporated centrally into every proposed design. I found the level of research to be deeper than other books on the subject, and mercifully free of simplistic analysis. Easy to read too; no academic poopadoodle at all. —JB

Redesigning the American Dream, Dolores Hayden
1984; 270 pp.; **$10.95**
($11.45 postpaid) from:
W.W. Norton
500 5th Avenue
New York, NY 10110
(212) 354-5500 ✻WEA

Nina West Homes for single parents and their children. The child-

care center is at the back of the site on the ground level; the corridor between apartments also serves as a children's play area. Kitchen windows offer easy observation of the corridor, and intercoms link units for easier babysitting.

•

Access to the public domain is especially difficult for older women. After age sixty-five, many women reap the results of a lifetime of low earnings, limited mobility, and self-sacrifice. In a study of 82,000 widows in Chicago, Helena Lopata found that over half of them did not go to public places, and over a fifth did not even go visiting. While 82 percent were not in a position to offer transportation to others, 45 percent had no one, of any age, to rely on for transportation.

The Living City

A report from the front lines where cities are being revitalized and destroyed — often at the same time. It's the Byzantine politics view, where City Hall often wins. Whole Earth doesn't often review what's-wrong books, but sometimes a close look at real failures and lost battles gives a realistic idea of what to do next. —JB

The Living City
Roberta Brandes Gratz
1989; 414 pp.; **$10.95**
($12.45 postpaid) from:
Simon and Schuster
Attn.: Mail Order Dept.
200 Old Tappan Rd.
Old Tappan, N.J. 07675
(800) 223-2348 ✻WEA

•

Sadly, the Vieux Carrés, the SoHos and the Old

The Granite Garden

Very much in the tradition of Jane Jacobs, Ian McHarg, and Christopher Alexander, this author examines the role of nature in cities. The critique here is easy pickings, because cities, whether severely planned or done laissez faire, almost always end up wrong. The value of this book is in its balance between problems and solutions. Spirn quickly makes it apparent that healthy, workable answers to the dilemma of urban designs are not scarce commodities — techniques abound. What is lacking is economic and political will, and enough of a sense of tradition to allow for perseverance. —Richard Nilsen

The Granite Garden
Anne Whiston Spirn; 1984
334 pp.; **$15.95** ($19.45 postpaid) from: Basic Books, Route 3 Box 20B Downsville Pike Hagerstown, MD 21740 (800) 638-3030 ✳WEA

The Riverway, Boston, ca 1892, showing graded embankments ready for planting. To the right, a mound separates the park from a recently installed trolley line. (Below) Approximately thirty years after construction, having achieved a wholly "natural" appearance, the adjacent trolley line now hidden behind mound and plants. Project was primarily for flood control.

Bioshelters, Ocean Arks, City Farming

"If the discoveries of the New Alchemy Institute are so important, why aren't you rich?" a Famous Person once asked John Todd, cofounder of the Institute. Good question. The answer is that ideas not obviously mainstream take a while to be accepted, no matter how wonderful. Convincing demonstrations don't necessarily help either; note that there have been practical solar homes for decades, but no solar building boom until builders, buyers, bankers and educators had sufficient incentive. Recent work, imaginatively reported, got things started.

The New Alchemy Institute's experiments (see p. 83) in aquaculture, bioshelters, small-scale farming and innovative architecture have proven successful, but so far have not ignited a massive thrust towards an ecologically sound, sustainable economy. Perhaps this has been because citizens haven't been able to see how these concepts might apply to their lives. This book elucidates an exciting collection of ideas that are a natural extension of New Alchemy thought — things that are now possible. It's a positive, hopeful view of what we can, and probably must, do soon. —JB
•
There is a science to working with existing forms and structures. It is comprised of a peculiar mixture of theory, research, and practicality — a science of "found objects." It does not attempt to build from scratch, but takes what exists and works to transform it to something useful or relevant. The French anthropologist Claude Levi-Strauss has described it as bricolage. Practitioners are bricoleurs, which translates rather clumsily as "enlightened tinkerers with what is at hand." In an

Bioshelters, Ocean Arks, City Farming
(Ecology as the Basis of Design) Nancy Jack Todd & John Todd; 1984; 210 pp. **$10.95** ($13.95 postpaid) from: Sierra Club Books, 730 Polk Street, San Francisco CA 94109; (415) 923-5500 ✳WEA

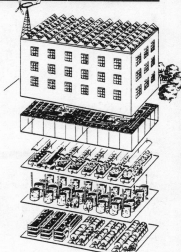

Warehouse Farm Company, Inner City or Suburban. 3rd floor: lettuces; 2nd floor: hydroponic peas, tomatoes, and cucumber; 1st floor: chickens, eggs and trout, catfish culture; basement: mushrooms and compost.

age of increasing scarcity, such a person is potentially a kind of hero, someone who can see with different eyes and utilize available resources. A lack or problem is not seen only as a burden, but an opportunity. A bricoleur can see what was, is, and can be as splendid continuum — one that must come full circle. Whereas most developers destroy before rebuilding, restorationists rebuild to recapture former glories, and designers prefer a clean slate, the bricoleur works from the assumption that the true potential of a house, a block, a whole town, or any other existing area, has scarcely been tapped.

Creating Successful Communities

Can inevitable growth be controlled? A quick look around any suburban area will convince you that there's no hope. Yet these authors say there is, and back their optimistic answer with a selection of effective strategies, many of which have been proven to work. The examples are presented from an insider's view, with enough detail to get you started taking on the black-hat locals messing up your space. The book is actually an action manual — particularly useful to folks whose annoyance has matured into outrage. For those that don't quite know what to do about it and are afraid of making naive mistakes, it's warpaint. —JB

Creating Successful Communities
Michael A. Mantell Stephen F. Harper & Luther Propst 1990; 230 pp. **$24.95** ($26.95 postpaid) from: Island Press Box 7, Covelo, CA 95428 (800) 828-1302 ✳WEA

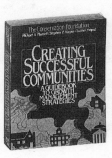

•

Growth Patterns

For many years, the Nantucket community had been trying to concentrate growth in existing village centers, away from open moors and beaches. However, every year more than 500 lots are subdivided on the island, and land prices jump about 20 percent. Off-island second-home owners buy about two-thirds of the real estate on the island.

Measures Taken

Other private and nonprofit efforts on the island, although without a direct role in the land bank, have preserved more than a third of the island over the past 25 years. The local land trust, the Nantucket Conservation Foundation, contributes enormously to preservation successes, and continues to demonstrate strong support. Recently, a 900-acre tract, equaling the acreage of all the lands acquired by the land bank, was donated to the Massachusetts Audubon Society in a will. The land bank program complements these private initiatives, and continued coordination with such efforts is important.

•
Towns of our cities are rapidly diminishing. Some that haven't fallen under the bulldozer of earlier "renewal" programs are being rediscovered and gradually rejuvenated. The real trick is, first, to make the citadel of power in every large or small community aware of the potential of the useful areas that remain, and, second, to extract a commitment to rejuvenation through "process," not "development" — through a process that includes participation of a spectrum of willing "small redoers," from individuals to small developers, instead of development only by project developers, and that also includes innovative strategies which involve more than physical rebuilding. That, in fact, is the consistent lesson of the string of revitalization stories just highlighted, starting with Ithaca. All these stories and the earlier ones of Savannah, the South Bronx, Cincinnati, Pittsburgh and Toronto underscore the appropriateness and success of the genuine rebirth *process* in contrast to misleading redevelopment *projects*.

•
Lincoln Center: Urban Devitalizer

I live near Lincoln Center, one of the earliest separatist centers, a trend-setter for marbleized entertainment centers that look more like giant mausolea than seats of culture. Lincoln Center is a self-contained center without streets, without any connection to its surrounding urban fabric, without anything to relate to its neighbors. It sits alone in isolated glory and could just as well be in the Mojave Desert.

Civic, cultural or shopping centers like this are alien schemes imposed on the texture of a singular place. They don't mend torn pieces of urban fabric. They destroy what exists. They replace. They are imbued with revitalization attributes they don't deserve. Their promoters use them to promise what can't be delivered. When the promise does not follow construction, few care enough to look back to recognize the mistaken assessment.

See Also . . .
Page 49, for more on urban climate control.

Living Simply

There *are* technologically and philosophically simpler ways of living, and they can work very nicely, thank you. It isn't obligatory to be part of a community of like-minded folks, but it helps. Best results seem to come when self-congratulation, flagellation or involuntary inducement is not involved. Ultimately, it's less a matter of hardware than of attitude — how you relate to the earth and its inhabitants. —*JB*

The Riddle of Amish Culture

The riddle of Amish culture in America is: how does it continue to dramatically prosper while unilaterally resisting the very core of mainstream American prosperity — technology? The surprising answer — adaptation and compromise — is given in loving detail in this great book. —Kevin Kelly

•

The Amish think modern children are spoiled by being driven from club to club and lesson to lesson in hopes that they will find and express their true selves. In contrast, Amish children are washing dishes by hand, feeding cows, hauling manure, pulling weeds, and mowing lawns. They are learning to lose their selves, to yield to the larger purposes of family and community. JOY, a widely used school motto, reminds children that *Jesus* is first, you are last, and others are in between.

The inconvenience of walking a half-mile to use a phone or taking messages from an answering service is a daily reminder that membership in an ethnic community exacts a price — a reminder that things that are too handy and too convenient lead to sloth and pride.

A community phone shanty shared by several farmers.

The Riddle of Amish Culture
Donald B. Kraybill; 1989; 304 pp.; **$8.95** ($10.95 postpaid) from: Johns Hopkins University Press, 701 West 40th Street, Suite 275 Baltimore, MD 21211 (800) 537-5487 ✳WEA

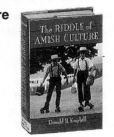

•

The Amish have been willing to negotiate. They have made numerous technological concessions that have reaped handsome financial benefits. While holding firm to some taboos, they have not allowed religious practices to erode the economic base of their community. Their flexibility has energized the fiscal and cultural vitality of their community.

Despite their flexibility, the Amish have insisted on the supremacy of the group over that of the individual. Excessive individualism, which threatens to splinter the collective order, is simply not tolerated. In both childhood and adulthood, the individual remains subordinate and submissive to community discipline.

•

They have adamantly opposed government "handouts," from Social Security to agricultural subsidies. This repudiation has baffled government bureaucrats. The Amish feared that members who were heavily insured and living on government "handouts" would have little interest in giving and receiving mutual aid. The Amish rejection of Social Security and other government subsidies was necessary to preserve two cherished ideals: community self-reliance and the religious belief that church members are obliged to provide for the economic welfare of their brothers and sisters.

Amish Society

The Amish are a religious community that originated in Europe during the Reformation and is now concentrated in Ohio, Pennsylvania, and Indiana. They are one of the most resilient subcultures in America and also some of our best farmers. Sociologists keep waiting for them to die out or otherwise homogenize into the goo of the American melting pot, but this they refuse to do.

This definitive study, by an Amishman turned college professor, is a fascinating history and provides a detailed look inside the Amish character. Their way of life, which from the outside may look hard or dull or quaint or boring, turns out to be a model for the necessary values embodied in the concepts of community and local politics. —*Richard Nilsen*

Amish Society, John Hostetler 1980; 432 pp.; **$9.95** ($11.95 postpaid) from: Johns Hopkins University Press 701 West 40th Street, Suite 275 Baltimore, MD 21211 (800) 537-5487 ✳WEA

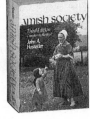

•

Amish communities are not relics of a bygone era. Rather, they are demonstrations of a different form of modernity.

The traditional barn-raising, a form of economic sharing in times of need, symbolizes the concern Amish members have for one another's welfare.

•

The Amish people maintain a human rather than an organizational scale in their daily lives. They resisted the large, consolidated school and the proposition that big schools (or farms) were better than small ones. A bureaucracy that places pupils together within narrow age limits and emphasizes science and technology to the exclusion of sharing values and personal responsibility is not tolerated. The Amish appreciate thinking that makes the world, and their own lives, intelligible to them. When human groups and units of work become too large for them, a sense of estrangement sets in. When this happens the world becomes unintelligible to them and they cease participating in what is meaningless.

The Simple Life

Those of us who would like to see the simple life become a norm in this great land of ours may find this a distressing book. Since Colonial times, numerous ideologies of and attempts at simple living have flamed briefly, only to be overwhelmed by the indomitable spirit of materialism and privatism that seems far more native to the American character than material simplicity. Nevertheless, plain living is an idea that can't be conquered, and in chronicling its history Shi relates a considerable sweep of this nation's history and higher yearnings. —*Stephanie Mills*

The Simple Life (Plain Living and High Thinking in American Culture), David E. Shi; 1985; 332 pp.; **$9.95** ($12.45 postpaid) from: Oxford University Press 16-00 Pollitt Drive, Fair Lawn NJ 07410; (800) 451-7556 ✳WEA

•

Essentially, it seems, the much-ballyhooed "frugality phenomenon" of the 1970s was limited to middle-and-upper-middle-class activists. Students, professors, environmentalists, consumer advocates, and idealists of various kinds were its most prominent and serious participants, and the predictions of a massive shift to simpler ways of living among the larger public were overstated.

•

The weaknesses seem clear. Proponents of the simple life have frequently been overly nostalgic about the quality of life in olden times, narrowly anti-urban in outlook, and too disdainful of the benefits of prosperity and technology. . . .

The radical critics of capitalism and promoters of spartan rusticity among the advocates of the simple life would be well advised to acknowledge that material progress and urban life can frequently be compatible with spiritual, moral, or intellectual concerns. As Lewis Mumford, one of the sanest of all the simplifiers, stressed in *The Conduct of Life*: "It is not enough to say, as Rousseau once did, that one has only to reverse all the current practices to be right. . . . If our new philosophy is well-grounded we shall not merely react against the 'air-conditioned nightmare' of our present culture; we shall also carry into the future many elements of quality that this culture actually embraces."

Down Home Country

Some people go to Amish country to gawk, as if they were visiting some sort of zoo. But many others go to take a look, to see for themselves how these gentle people manage to live so well. A consequent tourism has developed — serving up both tacky knick-knacks and marvelous calico, Disneyfied myth and the real thing. Amish furniture and craftwork abounds. The food tends to be hearty, cholesterol-ignoring and yummy. This tour guide features it all, from tacky to terrific. With maps. —*JB*

Down Home Country
Ora E. Miller, Editor **$5.95**/year (1 issue each spring) from: Down Home Publications, Inc. P.O. Box 418 Millersburg, OH 44654

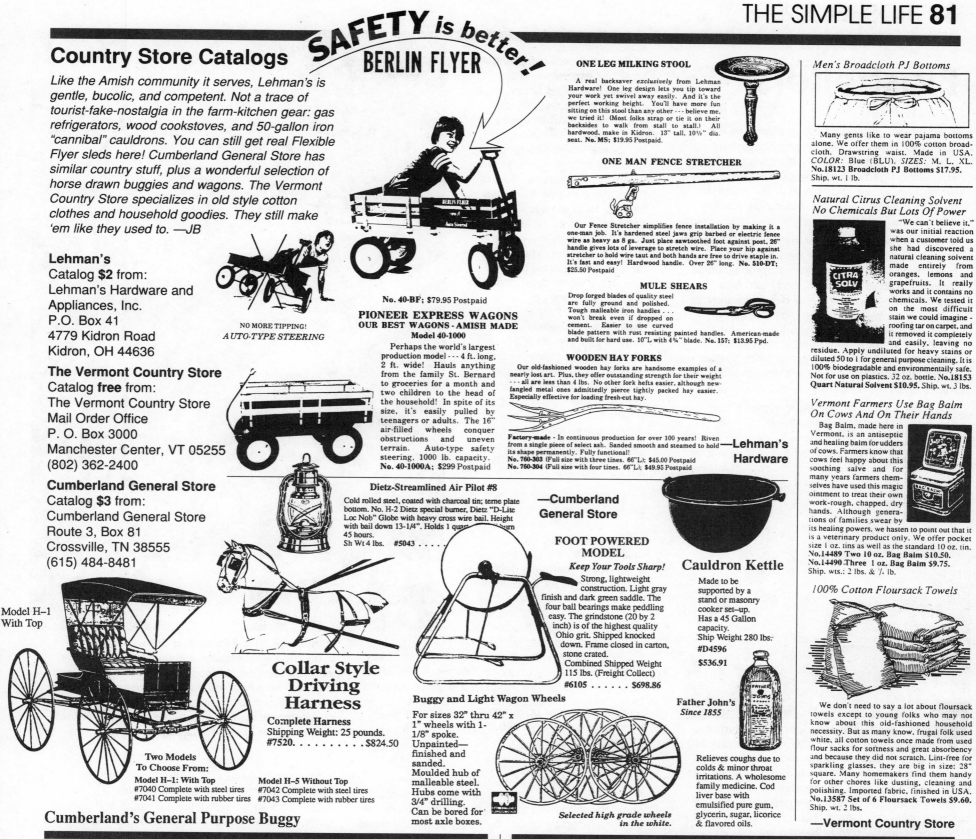

Country Store Catalogs

Like the Amish community it serves, Lehman's is gentle, bucolic, and competent. Not a trace of tourist-fake-nostalgia in the farm-kitchen gear: gas refrigerators, wood cookstoves, and 50-gallon iron "cannibal" cauldrons. You can still get real Flexible Flyer sleds here! Cumberland General Store has similar country stuff, plus a wonderful selection of horse drawn buggies and wagons. The Vermont Country Store specializes in old style cotton clothes and household goodies. They still make 'em like they used to. —JB

Lehman's
Catalog $2 from:
Lehman's Hardware and
Appliances, Inc.
P.O. Box 41
4779 Kidron Road
Kidron, OH 44636

The Vermont Country Store
Catalog **free** from:
The Vermont Country Store
Mail Order Office
P. O. Box 3000
Manchester Center, VT 05255
(802) 362-2400

Cumberland General Store
Catalog $3 from:
Cumberland General Store
Route 3, Box 81
Crossville, TN 38555
(615) 484-8481

Model H–1
With Top

Cumberland's General Purpose Buggy

Collar Style Driving Harness

Complete Harness
Shipping Weight: 25 pounds.
#7520 . . . . $824.50

**Two Models
To Choose From:**
Model H–1: With Top
#7040 Complete with steel tires
#7041 Complete with rubber tires

Model H–5 Without Top
#7042 Complete with steel tires
#7043 Complete with rubber tires

SAFETY is better!
BERLIN FLYER

NO MORE TIPPING!
AUTO-TYPE STEERING

No. 40-BF; $79.95 Postpaid
**PIONEER EXPRESS WAGONS
OUR BEST WAGONS - AMISH MADE**
Model 40-1000

Perhaps the world's largest production model - - - 4 ft. long, 2 ft. wide! Hauls anything from the family St. Bernard to groceries for a month and two children to the head of the household! In spite of its size, it's easily pulled by teenagers or adults. The 16" air-filled wheels conquer obstructions and uneven terrain. Auto-type safety steering, 1000 lb. capacity.
No. 40-1000A; $299 Postpaid

Dietz-Streamlined Air Pilot #8
Cold rolled steel, coated with charcoal tin; terne plate bottom. No. H-2 Dietz special burner, Dietz "D-Lite Loc Nob" Globe with heavy cross wire bail. Height with bail down 13-1/4". Holds 1 quart will burn 45 hours.
Sh Wt 4 lbs. **#5043** . . . . .

Buggy and Light Wagon Wheels
For sizes 32" thru 42" x 1" wheels with 1-1/8" spoke. Unpainted—finished and sanded. Moulded hub of malleable steel. Hubs come with 3/4" drilling. Can be bored for most axle boxes.

Selected high grade wheels in the white.

ONE LEG MILKING STOOL
A real backsaver *exclusively* from Lehman Hardware! One leg design lets you tip toward your work yet swivel away easily. And it's the perfect working height. You'll have more fun sitting on this stool than any other - - - believe me, we tried it! (Most folks strap or tie it on their backsides to walk from stall to stall.) All hardwood, make in Kidron. 13" tall, 10½" dia. seat. No. MS; $19.95 postpaid.

ONE MAN FENCE STRETCHER
Our Fence Stretcher simplifies fence installation by making it a one-man job. It's hardened steel jaws grip barbed or electric fence wire as heavy as 8 ga. Just place sawtoothed foot against post, 26" handle gives lots of leverage to stretch wire. Place your hip against stretcher to hold wire taut and both hands are free to drive staple in. It's fast and easy! Hardwood handle. Over 26" long. No. 510-DT; $25.50 Postpaid

MULE SHEARS
Drop forged blades of quality steel are fully ground and polished. Tough malleable iron handles . . . won't break even if dropped on cement. Easier to use curved blade pattern with rust resisting painted handles. American-made and built for hard use. 10"L with 4¾" blade. No. 157; $13.95 Ppd.

WOODEN HAY FORKS
Our old-fashioned wooden hay forks are handsome examples of a nearly lost art. Plus, they offer outstanding strength for their weight - - - all are less than 4 lbs. No other fork hefts easier, although new-fangled metal ones admittedly pierce tightly packed hay easier. Especially effective for loading fresh-cut hay.

Factory-made - In continuous production for over 100 years! Riven from a single piece of select ash. Sanded smooth and steamed to hold its shape permanently. Fully functional!
No. 760-303 (Full size with three tines. 66"L); $45.00 Postpaid
No. 760-304 (Full size with four tines. 66"L); $49.95 Postpaid

—Lehman's Hardware

—Cumberland General Store

FOOT POWERED MODEL
Keep Your Tools Sharp!
Strong, lightweight construction. Light gray finish and dark green saddle. The four ball bearings make peddling easy. The grindstone (20 by 2 inch) is of the highest quality Ohio grit. Shipped knocked down. Frame closed in carton, stone crated.
Combined Shipped Weight 115 lbs. (Freight Collect)
#6105 . . . . . . $698.86

Cauldron Kettle
Made to be supported by a stand or masonry cooker set–up. Has a 45 Gallon capacity.
Ship Weight 280 lbs.
#D4596
$536.91

Father John's
Since 1855
Relieves coughs due to colds & minor throat irritations. A wholesome family medicine. Cod liver base with emulsified pure gum, glycerin, sugar, licorice & flavored oils.

Men's Broadcloth PJ Bottoms
Many gents like to wear pajama bottoms alone. We offer them in 100% cotton broadcloth. Drawstring waist. Made in USA. *COLOR:* Blue (BLU). *SIZES:* M. L. XL. No.18123 Broadcloth PJ Bottoms $17.95. Ship. wt. 1 lb.

*Natural Citrus Cleaning Solvent
No Chemicals But Lots Of Power*
"We can't believe it." was our initial reaction when a customer told us she had discovered a natural cleaning solvent made entirely from oranges, lemons and grapefruits. It really works and it contains no chemicals. We tested it on the most difficult stain we could imagine - roofing tar on carpet, and it removed it completely and easily, leaving no residue. Apply undiluted for heavy stains or diluted 50 to 1 for general purpose cleaning. It is 100% biodegradable and environmentally safe. Not for use on plastics. 32 oz. bottle. **No.18153 Quart Natural Solvent $10.95.** Ship. wt. 3 lbs.

*Vermont Farmers Use Bag Balm
On Cows And On Their Hands*
Bag Balm, made here in Vermont, is an antiseptic and healing balm for udders of cows. Farmers know that cows feel happy about this soothing salve and for many years farmers themselves have used this magic ointment to treat their own work-rough, chapped, dry hands. Although generations of families swear by its healing powers, we hasten to point out that it is a veterinary product only. We offer pocket size 1 oz. tins as well as the standard 10 oz. tin.
No.14489 Two 10 oz. Bag Balm $10.50.
No.14490 Three 1 oz. Bag Balm $9.75.
Ship. wts.: 2 lbs. & ½ lb.

100% Cotton Floursack Towels
We don't need to say a lot about floursack towels except to young folks who may not know about this old-fashioned household necessity. But as many know, frugal folk used white, all cotton towels once made from used flour sacks for softness and great absorbency and because they did not scratch. Lint-free for sparkling glasses, they are big in size: 28" square. Many homemakers find them handy for other chores like dusting, cleaning and polishing. Imported fabric, finished in USA. **No.13587 Set of 6 Floursack Towels $9.60.** Ship. wt. 2 lbs.

—**Vermont Country Store**

Voluntary Simplicity

The theory of improving everything by simplifying one's life — save the Earth, save your civilization, save yourself. I figure, if it feels good, it'll happen. Fortunately it feels good. This book gives context and motivation, not how-to.
—Stewart Brand

•

Satisfactions: Life is a lot simpler — I no longer spend twenty-four hours a month shaving legs and curling hair and god knows how long driving back and forth to Safeway. Life is infinitely cheaper — releasing money for the real luxuries of life. Dissatisfactions: outward appearances suggest poverty, and this culture is very discriminatory toward the poor. . . .

(woman, twenty-eight, married, rural, west)

•

A self-reinforcing spiral of growth begins to unfold for those who choose to participate in the world in a life-sensing and life-serving manner. As we live more voluntarily — more consciously — we feel less identified with our material possessions and thereby are enabled to live more simply. As we live more simply, our lives become less filled with unnecessary distractions, we find it easier to bring our undivided attention into our passage through life, and thereby are enabled to live more consciously.

Voluntary Simplicity
(Toward A Way of Life that is Outwardly Simple, Inwardly Rich), Duane Elgin 1981; 312 pp.; **$7.95** ($9.45 postpaid) from: William Morrow & Co. P. O. Box 1219 39 Plymouth St. Fairfield, NJ 07007 (800) 843-9389 ✳WEA

Portable Dwelling Info-Letter

Would you live under a tarp in the forest? We're not talking bag-ladies here; there are folks who by choice live at the extreme limits of simplicity, using technology only where it would be nutty not to. They live lightly, as more-or-less permanent campers. How they do it is served by this modest newsletter. It's replete with helpful hints, news of friends, a bit o' philosophy, and the necessarily gritty details that attend life in the boonies.

Walden lives! —JB

Portable Dwelling Info-Letter
(formerly Message Post); **$5.50**
(six issues; $1 for sample issue)
from: Portable Dwelling Info-Letter
P.O. Box 190, Philomath, OR 97370

DWELLING WITHOUT DRIVE-WAYS. A case for living in portable self-contained structures on steep or rough lands left natural, to save money, energy, croplands. CORDIAL CO-OP CAMPING. SAVE RENT! PITCH A TENT (Set #D) All 3 for $1

WINGS & ROOTS: Choosing a Dwellingway. Compares 5 kinds of portability plus some settled ways. (Report#C) By S.Lund $1

WINTERING IN A TENT. Choosing tent and site. Making it warmer,drier. 12 LIGHT WAYS TO WINTER WARMTH,usual & unusual. WHAT KIND OF PORTABLE SHELTER? Good and bad features of various. TWIPI STUDY PLANS. This low cone-shaped shelter withstands rain, wind, sun, snow load. Body heat alone sufficient in most climates. (Set #W) All 4 for $1

We've never had any trouble entertaining friends during good weather as long as we are in a place where the owners of the place want to join in the party (i.e. we have the same circle of friends). We just throw a barbeque party, pull out the guitar, and sit around and sing.
While living in a house last winter, all of us were homesick for our yurt - except for our oldest boy because he likes cooking with the electric kitchen gadgets. Once I read that some Mongolians obtained a castle in which to live. They put their animals in the castle and pitched their yurts outside the wall. Now I feel the same way.

Anne

Bioshelters

By J. Baldwin

Conceptually, it's house-as-consumer vs. house-as-provider. Most homes import some combination of electricity, gas, oil, firewood, water and food. They export garbage and wastewater. A vast and expensive system of umbilical wires, pipes and roads makes this possible, but not particularly desirable.

In contrast, a bioshelter can be designed to make its own electricity and heat the wash water. It raises food (except for Twinkies), processes or recycles most of its wastes, and maintains the desired air temperature — all directly or indirectly with solar power. Think of a bioshelter as a pleasant greenhouse that you live in. A larger bioshelter with dwelling units around its perimeter might serve institutions or even whole neighborhoods. (Note that the necessity for some sort of road remains; bioshelters are not a cure-all).

The basic idea isn't new. Greenhouses have been around for about 400 years, though few have been rigged as fulltime living space for people. In 1945, Buckminster Fuller proposed a "Garden-of-Eden Dome" as an alternative to conventional homes.

Bucky and Anne Fuller pose for his 85th birthday at Windstar in 1981. Behind them is a prototype of his "Fly's Eye" dome and the one remaining Dymaxion car, both flown in for the party. Never marketed, the Fly's Eye currently stars in a traveling Fuller exhibit. The 1934 three-wheeled Dymaxion car lives at Harrah's Auto Museum in Reno. It sat eleven people, could top 120 mph and got 30 miles per gallon using a crude Ford V8 engine.

The idea was to erect a lightweight, transparent geodesic dome — he called it a "Skybreak" — under which the occupants could control the weather. The protected interior could be fashioned imaginatively and economically from local materials, expressing the inhabitants' creativity to a much greater degree than is possible in a conventional house. (This answered critics accusing domes of "peas in a pod" sameness). The controlled climate would make possible "living outdoors-indoors" with aquaculture, agriculture, and even trees. The dome shells were to be be high-tech, permanent, maintenance-free, and very economical of resources. They would be inexpensively mass-produced from materials that resist deterioration. Being state-of-the-art, they would defer technical and stylistic obsolescence. Building time would be measured in hours instead of months; equally simple disassembly would permit relocation. Domes can easily be made earthquake and hurricane proof. With this interesting potential why has no Garden-of-Eden dome or other bioshelter-home been built?

As with any evolving idea, experimenters have approached the building of bioshelters in a variety of ways, not necessarily as domes. Biosphere II

(p. 6) is the most comprehensive, and expensive. More modest controlled ecosystems have been successfully demonstrated by Carl Hodges — now deeply involved in Biosphere II — and by the New Alchemy Institute, as well as a host of imitators. Most of these systems use fish tanks as solar heat storage. The fish eat dark-colored, solar heat absorbing algae, insects, and vegetable scraps. The warm tank water, enriched by "fish exhaust," is periodically used to irrigate gardens or hydroponic troughs. Properly designed, bioshelters can raise commercial quantities of vegetables (and fish) even in the off season, eliminating shipping costs, and keeping customers' money in the local economy. Bioshelters also work well for related uses; John Todd's Solar Aquatic Systems wastewater treatment facilities (p. 85) for example.

I mention proper design because glasshouses have a history of fragility and energy hunger, with resulting high maintenance costs. Traditional greenhouse materials deteriorate quickly under siege from weather, sunlight, mildew, corrosion, and rot. There has also been the persistent problem of controlling temperature and humidity extremes without resorting to economically and philosophically unacceptable fossil-fuelled heating and cooling. And there are difficulties with anachronistic building codes that label such buildings — even experimental ones — as "unfit for human habitation." To my knowledge, no insulated, transparent, permanent structure enjoys mass production at this time.

In 1982, terminal rot brought down the New Alchemy Institute's 2x4 and fiberglass geodesic dome greenhouse after less than a decade. It has been replaced by one of my designs, a pillowdome framed with aircraft aluminum tubing and skinned with argon-inflated triangular "pillows" fabricated from DuPont's Tefzel®. This tough, inert material is more transparent than glass, and is one of the few plastics not degraded by sunlight. (At least not for 27 years, the time samples have been out in Florida sun.) The inert argon gas acts as insulation — it's much better than air — and built-in fire suppression. The 31 ft. diameter dome weighs only 1/2 lb. per square foot, yet it has withstood 130 mph winds and heavy snow loads without damage. Structural parts shade only 4% of the floor; conventional greenhouses shade as much as 25%. It makes a respectable year-round greenhouse, but the temperature varies too much for human comfort. Mass production awaits expensive tooling.

The Windstar Foundation's 50 ft. diameter Biodome was calculated by Amy Edmondson and executed by John Katzenberger in 1986. These domes are skinned with translucent,

The 50 ft. Biodome at Windstar.

Windstar's 50 ft. Biodome at Snowmass, Colorado, grows vegetables and fish all year despite subzero winters. No fossil fuel is used; electricity comes from photovoltaic panels and a small water turbine. You can buy one, though it needs more development for use as a home. For another look at a Biodome exterior, see page 50.

triple-layer polycarbonate panels mounted on an aircraft aluminum framework. Like New Alchemy's bioshelters, this one houses fishtanks and gardens, the latter arrayed on three decks. There are eight Biodomes up or a-building at this time; one in Denmark. Another is planned for Soviet Georgia. They're located in various climates, a good way to learn the food-raising procedures for maximum yield anywhere.

A separate company, Biospaces, Inc. (P.O. Box 1725, Basalt, CO 81621; 303/963-0114), has been set up to produce hand-built Biodomes in various sizes. If you need a big, permanent Biodome today, Biospaces, Inc. can build you one. But not to live in; as with the pillowdome, the temperature varies too much for all-season human comfort. Prices are not outrageous.

When will bioshelters be able to house human beings? Soon, I'd guess. Recent developments in solar drying of fine furniture woods include a heat pump specifically designed to dehumidify an interior space without throwing away the heat. This should solve bioshelter condensation problems. There has been progress in maintaining steady interior temperatures as well.

Suntek

Ten years ago, Day Chahroudi was instrumental in developing a coating known as Heat Mirror®. It permits the passage of visible light, but blocks certain heat-carrying infra-red wavelengths. Heat Mirror is widely available today in premium grade windows upon which it bestows superior insulation qualities. But Heat Mirror doesn't entirely block the sun; if it did, a building would not be able to capture solar heat in the winter. Shading needs another material. Day Chahroudi has come up with it at last. His company, Suntek, calls it Cloud Gel®. This material is sandwiched between two layers of transparent plastic. When the sandwich reaches its designed temperature, it quickly turns a sun-reflecting opaque white. As the temperature cools, full transparency is restored.

This neatly and automatically takes care of the biggest problem with transparent buildings:

summer overheating. The advantage is particularly notable in dome-shaped structures; if highly reflective, domes will automatically develop an air circulation phenomenon that dramatically drops the interior temperature to about 15% less than that of its surroundings.

(This effect was discovered by Buckminster Fuller during World War II. I can personally attest that it occurs as claimed, and that it will work whether the dome is insulated or not. PhD, anyone?)

The most effective temperature control will occur when Heat Mirror and Cloud Gel are used together as Day proposed in 1970 before either material had been developed. I would guess that it is being tried now, perhaps by Day himself in one of his Climatic Envelopes, a version of the bioshelter

This is a model of Suntek's proposed 4000 sq.ft. headquarters building. Imagine how it would feel working in there at your desk under the trees, the balmy interior climate controlled without resort to furnace or air conditioner.

New Alchemy Institute's 31 ft. Pillowdome is skinned with Dupont Tefzel® pillows inflated with inert argon gas for insulation. Despite weighing only 450 lbs., hurricanes and snow loads have not been a problem.

he proposed 15 years ago. In any case, Day's efforts make possible self-regulating buildings with skins that act rather like our own. This capability combined with twenty years of bioshelter greenhouse experience make possible a truly new architecture; buildings that give more than they take. The next move is clear.

Suntek (Energy Materials for Buildings Through Molecular Design), Information **free** from: Suntek, Inc., 6817A Academy Parkway Albuquerque, NM 87109

The New Alchemy Institute

Twenty-one years ago, the Alkies set out to "restore the lands, protect the seas, and inform the Earth's stewards" — all that in addition to raising kids, running homes, and scraping together the necessary money. They've found that money is there for exploratory work if it is done according to accepted scientific standards. New Alchemy has been careful to avoid a reputation for funkiness, and so has received support from a host of grant-givers, including the National Science Foundation.

Like many groups (including Whole Earth) loosely dubbed "New Age" by media dumbheads, New Alchemy eventually suffered from success. They've long advocated and innovated organic food-raising, alternative energy, conservation of resources, and nonpolluting, sustainable ways of living — all demonstrated on their 12 acre spread on Cape Cod. When they started, that sort of thing was unheard of. Now it's mainstream to the extent of being trendy. While success has stolen a bit of New Alchemy's thunder, it has also raised a demand for their expertise. Thus the Alkies enter their third decade as consultants and teachers. Oh, there's still plenty of research going on; good teachers must stay ahead of the game.

The Institute offers all manner of apprenticeships, training programs, kid's classes, courses for academic credit, and lectures. They host thousands of visitors every year. They act as a clearing house for worldwide environmental consulting, an act made easier by the small army of ex-Alkies out there (I among them) and the irrefutable usefulness of their past work. If I starred everything in this Ecolog that has been written, accomplished or directly influenced by New Alchemists and friends, it'd look like the Milky Way. —JB

The New Alchemy Institute, $35/year (includes a subscription to New Alchemy Journal, free admission for tours, reduced tuition for courses, 20% discount on publications); Information **free** from: The New Alchemy Institute, 237 Hatchville Road, East Falmouth, MA 02536; (508) 564-6301

The Windstar Foundation

John Denver and Thomas Crum founded Windstar in 1976, to help create a more healthy environment through demonstration, research projects, and education. Windstar programs have emphasized personal and interpersonal development as well as ecology, noting that all must be healthy in a sustainable community. Like New Alchemy, Windstar has extensive organic gardens, a commercial-scale bioshelter, and an energy-efficient headquarters. They give lectures and workshops and sponsor symposia, including their famous annual "Choices for the Future" event. The good work gets spread around — they have Windstar Connection programs all over the world, executing

The grapevine growing happily under the roof announces harvest time by dropping grapes into the hexagonal pool, changing the water to a pale pink.

projects that encourage the building of a sustainable society.

Windstar (now in partnership with the National Wildlife Federation) enters the 90s with advanced bioshelter research, and a comprehensive education effort that includes a cultural exchange program and lots of new publications from their Earth Pulse project (p. 109). Visitors, volunteers, participants, supporters, and sometimes apprentices, welcome. —JB

The Windstar Foundation, $35/year (includes subscription to Windstar Journal); Information **free** from: The Windstar Foundation, 2317 Snowmass Creek Road, Snowmass, CO 81654-9198; (303) 927-4777 or (800) 669-4777

Living Under Glass

Recent surveys have shown most people use their sunspace or attached greenhouse as a family room instead of as a garden. Sure, they have plants in there, but the main attraction is aesthetic. The natural light, the often (but not always) pleasant climate, and the feeling of being in a private, protected outdoors are charming effects, particularly in a city home. People like being under glass. That charm is captured nicely in this collection of exceptional color photographs of occasionally lived-in greenhouses, old and new, from many countries. They make you want live that way. In a bioshelter, perhaps? —JB

Living Under Glass (Sunrooms, Greenhouses, and Conservatories) Jane Tresidder and Stafford Cliff 1986; 166 pp. **$22.50** ($27 postpaid) from: Publisher's Central Bureau 1 Champion Avenue Avenel, NJ 07001 (201) 382-7960 **✱WEA**

*WEA — Available from Whole Earth Access, see p. 2.

We All Live Downstream

From the karst (limestone) watersheds of Eureka Springs comes the most radical support for waterless toilets. Plagued by underground pollution, The Water Center has produced the only in-print book surveying dry toilets — from commercial varieties to home-grown; from incinolets to moulder (cold, slow compost) varieties. I would like more about dry toilet headaches; flies, shock loading, maintenance, installation, quality of final compost. But there is no better access.

***Downstream** also surveys greywater systems and community water politics, knowing full well that water connects and our feces are but fine fertilizers for future food. An impressive, populist production. —Peter Warshall*

We All Live Downstream
(A Guide To Waste Treatment That Stops Water Pollution)
Pat Costner with Glenna Booth and Holly Gettings; 1986; 92 pp.
$6.95 ($7.95 postpaid) from: Bookpeople, 2929 5th St. Berkeley, CA 94710; (800) 624-4466 **✱WEA**
●

Our entire culture was toilet-trained to water in only a few generations. The fundamental measure of social competence and acceptability became the ability to relate successfully to a flush toilet. More than the car, telephone or television (and certainly more than the eagle), the water toilet is the symbol of our society.

In its change from novelty to apparent necessity, the water toilet also changed our culture's attitude toward water. The status of water plummeted from "sacred source of life" to "waste sump." At the same time, the water toilet changed our attitudes toward our body products. By interrupting the return of feces and urine to the soil, the water toilet hid their purpose as links in the food chain.

On-Site Wastewater Treatment Systems

This booklet gives you a look at conventional home septic systems and some available alternatives. All are explained and illustrated. Just what you need to read if you're considering a domestic wastewater treatment system. With glossary and annotated bibliography. —JB

On-Site Wastewater Treatment Systems
Technical Bulletin No. 6
Tad Montgomery
1990; 24 pp.
$4.50 ($6.50 postpaid) from: New Alchemy Institute
237 Hatchville Road
East Falmouth, MA 02536
(508) 564-6301
●

The EPA National Small Flows Clearinghouse, 258 Stewart Street, West Virginia University, Morgantown WV 26506; phone: 800-624-8301. This organization was set up in 1977 through the Clean Water Act in order to facilitate the design, planning and construction of innovative and alternative decentralized wastewater treatment facilities in areas where conventional systems are not economically feasible. Programs include a newsletter, computer bibliographies on topics ranging from composting toilets to failing septic systems, design modules to help in evaluating technologies ranging from mound systems to vacuum sewers, septage management and novel alternatives, and case studies of a number of different decentralized waste systems. A forthcoming project involves the videotaping of various aspects of select waste treatment technologies.

Gray Water Use in the Landscape

Waste has become synonymous with the American lifestyle, and our use of water is no exception. Altho government policy wastes water it isn't necessary that the individual do the same, so as agribiz empties aquifers it's possible for individuals to conserve their own.

*Despite our American lifestyle, middle-class sanitation hangups and archaic health codes, "gray water," anything that's not sewage, is still useful, even tho it may have just finished washing your dishes. Robert Kourik, author of the **Edible Landscape** book (p. 48), gives us some practical ways to convert household plumbing to a graywater system, diverting water that used to go down the tubes to irrigation instead.*

Kourik's pamphlet is based on his experiences during the last California drought, when he struggled with a bureaucracy that briefly relaxed the rules to permit legal experimentation. It's conservative, but will guide the conversion of a home plumbing system into a home irrigation system, a subtle form of un-American behavior that your local aquifer will appreciate. —Dick Fugett

*Once a year Edible Publications will produce a 26 page update to **Gray Water Use in the Landscape**. Also by the time you read this, Edible Publications will offer the "Graytest Little Catalog of Grayt Products" including gray water laundry*

Gray Water Use in the Landscape, Robert Kourik; 1988; 25 pp.; **$6** postpaid **✱WEA**

Graytest Little Catalog and update information

All from: Edible Publications P.O. Box 1841, Santa Rosa, CA 95402

soap with a NPK rating of 4-2.9-6.1 and 7.7 pH which comes out of your machine as gray water fertilizer, plus gray water reuse systems and components and much more. Can't wait to see it!!
—Susan Erkel Ryan

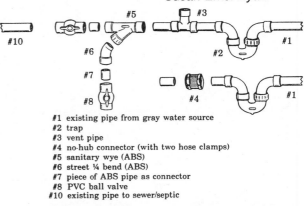

#1 existing pipe from gray water source
#2 trap
#3 vent pipe
#4 no-hub connector (with two hose clamps)
#5 sanitary wye (ABS)
#6 street ¼ bend (ABS)
#7 piece of ABS pipe as connector
#8 PVC ball valve
#10 existing pipe to sewer/septic

Always cut into your existing plumbing after (down hill from) the vent pipe(s). If you're cutting into metal pipe you must use a no-hub connector and tighten the two hose clamps carefully.

Septic Tank Practices

A modest title for a book that clearly lays out aspects of various types of on-site sewage treatment and their relationship to soil, water use, construction, maintenance, and politics. Written by a brilliant biologist who has integrated theory with a practical hands-on approach. —Sim Van Der Ryn

This book is wonderful — outrageous and authoritative simultaneously. —Stewart Brand

Septic Tank Practices; Peter Warshall; 1979; 177 pp.; **$4.95** ($7.95 postpaid) from: Whole Earth Access, Mail Order Dept., 2990 Seventh Street, Berkeley, CA 94710; (800) 845-2000
●

Turn the faucet, and magically "clean water" appears. Flush, and "magically" everything empties into the unknown.

Annals of Earth

*Is it possible to regularly publish news of applied ecology without endlessly reclothing the same old stuff in trendy garb? You bet your bippy it is! As edited by Nancy Jack Todd, **Annals** reports brave experiments — proposed and in progress, physical and intellectual — in articles by the experimenters themselves. It's a good place to keep up with the works of Ocean Arks (opposite) and the New Alchemy Institute (p.83) as well as a great assortment of other enterprises. This is one of the few publications I subscribe to. —JB*

Annals of Earth, Nancy Jack Todd, Editor; **$10**/year (4 issues) from: Annals of Earth 10 Shanks Pond Road, Falmouth, MA 02540

Low-Water-Use Toilets

Here's a bit of odoriferous trivia: If you sun-dried an entire year's worth of your excrement (downwind, I trust), it would fit into a couple of shoeboxes. It would also be a highly concentrated source of many useful minerals and other substances. If you're typical, you flush it away instead, propelling it with approximately 1800 gallons of purified drinking water that must be expensively dealt with in your septic system or municipal sewage treatment plant. The resulting discharge, "effluent," tends to be troublesome rather than helpful. The useful chemistry is, of course, lost. Add another 1800 gallons of water per year for each additional daily flush, and multiply that times population. Large-scale folly, yes? Matched only by the large-scale problems involved in doing something about it.

Low-water-use toilets are a good start. The best of them use only 1.5 gallons per flush — a mere drop in the bucket compared to an old-style water closet's 5 gallon thirst. Yes, 1.5 gallons will still rinse the toilet bowl and carry the load to where it must go (assuming the pipes are sloped according to code), but parents will find that diaper-sloshing doesn't work very well. New designs coming soon will take care of that problem. Even more water is saved by Japanese models not yet available here. They incorporate a hand-washing sink into the tank top. The "grey water" is then reused for flushing. Clever! And obvious, too, but nobody thought of it before because until recently, water supplies seemed inexhaustible.
—JB, who actually tried the shoebox bit.

Aqualine $175

Toto $130

Cascade $195

Veneto $350

Low water use toilets available from Resource Conservation Technology, p. 56, and Real Goods, p. 58.

Solar Aquatics

By John Todd

DURING THE 1970s I was part of a social and scientific experiment known as New Alchemy. New Alchemy was, and still is, a small, not-for-profit "think tank" that created working models of agricultural and architectural systems based upon the teachings of nature (p. 83). My time there convinced me that ecology would shape culture in the twenty-first century, that the next frontier lay in shaping economic life within an ecological framework. It seemed then, and still does, to be the only way to balance the needs of humanity and the dictates of the environment. Without such a balance our civilization would decay in its own poisons. The ecological imperative also seemed the only path to begin to right the inequities between rich and poor nations.

My experience had taught me that third-world people don't want any part of what they perceive as second-class technologies but respect those of the mainstream of industrial cultures. And by then the time seemed right to test my ecological business ideas in that mainstream. To be successful, a new kind of environmentally responsible wealth had to be created and the technologies to do so had to be accessible not only to the capitalist, but also to the peasant farmer on the hillsides of tropical America.

With two friends I formed a for-profit corporation to develop ecological technologies. It was to be a hybrid between a design studio and commercialization organization. We targeted ocean farming, wastewater purification and "smart" houses as potential areas to develop.

Our course was charted by my personal response to an impending local crisis. The drinking water of Falmouth, my town in Massachusetts, had deteriorated badly and our cancer rates were climbing alarmingly. The necessity of buying bottled water to help protect me and my family raised a problem I couldn't get out of my mind. Water is the basis of all life. I reasoned that the quality of water determines the quality of life from amoeba to butterfly to human. Thousands of toxic and cancer-causing substances are entering the planetary waters each day. Reflecting on the state of the water reorganized my priorities. For over fifteen years, beginning at New Alchemy, I had raised fish and had learned innumerable tricks to purify water in order to keep the fish healthy. It seemed logical to use the same biological techniques and apply them to purifying water, sewage and other waste streams. An ecosystem approach, while dramatically different from conventional waste engineering, seemed to me to be the best long-term solution to upgrading water quality not only on Cape Cod, but throughout the country.

Contemporary wastewater treatment technologies are major environmental polluters. They have failed on at least three fronts:

1. Technically, conventional water treatment produces a difficult to dispose of and often toxic by-product called sludge. Merely separating the solids from the liquids is not waste purification.

2. Chemically, conventional waste treatment is a failure in that the industry uses hazardous compounds in the treatment process all of which end up in the environment. Chlorine, for example, which is widely used in sewage treatment, can combine with organic compounds to produce chloramines which are known carcinogens. The chlorine industry is a multibillion dollar industry. Aluminum salts, often used to precipitate out sludge and phosphorus, have been implicated in a number of problems from the weakening of the forest to Alzheimer's disease. The list is long.

3. The third failure of the industry is cost ineffectiveness. Without the massive federal subsidies of the past, communities cannot afford to build and operate advanced waste-water facilities. Nor are the conventional waste treatment technologies designed to produce

This Solar Aquatics facility treats noxious municipal wastewater by natural means. It produces no recalcitrant sludge or nasty smells. No toxic chemicals or metals are employed or discharged; they're neutralized or collected for re-use. It costs far less to build and run. It works. It's available now.

economic by-products. The huge infrastructure of the waste treatment industry makes it difficult for it to change or adapt. In periods of economic scarcity and in looming energy pinches the drive to innovate is weakened.

Such facts cry out for new approaches to water management, and new approaches are based on new paradigms. The Center for the Protection and Restoration of Waters will help formulate such ideas. For example, what would the world be like if we had four basic rules for water?

1. Treat water at its pollution source.

2. Discharge as high or higher quality water than is received.

3. Prevent soil and land degradation. Healthy terrestrial ecosystems purify water.

4. Begin any endeavor, from farming to building shopping malls, by asking the question: "what does the water need?", and proceed in accordance with those needs.

As it turned out, it was the non-profit structure of Ocean Arks International which provided the bulk of the support for the new direction. Ecological water purification was too risky for venture capital, which unadventurously waits until risks are minimized or eliminated. But several environmentally concerned foundations liked our ideas for greenhouse-based sewage-purifying ecosystems and backed the construction and operation of a fifteen-thousand-gallon-capacity prototype at Sugarbush, a ski resort in Vermont. Without the foundation help our eco-technology plans would still be in the drawer.

The Vermont facility became the base for a number of breakthroughs in waste treatment. The ecosystems we designed removed toxic ammonia even during the extreme cold of a northern winter. Trout and small-mouth bass were integral to the system and they grew and thrived. Residual sludge was incorporated into the food chains leaving only modest amounts of sediments which were very low in volatile organic matter. This was important as sludge removal and deposition from conventional sewage treatment plants is reaching crisis proportions. Our ecological technology in Vermont created a beautiful, sweet-smelling aquatic environment in which wastes are transformed into pure water, plants, fishes and diverse life forms. No hazardous chemicals were used in the process.

In 1988, I subsequently designed and the Ocean Arks staff built a prototype aquatic ecosystem for the town of Harwich on Cape Cod to treat cesspool or septage wastes which are pumped by honey wagons from septic tanks into holding ponds. Septic wastes are as much as one hundred times more concentrated than sewage. No conventional current technology does a good, cost-effective job of treatment. Toxic substances, restaurant fats and greases, and industrial and hospital waste products wreak havoc with normal bacteriological processes.

We used complex, photosynthetically based ecosystems

How It Works

BY harnessing certain biological processes, Solar Aquatics imitates the way nature cleans dirty water, only much more quickly and thoroughly. The process appears simple, and in many ways it is. Briefly, and simply, this is how a system works:

Large, translucent, cylindrical tanks are placed in rows inside a greenhouse, positioned and piped in a series so that gravity is the driving force creating a stream through each line. The first tanks contain largely bacteria, algae, and snails, while subsequent tanks downstream contain more complex life forms, including higher plants, other mollusks and fish. Wastewater is pumped into the first tanks where microscopic bacteria attack or consume organic matter, or nutrients, which causes their populations to grow. Algae, in turn, thrive on nutrients released by the bacteria and grow rapidly because of the abundant food source. Snails then consume the algae, and on and on it goes: one organism thriving on another, consuming one thing and being consumed by something else, all the while transforming the wastewater. Further on plants are rafted on the water allowing their oxygen rich roots to fall beneath the surface where higher organisms graze. In the last tanks fish, such as tilapia and bass, swim around in clean water. Final purification takes place in an engineered marsh.

to absorb toxic shock and organic loading.

Inaugural Projects

THE Center's beginning project will involve Solar Aquatics: the sun-based method of purifying waste without hazardous chemicals. Our "flagship" is the Providence plant where, in cooperation with Ecological Engineering Associates and eight research and educational institutions, we are embarking upon a study of the potential of natural systems to transform wastes to useful and safe products. We will focus on the fate of toxic organics, pathogens and heavy metals in sewage-containing industrial wastes.

At Marion, MA, on the major marine estuary, Buzzards Bay, the Center, in partnership with the state of Massachusetts, the EPA, the Coalition for Buzzards Bay and Ecological Engineering Associates, has built a prototype facility to ecologically treat toxic waste pumped from boat toilets. Currently 14,000 acres of Buzzards Bay are closed to shellfishing, in part because of discharge from boats.

Most recently, in partnership with Ball State University Center for Energy Research, we have designed and built a small prototype Solar Aquatic facility to treat sewage in Muncie, Indiana. Additionally, plans are underway for several more Solar Aquatic System facilities in a variety of places.

The first Solar Aquatic System projects have been small. The Providence facility treats the wastes of approximately 125 households. The Harwich facility will treat the septage wastes of several thousand residences and can be expanded easily. Solar Aquatics can be used to treat millions of gallons daily. Since the systems are modular and adaptable to many different specifications of climate, waste streams, local geography and population requirements, it is possible to decentralize urban waste treatment and incorporate the processes into neighborhoods, producing local economies and environmental benefits.

IN addition to Solar Aquatic Systems, The Center for the Protection and Restoration of Waters is currently engaged in developing remedies for the effects of acid rain. To encourage the spread of such projects, teaching and training programs in water stewardship are offered, some for academic credit. Ask for information. —JB
The Center, $30/year (membership includes a subscription to *Annals of Earth,* reviewed opposite page) from: Ocean Arks International, 1 Locust Street, Falmouth, MA 02540; (508) 540-6801

IT'S EASIER to prevent a mess than it is to clean it up and only two strategies are likely to work. One is the technical fix — develop technologies that minimize pollution. More basic is to live in a way that minimizes demands that result in pollution. That turns out to be hard to do even for the best-intentioned of us, but at least it's clear where to start. —*JB*

Last Stand of the Red Spruce

The national debate on acid rain, begun nearly ten years ago, has been marked by as much scientific as political conflict over causes, effects, and solutions. The result has been a confused and often ill-informed public, too frequently focused on narrow parochial interests to appreciate the larger, and ultimately more serious, problems embodied in the acid rain issue. Author Robert Mello, a lawyer and amateur naturalist, has waded through an enormous body of scientific literature to produce a balanced, in-depth look at the complex relationships among acid rain, air pollution, and forest decline. His achievement is remarkable not only for the clear and concise manner in which he explains complicated scientific issues but also for his ability to weave the many diverse but related aspects of this problem together into a very readable and cohesive examination of the evidence. —Fred Schauffler

Last Stand of the Red Spruce
Robert A. Mello; 1987; 208 pp.
$14.95 ($16.95 postpaid) from:
Island Press, Box 7, Covelo
CA 95428; (800) 828-1302 ✱WEA

•

Inside the narrow band that extends from the ground to just 25 feet above the ground, 5 billion tons of air pass over the United States each day. For hundreds of millions of years, this air has brought to trees the carbon dioxide, hydrogen, and water they need to live. Since the beginning of the Industrial Revolution, the air has also brought increasing amounts of noxious pollutants. The burning of oil and coal by electrical power plants and manufacturing facilities, the combustion of gasoline by motor vehicles, incineration, the smelting and refining of copper, lead, zinc, nickel, and other ores cumulatively pour tens of millions of tons of particles and gases into the atmosphere every year. All of the particles and gases that go up ultimately come back down either as fallout or in precipitation. While they are in the air, however, the pollutants undergo a chain of chemical reactions, transforming some of the gases into more dangerous forms of pollution; thus, what comes back out of the air is worse than what was put into it. Many of these pollutants are known to be deadly to trees, depending upon the concentrations present and the length of time the trees are exposed.

National Toxics Campaign

The National Toxics Campaign provides leadership, coordination and ammunition to grassroots toxics activists across the nation. NTC and its research arm, the National Toxics Campaign Fund, also bring expert organizational and technical help to grassroots groups.

They orchestrated a "Superdrive for Superfund," which featured a caravan of trucks collecting water and soil samples from 200 toxic sites around the country. The samples were delivered to the Capitol steps to emphasize the need for stronger legislation.

The Superfund law was an important first step. While cleaning up the past sites is a major job, America has not yet accomplished the prevention measures that are needed to stop the poisoning of its people and environment. So NTC has forged ahead with a multifaceted effort to prevent toxic hazards in all of their forms:

• NTC is providing tools to grassroots activists who are demanding that local polluters provide the Right to Know, the Right to Inspect and the Right to Negotiate.

• NTC launched a campaign to persuade grocers to end the sale of fresh produce with cancer-causing pesticides by 1995. As of this writing, more than a thousand grocers had signed up, including five major food chains.

• NTC is circulating and providing support for model state policies to reduce the use of toxic chemicals and the production of hazardous wastes. Legislative versions of the policies have been enacted in two states, and filed in about ten others.

*• NTC publishes an excellent newsletter, **Toxic Times** [$15/year (4 issues) to NTC members].*

• During 1989, the organization established the first public-interest environmental laboratory. The lab provides truly independent testing for citizen activists who want to know the chemical ingredients of water, air, soil, sludges, wastes and tissues. —Sanford Lewis [An attorney for National Toxics Campaign]

National Toxics Campaign, 37 Temple Pl., 4th Floor, Boston, MA 02111; (617) 482-1477 *(Membership in NTC is $25 for individuals and $100 for organizations. Organizational membership includes discount prices on lab services and publications.)*

Nuclear Information and Resource Service

The Nuclear Information and Resource Service keeps an admittedly jaundiced eye on the nuclear power industry, then makes what they find available to you in this level-headed quarterly. At other times, you can stay current with NIRSNET, their computer bulletin board that keeps tabs on every nuclear facility in the US, or the legislative alerts that NIRS sends its members when the situation requires fast action. If you're baffled by jargon or complex proposals, there's a technical assistance program. NIRS also serves as a nuclear information clearing house. Commendable. —JB
[Suggested by Sandy Stewart]

Nuclear Information and Resource Service;
$20/year membership [includes a subscription to *Groundswell*, (4 issues a year) and access to Nirsnet for regulatory & legislative alerts, technical assistance & information clearinghouse] from:
NIRS
1424 16th Street NW
Suite 604, Washington
DC 20036; (202) 328-0002

Hazardous Waste in America

The compendium of information about the particular components of the 80 billion pounds of hazardous waste materials generated annually by American industries — 350 pounds per year for each inhabitant of the U.S. The book includes a directory of 8000 toxic dumps located in all 50 states; a field guide to locating undisclosed waste sites; a selection of case studies of toxic dumps and their tragic human toll; an excellent "citizen's legal guide to hazardous wastes"; and an intelligent, emphatic discussion of the political, legal, practical, and philosophical solutions to a toxic nightmare that is all too real. —Carol Van Strum

The cream of the crap, so to speak.
—Peter Warshall

Hazardous Waste in America, Samuel S. Epstein, Lester O. Brown & Carl Pope 1982; 593 pp.; **$27.50** ($32 postpaid) from: Sierra Club Books, 730 Polk Street San Francisco, CA 94109 (415) 923-5500 ✱WEA

•

Some wastes are effectively *immortal*; their toxic qualities are intrinsic to their elemental structure. The heavy metals are in this category, and, in a different sense, so is asbestos, whose toxicity is a function of its physical structure, which, for practical purposes, is indestructible. Some radioactive wastes, particularly uranium and plutonium, retain their radioactive properties for so long that we should also view them as immortal.

A second group of wastes is *semi-mortal*. Destruction or degradation occurs in the environment, but very slowly. Chlorinated hydrocarbons, especially complex ones, are semi-mortal in natural environments, but can be destroyed in high-temperature incinerators.

A third group of toxics is very short-lived or *mortal*, including acids and bases and other strongly reactive materials like cyanides, which are rapidly destroyed or neutralized in the environment.

Coping With An Oiled Sea

Our government's Office of Technology Assessment (OTA) analyses present oil spill recovery techniques and their limitations. A sobering read. They don't mention that if cars got better mileage (and we drove less), most tankers would not be necessary. —JB

•

While considerable public pressure exists to take immediate action to restore polluted shorelines to prespill conditions, this inherently costly, labor intensive undertaking has seldom had more than modest success, particularly on rocky shorelines. Moreover, in some instances, shoreline cleanup has resulted in more damage than good. Marshes and other wetlands are particularly vulnerable to mechanical cleanup methods, but cleanup of sandy and rocky beaches can also cause additional damage. In some instances, the best course of action, although not a satisfying one, is to do nothing and let the beach slowly recover naturally.

Coping With An Oiled Sea
Stock# 052-003-01183-2
$3.75 postpaid from:
Superintendent of Documents
Government Printing Office
Washington, DC 20402-9325
(202) 783-3238

See Also...
Environmental magazines, p. 112.
Pollution fighters get together, p. 104-107.
Worldwatch papers on pollution, p. 8.

The Electromagnetic Environment

By Robert Horvitz

SO ON THE ONE HAND *you have folks sticking their heads in electronic "tuning" fields, as some sort of brain-boost or nonchemical psychedelic, and on the other you have folks afraid of leakage from video monitors, microwave ovens, and powerlines. Are electromagnetic fields (EMFs) a neat high or a lethal hazard?*

Maybe both, maybe neither. Maybe we just don't know.

There's been an upsurge recently in public concern about the invisible fog of electromagnetism we live in. It must concern us because that fog has thickened so much this century, and it permeates our bodies. Every electric motor, appliance and current-carrying wire radiates energy as a byproduct of normal operation. We also use radio to communicate, as in broadcasting, cordless and cellular phones, beepers and CBs. Microwave ovens are popular. So are electric blankets and stoves. Radar is used by police departments, meteorologists, aviators and navies around the world. Metal detectors, remote controlled toys . . . the list goes on and on.

We can't see these emissions. That used to mean we ignored them. But now that a wide range of biochemical effects has been attributed even to weak EMFs, invisibility feeds fear: we don't know when or how much we're being exposed. Exposure is likely anywhere that electricity flows, and our dependence on things electric grows daily.

There's some consolation in knowing that this wave energy penetrates our bodies precisely because we absorb so little of it: we are nearly transparent to radio. And compared to sunlight, which can sear flesh in a few hours, low frequency EMFs are "soft." The sun's ultraviolet rays are a much more immediate health threat.

Which partly explains why research on the biological impact of EMFs got off to a slow, faltering start. Another reason is that bioelectricity seems to attract charlatans and quacks like no other subject. That has made funding agencies and serious scientists leery. Plus, some people in high places oppose research whose findings could impede "progress," raise business costs, establish liability, or encourage regulation. Shutting down the Environmental Protection Agency's research program on EMFs in 1986 was one of the Reagan Administration's many low-points.

Despite the prevailing skepticism and lack of funding, interest in EMF bioeffects increased during the 1980s, after some curious results were found in lab experiments, and statistical studies started showing some association between EMFs and serious illness. Federal inaction in the face of growing public fear led some local governments to impose tight restrictions on EMF sources. As the patchwork of local standards spreads, it's starting to look like the cost of *not* doing the research needed to establish consistent and reasonable safety standards may be higher than doing it right.

A few hints of consensus have started to emerge from the work done so far. With caveats galore (I'm no doctor, we still don't understand the mechanisms, not everyone agrees), this fool rushes in where a lot of other fools have already been mucking around:

• Many bio-effects seem to occur at specific combinations of frequency and power, suggesting that molecular resonance is involved. If that's the case, setting exposure limits across the broad spectrum

will be difficult. (To use a plumbing analogy, your pipes may "sing" when water flows through them at a specific rate. Decreasing the flow will stop the singing; but so will INCREASING it. And when the water is at a different temperature, the singing starts and stops at different flow-rates. This kind of nonlinear relationship between "dose" and effect means that at certain frequencies, a weak EMF might have more impact on a specific chemical reaction than than a stronger one does.) Until we sort everything out minimizing exposure in general is the safest strategy.

• The orientation of the field, the coherence and shape of the waves, the way they're modulated (AM, FM, or pulse), the peak versus average power density — any or all of these may be important variables. They complicate setting exposure limits, too.

• Magnetic fields may be more of a health problem than electrical fields, though they are often found together. TVs and video terminals, small motors (hairdriers, fans, and plug-in clocks), fluorescent lights and electric blankets, are typical sources of magnetic fields in the home. Magnetic shielding (as opposed to electrical shielding) is generally impractical. However, the magnetic fields from most appliances fade to below the background level a few feet or yards away.

• The magnetic fields of powerlines have a farther reach. They are more intense where there's an unbalanced load and the voltage is stepped down by a transformer. You can easily check for "hotspots" in your neighborhood by walking around with a portable radio tuned to a vacant channel at the low end of the AM band. As you near a radiating section, you'll hear a loudening buzz.

• If you have a microwave oven, have a professional repairman check the seal around the door at least once a year.

• Electric blankets have been singled out as something to avoid because they create strong fields and are meant to be used close to the body for long periods of time. Consider a down comforter instead.

It's important to keep in mind that not all of the recently discovered effects are necessarily harmful. Some may have no health impact at all, and some may ultimately prove beneficial. The real pay-off in EMF bioeffects research may not be just in minimizing risks, but in the development of positive applications. It is already clear that there are therapeutic uses — in bone-healing and pain relief — as well as new imaging techniques which eliminate the need for exploratory surgery. If EMFs can in fact promote or inhibit certain chemical reactions, we may able to harness that ability for desirable ends.

Artificial EMFs

Research is moving so fast in this field that newsletters are the only way to keep up. **"Microwave News"** and **"VDT News,"** both edited by Louis Slesin, are widely acclaimed by all sides as the best sources of reliable and current information. Slesin believes that emissions from computer monitors, and EMFs generally, are a serious health issue. But he's established a reputation as an "honest broker." When a well-done study is published showing no evidence of harm, or refuting a study that found something scary, Slesin reports it just as carefully, and with just as prominent a headline, as reports favoring the other side. As a result, he's been much more effective in changing the attitudes of researchers than more partisan reporters. Almost every study cited in **Currents Of Death** was first reported in either "Microwave" or "VDT News."

As you might have guessed, "VDT News" covers emissions from computer monitors, and worker-health issues related to office equipment in

general. "Microwave News" is less accurately titled. It covers the entire radio spectrum, not just microwaves, increasingly focusing on the low end of the spectrum (macrowaves?). "MN" is the more expensive of the two, but it has a lot more news per issue.

Microwave News
$250/year (6 issues)
P.O. Box 1799
Grand Central Station
New York, NY 10163
(212) 517-2800

VDT News
$87/year (6 issues)
P.O. Box 1799
Grand Central Station
New York, NY 10163
(212) 517-2802

For a one-off summary, a background paper published by the U.S. Congress's Office of Technology Assessment is a reasonable place to start. **Biological Effects of Power Frequency Electric and Magnetic Fields** addresses powerline issues, summarizing the research in a relatively accessible, non-alarmist way. Also discusses policy issues, recent regulatory actions, and ongoing research programs.

Biological Effects of Power Frequency Electric and Magnetic Fields, Office of Technology Assessment 1989; 103 pp.; Stock No. #052-003-01152-2; **$4.75** from: Superintendent of Documents Government Printing Office Washington, DC 20402-9325 (202) 783-3238.

Among recent books on these subjects, **Currents of Death** has certainly attracted the most attention. Brodeur gives a pretty good overview of material originally published in Slesin's newsletters. But he differs sharply from Slesin in taking any skepticism about even the flakiest claims of injury from EMFs as proof that the doubter must be part of a massive conspiracy hatched by the U.S. military, the electric utilities and the computer manufacturers, who want to wreak a holocaust on the public and cover up their evil plan. For Brodeur, there's no such thing as a different interpretation of ambiguous data. There are no errors in the research of the pro-harm camp, fatal errors in every study from the no-harm camp. Reasonable people don't disagree: you're either pro-Life or pro-Death.

This is nonsense. It does a real disservice to the complexity of the scientific issues, and to the honest researchers in both camps trying to figure them out. The breakthroughs in understanding which are likely to emerge from this controversy are probably still cloaked in unresolved questions that Brodeur would dismiss as lame excuses for reactionary caution. If you read this book, make sure you read the OTA paper for some sort of balance.

Currents of Death
(Power Lines, Computer Terminals, and the Attempt to Cover Up Their Threat to Your Health), Paul Brodeur 1989; 333 pp.; **$19.45** ($21.40 postpaid) from: Simon & Schuster, Mail Order Dept. 200 Old Tappan Road Old Tappan, NJ 07675 (800) 223-2336 ✱WEA

Profit from Pollution Prevention

Bucky Fuller said for years that pollution is just good stuff in the wrong place at the wrong time. This Canadian book offers hard evidence that not only can many pollutants be controlled but that the control can produce income. Experience has proven over and over that without economic incentive, polluters won't do much. Turns out that even with economic incentive, they won't be much inclined to do much until convinced. This book examines a host of common industrial polluting materials and practices. Alleviation tactics are discussed. For many nasties, successful case studies are presented. If you need to deal with a polluter, this book should be included in your homework. —JB

Profit from Pollution Prevention, Monica E. Campbell & William M. Glenn; 1982; 404 pp. **$25** (postage & handling fees depend on location) from: Firefly Books 250 Sparks Ave. Willowdale, Ontario M2H 2S4, Canada (416) 499-8412 **✶WEA**

●

Textiles

Every year, millions of pounds of sizing chemicals are generated as a result of desizing operations.

Size chemicals, which are applied to warp yarn to protect them during the weaving operation, represent a valuable material that may be recovered and then re-used in the slashing operation.

Spokesmen for the Canadian textile industry suggest that most Canadian plants tend to use starch as the predominant sizing agent. In the United States, use of polyvinyl alcohol (PVA) and carboxymethyl cellulose (CMC) are becoming increasingly prevalent.

The J.P. Stevens Company, one of North American's larger textile companies, has been recovering PVA size for about seven years at its Clemson, South Carolina plant.

At the Clemson plant, the size recovery technique is based on ultrafiltration technology (also known as hyperfiltration).

According to Gaston County (Stanley, North Carolina), the heart of their ultrafiltration system is a carbon tube/membrane filter which provides mechanical separation of liquid systems according to molecular or particulate size. The membrane consists of an inorganic coating mechanically bonded to a porous carbon tube. Both membrane and support tube possess a high degree of resistance to chemical and abrasion degradation, and tolerate wide pH and temperature ranges.

Carbon Tube with Ultrafiltration Loop

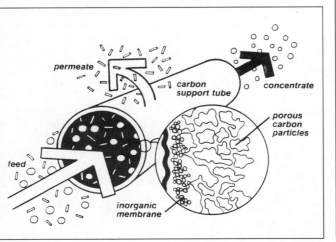

permeate

carbon support tube

concentrate

feed

porous carbon particles

inorganic membrane

We ALL KNOW that recycling of pretty near everything has got to happen sooner or later. Who is going to do it? How is it going to be paid for? (We know quite well *who* is going to pay, right?) How do we deal with vested interests — which apparently include the Mafia in some locales — that stand to lose money and power if recycling becomes, as it must, "the way we normally do things"? This is all being decided right now in the ponderous, messy dance that eventually gets things sorted out in this country. —JB

Garbage Reincarnation

This classroom manual on garbage recycling is the gem at the bottom of the trash heap and like all great "activity" books for kids, a book every adult will learn tons from. The authors are champions of human energy over the false application of high technology. —Peter Warshall

Garbage Reincarnation Sonoma County Community Recycling Center 1982; 51 pp.; **$5.95** postpaid from: Sonoma County Community Recycling Center P. O. Box 1375 Santa Rosa, CA 95402 (707) 584-8666

●

Sanitary Landfills

Twenty million tons of residential and commercial garbage enter the waste stream each year in California, and this amount is increasing each year. The majority of this is deposited into *sanitary landfills* where it is buried at a tremendous cost. This garbage, or resource, is, for all practical purposes, lost forever.

things to think about . . .

. . . where does all your garbage go?

. . . why does it go there?

. . . is *leachate* creating a problem at your *landfill*?

BioCycle

***BioCycle** is close to my feces-fertilizer-farm-food-feces revolving vision. It features my favorite Compost Guru, Clarence Golueke. I once thought their bumper sticker should read: "Have You Hugged Your Humus Today?" Herein, the creators of America's long-term wealth. —Peter Warshall*

BioCycle, Jerome Goldstein, Editor; **$55**/year (12 issues) from: BioCycle Box 351 Emmaus, PA 18049

●

REGIONAL ROUNDUP

St. Petersburg, Florida

YARD WASTE RECYCLING PROGRAM GRINDS OUT 7,000 TONS OF MULCH

Tom Lehmann, Environmental Sanitation Services Manager for St. Petersburg, is proud of the efficient way 7,000 tons of yard debris ("whatever residents can scrape up") are being processed into partially-decomposed mulch. A tub grinder (Mighty Giant) is moved as needed to any of the six dropoff sites, so material can be run through the machine prior to transport to a central windrowing site. Windrows are 8 to 10 feet high, 25 feet wide. "We windrow primarily to get rid of weed seeds, not to generate a finished compost," says Lehmann. After three months, mulch material is

---

Resource Recycling • Plastics Recycling Update

*This magazine is aimed at big-time recycling operators, government officials, and industries developing products that make recycling easier. The harsh facts of recycling economics are especially well attended, as they must be if large changes in public attitude are to be implemented. The same folks put out the monthly 6 page newsletter, **Plastics Recycling Update**, which keeps readers current in that rapidly developing field. (Its unfortunate price is typical of this breed of very-low-circulation specialty papers). Magazines and newsletters of this sort are a sure sign that recycling is becoming a major industry at last. —JB*

Resource Recycling Jerry Powell, Editor **$42**/year (12 issues)

Plastics Recycling Update; **$85**/year (12 issues)

Both from: Resource Recycling, Inc. P.O. Box 10540 Portland, OR 97210 (503) 227-1319

●

Plastics Waste Controls

Newark, New Jersey is one of the first communities in the U. S. to implement a ban on polystyrene packaging use in restaurants. Some 1,700 local businesses have received an education packet listing firms that sell paper and degradable packaging.

Several retailers are taking advantage of a recycling exemption which allows the outlet to escape the ban if it recycles 60 percent of its waste. Five McDonald's restaurants are trying this tactic, with collected plastics destined for Polystyrene Recycling Inc. in Brooklyn, New York. In

put in a storage pile, then transferred back to the dropoff sites for distribution to municipal agencies and residents.

●

Scott County, Minnesota

RECYCLING WHITE GOODS

When an amendment to the county's solid waste ordinance prohibited land disposal of appliances in 1988, Scott County didn't leave its residents looking for a place to dispose of their old water heaters, refrigerators and clothes dryers. Instead, the county worked with its only landfill, Louisville Landfill, and helped to fund a recycling program that last year processed approximately 3,000 appliances.

For $10, residents and private haulers can take major appliances to the landfill where they are stockpiled until being removed by Major Appliance of St. Paul. Major Appliance ships them to a processing facility where serviceable appliances are reconditioned. The rest are shredded and the materials sold to materials markets. Under a new program effective July 1, 1989, any hauler that provides the county with a receipt from an approved recycler will be reimbursed $15 per appliance by the county.

Al Frechette, Scott County's Environmental Health program manager feels that by providing the reimbursement, haulers will be able to pass the savings onto their customers and provide collection services for $5 per appliance or less and keep the material out of ditches and illegal dumps.

McDonald's recycling experiments in Portland, Oregon and Brooklyn, New York, customer compliance in separating plastics from other wastes ranges from 50 to 70 percent.

The ordinance includes a $1,000 fine for noncompliance. —*Plastics Recycling Update*

•

Seattle has won funding from the U.S. Environmental Protection Agency to pilot test a system of weight-based garbage collection, that it calls "Garbage by the Pound." The city hopes to retrofit several garbage trucks with scales and use barcode address systems that will allow each customer to be charged on the basis of the actual weight of the garbage put out for disposal. The city hopes that using a bar-code system, combined with a retrofit of the semi-automated garbage trucks, will lead to a operation that is fairer, but does not slow down or complicate collection.

—*Resource Recycling*

At a pilot latex paint recycling project in Seattle, paint is collected, sorted and consolidated. A study has estimated that Seattle could save $1 million in landfill disposal costs by recovering latex paint. —*Resource Recycling*

Garbage Reincarnation

We Should Be Doing This

In Sweden we have recycling of batteries, the main reason for this is the concentration of mercury (alkaline batteries) and cadmium (in most rechargeable batteries) and the difficulty of disposing of the batteries in a safe way.

Starting this year the battery companies must put a recycling symbol on all batteries with heavy metals over a certain percent (0.025% mercury — manganese dioxide batteries are below that limit) and pay about 10 cents in environmental tax for every battery sold.

The Government has put orange battery-recycling boxes beside the glass and clothes recycling stations, usually located within walking distance from most homes. You don't get paid, but after some advertisement and information campaigns, most people put their discard batteries in the orange boxes.

Now there are Alkaline batteries on the Swedish market (UCAR/Philips) with very little mercury, marginal price difference, and no need for recycling and no environmental tax.

—Erix Ericsson [via Peter Funk]

WASTE   By *Wendell Berry*

As A COUNTRY PERSON, I often feel that I am on the bottom end of the waste problem. I live on the Kentucky River about ten miles from its entrance into the Ohio. The Kentucky, in many ways a lovely river, receives an abundance of pollution from the Eastern Kentucky coal mines and the central Kentucky cities. When the river rises, it carries a continuous raft of cans, bottles, plastic jugs, chunks of styrofoam, and other imperishable trash. After the floods subside, I, like many other farmers, must pick up the trash before I can use my bottomland fields. I have seen the Ohio, whose name (Oyo in Iroquois) means "beautiful river," so choked with this manufactured filth that an ant could crawl dry-footed from Kentucky to Indiana. The air of both river valleys is seriously polluted. Our roadsides and roadside fields lie under a constant precipitation of cans, bottles, the plastic-ware of fast food joints, soiled plastic diapers, and sometimes whole bags of garbage. In our county we now have a "sanitary landfill" which daily receives, in addition to our local production, fifty to sixty large truckloads of garbage from Pennsylvania, New Jersey, and New York.

Moreover, a close inspection of our countryside would reveal, strewn over it from one end to the other, thousands of derelict and worthless automobiles, house trailers, refrigerators, stoves, freezers, washing machines, and dryers; as well as thousands of unregulated dumps in hollows and sink holes, on streambanks and roadsides, filled not only with "disposable" containers but also with broken toasters, television sets, toys of all kinds, furniture, lamps, stereos, radios, scales, coffee makers, mixers, blenders, corn poppers, hair dryers, and microwave ovens. Much of our waste problem is to be accounted for by the intentional flimsiness and unrepairability of the labor-savers and gadgets that we have become addicted to.

Of course, my sometime impression that I live on the receiving end of this problem is false, for country people contribute their full share. The truth is that we Americans, all of us, have become a kind of human trash, living our lives in the midst of a ubiquitous damned mess of which we are at once the victims and the perpetrators. We are all unwilling victims, perhaps; and some of us even are unwilling perpetrators, but we must count ourselves among the guilty nonetheless. In my household we produce much of our own food and try to do without as many frivolous "necessities" as possible — and yet, like everyone else, we must shop, and when we shop we must bring home a load of plastic, aluminum, and glass containers designed to be thrown away, and "appliances" designed to wear out quickly and be thrown away.

I confess that I am angry at the manufacturers who make these things. There are days when I would be delighted if certain corporation executives could somehow be obliged to eat their products. I know of no good reason why these containers and all other forms of manufactured "waste" — solid, liquid, toxic, or whatever — should not be outlawed. There is no sense and no sanity in objecting to the desecration of the flag while tolerating and justifying and encouraging as a daily business the desecration of the country for which it stands.

But our waste problem is not the fault only of producers. It is the fault of an economy that is wasteful from top to bottom — a symbiosis of an unlimited greed at the top and a lazy, passive, and self-indulgent consumptiveness at the bottom — and all of us are involved in it. If we wish to correct this economy, we must be careful to understand and to demonstrate how much waste of human life is involved in our waste of the material

goods of Creation. For example, much of the litter that now defaces our country is fairly directly caused by the massive secession or exclusion of most of our people from active participation in the food economy. We have made a social ideal of minimal involvement in the growing and cooking of food. This is one of the dearest "liberations" of our affluence. Nevertheless, the more dependent we become on the *industries* of eating and drinking, the more waste we are going to produce. The mess that surrounds us, then, must be understood not just as a problem in itself but as a symptom of a greater and graver problem: the centralization of our economy, the gathering of the productive property and power into fewer and fewer hands, and the consequent destruction, everywhere, of the local economies of household, neighborhood, and community.

This is the source of our unemployment problem, and I am not talking just about the unemployment of eligible members of the "labor force." I mean also the unemployment of children and old people, who, in viable household and local economies, would have work to do by which they would be useful to themselves and to others. The ecological damage of centralization and waste is thus inextricably involved with human damage. For we have, as a result, not only a desecrated, ugly, and dangerous country in which to live until we are in some manner poisoned by it, and a constant and now generally accepted problem of unemployed or umemployable workers, but also classrooms full of children who lack the experience and discipline of fundamental human tasks, and various institutions full of still capable old people who are useless and lonely.

I think that we must learn to see the trash on our streets and roadsides, in our rivers, and in our woods and fields, not as the side effects of "more jobs" as its manufacturers invariably insist that it is, but as evidence of good work *not* done by people able to do it.

Excerpted from **What Are People For?**, *copyright 1990 by Wendell Berry, published by North Point Press and reprinted by permisssion. Review on p. 97.*

Earth Care Paper

Some of the nicest note cards and Christmas cards I've seen come from Earth Care, a manufacturer of recycled paper products. But cards aren't the only thing they sell — envelopes, computer paper, and non-plastic food storage bags are just a few of the items in this, the latest catalog. The catalog is full of interesting blurbs about recycling, plastics, and other environmental concerns. 10% of their profit goes to various organizations dedicated to solving environmental and social problems. Best of all, prices are very reasonable.
—John Ruckes

Earth Care Paper, Inc.; Catalog **free** from:
P. O. Box 3335, Madison, WI 53704
(608) 256-5522

Index to Office and Printing Papers

	Letterhead & #10 Envelopes	Business Cards	Brochures	Note Cards	Newsletters	Photocopying	Typing & Office Use	Page Number
Cadence Linen Text	A		A			B	A	25
Cadence Linen Cover		A		A				25
Ultima Laid			A					26
Brockway Felt			B	A				26
Crestline Vellum Text	A		A		A	B	A	27
Coat of Arms Cover		A		A		B		27
Passport Speckle Text	A		A					28
Passport Cover		A		A				28
Sycamore Colors	A		A		A	B	A	29
White Offset	A		A		A	B	A	29
Copy-Bond						A	A	30
Computer Paper								30
Minimum Impact*	A		A		A	B	A	31

A = Ideally suited for this purpose   B = Works well in most situations
*(the most ecological printing paper made)

*This article is derived from **Total Recycling: Realistic Ways to Approach the Ideal**, a book by Daniel Knapp and Mary Lou Van Deventer, coming soon from the University of California Press. Their ideas are based upon lessons learned the hard way at Urban Ore, a precedent-setting recycling operation still growing vigorously in Berkeley, California. —JB*

How to Design Total Recycling Systems

By Daniel Knapp, Ph.D.
& Mary Lou Van Deventer

Total recycling is a big vision — it means not wasting anything. It means a technological, economic, and cultural system built for convenient, effective reuse and recycling of anything we can no longer use. It means wasting and attitudes that permit waste are unacceptable. It has been considered presumptuous even to think of such a thing — until now. Now it is necessary.

But in a world of sound bites and attention spans shortened by television, big visions must be reduced to microbits to be seen at all. Which is okay, so long as the microbits expand on command. These principles are presented as microbits that could be expanded into a huge industry called total recycling:

1. **Waste isn't waste until it's wasted.** Conventional disposal systems waste resources by mixing unlike things together, often in the name of efficiency. The first step in avoiding waste is avoiding mixing.

2. **Recyclers handle discards, not wastes.** Discards can be recycled or wasted. We will always have discards, but we can deny people the option to waste them.

3. **Recycling upgrades discards to resources** instead of downgrading them to garbage. Garbage represents a design failure in the disposal system. Recyclers sometimes waste things, but their ultimate goal is to waste nothing.

4. **Recycling manages the supply of discards,** not the "solid waste stream." The term "waste management" should be reserved for the garbage disposal industry.

5. **Recycling is a form of disposal.** Disposal by recycling is not destruction; it is orderly placement. Auction houses also dispose of things, as do estate sales. Only the garbage system disposes of things by destroying their value.

6. **Disposal fees can power recycling** disposal just as they do garbage disposal. There are fees for disposal services rendered. Recyclers must be allowed and encouraged to compete with garbage interests for disposal fees. This will unlock the potential for recycling businesses to handle vast quantities of material and eventually to replace the garbage system.

7. All of what now becomes garbage can be sorted into **twelve master categories** of recyclable materials.

8. A discard management system in which recycling is the preferred disposal technology must begin with a **discard composition study.** Such a study analyzes today's discards to establish the proportion and volume of each of the twelve master categories of recyclables. Observational studies that sort and weigh are preferable to desktop studies that import data from other localities or use other esoteric methodologies.

9. **Each locality should do its own composition study**, and results should be made public.

10. A comprehensive recycling system provides opportunities to recycle all twelve of the master discard categories. Recycling systems should not be called comprehensive until all twelve master categories are provided for.

11. Using the twelve master categories provides a way to **estimate progress toward the goal** of total recycling. The steps are: (A) estimate the amount of each master category within the total supply of discards; (B) estimate the amount being recycled within each master category (include long-extant scrap industries); (C) add the discards wasted to the discards recycled; and (D) divide the discards recycled by the total discards. The resulting percentage will be the **recycling rate.**

12. Our culture will move toward total recycling in **incremental steps,** not all at once.

13. **Banning and precycling** (source reduction) are valid and useful tools for achieving the goal of total recycling. Some things will never be recyclable.

14. **All closed landfills should be evaluated** for their suitability as sites for comprehensive recycling transfer stations. This is the largest single option for increasing discard disposal capacity for any community. It will also immediately reduce pressure on remaining landfill capacity.

15. Systematic research should be conducted on the feasibility of **mining old landfills** to recover some resources, but more important, fill space.

The Twelve Master Categories Of Recyclable Materials

As we mentioned, designing a comprehensive recycling system requires a discard composition study. To do the study, one must observe and record what is being tossed out. Categories become important at this stage, because watching the variety of things dumped at a landfill can be overwhelming.

To pull order out of the chaos, similar things must be grouped together. But the category list is crucial; a study will see only what its categories provide for. Inadequate categories will leave a lump of unidentified residue called "miscellaneous" or "garbage." The list has to be big enough to cover everything, and small enough to be useful.

Different sizes of lists are possible, depending on one's idea of what will ultimately happen to the discards. Composition studies for incinerators often have only two categories: burnable and nonburnable. A study for a garbage composting plant might use only four or five.

How many categories are best for a total recycling system? It turns out there are twelve. (The examples after the category names are intended to suggest expansion; they are not limits by any means.)

1. **Reusable goods**, including intact or repairable home or industrial appliances; household goods; clothing; intact materials in demolition debris, such as lumber; building materials such as doors, windows, cabinets, and sinks; business supplies and equipment; lighting fixtures; and any manufactured item or naturally occurring object that can be repaired or used again as is.

2. **Paper**, including newsprint; ledger paper; computer paper; corrugated cardboard; and mixed paper.

3. **Metals**, both ferrous and nonferrous, including cans; parts from abandoned vehicles; plumbing; fences; metal doors and screens; tools; machinery; and any other discarded metal objects.

4. **Glass**, including glass containers and window glass.

5. **Textiles**, including nonreusable clothing; upholstery; and pieces of fabric.

6. **Plastics**, including beverage containers; plastic packaging; plastic cases of consumer goods such as telephones or electronic equipment; films; and tires.

7. **Plant debris**, including leaves and cuttings; trimmings from trees, shrubs, and grass; whole plants; and sawdust.

8. **Putrescibles**, including animal, fruit, and vegetable debris; cooked food; manures; offal; and sewage sludge.

9. **Wood**, including unreusable lumber; tree rounds; and pallets.

10. **Ceramics**, including rock; tile; china; brick; concrete; plaster; and asphalt.

11. **Soils**, including excavation soils from barren or developed land; and excess soils from people's yards.

12. **Chemicals**, including acids; bases; solvents; fuels; lubricating oils; and medicines.

Estimated and Actual Percentages of Recyclables in the Total Discard Supply

From incomplete empirical studies and countless unsystematic real-world observations, we can build up a composite picture of the way the twelve master categories are probably related. This is a best guess and is not accurate for any specific locality, but it is still quite useful because it provides an overview showing that although discards viewed en masse are chaotic and psychically overwhelming, they are nevertheless finite and can be accounted for.

Percentage of Recyclables in the Discards

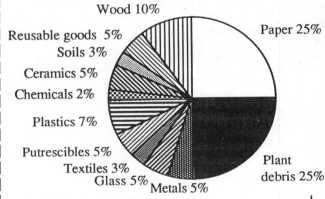

Wood 10%
Reusable goods 5%
Soils 3%
Ceramics 5%
Chemicals 2%
Plastics 7%
Putrescibles 5%
Textiles 3%
Glass 5%
Metals 5%
Paper 25%
Plant debris 25%

This generic chart lets us make these big and very useful observations:

• Just two categories, paper and plant debris, make up 50% of the total discards.

• About 85% of the discards are organic, carbon-based compounds.

• The original "Earth Day" recycling focused on post-consumer cans, bottles, and newsprint. We have not achieved total success in these categories — really subcategories — but if we did, that would give us a recycling rate somewhere between 15% and 25%.

• From an entrepreneurial point of view, the current public preoccupation with plastics recycling obscures much more viable business opportunities with bigger potential impacts. Reusable goods, plant debris, soils, ceramics, putrescibles, and textiles can be harvested more easily and profitably than plastics, and they represent 56% of the total, compared to plastics' 7%.

• Had the early recyclers concentrated on reusable goods — the single most valuable category per ton of the twelve — they could have tapped into a financial resource that would have stabilized and underwritten their losses elsewhere without diminishing the environmental impact of their efforts. Reusable goods are equal in volume to glass and metal, and salvaging them conserves the manufacturing energy embodied in them.

Some Parts of the Total System and How They Work

No fully operational twelve-category recycling system is currently up and running anywhere at this time. But for every one of the master discard categories, there are recycling enterprises somewhere reliably disposing of all or part of the supply.

Lars Benson relocates some of Urban Ore's sink collection. Separating reusables involves lots of handwork.

Urban Ore's Compost Farm turns plant debris into a salable product, saving landfill space and reducing the need for chemical fertilizer. Probably the most underrated part of a comprehensive recycling system is composting. Clean brush and yard debris accounts for about 25% of the total discard supply, not only in sunny California, but also in New Jersey, Illinois, and most other states. Americans love gardens, gardens grow, and they need regular trimming — or pruning in the winter. Winter in cold climates offers a supply of dead leaves and woody debris.

Recycling Reusables with Urban Ore

Just before the Berkeley landfill died, it gave birth to Urban Ore, Incorporated.

"Urban Ore" was originally the title of a research proposal written to the National Science Foundation. We wanted to study the feasibility of digging some test holes in the landfill, recovering what we could for recycling, and composting the rest. What we were really after was not materials at all, but more space to fill while we developed a big, comprehensive recycling system on the landfill surface.

We wanted to extend the life of the landfill.

The funding never came through, though, so we had to stop thinking of ourselves as scientists in lab coats. We adopted a new identity as urban scavengers.

In the wild and woolly environment of the dump, just surviving from one day to the next was a major feat. We went after reusable goods because they had more survival value than anything else. When we wanted tools, we found them in the dump. When we wanted clothes, we found them, too. When we wanted money, we sold the things we found: scrap metals, building materials, furniture, equipment, books, toys. We learned the salvage trade by trial and error, and by necessity.

We learned business so we could become established, legitimate, and recognized. We passed a major city audit and when the landfill closed on schedule, we were invited to be part of the recycling system at the new transfer station. We even prevailed in a major battle with our host public works department over an incinerator they wanted to build.

That political victory was necessary to our survival because it protected our supply. Nevertheless, it cost a lot of effort and money, and it dug a gulf between our regulators and us that took years to bridge.

We've had our ups and downs, just like any other business. But overall, we've grown and prospered. Ten years later, Urban Ore generates over $600,000 per year selling reusable goods. It employs fifteen people at wages ranging from $8.00 to $12.00 per hour. Its employees enjoy a company-paid health plan. Customers include flea-market vendors, artists, realtors, house-restoration contractors, property managers, landlords, renters, collectors, students, newlyweds, movie and theater companies, and just about anyone else looking for bargains, surprises, and sometimes just ideas. ▪▪▪▪▪▪▪▪▪▪▪▪▪

Cities and transport systems use vast amounts of ceramic materials. The steel skeleton of a typical highrise holds up cement floors and a stone and glass exterior. Aqueducts, freeways, subways, and airports are frozen rivers of cement or asphalt. Repair, remodeling, and reconstruction of these facilities produces millions of tons of stone-like rubble annually. Broken concrete is crushed into gravel, reducing need for both land fill space and gravel mining.

Urban Ore
(415) 526-7080

A small part of the wood sash department at Urban Ore Building Materials. Studies show that selling used building parts does not steal customers from building supply houses.

Materials tipped into this conventional pit-type transfer station *(below)* are crushed and mixed, making recycling impossible. The best transfer stations have yet to be built. These transfer stations will offer separate unloading areas for each of the twelve master discard categories. Each station will charge a fee or pay one for the materials it handles. The only materials that will get through to the end will be grossly contaminated by careless handling, or will have been designed and built so they can't be recycled. The highest tipping fees will be at the end of the line.

Recycling transfer stations will anchor the total recycling systems of the future, but the boundaries will be fuzzy. Large and small businesses will function as parts of a whole resource-handling system, and where primary production stops and recycling begins will be less distinguishable as time goes on. The entire economic structure will simply assume frugality and overall resource efficiency.

Giant hydraulic splitter turns recalcitrant stumps into salable firewood.

IVAN ILLICH once commented rather impolitely, "If you insist on working with the poor, if this is your vocation, then at least work among the poor who can tell you to go to hell." He suggests that you work nearer home. When relatively rich North Americans work abroad, they often do more harm than good, especially by exporting our values — often the worst ones — into an area where they have no natural enemies to keep them in balance. I agree; my own overseas efforts have produced no significant lasting benefits to anyone. (Except me. "Doing time" is a great way to learn.) A contribution of my airfare would probably have been more effective. Nonetheless, there are more and more examples of projects where a spirited, humble application of expertise *has* done some good; people are learning how to help in an effective way at last. The most successful seem to be those that deeply involve local people. —JB

ITDG

The Intermediate Technology Development Group of North America, Inc., is a child of the original British ITDG founded by the late E.F. Schumacher of *Small Is Beautiful* fame (p. 98). ITDG has designed and executed some of the very best AT projects yet seen domestically and worldwide. They publish and distribute many of the most useful AT books and other literature. They're too multifaceted to present here in all their glory. If you'd like to work with them, give them a call. Their publications catalog offers entry into what has become a major world movement marked by increasing cooperation and information exchange. It's also a fine source for English language versions of international publications.

ITDG produces a fine magazine too — appropriately called **Appropriate Technology Journal.**
—JB

ITDG Catalog **free**; **Appropriate Technology Journal**; **$23**/year (4 issues). Both from: Intermediate Technology Development Group of North America, Inc., 777 United Nations Plaza, Suite 9A, New York, NY 10017; (212) 953-6920

●

UNACCEPTABLE BIOGAS. The other aspect of the growth in information available to us all through data bases is that it is not usually cross indexed according to the social context or 'genetic code' that produced it. We have all heard of the plans available for all sorts and conditions of biogas digesters, all keenly studied by organizations throughout the world, and all seeming to reflect a keen interest in a usable and sustainable technology suited to the Third World's mix of resources. And yet the only places where there is widespread use of this technology are China and India.

There is something in the social context of biogas technology which makes it seem inappropriate and unacceptable in many places where, on the face of it, it would seem very relevant. In most of these places the reason seems to me very simple — the people for whom it is being considered don't like handling shit (and who's to blame them?). Rare, however, is the technical manual which says that one of the parameters to be considered for using digesters is a willingness to handle shit: mostly it's all talk about recycling oil-drums, gas pressures, ranges of temperature, etc, etc.

And finally, so much information that becomes

Appropriate Technology Sourcebook and Microfiche Library

More than 1000 of the proven-best-worldwide AT books are sorted out, indexed, and given succinct reviews in this most useful book. Even more remarkable is that the book also serves as the annotated index to a matching portable microfiche library containing the entire contents of every one of those books, illustrations and all. That's more than 140,000 pages! The library fits into one sturdy tacklebox. A choice of 'fiche readers is available, including 240 volt and 12 volt (as in vehicle battery or solar panel) models. The price of the whole set is an amazing bargain at less than 5% of the cost of the actual books (not to mention the cost of shipping and storing them abroad). It's the best single idea I've seen in my 25 years of AT action. If you work in developing countries, you need one of these sets. Hatched and executed by Ken Darrow of VIA (Volunteers in Asia). —JB

Appropriate Technology Sourcebook, Ken Darrow and Mike Saxenian; 1986; 800 pp.; **$17.95** ($19.95 postpaid)✱WEA. Appropriate Technology **Microfich Reference Library**; Information **free**; Library & case **$695**, Fiche Reader **$250-350** (postage and handling varies by destination). Both from: Appropriate Technology Project, Volunteers in Asia, P. O. Box 4543 Stanford, CA 94305; (800) 648-8043; [in California (415) 326-8581]

●

The Rower Pump, MF 14-368, reports and brochures, 1984 and later, available from Mirpur Agricultural Workshop and Training School (MAWTS), Mirpur Section 12, Pallabi, Dacca-16, Bangladesh; or Mennonite Central Committee, 1/1, Block "A" Mohammadpur, Dacca, Bangladesh.

Thousands of low-cost direct action handpumps made of pvc pipe are being used in Bangladesh for low-lift irrigation of small plots. The Rower pump can be easily made in developing countries, and the farmer can do his/her own simple repairs. The pump pays for itself in one crop.

The extremely low cost of the hand-pump (approximately US$15) and pvc tubewell installation (approximately US$30-45) and the large economic return from small plot irrigation together make this technology an excellent investment for farmers in

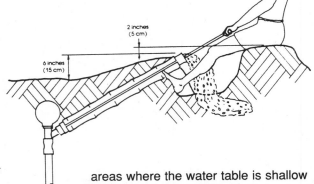

Rower Pump Installation for Irrigation

areas where the water table is shallow (15 feet or less). The Rower pump is probably one of the most important agricultural tools invented in the last 20 years.

Readers seeking information on the Rower pump can write to the manufacturer (MAWTS) for a brochure with technical details. Some of the same material is reproduced in *Handpumps Testing and Development: Progress Report on Field and Laboratory Testing*. The results of an extensive laboratory test are described in *Laboratory Testing of Handpumps for Developing Countries: Final Technical Report* . The relevant pages from both of these books are reproduced in the A.T. Microfiche Library as MF 14-368.

TRANET

Networking and information exchange is increasingly the name of the game, and TRANET (from Transnational Network for Appropriate/Alternative Technologies) has been doing it more comprehensively than anyone else for about 15 years now. Their lively bi-monthly newsletter has brief reviews of useful books, lots of news from the front, a member's bulletin board, and reader commentary — much of it uncomplimentary to the establishment. That last characteristic gives it a noticeably '70s character, but the level of information exchange is very much of today. The TRANET crew is often the first to spread the news globally among people taking control of their own lives. We read every issue. —JB

TRANET; **$30**/membership (includes subscription to bi-monthly newsletter) from: TRANET, P.O. Box 567, Rangeley, ME 04970

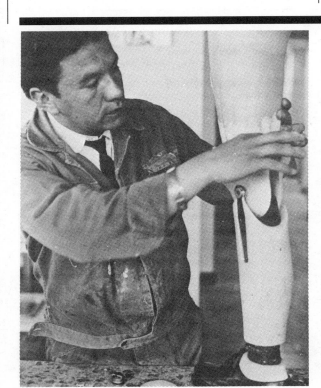

available is not involved with looking at the actual world of the poor and assessing the value of practices and knowledge which have kept such people going for a long time, but in thirsting for new knowledge which, on the face of it, looking at the situation of the Third World today, has not been of great help. So often the solution to a problem of the poor is much more likely to be found among slightly less poor people in a culturally similar environment in some other part of the world who have faced the same problem and have found a working solution to it. If only new ideas, which are often preceded by a literature search, could be preceded by a culture search, and preferably one which is organized along ecological parameters, since the lives of the poor are bound by the natural products around them.
—*Appropriate Technology Journal*

Technologies developed for disabled people can provide income-earning possibilities for other people. —*Appropriate Technology Journal*

VITA

For 25 years, Volunteers in Technical Assistance has been a reliable source of expert advice and an experienced stack of publications. You don't join VITA as you would the Peace Corps, for instance, but you can make your special knowledge available through them. Their record of action is inspiring; see for yourself in **VITA News.** *—JB*

VITA News, Margaret Crouch, Ed.; **$15**/year, (4 issues), from: Volunteers in Technical Assitance 1815 N. Lynn St., # 200 Arlington, VA 22209 (703) 276-1800

•

Packet radio allows communication in areas where the only power available is batteries or solar cells.

Each station in a packet radio system consists of a personal computer, radio transceiver, terminal node controller (TNC) — a modem-like device — a printer, and an antenna. Messages are entered into the computer. In swift bursts of energy, the TNC breaks the message into small pieces (packets) that are transmitted by radio to the receiving computers. There, another TNC decodes the packet, which appears on the computer screen and can be printed.

Hamid Ali Mohamed sends the first packet radio message in Sudan. The radio network was installed and local operators were trained by VITA Volunteers Mark Oppenheim and David Henderson.

Bridging the Global Gap

The first comprehensive guide that connects you to the many groups engaged in people-to-people exchanges between the First and Third Worlds. The authors cover the spectrum of popular initiatives: alternative trade organizations, sister-city programs, technical assistance programs for the Third World, peace groups, alternative tourism and more. The first part of the book consists of first-person accounts by veterans of grassroots global exchanges, and the final third is a well-designed resource guide to organizations. Global Exchange, the organization that spawned this guidebook, has performed a mighty service to anyone who, in the

Bridging the Global Gap
Medea Benjamin and Andrea Freedman; 1989; 336 pp. **$11.95** ($13.75 postpaid) from: Global Exchange 2141 Mission Street #202 San Francisco, CA 94110 (415) 255-7296 ✱WEA

ifda dossier

This little journal is a forum for ideas and techniques intended to improve the lot of those living under unfortunate circumstances. The articles tend to address issues you don't see in slick magazines and university papers, the sort of things comfortable people don't often think about. Lots to learn here. Even the most humble article will reveal to most USA readers the naive simplemindedness of our worldview. —JB

•

The "carnivorous" fishermen of the coasts of Gujarat and Maharashtra, once considered as the lowest of the low, devoted the fruits of their *bhakti* to the creation of "floating temples" or *matsyagan-*

TOOL

Netherlands-based TOOL is another lively technical assistance organization working all over the world. A written description of their work would sound a lot like ITDG, though I'm sure that members of both groups would be quick to point out differences. From what I've seen, there is no difference in competence. TOOL maintains a huge reference library, and 500-item publications list of interest to those actually working in the field. Their

TOOL
Catalog **free** from: TOOL-Reference Centre Entrepotdok 68a/69a 1018 AD Amsterdam, The Netherlands; (0) 20-264409 **AT-SOURCE**; Dfl**25**/year (4 issues) from: AT-SOURCE, P. O. BOX 41 6700 AA Wageningen The Netherlands

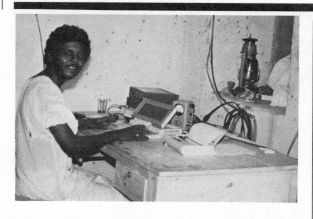

face of dismal news about rainforests and poverty, longs to stop wringing hands and do something to connect to the world beyond our borders. There's nothing else like it available. —Richard Schauffler

•

The internationalism we describe in this book is based on a healthy combination of honest self-interest mixed with deep compassion. It recognizes that the interests of the Third World poor coincide with the interests of the majority of North Americans. Less poverty abroad would mean fewer companies abandoning the United States in search of cheap labor; higher standards of living in Third World countries would mean more markets for our goods; greater democracy overseas would mean less U.S. tax dollars wasted on military aid to repressive regimes. As the late President of Mozambique, Samora Machel, stated, "International solidarity is not an act of charity. It is an act of unity between allies fighting on different terrains toward the same objectives. The foremost of these objectives is to aid the development of humanity to the highest level possible."

dhas. The name refers to the first incarnation of God Vishnu as a fish. Here again, the idea started with a number of fishermen (Dada calls them sagarputras *or sons of the sea) who knew only how to fish and to navigate. Dada suggested that they offer their* bhakti *by setting a day's fish of their catch in a month for buying motorised boats, tools and tackles.*

Although the experiment is only 8 years old, the "impersonal wealth," thus produced, has already enabled the fishermen to buy over 14 boats.

ifda dossier; **$32**/year (6 issues) from: IFDA, 4 Place du Marché, 1260 Nyon, Switzerland Phone 41 (22) 61 82 81

quarterly magazine — **AT Source** *— features extensive, detailed background information articles on problems needing and receiving attention. A student of mine found that the March 89 issue on the world firewood shortage was the best overview available. TOOL publishes in English. —JB*

When cultivating new land, the rural population have since time immemorial spared specific valuable trees.

Micro-Hydropower Sourcebook

We review this book as an example of the current crop of incredibly detailed and experienced technical books now available. This one is admittedly above average, so in addition to being a peerless presentation of the subject, it serves as an inspiration to other authors. With **Sourcebook** *in hand, just about any intelligent, English-literate, shop-savvy person could manage the development of a small hydropower system. The basic engineering is done in layperson's terms, along with a little lesson in how to think about it. The drawings show what you need to know, and they don't waffle over difficult details that must be right. (There is ample opportunity for disaster and chagrin in the small hydropower business.) I don't think I've ever seen a better working manual, especially for something so complex. —JB*

Micro-Hydropower Sourcebook, Allen R. Inversin; 1986; 285 pp. **$32.50** ($36.50 postpaid) from: NRECA International Foundation Attn.: Sourcebook, 1800 Massachusetts Ave. N.W. Washington, DC, 20036 (202) 857-9500

A Multi Purpose Power Unit runner being fabricated, Kathmandu, Nepal.

The Next Economy

Economic civilization is going around a corner the like of which it's never seen before. This is the only guidebook so far. Customers and citizens and adaptive businesses are leading the way. Governments and major corporations are following. Where we come out is better. The now waning Mass Economy amassed fabulous wealth. The emerging Information Economy may not be so opulent, but it presents greater opportunity for wholeness and happiness.

Because Hawken is a businessman — the only economist who is (Smith and Hawken tools, p. 41) — his writing has a street savvy you find nowhere else (except Peter Drucker). His economics is rooted in the individual. It speaks clearly to individual understanding and gives good counsel for individual behavior — "how to invest your life" — which in turn benefits the commonweal as well as the individual. —Stewart Brand

The Next Economy
Paul Hawken; 1983; 242 pp.
$3.95 ($5.95 postpaid) from
Random House
400 Hahn Road
Westminster, MD 21157
(800) 726-0600 ✱WEA

●

In a informative economy, we change from an affluent to an *influent* society. If you are affluent, goods and services flow toward you; if you are influent, the information contained within goods flows into you. An affluent society may possess an opulent and abundant amount of goods, but that does not mean it will be able to utilize, appreciate, and maintain them. An influent society will have less, but its relationship to what it has will be more involved and concerned; people will take care of what they have, and what they have will mean more to them. In other words, an affluent society amasses goods, while an influent society processes the information within goods.

●

The informative economy requires more intelligence from everyone — management, labor, consumers, governments. Those who do not become learners again, regardless of age or rank, will find themselves at an increasing disadvantage as the informative economy takes root.

The Wall Street Journal showed two different energy forecasts. The first was the Exxon/Shell/ CIA model used in the mid-to-late seventies that projected inelastic energy demand clashing with limited supply, a forecast that would result in soaring energy prices. The second model was a simple supply-and-demand curve, in which the rising price of a commodity lowers demand while simultaneously drawing forth more supplies .

The Journal cited an editorial printed five years earlier that said the free market would solve the energy problem if left to its own workings. And so it has.

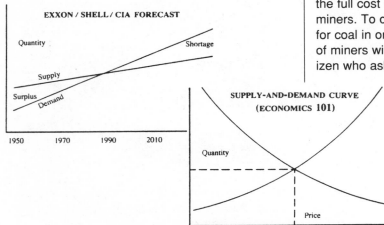

For the Common Good

An economist and a theologian get together in this disturbing book. They give the related causes of world economic and environmental problems a good shake, and make conventional economics look rather odd while doing so. Could all those theoreticians and makers of policy be so blind? And that's what's so disturbing. Daly and Cobb are essentially correct in their analysis and proposed solutions. The question is, how are the changes to be made when the Powers That Be don't particularly care to make the changes? Now that all this has been so nicely laid out and discussed, what's the next move? After all, in 1929, greedy folks chose to bring down the entire system rather than mend their ways. Easily read, and rather scary.
—JB

For the Common Good
(Redirecting the Economy
Toward Community, the
Environment, and a Sustainable Future), Herman E.
Daly and John B. Cobb, Jr.
1989; 482 pp.; **$24.95**
($27.50 postpaid) from:
Putnam Publishing, 390
Murray Hill Parkway, East
Rutherford, NJ 07073; (800) 631-8571 ✱WEA

●

How can we guard against misplaced concreteness in economics? For one thing, we could warn students about it in the early chapters of economic principles texts, as we already do for the fallacy of composition, *post hoc ergo propter hoc, petitio principii*, and other Latin crimes against reason. As far as we have been able to ascertain, no text mentions the fallacy of misplaced concreteness. They do talk about abstraction, but mainly in order to emphasize its powers, not its dangers.

There are nevertheless two rules of thumb that will help us to minimize misplaced concreteness. One is, in Whitehead's words, "recurrence to the concrete in search of inspiration." One technique for getting back to the concrete is to look at all four of Aristotle's notions of cause. These four causes (material, efficient, formal, and final) can be explained with reference to a house. The material cause is the lumber, bricks, and so forth from which the house is made. The efficient cause is the carpenter and his tools, which effect a change of form in the material. The formal cause is the blueprint that the carpenter is following. The final cause is the purpose for building the house — for example, shelter and privacy. In economics our attention is overwhelmingly focused on efficient and formal causes. If we remember material and final causes as well, we will be less likely to commit the fallacy of misplaced concreteness. Whitehead said, "A satisfactory cosmology must explain the interweaving of efficient and final causation". Likewise for a satisfactory political economy.

●

Coal mining companies could be required to pay the full cost of black lung disease among coal miners. To do this they would charge a higher price for coal in order fully to cover all medical expenses of miners with black lung disease. To the naive citizen who asks, "But can our society afford to pay those costs?" — the answer is that society is already paying them.

. . . if the general public rather than the producers and consumers of coal pay for black lung, then the coal industry will find it unprofitable to take any measures at all to reduce black lung disease, since the cost is being paid by others.

The Politics of the Solar Age

This edition of Hazel Henderson's 1981 classic shows that her revisionist economic ideas have not only aged well, they are still well ahead of the conventional theories that are proving to be just plain dangerous. Ms. Henderson was one of the first to see that economic calculations must take into account the costs of environmental and human degradation — an idea still considered heretical by establishment economists. Even some of the more enlightened economists stand their fur straight up at the mere mention of her name — possibly because she is self-taught. No degree, tsk. Perhaps even worse, she is notorious for publicly deflating windbags with her deadly accurate verbal knifework. You debate Hazel Henderson, and you had better have done your homework. Um, now for the delicate question: can you read her stuff without falling out of your chair? It is, after all, economics. I am happy to say that you can, and what's more, you will probably enjoy the trip. (You might also like her earlier book: Creating Alternative Futures, the End of Economics, also available as a TV series she produced (and paid for) herself.

These days, she keeps busy advising the Calvert Social Investment Fund, and is a partner in Commons Capital. She also is consultant to a number of foreign governments on the necessity for a more useful measure of prosperity than the GNP. And she always seems to be lecturing someplace; if she comes your way, I guarantee you won't be bored. —JB

The Politics of the Solar Age
(Alternatives to Economics)
Hazel Henderson; 1988; 433 pp.
$14.95 ($16.95 postpaid)
from: Knowledge Systems, Inc.
7777 W. Morris Street
Indianapolis, IN 46231
(317) 241-0749 ✱WEA

●

The underlying model of my "devolution scenario" is that of "self-organizing systems" (i.e., organic, and biological, systems incorporating both positive and negative feedbacks and displaying behavior modes both of deviation-damping morphostasis and deviation-amplifying morphogenesis). As the crisis of unmanageability unfolds, individual and group responses include:

1. Increasing demands for citizen participation at all levels of decision making.

2. Rapid societal learning via citizen movements (that are adult-education-based on the "each one teach one" model).

3. Proliferation of heterarchical (as opposed to hierarchical) communication in, for example, citizen-based media, newsletters, telephone trees, study groups, consciousness raising, and networking of new perceptions both within and across existing organizations.

4. Multiple-leadership model, i.e., heterarchy. As information-handling overwhelms hierarchical decision centers, they become bottlenecks. Normal channels for data input become overloaded. Similarly, there is insufficient capacity in existing political channels.

5. Retaking of individual responsibility. Public-interest-oriented individuals and public-issue-oriented groups appear at all levels of government.

●

The term hierarchy implies that all such systems have definitive boundaries, rather than the reality: that, like all biological systems, they are open and have "leaky" boundaries.

Economic Renewal Program

The Rocky Mountain Institute crew is justly famous for the depth of their investigations of energy and resource efficiency (p. 57). Their **Economic Renewal Program** *integrates these (ongoing) studies, utilizing their conclusions as a basis for improving local economies. RMI works with the people involved, helping them to identify what they want and how best to achieve it through their own enterprise. Workbooks (guidebooks, really) detail successful, proven strategies and encouraging case histories. The RMI publications list offers a number of introductory booklets that will help you get things started. Actual programs are custom-fit to your needs after appropriate negotiations. Results have been encouraging. —JB*

Rocky Mountain Institute Economic Renewal Publications: ER86-28 *Four Steps to Self-Reliance* (6 pp.) **$3**; ER88-2 *Facilitator's manual* (8 pp.) **$4;** ER88-25 *Financing Economic Renewal Projects* (71 pp.) **$20**; ER88-39 *Business Opportunities Casebook* (52 pp.) **$20**; ER88-40 *The Economic Renewal Program*: A *Colorado Innovation from Colorado Municipalities* (6 pp.) **$2**; ER89-9 *Introduction to the Economic Renewal Program* (15 pp.) **$3**; ER89-19 *Summary of the Economic Renewal Program* (4 pp.) **$2** (all postpaid); Information **free**, all from: RMI, 1739 Snowmass Creek Road, Snowmass, CO 81654-9900

Institute for Local Self-Reliance

ILSR specializes in urban community economic development that isn't dependent on welfare handouts. Unlike many similar organizations, they develop clever technical solutions to problems — they've been particularly successful in materials recovery and other schemes to reduce waste. Their experience and thoroughly professional demeanor, together with a Washington DC location has enabled them to be influential in policy decisions. No room here to list all their accomplishments; it's an impressive list. If your community is being pushed around by unfortunate economic circumstances, you should give these folks a call before giving up. —JB

Institute For Local Self-Reliance
Contributions tax-deductible; information **free** from: Institute for Local Self-Reliance 2425 18th Street, NW, Washington, DC 20009 (202) 232-4108

•

Advocate Alternatives to Incinerators

Southern California — ILSR worked with Black, Latino, and White community organizations to halt a plan for six waste incineration plants in Los Angeles. With ILSR assistance, the Los Angeles groups then formed a working coalition among groups throughout southern California that successfully campaigned to have 15 additional mass burn plants cancelled between 1985 and 1988 in favor of recycling technologies.

•

"Removing citizens and neighborhoods from a dependent relationship on government is a conservative cause. But involving and empowering ordinary citizens in the decisions that affect their commonwealth is part of the classic liberal agenda. Thus, ILSR has remained important and respected regardless of the political and philosophical winds of the moment."
—Howard E. Quirk, Executive Officer Victoria Foundation

Community Regeneration Network

This organization is yet another good idea from the redoubtable Robert Rodale. The basic idea is to help individuals and organizations to improve their own communities by working together with the resources they already have. First step is membership in the Community Regeneration Network. That brings you **Regeneration,** *an encouraging newsletter, plus access to the unique and powerful Rodale resource files, and membership database. The real work is done through a variety of inspiring community regeneration workshops led by Rodale's expert facilitators. The word* catalyst *comes to mind. —JB*

Community Regeneration Network; $25/year (membership includes 6 issues of **Regeneration**), publications list **free** from: Community Regeneration Network 222 Main Street Emmaus, PA 18099-0086 (215) 967-5171

•

Timber brought immigrants to the area in the 1880s, and when the tall white pines had all been cut, industrialists turned to the rich deposits of iron ore. . . . Iron supported the region for two generations. By the early 1980s several thousand people were employed by the mines in well paying jobs. But in 1986, the protracted boom went bust. The major employer, Reserve Mining, went bankrupt and 2,500 jobs were lost.

What was left, after the exodus of those who went in search of employment elsewhere, was a tough, resilient, self-reliant core of "Rangers" who decided that they would do better than survive. They would make the Range an even better place to live. Thus, in 1986, Greta Wood, founder of Voyageur Vision, enlisted the aid of 91 volunteers from the communities of Ely, Babbitt, Tower, Sudan, Embarrass, and Winton, Minnesota, to find what potential lay in area home-based businesses.

In conjunction with Babbitt/Embarrass Area Development Association (BEADA) and the Minnesota Project, a nonprofit technical assistance organization, Voyageurs developed an eight-page questionnaire to which 1,500 households, 43 per-cent of those surveyed, responded. They found that people in the area were making everything from blueprints to canoes at home.

More than 400 households were interested in making money through the sale of handwork and nearly 300 households wanted to earn money by providing a homebased service.

•

Q: Our community engages in a lot of fingerpointing. Cultural, church and civic groups all blame each other for our problems: drugs, absentee landlords, rubble-strewn vacant lots. How can we ever get over this hump.?

A: Community Regeneration workshop facilitators will help reintroduce community members to one another. Through the exercises and skills learned in Regeneration workshops, teachers and students, single parents and pastors, varied races and religions, all work together to discover solutions and uncover their communities internal resources.

We're available for both long- and short-term projects. Using our workshops and our consulting services, a community receives the broadest range of assets-oriented expertise available. We draw on a network of individuals from around the country who are tops in the fields of economic development, waste management, the environment, education and agriculture, to name a few.

Working Assets

Do you have an investment portfolio? Does it contain stock in nasty companies you'd rather not be associated with, much less help capitalize? Would you invest in socially responsible companies if the rate of return was respectable? Many people seem to think that it might be nice to support worthy enterprises, but are afraid to stray from well-known names no matter how despicable.

You don't need to do that. Working Assets Money Fund is about as clean as you can get these days, and its rate of return has been respectable. They're the biggest "social-conscience" investment company. The Fund does not invest in companies with substantial military contracts, that build or operate nuclear power plants, that do business in South Africa, that have a record of environmental violations, or that have a poor record on employee discrimination or safety. Have at it! —JB

Working Assets Money Fund
230 California Street, San Francisco, CA 94111 (800) 533-3863

Period	Average Annual Rate	Effective Annual Yield
3Q	8.07%	8.32%
4Q	7.71%	7.94%
Year	8.21%	8.43%
1990		
1Q	7.40%	7.61%

Council on Economic Priorities

In 1969, Alice Tepper Marlin compiled a list of companies that were not involved in supplying the Vietman war. Her fledgling organization has grown to today's CEP, a respected and feared assessor of corporate social character.

Their **Shopping for a Better World** *(p.109) has had considerable effect, and will doubtless have increasing influence as it appears in classrooms. Their* **Research Reports** *(they come with membership) are a good place to get the level-headed lowdown on corporate lowlife, and — huzzah! — good guys too. —JB*

Council on Economic Priorities; $25/year (membership includes monthly newsletter) from: CEP 30 Irving Place New York, NY 10003 (800) 822-6435

•

It's Not Easy Being Green

Many questions about green products remain unanswered. Who will distinguish between true environmental product improvements and false ones? Is there any agreement about what "safe for the environment" really means? Do standards exist for assessing a product's environmental impact? Who will verify manufacturers' claims? Marketing Intelligence Service, for instance, doesn't check up on company claims. If the company markets a product as green, Marketing Intelligence Service categorizes it as green.

Eco-labelling Symbols

Canada's Environmental Choice

Japan's Eco-mark

West Germany's Blue Angel

Buckminster Fuller

Buckminster Fuller is often represented — not always positively — as the ultimate champion of technology. He insisted that intelligently deployed, efficient technology is the only means to a healthy, fulfilling life for all humans, and that this can be accomplished even for greater populations than now have (see page 9). He called for "comprehensive, anticipatory design." To demonstrate the possibilities, he developed a number of resource-efficient artifacts, including his famous geodesic domes which shelter a space with only 1/50th the material of conventional structures. (Examples on page 82.)

*Bucky's everything-is-connected-to-everything vision and detailed language can make much of his writing and lecturing difficult to follow if you are new to it. I'd start with a book about him, **Buckminster Fuller**. Next you might try the easily understood **Critical Path,** a book that chronicles human evolution to the present, then outlines the path that we must take for species survival. To understand the underlying principles, you'll work very hard reading and comprehending **Synergetics 1** and **2**, but you now have help in **A Fuller Explanation** by Amy Edmondson who was Fuller's collaborator and mathematician at the time of his death in 1983. There are many other books by and about him, as well as a video and an astounding 57 hours of taped lectures called **Everything I Know**. All this, along with lots of other artifacts and a newsletter — **Trimtab** — is available from the Buckminster Fuller Institute. Many of Bucky's insights are proving to be critical and even prescient, often being adapted without credit these days. We give him credit though, as one of the inspirers of the original **Whole Earth Catalog**.*

—JB

Buckminster Fuller
Robert Snyder, Editor
1980; 218 pp.
$15.95 ($18.95 postpaid)

Critical Path
R. Buckminster Fuller
1981; 471 pp.
$10.95 ($13.95 postpaid)

Synergetics
R. Buckminster Fuller
with E. J. Applewhite
1975; 876 pp.
$13.95 ($16.95 postpaid)

Synergetics 2
R. Buckminster Fuller
1979; 592 pp.
$13.95 ($16.95 postpaid)

A Fuller Explanation
Amy C. Edmondson
1987; 302 pp.
$37.50 ($42.50 postpaid)
    All above also ✳WEA

Everything I Know
Seven six-cassette volumes
$35 per volume ($38 postpaid) **$225** complete set
($232 postpaid)

Trimtab Bulletin
Included with **$20**/year membership in Buckminster Fuller Institute (4 issues)

All from:
Buckminster Fuller Institute
1743 S. La Cienega Blvd.
Los Angeles, CA 90035
(213) 837-7710

•

I'm sure none of you know what you're doing with your supper. All you know is you've loaded it in, and you're not saying, "I'm going to send some of it off to this gland and some to that, and tomorrow morning I'm going to grow some hair." I'll simply assert all of you are almost completely automated and always have been. And you talk about automation as though it were something new and rather scary. —*Buckminster Fuller*

•

A sphere is the only shape in which every axis is a neutral axis, which is to say, a sphere's width is the same in every orientation. Therefore, this shape resists compression from any direction; it cannot buckle. Hence the ball bearing. This tangible example illustrates the ideal design for compression.

What about tension? Evidence of longer, thinner, and ever more resilient tension materials suggests that there's no inherent limit to length.
—*A Fuller Explanation*

•

Mast in the Earth: In his primary regard for compressional structuring, man inserts a solid mast into a hole in the "solid" Earth and rams it in as a solid continuity of the unitary solid Earth. In order to keep the wind from getting hold of the top of the mast and breaking it when the hurricane rages, he puts tension members in the directions of the various winds acting at the ends of the levers to keep it from being pulled over. The set of tension stays is triangulated from the top of the masthead to the ground, thus taking hold of the extreme ends of the potential mast-lever at the point of highest advantage against motion. In this way, tension becomes the helper. But these tensions are secondary structuring actions. They are also secondary adjuncts in man's solidly built, compressional-continuity ships. He puts in a solid mast and then adds tension helpers as shrouds. To man, building, Earth, and ship seemed alike, compressionally continuous. Tension has been secondary in all man's building and compression has been primary, for he has always thought of compression as solid. Compression is that "realistic hard core" that men love to refer to, and its reality was universal, ergo comprehensive. Man must now break out of that habit and learn to play at nature's game where tension is primary and where tension explains the coherence of the whole. Compression is convenient, very convenient, but always secondary and discontinuous. —*Synergetics*

•

A human being is what I call a pattern integrity.

I'm going to take a piece of manila rope, and then I'm going to splice into it a piece of cotton rope. I splice into the other end of the cotton rope a piece of nylon rope. I'm going to make the very simplest knot I know, which is to go around 360 degrees in this plane and 360 degrees in that plane.

I'm not going to pull it tight. There's the knot.

The rope has not done this, I have done it to the rope. At any rate, I can slide it along . . . and now it's on the nylon — suddenly, it's off the end. We say: "The knot was a pattern integrity." It wasn't manila, it wasn't cotton, it wasn't nylon.

Cotton, nylon, and manila — any one of them is good to let us know its shape, what its pattern was; but it wasn't that: it had an integrity of its own. —*Buckminster Fuller*

Questioning Technology

Does our industrial techno-society have you worried? You should be, and the thirty-one writers in this anthology tell you why as they present most of the principal anti-tech arguments. We're not talking emotional air-head stuff here, either — this is the carefully thought-out view. And only the negative view; there are no balancing arguments or suggestions for correcting the problems. (Maybe no corrections are possible?) The editors say that this collection is intended to be thought-provoking. It certainly is. Your worst fears will be abundantly confirmed. Perhaps this will goad you into appropriate action.
    —JB, unreconstructed technotwit

Questioning Technology
John Zerzan & Alice Carnes, Editors; 1988; 288 pp.; **$11.95** ($13.45 postpaid) from:
Left Bank Distributors
4142 Brooklyn NE, Seattle, WA
98105; (206) 632-5870 ✳WEA

All European tradition, Marxism included, has conspired to defy the natural order of all things. Mother Earth has been abused, the powers have been abused, and this cannot go on forever. No theory can alter that simple fact. Mother Earth will retaliate, the whole environment will retaliate, and the abusers will be eliminated. Things come full circle, back to where they started. *That's* revolution. And that's a prophecy of my people, of the Hopi people and of other correct peoples.
— Russell Means

•

The vitality of democratic politics depends on people's willingness to act together — to appear before each other in person, speak their minds, deliberate, and decide what they will do. This is considerably different from the model upheld as a breakthrough for democracy: logging onto one's computer, receiving the latest information, and sending back a digitized response. No computer enthusiasm is more poignant than the faith that the personal computer, as it becomes more sophisticated, cheaper, and more simple to use, will become a potent equalizer in society. Presumably, ordinary citizens equipped with microcomputers will counter the influence of large, computer-based organizations. This notion echoes the eighteenth- and nineteenth-century revolutionary belief that placing firearms in the hands of the people would overthrow entrenched authority. But the military defeat of the Paris Commune in 1871 made clear that arming the people may not be enough. Using a personal computer makes one no more powerful vis-a-vis, say, the U.S. National Security Agency than flying a hang glider establishes a person as a match for the US Air Force. —Langdon Winner

•

As the rhythm of the workplace speeds up to match that of the computer, the resulting increase in both load and rate of work, aggravated by the reliance on symbols and abstractions that the computer demands, creates new physical and psychological pressures. —Craig Brod

•

Western science would have us all stand in an adversarial relationship to our environment. If we are to study and control nature, then we must distinguish it from ourselves, *alienate* ourselves from it. The limited epistemology and the questionable values of science allow us to make that separation. As a consequence we can "do to" other entities what we would never think of doing to ourselves. If we perceive an "other" to be a part of ourselves, then we deprive ourselves of the luxuries we have become so dependent upon.
—Sally Gearhart

What Are People For?

Wendell Berry takes us backstage in our own theater in order to show us the basis for, and consequences of, our illusions and actions. Because he's not afraid to include himself in the discussion, there is a feeling of essential truth in what he says; arguable but undeniable. Reading his stuff sometimes makes me feel like I've walked smack into a very clean glass door, stopped cold by something very real but difficult to see unless you pay very close attention. (There's a whole chapter from this book on page 89.) —JB

What Are People For?
Wendell Berry; 1990
210 pp.; **$9.95** ($11.45
postpaid) from: North Point
Press, 850 Talbot Avenue
Berkeley, CA 94706
(415) 527-6260 ✱WEA

●

Emerson writes:

I grasp the hands of those next me, and take my place in the ring to suffer and to work, taught by an instinct, that so shall the dumb abyss be vocal with speech.

Emerson's spiritual heroism can sometimes be questionable or tiresome, but he can also write splendidly accurate, exacting sentences, and that is one of them. We see how it legislates against what we now call "groupiness." Neighborhood is a given condition, not a contrived one; he is not talking about a "planned community" or a "net-

work," but about the necessary interdependence of those who are "next" each other. We see how it invokes dance, acting in concert, as a metaphor of almost limitless reference. We see how the phrase "to suffer and to work" refuses sentimentalization. We see how common work, common suffering, and a common willingness to join and belong are understood as the conditions that make speech possible in "the dumb abyss" in which we are divided.

This leads us, probably, to as good a definition of the beloved community as we can hope for: common experience and common effort on a common ground to which one willingly belongs.

●

Like any other public institution so organized, the organized church is dependent on "the economy"; it cannot survive apart from those economic practices that its truth forbids and that its vocation is to correct. If it comes to a choice between the extermination of the fowls of the air and the lilies of the field and the extermination of a building fund, the organized church will elect — indeed, has already elected — to save the building fund. The irony is compounded and made harder to bear by the fact that the building fund can be preserved by crude applications of money, but the fowls of the air and the lilies of the field can be preserved only by true religion, by the *practice* of a proper love and respect for them as the creatures of God. No wonder so many sermons are devoted exclusively to "spiritual" subjects. If one is living by the tithes of history's most destructive economy, then the disembodiment of the soul becomes the chief of worldly conveniences.

Ecotopia

Fifteen years have passed since Ernest Callenbach wrote this lively examination of the world-we-could-have. Northern California, Oregon and Washington have seceded from the USA and become a country called Ecotopia. Their technology is environmentally benign; society and nature are in balance, to the betterment of both. The story makes Ecotopian life believable and so desirable — and to some, infuriating — that the very word ecotopia has become a part of our language. If anything, fifteen years have added to the seductive charm of the Ecotopian ideal. Only the sex seems dated today — there was no AIDS at the time it was written. Sigh. —JB

Ecotopia, Ernest Callenbach
1975, 1990; 181 pp.; **$8.95**
($10.95 postpaid)from: Bantam
Books, Inc.,414 E. Golf Rd.,
Des Plaines,IL 60016
(800) 223-6834 ✱WEA

A version of Ecotopia is
available on tape. **Ecotopia**:
An Audio Novel, **$15.95** ($17.05 postpaid) from:
St. Martin's Press, 175 5th Ave., New York, NY
10010; (800) 221-7945

●

"Probably our greatest economies were obtained simply by stopping production of many processed and packaged foods. These had either been outlawed on health grounds or put on Bad Practice lists."

This sounded like a loophole that might house a large and rather totalitarian rat. "What are these lists and how are they enforced?" I asked.

"Actually, they aren't enforced at all. They're a mechanism of moral persuasion, you might say. But they're purely informal. They're issued by study groups from consumer co-ops. Usually,

when a product goes onto such a list, demand for it drops sharply. The company making it then ordinarily has to stop production, or finds it possible to sell only in specialized stores."

"But surely these committees are not allowed to act simply on their own say-so, without scientific backing or government authorization?"

The Assistant Minister smiled rather wanly. "In Ecotopia," he said, "you will find many many things happening without government authorization."

●

After some drinks the conversation got livelier and more personal. Thought I'd do some probing. "Doesn't this stable-state business get awfully static? I'd think it would drive you crazy after a certain point!"

Bert looked at me with amusement, and batted the ball back. "Well, don't forget that we don't have to be stable. The system provides the stability, and we can be erratic within it."

●

Ecotopians treat as severe breaches of the peace many actions we consider white-collar crimes seldom deserving of police or court action. Deliberate pollution of water or air is punished by severe jail sentences. "Victimless" crimes such as prostitution, gambling, and drug use are no longer on the books, but embezzlement, fraud, collusion, and similar "gentleman's crimes" are dealt with just as severely as crimes like assault and robbery — which are, by the way, rare in Ecotopia, perhaps because of the personal nature of their neighborhoods and the virtual impossibility of anonymity in them. (Strangers get a lot of attention in Ecotopia, but the motives for this may not be entirely friendliness.) Ecotopian courts mete out fines very seldom, it appears, preferring to rely on imprisonment, which is felt to affect convicted persons more equally. I hope to visit an Ecotopian prison soon; I am told that all prisons require the inmates to work, and rumors have circulated that some verge on slave-labor camps.

Notes on the Underground

Rosalind Williams gets rolling fast with a wide open question: "What are the consequences when human beings dwell in an environment that is predominantly built rather than given?" An uncommonly astute and provocative array of answers are examined through the metaphor of living underground, literally and in literature. Frankly, when I started reading, I expected some sort of dry exercise in effete literary criticism — an impression reinforced by the mass of footnotes at the back of the book. Instead, I found a spellbinder. I started dog-earing pages for future reference, but soon the whole damned book was dog-eared, the margins filled with scribbled notes. I found my own technical experience and ideas clarified by a new perspective; sometimes strengthened, and occasionally definitively shot down. Ms. Williams has given us the rare vantage point that permits self-examination at a critical time. —JB

Notes on the Underground
(An Essay on Technology,
Society and the Imagination)
Rosalind Williams; 1990; 265 pp.
$24.95 ($27.45 postpaid) from:
The MIT Press, 55 Hayward St.
Cambridge, MA 02142
(617) 253-2884 ✱WEA

●

What is unique about the natural environment, what can never be replaced by the technological one, is its independence of the social order.

From this viewpoint, the concept of environmental politics takes on new meaning. The very existence of nature, its sheer being, challenges the life-denying, past-denying values of a machine-oriented collectivity. Because nature itself escapes from social determinism, it offers a reference point so human beings too can escape from social determinism. E. M. Forster writes in a pastoral tradition that "asserts or implies a continuity between the human spirit and the natural universe that is distinct from social definitions or placements of character." Were nature hidden or destroyed, people would have no independent source of value by which to judge the dominant order. To appeal to the physical world is to appeal to a moral and political counterforce.

In that case, the real danger to the environment is not desacralization but destruction. To Forster, nature cannot be desacralized. That is precisely why the Committee of the Machine wants it destroyed — to get rid of an opposing source of authority. Pollution, then, is to be taken seriously in its ritual meaning as desecration. The disappearance of the untainted, the untouched, is not just an example of lamentable but correctable mismanagement. The destruction of nature is also an expression of powerful, possibly ineradicable aggressive impulses. "If man *must* conquer nature in order to survive," Daniel Callahan writes, "he also *wants* to conquer nature as an expression of his omnipotence. . . ." Natural despoilation is not just a result of economic pressures; it is also a political action aimed at removing a source of subversion.

●

We have always lived below the surface, beneath the atmospheric ocean, in a closed, sealed, finite environment, where everything is recycled and everything is limited. Until now, we have not felt like underground dwellers because the natural system of the globe has seemed so large in comparison with any systems we might construct. That is changing. What is commonly called environmental consciousness could be described as subterranean consciousness — awareness that we are in a very real sense not on the earth but inside it.

A *Maxine!* cartoon by Marian Henley. Reprinted by permission.

Small is Beautiful

I doubt if Americans have been so influenced by printed eloquence since Thomas Paine's **Common Sense** *helped focus our founding independence. Schumacher is fighting a similar oppression, only this time we colonized ourselves, as he reveals by subtitling his book "Economics as if People Mattered."*

The wonder of Schumacher's work is his eminent practicality, based on his years with the British Coal Board.

With good sense and a mature spirituality, Schumacher comes on like John Henry against the mega-machine, sure that he will win, and he is.
— *Stewart Brand*

Small is Beautiful
E. F. Schumacher
1989; 352 pp.; **$9.95** ($13.45 postpaid) from: Harper & Row
Keystone Industrial Park
Scranton, PA 18512-1596
(800) 638-3030 ✳WEA

A Sand County Almanac

The most important book on ethics ever written on American soil — honest, clear, graceful, superbly crafted — It begins: "There are some who can live without wild things, and some who cannot. These essays are the delights and dilemmas of one who cannot." For Leopold, like Thoreau, human nature and nature's nature are inseparable natures and anything worth saying must be born from both. So the **Almanac** *exposes, reflects on, and strays into "values" that humans might cherish but it never strays too far from wildness, that teacher of many minds. In short, this is the bible of "oikos-logos" — the governing principle of our communal home — "ecology." —Peter Warshall*

•

Thinking Like a Mountain

A deep chesty bawl echoes from rimrock to rimrock, rolls down the mountain, and fades into the far blackness of the night. It is an outburst of

A Sand County Almanac
Aldo Leopold; 1968; 226 pp.
$7.95 ($10.45 postpaid) from:
Oxford University Press, 16-00
Pollitt Drive, Fairlawn, NJ 07410
(800) 451-7556 ✳WEA

wild defiant sorrow, and of contempt for all the adversities of the world.

Every living thing (and perhaps many a dead one as well) pays heed to that call. To the deer it is a reminder of the way of all flesh, to the pine a forecast of midnight scuffles and of blood upon the snow, to the coyote a promise of gleanings to come, to the cowman a threat of red ink at the bank, to the hunter a challenge of fang against bullet. Yet behind these obvious and immediate hopes and fears there lies a deeper meaning, known only to the mountain itself. Only the mountain has lived long enough to listen objectively to the howl of a wolf.

As Gandhi said, the poor of the world cannot be helped by mass production, only by production by the masses. The system of *mass production,* based on sophisticated, highly capital-intensive, high energy-input dependent, and human labour-saving technology, presupposes that you are already rich, for a great deal of capital investment is needed to establish one single workplace. The system of *production by the masses* mobilises the priceless resources which are possessed by all human beings, their clever brains and skilful hands, *and supports them with first-class tools.* The technology of *mass production* is inherently violent, ecologically damaging, self-defeating in terms of non-renewable resources, and stultifying for the human person. The technology of *production by the masses,* making use of the best of modern knowledge and experience, is conducive to decentralisation, compatible with the laws of ecology, gentle in its use of scarce resources, and designed to serve the human person instead of making him the servant of machines. I have named it *intermediate technology* to signify that it is vastly superior to the primitive technology of bygone ages but at the same time much simpler, cheaper, and freer than the supertechnology of the rich. One can also call it self-help technology, or democratic or people's technology — a technology to which everybody can gain admittance and which is not reserved to those already rich and powerful.

•

The cultivation and expansion of needs is the antithesis of wisdom. It is also the antithesis of freedom and peace. Every increase of needs tends to increase one's dependence on outside forces over which one cannot have control, and therefore increases existential fear.

•

The type of realism which behaves as if the good, the true, and the beautiful were too vague and subjective to be adopted as the highest aims of social or individual life, or were the automatic spin-off of the successful pursuit of wealth and power, has been aptly called "crackpot realism." Everywhere people ask: "What can I actually *do*?" The answer is as simple as it is disconcerting: we can, each of us, work to put our own inner house in order. The guidance we need for this work can not be found in science or technology, the value of which utterly depends on the ends they serve; but it can still be found in the traditional wisdom of mankind.

Filters Against Folly

Twenty years ago, Garrett Hardin published a deadly essay titled "The Tragedy of the Commons." In it, he showed irrefutably that individual citizens attempting to better their lot by adding one more sheep to the commonly owned pasture would inevitably bring ruin to all. This concept opposed the view held by many economists that the sum of individual strivings for advancement will benefit society as a whole. Hardin has aroused further controversy by advising that the U.S. not send aid to countries with rapidly expanding populations, claiming that such aid only brings worse problems later. "We Are The World" fundraising isn't necessarily a good idea.

This book further elucidates the idea of "commons" — it's easy to conceive of many that have little to do with sheep. More important, Hardin offers us a lesson in critical thinking so that we may be better able to avert lurking ecological catastrophe. He suggests that we subject incoming information from all sources — friend and foe — to three filters: Literacy — what's really being said; Numeracy — insisting upon quantification and careful interpretation of numbers; and Ecolacy — examining the long-run complex effects of our ac-

Filters Against Folly, Garrett
Hardin; 1986; 256 pp.; **$8.95**
($10.45 postpaid) from:
Penguin USA/Cash Sales
120 Woodbine Street
Bergenfield, NJ 07621
(800) 526-0275 ✳WEA

tions. Even though I've been analyzing information in this way for some time now (I base a college course I teach on Hardin's ideas), seeing the concepts put so clearly and accessibly is most helpful in cutting the crap. You may find likewise. —JB

•

The Marxist system is critically sensitive to scale. Hutterites found this out long ago when they noticed that as their community grew in size, the relative numbers of goldbricks increased. Workers found excuses for going into town "to get a part for the tractor" or whatnot, lingering for a long time before returning. What were at first the actions of a few became the actions of many, as some of the hardest workers decided they were unwilling to carry the burden of the whole community. Altruism diminished as envy and resentment took over. Instead of working, people argued about working. Exercised abilities declined; expressed needs increased.

The answer, the Hutterites found, lay in controlling the scale. As long as the community was less than some apparently critical number (about 100 to 150), the Marxist distribution system worked. Above that not precisely defined number the system failed, and failed ever more badly as the number increased. So the Hutterites adopted a development program that plans for the automatic splitting of a community into two as soon as its numbers have doubled. One farming community becomes two, two become four, and so on, at intervals of about fifteen years. So long as abilities and needs are determined within a really small community, commonism works.

Technics and Civilization

I first read this book in 1957, and twice since then. Here are the first lines of the book:

During the last thousand years the material basis and the cultural forms of Western Civilization have been profoundly modified by the development of the machine. How did this come about? Where did it take place?

Lewis Mumford was an unusual man. He wasn't an engineer or a scientist, he wasn't an historian or sociologist, you can't identify him as a business man or a literary man or an academic. He seems beyond all those roles. This made him especially attractive to me when I was 19 because his style smelled of the place I wanted to go. He was profound, poetic, knowledgeable. He took care of the large and small things in his books.

How I have used him: all through my twenties I used him as my guide. —Steve Baer

●

Once we have generally reached a new technical plateau we may remain on the level with very minor ups and downs for thousands of years. What are the implications of this approaching equilibrium?

First: equilibrium in the environment. This means first the restoration of the balance between man and nature. The conservation and restoration of soils, the re-growth wherever this is expedient and possible, of the forest cover to provide shelter for wild life and to maintain man's primitive background as a source of recreation, whose importance increases in proportion to the refinement of his cultural heritage. The use of tree crops where possible as substitutes for annuals, and the reliance upon kinetic energy — sun, falling water, wind — instead of upon limited capital supplies. The conservation of minerals and metals: the larger use of scrap metals. The conservation of the environment itself as a resource, and the fitting of human needs into the pattern formed by the

Technics and Civilization
Lewis Mumford; 1934; 1963;
495 pp.; **$14.95** ($16.95 post-paid) from: Harcourt Brace
Jovanovitch, 465 South
Lincoln, Troy, MO 63379
(800) 543-1918 ✱WEA

region as a whole: hence the progressive restoration out of such unbalanced regions as the over-urbanized metropolitan areas of London and New York. Is it necessary to point out that all this marks the approaching end of the miner's economy? Not mine and move, but stay and cultivate are the watchwords of the new order. It is also necessary to emphasize that with respect to our use of metals, the conservative use of the existing supply will lower the importance of the mine in relation to other parts of the natural environment?

[He said this in 1934! —JB]

●

The important thing to bear in mind is that the failure to evaluate the machine and to integrate it in society as a whole was not due simply to defects in distributing income, to errors of management, to greed and narrow-mindedness of the industrial leaders: it was also due to a weakness of the entire philosophy upon which the new techniques and inventions were grounded. The leaders and enterprisers of the period believed that they had avoided the necessity for introducing values, except those which were automatically recorded in profits and prices. They believed that the problem of justly distributing goods could be sidetracked by creating an abundance of them: that the problem of applying one's energies wisely could be cancelled out simply by multiplying them: in short, that most of the difficulties that had hitherto vexed mankind had a mathematical or mechanical — that is a quantitative — solution. The belief that values could be dispensed with constituted the new system of values.

Rediscovering America's Values

Lappé sets up a dialogue between an unbridled free-market apologist and herself — an advocate of socialist-leaning reforms. These two voices then have at each other on fundamental topics such as freedom, market efficiency, civil liberties, and human nature.

The book's debate succeeded in its stated aim: provoking me into questioning my own assumptions on fairness and what security democratic governments should and can provide. Unfortunately the book falls down in creating as strong an argument for Lappé's philosophy as I had hoped for. I agree with Lappé's intentions, so I wanted her argument to be the outstandingly more convincing one. But the free-marketeer, while espousing tough-luck policies, came out sounding sometimes more logical than Lappé. Still, as Lappé herself says, some of our now most taken-for-granted rights — universal suffrage, desegregation — were changes pushed for by visionaries who sounded illogical to their contemporaries. I wouldn't quite call Lappé a visionary, but then she's certainly not illogical either. Indeed, the book is well-written and thought-provoking. I strongly recommend it as a tool for reopening a debate on basic values. —Mary James

●

(Conventional Liberal) If individuals feel strongly enough about something they should be willing to use their dollar-votes to make their point in the marketplace. They can choose to boycott, choose to recycle, choose to buy from firms they think are

Rediscovering America's Values, Frances Moore
Lappé; 1989; 325 pp.
$22.50 ($25.88 postpaid)
from: Institute for Food &
Development Policy
145 Ninth Street
San Francisco, CA 94103
(415) 864-8555 ✱WEA

better for whatever reason. That's one great advantage of the market system. We as individuals can express our views. You want the government to be a parent, forcing you — and, of course, others — to do what you aren't disciplined enough to do by yourself!

(Lappé) No, that's not it. Thinking about it, I realize that if I failed to recycle it would not be out of laziness; it's that I would know my individual decision would have little impact — so why bother? Whereas if everybody is doing it, my individual effort will matter, and, what's more, systems will be set up to make recycling practical. As citizens, we can organize our common lives to make it practical to do what as individual consumers we wouldn't do — but what in our hearts we know is right.

If we had only interests and no principles, we wouldn't need a polity at all; we could get by with just an economy in which all transactions — from education to law enforcement to saving endangered species — are left to the market. Indeed, if you were right, there could be no such thing as a civil servant. Motivated only by rational self-interest, officials would just respond to bribes of one sort or another.

Turtle Island

To understand whole *evidently requires understanding with more than rational consciousness. I mean, with experience, with dreams, with art, with poetry — (not-quite synonyms for knowledge which is real but not nameable). Gary Snyder's poetry addresses the life-planet identification with unusual simplicity of style and complexity of effect.*
—Stewart Brand

Turtle Island
Gary Snyder
1974; 114 pp.
$5.95 postpaid from:
W. W. Norton & Co., Inc.
Keystone Industrial Park
Scranton, PA 18512
(800) 233-4830 ✱WEA

●

TOMORROW'S SONG

The USA slowly lost its mandate
in the middle and later twentieth century
it never gave the mountains and rivers,
    trees and animals
        a vote.
all the people turned away from it
    myths die; even continents are impermanent

    Turtle Island returned.
    my friend broke open a dried coyote-scat
    removed a ground squirrel tooth
    pierced it, hung it
    from the gold ring
    in his ear.

We look to the future with pleasure
we need no fossil fuel
get power within
grow strong on less.

Grasp the tools and move in rhythm side by side
    flash gleams of wit and silent knowledge
        eye to eye
sit still like cats or snakes or stones
    as whole and holding as
        the blue black sky.
gentle and innocent as wolves
    as tricky as a prince.

At work and in our place:

    in the service
    of the wilderness
    of life
    of death
    of the Mother's breasts!

Ecophilosophy

A much-needed "mini-bibliography" of eco-related values. 238 books are listed with a brief annotation — enough to get a feel for the books you want.

Also included are separate listings of periodicals and organizations, plus an index to the whole book. A really useful book, as eco-philosophy is a hard subject area to define. You would otherwise have to wade through hundreds of listings in standard reference works. Great for libraries, bookstore use and for people looking to find good books in this hot area. My hat's off to the author and publisher! —Cliff Martin

Ecophilosophy (A Field Guide
to the Literature), Donald
Edwards Davis; 1989; 137 pp.
$8.95 ($10.45 postpaid) from:
R & E Miles
P. O. Box 1916
San Pedro, CA 90733
(213) 833-8856 ✱WEA

Corporate Environmentalism

By Art Kleiner

DuPont's chairman makes speeches, proclaiming himself to be an environmentalist. Weyerhauser boasts, in its advertising, about the number of trees it plants. Royal Dutch/Shell funds a group of energy conservation activists coordinating efforts to respond to global warming. And this year, more than one major corporation tried to become a full-scale sponsor of Earth Day 1990 — as if it were the Superbowl or the Olympics. In the wake of incidents like Valdez and the Boesky/Milken indictments, it's easy to be cynical about the intentions behind corporate environmentalism. Indeed, many efforts by large companies begin as nothing more than public relations and damage control. But some efforts go further.

A movement towards corporate environmentalism has existed for at least a decade. It's diffuse and scattered; people in different companies are rarely aware of each other. Often, the movement operates semi-covertly, fueled by individuals who believe that they can influence their part of the firm to halt a bad practice or start a good one — usually in some small way. In some cases, it takes years for that change to take effect. While few corporations (if any) can yet be called "environmentalist" in a way that would satisfy, say, Greenpeace, it is nonetheless becoming clear that there are ways to prompt even the largest corporations to behave more responsibly. Public criticism and boycotts, like that against Exxon after Valdez, tend to lead to stonewalling; it works better to find the people who are ready for a change of heart, and to help them deal with the cultural contradictions between the profit motive and ecological values.

The tragedy of corporate-environmentalist disagreement emerged from cultural differences. Corporations typically had put ill-trained public relations flacks in charge of environmental issues, or over-trained engineers; the depth of their training made it inevitable that they would see environmentalists as flakes and blowhards. Environmentalists (especially those dealing with issues like toxic waste) had often been wounded by birth defects in their children, or cancer in their neighborhood, or the loss of a beloved place. They came in fear and bitterness, which made it difficult to realize that most individuals in corporations see themselves as fundamentally moral and responsible — and are willing to act to live up to that morality. The two groups met in courtrooms, where no one could admit fallibility for fear of making the company (or group) they represented more vulnerable. Nor could they talk frankly, as people — for fear of being co-opted.

Stalemates like this end slowly, and only by giving up the need for the other side to give in. But we live in an era of stalemate-ending. Consider, for instance, the Dow Chemical Company. In the 1970s and early 1980s, Dow Chemical was one of the most antagonistic corporations to environmentalism in America. They refused to release statistics on their smokestack emissions, and sued the EPA for flying airplanes overhead. Dow executives spread rumors that Greenpeace workers had syphilis; and fought bitterly with Oregon residents over responsibility for dioxin poisoning associated with their herbicide 2,4,5-T. (Carol Van Strum described the heartbreaking battle in her book, "A Bitter Fog.") Beginning in 1982, however, there was a dioxin scare in Dow's small Michigan hometown, Midland. At first, Dow engineers pooh-poohed the danger; they had, in fact, triggered the

See Also . . . Values, pages 98-99.

Earth Communications Office (ECO) • Environmental Media Association (EMA)

When you see an environmental activist character on thirtysomething, you know something's up. Who decided to put them into the plot? Who checked the lines to make sure they weren't nonsense? Who organized a superstar trek to the rainforest for a firsthand look at what they've agreed to help save? Something has changed in Hollywood. At work are two young organizations. EMA seems aimed mostly at influencing and educating producers and other top management; ECO seems to include everybody right down to the floor sweepers. Both seem effective in their goal of assisting the entertainment industry in promoting environmental concerns within itself and the public. Even better, both groups seem able to tell the difference between faddish eco-chic and the real thing. What a great idea!
—JB [Suggested by Esther Feldman]

For more information write to:

Earth Communications Office (ECO)
1925 Century Park East, Suite 2300
Los Angeles, CA 90067

Environmental Media Association (EMA)
10536 Culver Boulevard, Culver City, CA 90232

scare by developing a method of measuring much smaller quantities of the chemical waste than had ever been measured before. But the reaction did not die down; and Dow executives, seen as villains for the first time by their own neighbors, found themselves changing their attitudes.

I have interviewed Dow executives and environmentalists who dealt with them, and I don't pretend to know for certain whether Dow is now an environmentalist company. Some policies are certainly different: Dow now invites the EPA to tour their plants. Before designing a new chemical plant, they seek out local environmental groups. And they have become deeply involved in plastic recycling research, and in lobbying for heavier government restrictions on toxic waste. On the other hand, they still manufacture herbicides, and they admit that their campaign for plastic recycling is a way to stave off restrictions against plastic packaging (like those passed recently in Portland, Oregon).

Several environmentalists (including Carol Van Strum) have told me that they believe the new Dow attitude is all lip service and public relations. Others have praised Dow for substantive changes. I happen to believe that part of the problem is their "Great Things" commercials, which are so slickly emotional that they seem insincere. But the Dow people I've talked to are sincere. The question is, how effective can they be at tackling the truly difficult questions — such as whether herbicides or some plastics should be manufactured in the first place?

Of course, there are ulterior motives for some corporate involvement — environmental cleanup is profitable (though that's not one of Dow's businesses), and the inundation of coastal cities with seawater is presumably bad for business. Behind the stereotypes on both sides is a deeper truth; no company can prosper without long-lasting ecological safety. You don't have to be, as business people say, a rocket scientist to realize the principle. The trick is getting the large firms to act on it, and to provide more communities that encourage mainstream corporate people and environmentalists to talk to each other. Both sides need to educate each other.

Our Common Future

A United Nations Commission proposes that without economic growth, there can be no environmental protection. Nor without environmental protection can there be economic growth. The "Brundtland Report" (named after Norwegian President Gro Brundtland, who chaired the commission) is less valuable for its worthwhile overview of global environmental problems than for its influence. In many countries (not the United States), councils now meet to figure out ways in which industries can assume some of the responsibility for handling environmental problems. The Brundtland vision of the future is impossibly utopian; local countries around the world are to bring together citizens' groups, government agencies, and industry, and work diligently to raise everyone's standard of living and natural purity simultaneously — outflanking local corruption, and keeping cultural diversity intact. It's hard to believe it could happen. It's sobering to read what the Brundtland commission expects will take place if humanity doesn't achieve that impossible goal. And it's inspiring to read the reasons why they believe we can. —Art Kleiner

Our Common Future, World Commission on Environment & Development; 1987; 400 pp. **$10.95** ($12.95 postpaid) from: Oxford University Press 2001 Evans Rd., Cary, NC 27513; (800) 451-7556 ✳WEA •

A world in which poverty and inequity are endemic will always be prone to ecological and other crises. Sustainable development requires meeting the basic needs of all and extending to all the opportunity to satisfy their aspirations for a better life.

. . . Perceived needs are socially and culturally determined, and sustainable development requires the promotion of values that encourage consumption standards that are within the bounds of the ecologically possible and to which all can reasonably aspire.

Normal Accidents

It's your worst fears confirmed: accidents in complex technological systems are inevitable, unpreventable, and must, like a little dishonesty, be considered a normal fact of life. The sociologist author makes a worrisomely good case for this view, though his credibility is superficially tarnished by poor science editing and careless proofreading. Put aside those annoyances, and you'll find ample proof that dangerous technologies are not entirely controllable, even if the folks in charge are models of social and environmental responsibility. Horrendous examples — including nuclear — are detailed, but they aren't nearly so disturbing as the dishonesty that accompanies disasters. Ass-covering prevarications are expected. The less-expected intellectual dishonesty short-circuits the learning process that can prevent the same sort of thing from happening again even when profits and prestige are not at stake. The question is whether certain technologies should be permitted at all if the consequences of failure are drastic. The answer is no, of course, but the author offers few solutions. We'd better get to work. —JB

Normal Accidents
Charles Perrow; 1985
386 pp.; **$14.95** ($17.95 postpaid) from: Harper & Row, Attn: Order Dept., Keystone Industrial Park, Scranton, PA 18512; (800) 242-7737 ✳WEA

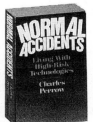

Life Work

By Jim Dodge

A basic rule of human habitation has always been "Don't shit in camp." When the number of human inhabitants reached five billion, "camp" became the planet, the common ground of the global village and everyone's backyard. This recognition that our species' pollution and pillage in disparate locales now threatens, by cumulative insults, to foul the collective nest has been relatively sudden (the last thirty years of human occupation) and perhaps too late. But if necessity is the mother of invention, species-survival may prove downright inspirational.

The notion of "right livelihood" — work that is individually satisfying and for the common good — is beginning to exert its simple wisdom on a wider scale. If we spend about a third of our lives sleeping and a third at work, a comfortable bed and a fulfilling job are obvious provisions for getting a jump on happiness. A recent Columbia University study of people over 95 years old asked the elders what they'd change if they could re-live their lives. Among the three most frequent answers was "Create something that would last beyond death." (The other two were "Take more risks" and "Stop and smell the roses.") Restoration work not only offers right livelihood at a time when we seem sick-to-puking with meaningless labor for the poverty of dollars, it also, according to our elders, insures us against regret. Work is work, but it's a pleasure to sing for one's supper when the song itself provides sustenance.

Restoration, like any art, seeks a greater understanding of existence, which tends to deepen our appreciation, gratitude, and humility, salubrious states of mind that are less fringe benefits than compelling requisites for further work. Moreover, the art of restoration is finely balanced between mind and body, thought and sweat. The work is heads-up and hands-on: figuring out by guess, gut, experience, and calculation how many trees to plant on the hillside, what species, when, and to what immediate and long-term consequence, then picking up your hoe-dad and doing it. Even better, it's outside work, so you don't have to make a special trip to smell the roses or feel the rain on your face. Compared to restoration, the other arts seem dangerously self-involved and boringly one-dimensional.

from the
Farming Game, review p. 44

It's my feeling, one that swings between conviction and wild hope, that we're at a point in species' consciousness where we're about to grasp both the importance and rightness of helping the planet heal the injuries we've mindlessly inflicted. It's tempting to think of restoration as a new genre of the healing arts, but in fact we have hardly begun to wash the wounds, much less address the psycho-social pathologies and self-destructive contempt that fuel the affliction. In caring for the earth, we may heal ourselves, but at present the art of restoration is more janitorial than medicinal. We've made a mess of creation, and now we need to clean it up.

Doing What Needs to be Done

"**I** felt then . . . that it could be that instead of trying to think about: *How do I earn a living? . . . how do I survive? . . .* that we ought to be looking around and saying '*what is it that my experience teaches me that needs to be attended to, which, if properly attended to, could bring advantage to all humanity, and which, if not attended to properly, could find humanity at great disadvantage?*'

"If you have had anything in your experience say that to you insistently, you ought to do something about it. . . and pay no attention to the earning of a living." —R. Buckminster Fuller

I took Bucky's advice when I was 18 and have not sought employment since. It's been a good, if not affluent, life. Virtually all the people I know who have elected to take this route have done OK — "Had good luck", as some detractors sneer. Would I do it again if I were 18? Yes, only with more hubris and trust. Are there any tricks to the game? Yup: Do your homework, stay awake and be ready to pounce, be cool when you get the heebie-jeebies watching just about everyone else work hard for "security" while you snoop around the Universe on odd quests. —JB

The National Parks Trade Journal

For those of you who missed the first two editions of this sassy publication, it's a book with a magazine's title and contents. Definitely not the official Washington viewpoint, the journal nevertheless offers reliable and detailed park-by-park information that'll help you choose and nab a job in a national park. That'd be reason enough to take the book home, but there's more. Poetry, art, adventure stories, comments on outdoor equipment, and a great selection of advertisements for environmentally Right Stuff is mixed with articles on international environmental organizations. This journal has become a kind of in-house magazine for park workers, but one they want to share with you, inviting you to join their way of life. If you're wondering what to do next, or you've considered maybe working in a park, start reading. Prepare to be seduced. —JB

•

National Parks Underwater. These units of the National Park System contain more than 2,250,000 acres of submerged land, an area equal to the size of Yellowstone National Park. Yet we know more about the most remote parts of Yellowstone than we do about these underwater areas. There are 80 parks which lie on or near large bodies of water, including well-known parks like Channel Islands, Isle Royale, Virgin Islands, Cape Hatteras, Biscayne or Fort Jefferson. There are lesser known areas, too, including parks on rivers or smaller lakes.

The National Parks Trade Journal, Dave Anzalone, Editor 1984, 1989; 345 pp.; **$12.95** ($14.50 postpaid) from: National Parks Trade Journal Wawona Station, Yosemite National Park CA 95389; (209) 375-6552

The Complete Guide to Environmental Careers

You may not end up Trumpishly rich as an environmental worker, but you surely will be riding the first wave of a huge new profession. I liken the potential to what alert early birds experienced in '50s television; get in now and be a manager soon. As this very savvy book makes clear, the field is so new that it is still possible to define your own job. (If you feel better as a typical government slot-filler, there are those positions available too.) Of course, a new field is also harder to define, and it is likely that you will help define it. That will demand an unusual level of creativity and personal responsibility — a sign of interesting work. This book delivers an intimate, detailed lowdown on how to seek, recognize and nail the job you want. It's divided up into specific areas of interest: Planning, Education, Communications, Solid Waste Management, Hazardous Waste Management, Air Quality, Water Quality, Land and Water Conservation, Fishery and Wildlife Management, Parks and Recreation, and Forestry. Each chapter is a good look at the specialty, what is required, and how to break in. Internships are discussed in detail. It's an insider's view. Tips abound. If your competition (and there's plenty for the good jobs) reads this book and you don't, you'll get left behind to sell used cars. Note: The bookjacket emphasizes young seekers, but the advice will work just fine for mid-life crisis course-changers and other agile veterans. —JB

The Complete Guide to Environmental Careers The CEIP Fund; 1989 328 pp.; **$14.95** ($16.95 postpaid) from: Island Press Box 7, Covelo, CA 95428 (800) 828-1302 ✳WEA

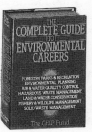

•

Internships: your first job.

The first work experience of most environmental professionals is an internship, seasonal, or volunteer position. It is now almost a prerequisite for environmental employment, to demonstrate your abilities and, more important, show employers that you are committed to the field. One employer pointedly asks, "If they haven't been able to do some hands-on work in all their years of education, why would they even think I might pick them over the 95 percent who have one and usually several such experiences?"

In Business

This magazine caters to the needs of small environmentally aware businesses. They've done a special issue (April 1990) featuring a very useful and inspiring Directory of Environmental Entrepreneurs (180 of them). It's worth sending for as a back issue, or looking up in the library. —JB

In Business (The Magazine for Environmental Entrepreneuring) Jerome Goldstein Editor; **$21**/year (six issues) from: In Business Box 323 Emmaus, PA 18049 (215) 967-4135

See Also . . . Economics, pages 95-95.

Tourists *are an infestation that degrades the society and environment being visited.*

Tourists are economic salvation and the strongest encouragement for the preservation of indigenous societies and the beauties of nature.

Sad examples are not hard to find; tourism is an example of Garrett Hardin's Tragedy of the Commons *(p. 98) with that which is being toured as the commons. But affluent people spend about $150 billion a year just for international travel; tourism is the largest single industry in the world.*

Since people are going to traipse around the planet, efforts are being made to reduce the deleterious effects. The best ecotourism strategies may actually bring benefit to the people and land being visited. The worst merely preserve a fakey stage-set showpiece with the locals as low-paid actors. Obviously it is impossible to have no effect at all. These things are still being worked out, so there is a wide range of eco-conscious travel available, not all of it beyond reproach. Take time to snoop around a bit and find an outfit that feels right to you at this time. Obviously, we can't list all available tour firms; the following are just a sample. —JB

Hike to the fantastic spires of the *Cuernos* (horns) of Paine on our *Patagonian Wildlands Safari*.

North American Coordinating Center For Responsible Tourism

This worthy organization is probably best known for its Code of Ethics for Tourists, but the Center is active in many areas, including such arcane matters as the treatment of hidden crewmembers on fancy cruise ships. (You might be surprised at what's going on out there.) Here's where to find out how to travel in a manner less likely to damage your hosts. You'll feel less guilty, and you might even do them some good. —JB

•

RESPONSIBLE TRAVELING
When planning a trip or buying a package tour, ask yourself these questions:
* **D**oes the tour organizer or travel agent demonstrate a cultural and environmental sensitivity to your questions?
* **H**ow are the local people and the culture you are to visit portrayed in advertising brochures and orientation materials?
* **W**ho benefits from the costs of your trip? Which sectors of the host country benefit? What percentage of your money stays in the country you visit rather than leaking out to the transnational travel industry, the hotel chains, and airlines?
* **I**s a realistic picture of your host country presented, or is it a version packaged for tourists?
* **W**ill you use accommodations, transportation,

and food used by members of the local society?
* **D**oes your schedule allow adequate opportunities for meeting with local people? Does its pacing provide time for you to create and/or accept opportunities for interacting with local people?
* **A**re you committed to engage in a pre-trip orientation program? Have you thought through ways to share your experiences when you return home, to maintain contact with people you meet, and to keep informed about the country you visit?
* **A**re you allowing sufficient lead time when opting for alternative local travel services?
* **D**o you inform your travel agent/tour organizer about your concerns for justice in travel?

North America Coordinating Center for Responsible Tourism; 45¢ stamped self-addressed envelope for more information about the work of The Center.

SASE for resource list of basic materials and reprints available from The Center.

Responsible Traveling Newsletter, Betty Stott, Editor; **$10**/year (four issues)

All from: The Center for Responsible Tourism
2 Kensington Road, San Anselmo, CA 94960
(415) 258-6594

New World of Travel 1990

There are thousands of travel books in print. I wouldn't be exaggerating much to say I've seen them all. This is the only one of them that has lots of tricks and savvy tips new to me. It's a menu of alternative, rewarding traveling possibilities, by the guy who invented "Europe on $5 a Day" in the 1950s. Mostly it's about practical and inspirational ways to go, and not about what to see. For the past several years Whole Earth has wanted to do a Whole Earth Travel Catalog. Now we don't have to. This book did it, and did it superbly.
—Kevin Kelly

•

SUMMER CAMPS FOR ADULTS
Sierra Club "Base Camps," Sample base camp stays planned for 1989: in the Tahoe Forest of California/Nevada, near early Indian habitats, abandoned mines, and ghost towns; near the Donner Pass amid majestic rock cathedrals and trout-stocked lakes; on a Navajo reservation near Canyon de Chelly National Monument of Arizona; in a nationally protected area of fossil beds in Oregon; in the densely wooded Monongahela Forest of West Virginia. Though the accent throughout is on fun — the sheer pleasure of removing oneself for a week or two to an untouched, untrammeled wilderness — participants (of all ages, and including families) have the added opportunity to "network" with other kindred sorts, the dedicated environmentalists of our nation.

The New World of Travel 1990, Arthur Frommer 1990: 381 pp.; **$16.95** ($19.95 postpaid) from: Simon & Schuster, Inc. 200 Old Tappan Road Old Tappan, NJ 07675 (201) 767-5937 **✱**WEA

Journeys

For fourteen years, these folks have offered adventure tours led by local residents. A portion of your land fee goes to the Earth Preservation Fund which is used to help nurture the land and the way of life of the people you are visiting. Fancy stuff is not what you're there for; you may get dirty.

The Nature Conservancy

In addition to their highly effective environmental work (see p. 111), The Nature Conservancy offers trips for folks who wish to see what needs to be, or is being, conserved. They offer inspiring field trips and tours to a variety of locations in the States and Latin America. Trips are led by Conservancy members and local guides who of course make sure that the proper sensitivities and attitudes are celebrated. Many find that it is a special pleasure to travel and learn in a group with similar concerns. You'll be helping out a bit, too; part of your fee is a contribution to Nature Conservancy's efforts. —JB

The Nature Conservancy; **$15**/year membership (includes bimonthly magazine & newsletter which lists field trips & tours in the states)

The Nature Conservancy's International Trips; Information **free** from: Sarah Bolon, Latin America Division

Both from: The Nature Conservancy
1815 N. Lynn Street
Arlington, VA 22209; (703) 841-5300

•

ECUADOR + GALAPAGOS ISLANDS, Aug. 1, Sept. 5. Visit the environmental education center and the montane forest of Pasachoa Reserve. Contrast this with the jungle world of Cuyabeno Reserve, an unspoiled tropical rainforest in the Amazon basin. Extend your adventure to the Galapagos Islands. Enjoy land tortoises, magnificent frigate birds, and perhaps a waved albatross in this tremendous archipelago. $2598. Galapagos extension, $1398.

Each trip is hosted by a Conservancy representative and includes visits or lectures by local conservation experts, as well as the services of a trained in-country naturalist.

Groups are small and arranged for compatibility. Families are welcome on many trips. Custom arrangements can be made. I have not travelled with Journeys, but I know people who have. They say it's a class act, complete with homework background books on the cultures you are about to visit. —JB

Journeys (Worldwide Nature & Culture Explorations); Catalog & quarterly newsletter **free** from: Journeys, 3516 NE 155th, Seattle, WA 98155; (800) 345-4453 [in WA (206) 365-0686]

●

YOUR GUIDES IN ARGENTINA: Our expedition director is Argentine conservationist and ornithologist, Ricardo Clark. You couldn't find a more qualified guide to show you the wildlands of Argentina. Ricardo is a former naturalist for the Argentine National Park Service and author of a field guide: *The Birds of Tierra del Fuego*. Domingo Galussio, our expert in Tierra del Fuego, is completing a field guide to the plants of the region and is considered the best guide on the island. Carol Passera is a lifetime resident of the Peninsula Valdes, a published photographer and author on conservation of the Magellanic penguin. Ricardo Gregorio, a farmer and mountaineer, is an assistant guide in charge of equipment, supplies and pack animals.

●

CALIFORNIA, **Santa Cruz Island** (May 10-13, Oct. 18-21). To the Island Chumash people, it was the center of the world. To geologists, it poses mysterious questions. To naturalists, it is a treasure trove of unique plants and animals. To the Conservancy, Santa Cruz Island is the "crown jewel" of preserves, an island sanctuary protecting 42 plants and 13 animal species that exist nowhere else on Earth. We'll explore pine forests, oak woodlands, volcanic peaks, and deserted beaches. By night we'll enjoy the hospitality of the historic rancho following daily bird, wildflower, and geologic forays. Limited to 8 people. Cost: $1650

Directory of Alternative Travel Resources

This unique catalog lives up to its billing as "250 alternative and socially responsible travel options." There's a wonderful variety — I'll bet you and your travel agent have not heard of most of the offerings. Some are church-associated. This is certainly worth checking if you crave something out of the even very nice ordinary; Club Med, it's not. —JB

Directory of Alternative Travel Resources Dianne G. Brause; 1988; 26 pp.; **$7.50** postpaid from: One World Family Travel Network 81868 Lost Valley Lane, Dexter, OR 97431 (503) 937-3351

●

Earthstewards Network/Holyearth Foundation P. O. Box 10697, Bainbridge Island, WA 98110 (206) 842-7986, (206) 285-7363 Contact: Danaan Parry

The Earthstewards Network organizes year-round citizen diplomacy trips to the USSR, Northern Ireland, and Costa Rica to promote sharing and working with others in their homes, workplaces, and schools. Several 3-4 week specialized groups, such as women, children, sheep farmers, gardeners, and the disabled have been organized. They also have a "Peace-Trees" project with Soviet, US, Indian & Costa Rican teenagers, an exchange between US & Soviet Veterans of recent wars and an on-going global network of members.

Earthwatch

Would you like to participate in a real scientific expedition? You can, by joining one of the many sponsored by this group. Yeah, you have to pay them instead of them paying you, but you'll learn a lot, and you'll actually be doing something useful with your time and (tax-deductible) money. There's a wide range of expeditions, here and abroad. You get to choose from numerous projects in rainforest ecology, archeology, geology, marine sciences, life sciences, and social sciences. You're going to work hard, though most schedules include time off for local explorations. I've heard few complaints. Fellowships may be available. You must be 16-85, and in appropriate health. Tempting! —JB

Earthwatch, **$25**/year membership (includes bimonthly Earthwatch magazine with list of expeditions, invitational events, eligibility for all expeditions) from: Earthwatch, 680 Mt. Auburn Street, P.O. Box 403, Watertown, MA 02172 (617) 926-8200

●

Island Rain Forest *(Ilha do Cardoso, Brasil) Field Conditions:* Teams, working in shifts day and night, will search for caiman nests; observe the animals' behavior; record the local habitat; map streams, swamps, and other topographic features; photograph animals and their habitats; and enter data in computers. They will also set traps for other reptiles and amphibians, collect any animals that are caught (snakes will be handled only by staff members), and help set up a photographic

Elderhostel

*We have reviewed Elderhostel in our earlier Catalogs as an excellent program for people over 60 (spouses under 60 and companions over 50 are welcome too) who want to learn and travel both in the U.S. and abroad inexpensively. But what makes it of particular interest for this **Ecolog** is that among the huge assortment of wonderful classes and seminars offered in the U.S. and Canada there are over 120 environmental programs each year.*

From Alaska to British Columbia to Maine and all those parts south to the Mexican border classes are given in Environmental Defense, How We Use Our Forests, Organic Gardening, Desert Ecology, Environmental Theater, Biosphere II Project, Old Growth Forest Ecology and Management, Environmental Ethics, and over 100 more.

I know first and second hand experience of Elderhostel's wonderfulness. My in-laws have participated in five different Elderhostel programs in the last three years and have enjoyed them thoroughly. From my own experience I found the staff at Elderhostel most helpful and willing to accommodate special needs.

Elderhostel is a great way to travel, meet like-minded people from different places, and learn how to do your part. —Susan Erkel Ryan

Elderhostel; Catalog **free** from: Elderhostel, Inc 80 Boylston Street, Suite 400, Boston, MA 02116; (617) 426-8056

BRITISH COLUMBIA, **Galiano Island/Therah Learning Center**. Galiano Island, a jewel in the Gulf of Georgia, is just an hour's ferry ride from Vancouver or Victoria. Many of this rural island community's 850 residents are artists and craftspeople who draw inspiration from the delightful environment. A year-round mild, sunny climate, magnificent arbutus trees, sculpted sandstone seashores and a diversity of wildlife entice explorers. Accomodation at Bodega Resort — large

index of the island's species.

Teams will stay in research station houses and dormitories, which have some electricity, running water, and flush toilets. Meals will be prepared by station staff. Because the island is so close to shore and major cities, there will also be occasional access to restaurants. Music makes up a regular part of the Brazilian culture and the life of the camp as well. Both Moulton and Magnussen play instruments; as do most of the Brazilian staff members; volunteers are encouraged to join in. *Related interests: photography, mapping, computers, biology, drawing.*

With each rainforest tree cut down, the broad-nosed caiman is a little closer to extinction. Caimans are primarily tropical, small crocodiles; Latin America has spawned a proliferation of species. Most are under seven feet long, but the black caiman can reach fifteen feet (including the powerful tail).

comfortable chalets and dining hall set on 25 seaview acres.

* *Trees—Guardians of the Earth*, Apr 1-7, 1990, #61410-0401-1. Forests are to some the earth's sacred mantle and to others a resource to be extracted. Explore the symbolic and environmental significance of trees and forests and compare industrial tree farming with community forestry.

Good Life Study Tours

A month-long homestay in Kerala in South India will change your sense of what is and is not necessary for the good life. These modest tours are actually seminars consisting of ten of you and ten English-speaking local associates, working together on problems of consumption, development, and living lightly as world citizens. It is not, as the brochure makes plain, "a thinking person's Club Med," and neither is the price. Adventure seems likely. It's too new for a personal recommendation, but it does seem like a good idea. If you give it a try, let us know how it went. —JB

Good Life Study Tours; Information **free** from: Institute for Food and Development Policy Good Life Study Tours, 145 Ninth Street San Francisco, CA 94103; (415) 864-8555

●

The modest consumption patterns of Kerala are a major factor maintaining life quality. Garbage and junk are nearly unknown. Air is free of industrial pollutants. Intensive farming satisfies vegetarian diets supplemented by fish. The combination of good life with very low per capita incomes is an unexplained mystery in modern economic science. We must seek our understanding of the Kerala good life in older, non-monetary virtues such as compassion, cooperation, thrift, and artistry.

See Also . . .
Oceanic Society Expeditions, page 15.

A Wildlife, Coastal & Parkland Conservation Act

Proposition 70, is what it was called on the 1988 California ballot. There was very little opposition, and it passed easily, netting $776 million for a variety of environmental projects all over the state. Where were the traditional foes of such legislation? The organizers fielded 20,000 volunteers to gather the 730,000 signatures that got the measure on the ballot. How was this done? The assistant campaign director, Esther Feldman, tells how in this booklet from the organization that did the deed, the Planning and Conservation League. PCL strategies and tactics are basically non-contentious: get opposing sides to identify what they can agree on, and go for that; spread the benefits over a wide constituency; thoroughly organize the effort in an impeccably professional manner. It works. PCL has been involved in the passage of every major piece of California environmental law for the past 25 years, making it one of the most effective lobbying organizations in the country. This booklet presents their generic recipe in sufficient detail that you can go and do likewise in your situation. The advice is well-written, utterly clear, toughened and honed by a quarter century of successful campaigns. It's the best manual for environmental political action I've ever seen. —JB

A Wildlife, Coastal & Parkland Conservation Act, Esther Feldman 1988; 39 pp.; **$10** postpaid from: Planning and Conservation League Foundation, 909 12th Street, Suite 203, Sacramento, CA 95814 (916) 444-8726

•

Each land acquisition project must meet the following <u>minimum</u> criteria:

1) There must be willing sellers. This is to avoid any possibility of controversy.

2) It must be a sound environmental project, with good reasons for being perserved.

3) The proposed acquisition should be part of a local or state general plan if at all possible. (We waived this requirement in a few cases.)

4) The project must be absolutely non-controversial, particularly with respect to landowners.

* This cannot be stressed strongly enough! Don't create a constituency that will oppose you with a funded campaign.

5) The project must have local political support. We asked for a resolution or other written support from the appropriate city or county.

6) The project must have strong support from local conservation groups, and from statewide groups if applicable.

7) There must be an entity willing to operate and maintain the area once it is bought.

Notes

*Use caution

*Avoid controversy

*Research each proposed project carefully

*Identify a reliable contact person for each project

•

You must be ABSOLUTELY CERTAIN that your petitions are in complete conformance with the law in your state. This includes the title, the type size, margin widths and the placement of different parts of the text on the petition. Have several people who know the regulations review the final text and layout of the petition before you print them. If you do something wrong, all of your petitions could be considered invalid. Check and recheck, and be certain of the legality of everything that you do! The smallest mistake could result in all of your petitions being thrown out.

VOTE YES

WILDLIFE, COASTAL & PARKS INITIATIVE

Resolving Environmental Disputes

A survey of a decade of eco-mediation with an interesting appendix of case studies. —JB

•

STORM KING

The dispute: Opposition to Consolidated Edison Company of New York's plans to build a hydroelectric and pumped storage plant at the foot of Storm King Mountain in the Hudson River highlands first arose when the Scenic Hudson Preservation Conference was formed late in 1963. Over the years, the issues involved in the dispute spread from simply whether the plant would unacceptably mar the scenic beauty of the Hudson to broad questions of the total effect of several utility plants on the water quality and fish life of the Hudson River.

The process: After a decade and a half of litigation and administrative hearings, attorneys for the environmental groups and Consolidated Edison discussed negotiating face to face and, in March 1979, asked Russell Train to mediate the dispute. Train spend several months laying the groundwork for negotiations and began them in August 1979. On December 18, 1980, 11 parties signed an agreement that ended the dispute.

The result: Consolidated Edison forfeited its

construction license for Storm King and turned the land over to the Palisades Interstate Parkway Commission. To protect striped bass and other fish species, the utilities agreed to establish a fish hatchery and to reduce, for 10 years, their withdrawals of water from the river during the summer months. They further agreed not to build any new power plants without cooling towers above the George Washington Bridge for 25 years, to endow a river research organization, and to reimburse legal fees to the environmental groups. In return for these concessions, EPA dropped its demand for expensive cooling towers at several of the existing plants, and the environmental groups dropped legal and administrative challenges against the utilities.

A year after the settlement, New York State issued discharge permits, incorporating the terms of the mediated settlement, to the utilities. All aspects of the settlement have been implemented.

Resolving Environmental Disputes, Gail Bingham 1986; 284 pp.; **$15** ($l7 postpaid) from: World Wildlife Fund, P.O. Box 4866, Hampden Station, Baltimore MD 21211; (301) 338-6951

Land-Saving Action

The last decade has seen a tremendous expansion of private-sector preservation of open space lands. This book, with chapters by 29 experts, embodies the experience that ten years has produced, and will serve as a bible for anyone who loves a piece of land enough to want to find out how to save it. —Richard Nilsen

Land-Saving Action
Russell L. Brenneman and Sarah M. Bates, Editors; 1984; 250 pp. **$24.95** ($26.95 postpaid) from: Island Press Box 7 Covelo, CA 95482 (800) 828-1302 ✱WEA

•

Community support is vital in determining surrounding land uses. The uses of the land surrounding the preserved agricultural land are of vital concern. A single farming operation, no matter how well laid out and managed, faces tremendous odds without compatible neighbors. Nuisance ordinances outlawing livestock operations and restricting spraying emerge in communities where too many farms have turned into ranchettes and other homesites for city folk. Protecting one parcel of agricultural land requires consideration of the guarantees that ensure that the surrounding land uses will stay compatible. Otherwise, that parcel is likely to become the preserved open space for adjacent development.

PeaceNet/EcoNet

PeaceNet, a computer messaging service, hosts over a hundred on-line conferences for peace and social activist groups: EcoNet (ecological issues), HomeoNet (a homeopathic doctors' conference), the National Freeze Campaign, the Christic Institute, the Central America Resource Network, the Center for Innovative Diplomacy, Institute for Security and Cooperation in Outer Space, etc. It's worth joining not just for the news-postings and calendars of events (e.g. American Peace Test's schedule of nuclear blasts at the Nevada test site), but because participating groups often use PeaceNet to administer themselves. It's a treat to follow discussions of international issues, goals, strategies and tactics, and most times kibitzers can add their two cents. Openness is an important principle for many of these groups; PeaceNet makes that ideal both practicable and involving. (The system has limited-access sections and electronic mail facilities, too.) —Robert Horvitz

EcoNet is an excellent environmental tool. Not only is it an on-line conference covering a wide range of environmental issues such as Global Warming, Acid Rain, Toxics, and Energy, it is also a great information resource. It gives listings of directories including The National Wildlife Federation Directory and the Environmental Grantmakers Association Directory, and grant lists, and news reports from such groups as the Sierra Club and the International Union for Conservation of Nature. With over 2000 members, including most of the major environmental organizations in the U.S., it is a true conglomeration of ecology in action.
—Susan Erkel Ryan

PeaceNet/EcoNet, costs **$10** per month, users get one free hour of peak time. Additional time is charged at $5 an hour off-peak time; $10 an hour peak time (7 am-6 pm, M-F, user's local time). From: PeaceNet, 3228 Sacramento St., San Francisco, CA 94115; (415) 923-0900

Getting to Yes

This book on negotiation comes as a great personal relief to me and may well to you. I've always avoided situations that involved bargaining because of all the dishonesty that seemed to be required. When I was forced, by life, to bargain anyway, I usually did poorly, which reinforced my reluctance. All that is now cured by this modest 163 pages of exceptional insight and clarity.

The point is to negotiate on principle, not pressure — on mutual search for mutually discernible objectivity, patiently and firmly putting aside every other gambit. The book is a landmark, already a bible for international negotiators but just as useful for deciding which movie to see tonight or which school to send the family scion to.

***Getting to Yes** is a model in every way of ideal how-to writing. —Steward Brand*

Getting to Yes, Roger Fisher and William Ury; 1981; 161 pp. **$7.95** ($9.95 postpaid) from: Penguin USA, 120 Woodbine, Bergenfield, NJ 07621 (212) 366-2000 ✳WEA

•

A variation on the procedure of "one cuts, the other chooses" is for the parties to negotiate what they think is a fair arrangement before they go on to decide their respective roles in it. In a divorce negotiation, for example, before deciding which parent will get custody of the children, the parents might agree on the visiting rights of the other parent. This gives both an incentive to agree on visitation rights each will think fair.

•

A good negotiator rarely makes an important decision on the spot. The psychological pressure to be nice and to give in is too great. A little time and distance help separate the people from the problem. A good negotiator comes to the table with a credible reason in his pocket for leaving when he wants. Such a reason should not indicate passivity or inability to make a decision.

•

A good case can be made for changing Woodrow Wilson's appealing slogan "Open covenants openly arrived at" to "Open covenants privately arrived at." No matter how many people are involved in a negotiation, important decisions are typically made when no more than two people are in the room.

•

Reconciling interests rather than compromising between positions works because behind opposed positions lie many more interests than conflicting ones.

Green Line™

Green Line™ is a national, interactive, environmental 900 number service. Using a touch-tone phone, callers can "drive" through a constantly updated system that responds almost immediately to their requests for information on a wide range of subjects including: News — daily environmental bulletins, environmental events calendar; Action — legislative action line service, simple things you can do to help; Connections — contact/join/donate to organizations, 'green' marketplace info; Issues — information on key environmental issues.
—Gil Friend

Green Line™, **$.95** per minute billed to your home phone. For 900# and more information contact: Green Line, 758 Gilman Street, Berkeley, CA 94710; (415) 526-3900

Environmental Justice

By Mary James

"**O**ur right to breathe free is non-negotiable. Safe drinking water, that's non-negotiable. We must have a commitment and a timetable from Chevron to clean up the environment." These words could have come from any number of environmentalists speaking to a group of Sierra Clubbers. But they didn't. This was Jesse Jackson talking to members of the Missionary Baptist Church in Richmond, California.

Jackson, as part of Earth Day 1990 activities, teamed up with Denis Hayes and visited six minority communities to bring attention to local pollution problems. That more hasn't been done to clear up these problems, Hayes blamed on the predominantly white, upper middle class nature of the environmental movement. The base of support has been too narrow, says Hayes.

"Minorities are disproportionately affected by environmental issues," asserts Black environmental activist and consultant David Hahn-Baker. Studies have shown that hazardous waste sites are overwhelmingly located in minority and low-income communities. Yet traditional environmental groups tend to be mostly white. Fewer than two percent of field and management staff hired by environmental organizations in the past five years have been minorities, according to an informal survey. Of the 152 professionals at the National Audubon Society only five are minorities. Eight minorities out of 96 employees work at the Environmental Defense Fund. The Sierra Club reportedly has one Hispanic employee out of a total staff of 290.

While these figures paint a bleak picture for a true mass movement, signs of change are emerging. On the local level, minority-led coalitions fighting pollution problems — the West County Toxics Coalition in Richmond, for example — are growing in number and size. On the national level, major environmental groups have begun to target issues, such as toxics and urban habitats, that strongly affect minority communities.

Environmentalists are coming to realize that protecting endangered species might include protecting, and working with, vulnerable human populations. Earth Island Institute (see p. 110) is creating an Urban Habitat project to address the connections between race, poverty, and ecological restoration of cities. Carl Anthony and California Rural Legal Assistance Foundation attorney Luke Cole brought out the first issue of their Race, Poverty & the Environment newsletter just days before Earth Day 1990. This increasing recognition of environmental justice as an issue is pushing traditional environmental groups to end their homogeneity — a homogeneity that is creating problems for both the environmental and minority communities.

"Not only is working to diversify environmental groups the right thing to do," states Hahn-Baker, "but it's necessary if environmentalists want to accomplish their goals." Minorities make up over a third of the U. S. population, and that percentage is growing. Unless more minority communities — and the politicians representing them — perceive environmental issues as critical, these issues won't get the attention they need. In 1986 Washington, D. C., voters defeated a bottle-deposit bill thanks to a beverage industry campaign aimed at the black community. But environmental groups will lose more than minority support if they don't diversify.

"We will also miss the opportunity to enhance the work of our organizations by bringing a broader and more representative perspective to it," says Gerry Stover, executive director of The Environmental Consortium for Minority Outreach, a Washington-based coalition of major environmental organizations.

"Environmental groups had paid lip service to increasing minority representation, but nothing much had been done," claims Stover. "We had to make more than a verbal commitment. Even just recruiting isn't enough." While the consortium does recruit minorities for staff and board of directors positions, it also educates the environmental and minority communities about issues that concern them both. Stover is helping prepare a curriculum to expose schoolchildren to environmental topics and pulling together information on the socioeconomic effects of environmental issues.

Meanwhile several leaders of minority, low-income environmental groups have taken their own steps to speed up change. This January Pat Bryant, director of the Gulf Coast Tenant Leadership Development Project, and several other leaders sent a letter to eight major environmental organizations demanding that in the next 60 days they increase minority representation to 30 to 40 percent of their staff or stop working in minority communities. Benjamin Chavis, director of the United Church of Christ's Commission for Racial Justice, followed up the letter with a call for a summit meeting between leaders of national environmental organizations and ethnic environmental grassroots organizers.

Bob Norman, director of human resources for the National Audubon Society, says, "We want to be cooperative, but we can't solve this big of a problem overnight." He says he hasn't received enough applications from qualified minority scientists to fill the Society's needs, despite the Society's full-blown affirmative action program instituted two years ago.

"There's no denying we need to do a better job of reaching out to minorities," says Fred Krupp, executive director of the Environmental Defense Fund. Until recently, though, minorities interested in cause-oriented work have gravitated toward poverty and discrimination issues, rather than environmental concerns. That situation is changing now — fortunately. "The environmental movement will be stronger when we have a more diverse work force," he says. Unfortunately, once on the inside, minorities face other hurdles created by their years on the outside.

"The working environment is still lonely for minorities. It's an old boys' network so often," says Marcia Chen. For eight months she worked with the Boston-based CEIP Fund, an organization promoting environmental careers. By the end of her stint with CEIP, Chen had put together a comprehensive report on ways to increase minorities' presence in the profession. The Fund hosted a conference this April for minorities interested in environmental jobs, but Chen wasn't there. She had already left the field.

"Efforts at diversity are moving much faster now than at any time in the last ten years, but they're still chugging along slowly," says Hahn-Baker. "Because of the Gulf Coast letter, though, the joint is jumping." Still, for Hahn-Baker, diversifying the traditional environmental groups remains the little picture in today's movement. Redefining environmentalists as people who care about birds *and* low-income housing, toxic waste dumps *and* access to health care — that's the big picture.

When **LEGAL OPTIONS** have been **subverted**, when <u>government</u> once again puts a *fox* to <u>guarding</u> the **chickens**, when *time's a-wastin'*, the only remaining answer may be *immediate, possibly "<u>illegal</u>" action.* If the **ACTS** are well chosen and carried out with intelligence and *theatre*, the public is at least **awakened**, if not totally <u>OUTRAGED</u>. Straight folks, and of course those targeted, engage in much *hand-wringing* and talk of **TERRORism**. But a look at the recent past will show that *courageous **Earth First!-ers*** and *Greenpeace* squads have often been the *first to* stir up what later became major causes championed by less **CONTROVERSIAL organizations** with offices in <u>Washington</u>. I'm glad there are folks out there *with the **GUTS** to do this* sort of thing. —JB*!*

Greenpeace

Whenever you see a tiny rubber boat (a Zodiac or "Zode") obstructing a huge ship that's doing something environmentally despicable, you can bet Greenpeace is at work; nonviolent action is what they're famous for. Greenpeace also engages in less dramatic stuff too. They prepare well-researched briefs that help media, government, and courts get their facts straight; they make presentations at all levels of government, from town meetings to Congress; they produce slides, films, and videos. Greenpeace now includes scientists on their staff, adding academic credibility and political clout to a reputation for dramatic confrontation. That move — a mark of brilliant management — and a host of authoritative publications has made Greenpeace one of the most effective of all environmental organizations. Their list of hard-won accomplishments is long and inspiring. —JB

Greenpeace; **$15**/year (membership includes six issues of **Greenpeace** magazine) from: Greenpeace, P.O. Box 3720, Washington, DC 20007

•

Accomplishments

*In 1989, A Greenpeace-led Icelandic fish boycott forced Iceland to stop whaling.

*Greenpeace continues to maintain the only nongovernmental base camp in Antarctica.

*In the fall of 1989, thousands of activists called on the EPA to demand that states be required to emphasize waste prevention, not incineration, in hazardous waste "Capacity Assurance Plans." EPA rewrote its guidelines for the plans in an attempt to address the demands raised by the "Phone-In for Prevention" campaign.

*In 1988 and '89, Greenpeace Action educational campaigns contributed to pressure on the Department of Energy, which resulted in the indefinite closure of the Savannah River Plant reactors in South Carolina as well as the Hanford Reservation N-reactor and PUREX reprocessing facility in Washington.

The Monkey Wrench Gang • Hayduke Lives!

*Fifteen years after publishing **The Monkey Wrench Gang** and one year after his death, Edward Abbey has left us with a posthumous sequel, **Hayduke Lives!** Considering the author's circumstance (the book was written while Abbey was dying) and the story's optimistic ending, it is a gift to anyone concerned with re-routing the industrial juggernaut of late twentieth century civilization.*

*Abbey writes fiction with real-life consequence — his advocacy of anti-industrial sabotage in order to protect wilderness in **The Monkey Wrench Gang** inspired the radical environmental group Earth First! This summer, as fictional bombs turn into real-life explosives and we watch the establishment begin to give Earth First! the same treatment accorded the Black Panther Party in the late sixties, these books take on a chilling immediacy.*

*Everything you love to hate about Abbey, the redneck, bad-boy philosopher, is here in the final work — asinine macho posturing, hopeless stereotyping, and his intense dislike of essentially anyone not like himself. Both these novels are composed more of caricatures than characters; that's one reason the R. Crumb illustrations that grace the pages of the current edition of **The Monkey Wrench Gang** work so well. But there is humanity and humor driving the hatred and anger; Abbey's description in **Hayduke Lives!** of two overweight Mormons attempting to make baby number twelve, while an ultraviolet bug-zapper kills insects outside their bedroom window, is a short comic masterpiece.* —Richard Nilsen

*Dream Garden Press, which publishes **The Monkey Wrench Gang**, also sells T-shirts with R. Crumb's great artwork of the Gang and a wonderful calendar with stunning desert photographs of Abbey's hangouts as well as quotes from his various works.* —Susan Erkel Ryan

The Monkey Wrench Gang
Edward Abbey, Illustrations by R. Crumb; 1990; 356 pp. **$21.95** ($23.45 postpaid)
✶WEA

T-Shirts $15 each ($17 postpaid) *The Gang, The Wrench, Hayduke Lives!, Bonnie, Seldom Seen, Doc Sarvis (kicking t.v.)*

The 1991 Edward Abbey Western Wilderness Calendar; $9.95 ($11.95 postpaid)

All from:
Dream Garden Press, P.O. Box 27076
Salt Lake City, UT 84127; (801) 467-1490

Hayduke Lives!
Edward Abbey
1990; 308 pp.
$18.45 ($20.45 postpaid) from:
Little, Brown & Co.
200 West Street
Waltham, MA 02154
(800) 343-9204 ✶WEA

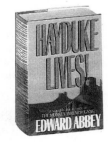

•

SYN-FUELS GO HOME. EURO-TRASH GO HOME. BACK TO BRUSSELS WITH GOLIATH. SAVE OUR GRAND CANYON. WHOSE LAND IS THIS ANYHOW?

The banners flew, the flags rustled, the paper placards snapped and popped and crackled, held aloft by proud little boys and pigtailed bright-eyed brave little girls. The messages, however, would not appear on your home viewing screen. Why not? Because the "media," though invited, had once again failed to appear. Why? Such decisions

"AS THE TIPOVER POINT APPROACHED THE TRACTOR ATTEMPTED (SO IT SEEMED) TO SAVE ITSELF: ONE TREAD BEING MORE ADVANCED INTO THE AIR THAN THE OTHER, THE TRACTOR MADE A LURCHING HALF-TURN TO THE RIGHT, TRYING TO CLING TO THE RIM OF THE MESA AND SOMEHOW REGAIN SOLID FOOTING."

are made discreetly, quietly, by a few important people meeting on the golf course, in the boardroom, at lunch in the Brown Palace in Denver, at the Biltmore in Phoenix. A few brief phone calls to the appropriate TV, radio and newspaper bureau chiefs settled the matter. After all, some events make worthy news and some do not. Another orderly protest demonstration against racial segregation in South Africa, for example, comfortably carried out on the campus of Berkeley or Stanford or Harvard or Yale ten thousand miles away, troubles no one, causes no embarrassment to anybody, allows all involved to look good, feel virtuous, risk nothing. But let a bunch of hairy redneck rabble in some wasteland western American state interpose their living bodies between the industrial megamachine and a little patch of free country, open space, old-growth forest, natural nature, wildland and wildlife, and the horror runs deep through the hierarchy of upper management. That kind of subversion (non-commercial) cannot be accepted; will not (anti-business) be tolerated; has to (pro-populist) be most severely punished both legally and — in so far as possible — illegally; and last but categorically imperative, shall not be encouraged through the power of example by publicity in any form. As in any well-ordered oligarchy, not only the event itself must be suppressed but all news of it as well.

Therefore the "media" did not appear.

—*Hayduke Lives!*

The Earth First! Li'l Green Songbook

*Music is the voice of the soul. For a movement to be successful, when the odds are against it but the heart is for it, it helps to have the soul speaking. Thus evolved the **Earth First! Li'l Green Songbook**.* —Susan Erkel Ryan

The Earth First! Li'l Green Songbook
Johnny Sagebrush and Friends 1986; 102 pp.; **$5** ($6.26 postpaid) from: Ned Ludd Books P.O. Box 5141, Tucson, AZ 85703; (602) 628-9610 ✶WEA

•

What's Left of the West

(Words and music by Greg Keeler)

Manifest destiny ain't had a rest

Ever since Horace Greeley said, "Young man go west."

Earth First!

Out on the front lines of eco-defense is Earth First!. "No compromise in the defense of Mother Earth!" Direct action against the machinery (not people) and eco-theatre is their modus operandi. Because many environmental groups have become top-heavy with managerial salaries and glossy promotions, Earth First! attracts more youth and makes more efficient use of limited funds.
—Peter Warshall

A subscription to **Earth First! The Radical Environmental Journal** *is not the same as joining the movement. There are Earth First! groups all over the world. In addition to lots of reports from the front lines, the* **Journal** *includes a directory of where they are. Last year, Earth First! founder Dave Foreman was busted by the FBI (in bed, at gunpoint, a set-up). Since then, there has been a lot more official action against Earth First! activists*

Earth First! Journal; **$20/ year** (eight issues) from: Earth First! Journal, P.O. Box 7, Canton, NY 13617

— a tribute to their effectiveness. The result has been an Earth First! you can see, and one you can't. The ranks are growing. —JB

•

How do you change society when you are apart from it? How do you understand yourself when you deny the social environment that produced you? How can you gain support for your goals and actions when your behavior alienates potential supporters?

Wise guerrillas know that they are part of society and need support from the population base. The isolated, alienated guerrilla is just as lost and vulnerable as the isolated, alienated gorilla. We primates are social animals. We have a long, deep heritage of being part of a tribe, of defining ourselves by the cultural context in which we were born.

We deny human ecology when we argue that we can operate totally apart from the mores of society, when we define ourselves as ethical islands, beholden to no one, without responsibility to others for our own actions. There we enter uncharted waters, beyond anthropology, beyond biology, into modernist alienation and nihilism, into Hobbe's nightmare of all against all, a dark and fearful place as far from the wilderness as we can imagine. —Dave Foreman

Ecodefense

Inspired by Ed Abbey's **The Monkey Wrench Gang, Ecodefense** *sports proven techniques of tree spiking, road spiking, disabling heavy equipment, fence cutting, trap clearing, lock jamming, billboard trashing, and sundry skills of propaganda, camouflage, sneaking around, escape and evasion, and the like. Fascinating stuff; best not to skim and try, but really study before trying — for two good reasons. One is that monkeywrenching mostly takes place in country where retribution is not only in the courts but also by direct action: you get the living shit beat out of you. The second is that monkeywrenching the wrong target is grotesquely counterproductive; you have not only to be right every single time, but conspicuously right, or you're just another random vandal making everyone else feel sick about being alive. The book constantly warns about knowing your target cold before making a move, and if in doubt, don't.*
—Stewart Brand

Ecodefense
Dave Foreman, Editor
1985; 1989 revised 2nd ed.
197 pp.; **$12** ($13.50 postpaid) from: Ned Ludd Books, P.O. Box 5141 Tucson, AZ 85703 (602) 628-9610 **✷**WEA

•

Try to break down the power of the billboard ad by *answering* it, looking at the space available and the way in which the words and images lend themselves to addition, alteration or comment. Humor is extremely effective in exposing the advertiser's real intentions — turning the ad's message back on itself. (Be sure to avoid spelling mistakes!)

If the offending billboard proves too high to reach, you can either get a ladder (which isn't particularly convenient) or build a spray can extension rod:

Obtain a broom handle or another solid, strong but lightweight wooden pole (see illustration, #1). At one end, cut out a wedge, half the width of the pole. Fit a flat metal bar to the remaining wood (#2). About one foot from this bar (or the height of your spray can), attach a support clamp on which the can will rest (#3). Fit an angle bracket on each side of the pole, about 8 inches from the end (#4). The spray can should fit between these brackets. Tie a length of plastic coated wire to the flat metal bar (#2) and feed it through a hole in the support clamp (#3) and screw eyes attached the length of the pole (#5). This wire, when pulled, will press down the nozzle of the spray can and paint will spray out. An optional extra is the roll-top of a deodorant bottle, fitted to the support clamp (#6). This will help maintain an even distance between the spray can and billboard. You may have to experiment a bit to get the right measurements to fit a can of spray paint.

Although these spray can extension rods are clumsy to use at first, with practice they become very effective.

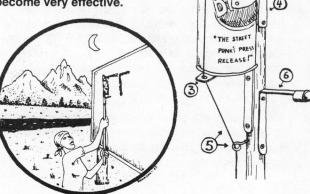

The Muckraker's Manual

Amateur investigation is arduous but fun, and one of the few do-it-yourself ways to effectively change the political scene. It's a shame more people don't try it. Muckraking is an accessible craft for anyone who can handle massive files of paper and long hours of interviews. There is a weird psychological split sometimes; you'll bare your soul to someone at breakfast, then expose them in print or court two months later. (On the other hand, a couple of my most valued friends started out as reporter's "sources.")

The Muckraker's Manual *is one of those exceptional books that way outclasses everything else on the subject. Though signed with a pseudonym, it's solid enough to be trusted. —Art Kleiner*

•

Often, you will be surprised at just who some of your friends and acquaintances do know. As an example, I recently finished an investigation of the networks that smuggle foreign nationals into the United States illegally to work for slave wages. I

knew I wanted to make contact with two groups: smugglers and the people who "bought" the undocumented immigrants. For a person who lives a relatively quiet, middle-class existence, this possibility seemed very remote. But I did what I always do. I talked about my investigation to my friends. As it turned out, one of my friends had a brother who "bought" undocumented immigrants. Another friend had a lover who had previously lived with a smuggler. Because I had developed these "inside" sources through my extended friendship network, both of them trusted me enough to talk to me about their experiences. They also were able to give me more leads.

The Muckrakers Manual
(Handbook for Investigative Reporters), M. Harry
1984; 145 pp.; **$11.95** ($14.95 postpaid) from: Loompanics Unlimited P.O. Box 1197, Port Townsend, WA 98368 **✷**WEA

So we've chewed up the mountains and spit out the plains

While we get indigestion from each acid rain.

It's gotten so bad, the West ain't any place.

I'll ask ya "How are ya?" and you'll stare into space.

What's left of the West's where we've already been.

So Alaska Hawaii again.

Chorus:

And Honolulu's no lulu. Fairbanks ain't so fair.

Take a sip of the water; take a whiff of the air.

Take some pictures of the wildlife: take a leak in the stream.

Take a jet back to Cleveland and dream.

If trees went to congress and forest could vote,

Our chances of survival might not be so remote.

But since we don't give a damn as to who they'd elect,

Their absentee ballots are the greenhouse effect.

What's a boatload of timber? What's the whole human race?

I'll ask ya, "How are ya?" and you'll stare into space.

What's left of the West's where we've already been,

So Alaska Hawaii again.

Chorus

We scrub up with phosphates then flush down the suds

Till the banks of our rivers is bubbles and mud.

Just to stay sanitary, we've gone to these lengths.

Now our whole ecosystem's industrial strength.

It's so simple to screw up what can't be replaced.

I'll ask ya "How are ya?" and you'll stare into space.

What's left of the West's where we've already been,

So Alaska Hawaii again.

Chorus

Karen Christensen is an American writer living in London. She was one of the judges of Britain's 1990 Green Book Fortnight. Karen is the author of **Home Ecology** *(London: Arlington Books, 1989; Denver: Fulcrum, October 1990), and is contributing a chapter on personal action and lifestyle change to* **Green Light on Europe** *(Heretic Books, 1991). —JB*

Green **I**nk in **B**ritain

By **K**aren **C**hristensen

OVER 500 libraries and 1100 bookshops, including Britain's major chains, took part in the second Green Book Fortnight in April 1990. There were displays of green books, posters highlighting selected titles, and free catalogs listing 200 books submitted by over 50 publishers. The catalog gave special prominence to the twelve books which were chosen by four judges as "the most representative books on environmental issues published over the last twelve months."

In a press release, the organizers of Britain's 1990 Green Book Fortnight explained the primary reason for the Fortnight: "The book trade, in its privileged position as a major provider of information to the general public, should make a contribution to the fight to save the planet." **Seeing Green**, **Green Pages**, **Teaching Green**, **Green Design**, **Green Parenting**, **Green Parties** (political parties, that is, not organic wine and cheese), **Great Green Limericks**, **Green Woodwork**, and **The Green Age Diet**, are among the "green" titles in print in Britain. Hundreds of books can be loosely categorized as green, and many more are on the way. There was considerable fuss about a "green wedding of the year" this summer, between two environmentalists; expect a **Green Bride Book** next spring.

When I first sat down to write this article I intended to say nothing but nice things about green books. On reflection, I realized that this wouldn't help save the planet, and that to point out some of the debates about British green book publishing would be more useful.

Clearing the ground, making room in the publishing sphere for the books we need to inform and inspire us, is an essential and demanding task. The truth, however, is that the first couple of years' cultivation of the mass market green book patch is producing a prolific crop of weeds, and they threaten to overwhelm the few flowers.

Ebury Press brought out a book this spring which they described, without irony, as the "first green gift book." During the Green Book Fortnight I was repeatedly asked by interviewers if publishers weren't "just jumping on the green bandwagon." The answer is that of course they are. But why should we expect them to be purer than car manufacturers, sit-com stars, and politicians?

No green would deny the importance of books in changing the world. Writing a book is not only a way of recording ideas but an opportunity to develop them. Since many green ideas are in their infancy, books are a crucial part of the process of developing coherent green strategy. Greens themselves tend to be particularly bookish; I've never seen such a frenzy of bookbuying as at the annual Schumacher lectures, held in Bristol every October. When the **Observer** newspaper ran a general knowledge competition a couple years ago, Green Party supporters got top marks (Conservatives were last).

One of the least green things about the book trade is its obsession with new titles, at the expense of backlist books. There is an increasing tendency for publishers to see books as disposable items.

When I expressed concern about whether books printed on recycled paper would hold up, a friend (and prolific writer) said reassuringly, "Nobody keeps books more than a year or two anyway."

Tessa Strickland, when managing editor at Viking Penguin in London and one of the founders of the Green Book Fortnight, raised this issue in an article in the **Bookseller** magazine, concluding that "The heart of the message has been around for a long time. If it was not only read about but also acted on, we would all flourish in a world of fewer books — and many more trees." (I wonder whether there was any connection between this article and Strickland's being made redundant several weeks later.)

Adrian Howe, director of Books for a Change, worries that the Fortnight could actually be bad for the environment, if it encourages publishers to produce green gift books.

An unfortunate effect of the Fortnight was that publishers rushed books out in order to take part. The results of haste, and poor editing, include mind-numbing prose ("It is not clear what role, if any, television has to play in the lives of Green toddlers. It is not necessary as a socializing medium since the child is not at an age where discussions with peers of common but absent interests take place, and she is also not yet subject to peer-group pressures as she will be later." —*Green Parenting*) and carelessness about facts (one prolix green writer does his own statistical estimates when he can't find what he needs in reference books).

Authors suffer from their publishers' sense of urgency. When I started writing **Home Ecology** in 1987, my publishers insisted on an early deadline "because there's so much interest in the environment, it'd be a pity to miss it." I find it extraordinary that publishers still think that the environment is a temporary fad.

Green publishing has several special difficulties. Libel suits by big businesses are an increasing problem, since many businesses are now trying to present an environment-friendly face to the public. This year, three green books were not on the shelves during the Green Book Fortnight because of legal threats from the McDonald's Corporation of Oak Brook, Illinois. One of these was **The Coming of the Greens**, by Jonathan Porritt (*the* green in our country) and David Winner. Also under threat, and therefore withdrawn from distribution, were Fred Pearce's **Turning Up The Heat** and my **Home Ecology.** This is probably the first case of a concerted assault on environmental books by a major international company. Most authors, whose contracts indemnify their publishers against libel actions, cannot afford to fight. Newspapers and publishers find it cheaper to apologize than to argue the case or defend their writers.

Another problem, highlighted by the Fortnight, is the superficiality of many environmental books. Practical guides are turning up everywhere, and here, as in the U.S., there is a lot of emphasis on 'simple things' — small things you can do without affecting your life or taking up much time. Not a bad idea, but the implication that cleaning up the environment is the equivalent of losing ten pounds before bikini season is pretty short-sighted. No one has yet suggested that you can solve the world hunger problem by clearing your plate.

As the author of a practical guide I am all for empowering the individual, but I find that the Earth Day hype, well-intentioned though it was, left many people feeling confused and guilty. Anyhow, it's patronizing to tell people that they can cure the greenhouse effect (or is it the ozone hole?) by fixing a leaky faucet. The notion that consumers can change industry simply by asking for environ-ment-friendly products is fraught with contradictions. It shifts the blame for environmental problems, and the responsibility for solutions, onto the individual and away from corporations and government.

The most important consequence of the Green Book Fortnight is that it has established green books as a selling category. Until recently, they were apt to turn up in Natural History or Politics. I have found **Home Ecology** on the thinner thighs shelf, and at Blackwell's in Oxford it was squeezed in with the biology textbooks. Green is a handy and accurate category, spanning everything from Third World development, organic farming, and electromagnetic radiation to alternative economics. 'Books for a change' sums it up.

"Green"

The word "green" hit the U.S. early this year, and is being taken up by the advertising industry to mean 'environment-friendly'. In Europe, 'green' is a much broader concept.

There are two distinct strands to the green movement here. The commercial greens, who rejoice that the new trend is also a color which can be splashed on packages and banners, know a good business opportunity when they see it. Their advertising targets people who are willing to pay more for products which aren't so hard on the environment, products which make you feel good.

On the other hand, there are the dark greens, who take a dubious view of green marketeering, deny that there is such a thing as "green growth," and insist that we cannot buy our way to a better world. Dark green thinking is a frequent target for noisy propaganda — the tabloid newspapers squealed 'They want to take away your VCR' during the Green Party Conference last September, after the UK Green Party had received 15% of the vote in the 1989 European elections, the best result a green party has ever achieved. A good dark green, and unabashedly political, book is **A Greenifesto** (Sandy Irvine and Alec Ponton, London: Optima, 1988), which was selected for the Green Book Fortnight last year.

The American Green Committees of Correspondence, the closest thing the U.S. has to a Green Party, have agreed on a succinct "Ten Key Values." (They have difficulty, however, in agreeing on much else, including definitions of the key values.) These are: ecological wisdom, decentralization, respect for diversity, non-violence, personal and social responsibility, global responsibility, grassroots democracy, post-patriarchal values, community-based economics, and future focus/sustainability. (In spite of organizational problems, there are strong moves to establish a policy-oriented Green Party in the U.S.) —KC

Books for a Change

You can obtain copies of all the selected books (and hundreds more) by mail from London's specialist green bookshop, Books for a Change. They are happy to send orders to American customers. A subscription to their catalog/magazine (which includes reviews and articles) is a good way to keep up-to-date on European green issues. —KC

Books for a Change
Sample catalog **free**
They accept MasterCard and VISA.
52 Charing Cross Road
London WC2H 0BB, England
Phone 071-836 2315
FAX 071-497 1036

The Global Ecology Handbook

*At some risk of being (pine) tarred and feathered (with feathers gathered from the ground beneath the nests of forest-dwelling sparrows) by the authors and publishers of the waist-high stack of save-the-Earth books that now resides in our also-ran box, I hereby subjectively proclaim this book the most useful of the bunch. It's authoritative, whine-free, comprehensive, detailed enough to be truly instructive, and backed by a great wad of notes. A tasty bibliography garnishes each section. It's the official backup for the PBS **Race to Save the Planet** series. Earth-saving authors tempted to join the fray late had better read this first; it'd be hard to do better. —JB*

The Global Ecology Handbook (What <u>You</u> Can Do About the Environmental Crisis) The Global Tomorrow Coalition; 1990; 414 pp. **$16.95**; Beacon Press 25 Beacon Street Boston, Massachusetts 02108-2800 (617) 742-2110

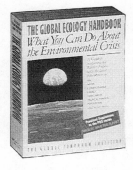

●

"Biosphere reserve" is an international designation made by the United Nations Educational, Scientific, and Cultural Organization (UNESCO) as part of its Man and the Biosphere (MAB) Program. As of early 1987, of more than 110 countries participating in the MAB Program, 70 countries had established some 260 biosphere reserves.

If protected areas are to survive, they must be seen as meeting the real needs of people — not simply fulfilling the esoteric interests of nature enthusiasts. This is especially true in the Third World, where the pressure on protected areas for agricultural use is greatest.

When a critical habitat is made into a national park or a nature preserve, laws must be enforced and local people educated so they can understand the preserve's importance and help support its existence.

In addition to on-site preservation of genetic diversity in parks, reserves, and other protected areas, the off-site preservation and breeding of animals and plants in zoos, aquariums, and botanical gardens is an important part of the overall strategy for preserving biological diversity.

Schematic plan of a Biosphere Reserve

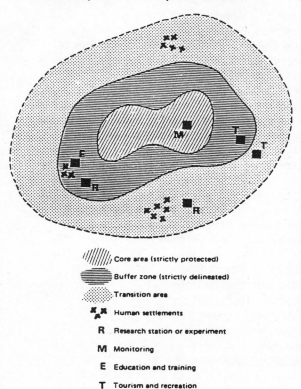

///// Core area (strictly protected)

◼ Buffer zone (strictly delineated)

Transition area

x▲x Human settlements

R Research station or experiment

M Monitoring

E Education and training

T Tourism and recreation

EarthPulse Handbooks

Each booklet in this series concentrates on a single subject such as Recycling or Energy. You get a pretty good basic or refresher course, with facts, figures, and advice delivered in a way that is easily remembered. The writing is good enough to keep you awake (that's unusual for this sort of thing, believe me). Some of it is sharp enough to quote at the heathen. Presenting information in this organized, economical manner is a lot less likely to bury you in despair and indecision. When I have to come up with quick answers to phoned-in questions I look here first because the answers are so easy to find. From Windstar (p. 83). —JB

EarthPulse Handbooks
Susan Hassol & Beth Richman **$3.95** each postpaid from: The Windstar Foundation 2317 Snowmass Creek Road Snowmass, CO 81654 (800) 669-4777

●

In a 10-week test of an intensive recycling system by 100 families in East Hampton, NY, 84% of their trash was recovered as marketable materials. The system is at least 35% cheaper than incineration, as well as more beneficial to the local economy and the environment.

●

Americans go through 2.5 million plastic bottles every hour.

One technical problem with recycling plastics is that more than 46 different plastic resin compounds, often used in combination, are currently in common use. A squeezable ketchup bottle, for example, is made of six different layers of plastic, each engineered to do a different job. Few recycling processes can handle more than one type of plastic; those which *can* produce an end product of lower grade than the incoming waste. Plastic containers, bottles, and packaging thus become ingredients for plastic lumber, outdoor furniture, paving materials, or insulation. So unlike the recycling of glass, paper, and aluminum which result in more bottles, paper and cans, recycling of plastic still requires the use of virgin materials to make new plastic bottles.

Shopping for a Better World

Shopping? Well, yeah . . . no matter how righteous you are, it's pretty hard to avoid buying things. But wouldn't it be nicer, or at least make you feel a bit better, to buy from folks whose sense of social responsibility matches your own? So here's a listing of 168 major companies and the brand names of what they make. Each company is scored as to their record on charitable giving, women's advancement, advancement of people of color, military contracts, animal testing, willingness to disclose information, community outreach, nuclear power, South Africa, environment, and family benefits. The pocket-size guide is arranged in a way that makes it easy to check on a company or product type; e.g., you can look up Salad Dressing and see who you'd rather buy it from, based on whichever of the categories you consider important. Bear in mind that any guide of this sort is not black-or-white perfect in every way; companies, like people, are rarely malicious baddies or angelic goodies. —JB

Shopping for a Better World, Ben Corson, et al., 1989; 289 pp., **$5.95** postpaid from: CEP, 30 Irving Place, New York, NY 10003 (800) 822-6435 ✳WEA

Encyclopaedia of Social Inventions

Tired of the obligatory squash-your-cans-to-save-the-planet line? This wad of 500 interesting (to say the least) ideas should keep you awake. It's a wonderful mixture of schemes that have been, might have been, and maybe should be, attempted, if our quality of life is to improve. (There are also a few in there that we can thank our stars were never tried.) Technical fixes are not the focus; social (as in economic) matters are. The range is wide — environment, taxation, crime, education and death are among the subjects. It's all quite, um, stimulating — plenty of flammable materials here ready for ignition. I've not encountered a better antidote to political correctness anywhere.

*The Encyclopaedia is a child of **The Institute for Social Inventions**, whose catalog lists a number of publications in a similar vein, including a periodical called **Social Inventions**. You might say that the whole operation is a social invention in itself. —JB*

Encyclopaedia of Social Inventions
Nicholas Albery and Valerie Yule, Editors 1989; 294 pp. **$34** postpaid

Social Inventions £17/year (4 issues)

Both from: The Institute for Social Inventions 24 Abercorn Place London, England NW8 9XP Phone: 01 208 2853

Unitax has much in common with the Polluter Pays Principle by acknowledging that the consumer should pay for the use of a polluting product or one that caused pollution in its production. However, there is a difference between selecting environmentally 'undesirable' items for penalty (Pearce), and a universal cost as in Unitax in which the market selects the most environmentally 'efficient' item. For example, if the Unitax cost brings the price up, the percentage of real value (by labour) can be increased without the same percentage being added to price. A discerning market can therefore consider cost-benefit and opt for more durable goods with higher (ambient or human) added value: quality. In turn this reduces the production volume and rate ('growth') and waste — but reducing neither the wealth of the nation nor the quality of life — nor incomes — in fact providing ultimately a basic income: shorter working hours equate with a reduction of pollution. These adjustments further reduce the cost of labour, cut deeply into the consumption of Uni-taxed base material resources and improve the quality of life —*Encyclopaedia of Social Inventions*

Company or Product	Abbr	$	♀	⚥	🗡	🐾	✍	🏘	⚛	🌍	👪	ALERT
Good Humor	UN	✗	✓	✓	No	✓•	✓	✗	No	Yes†	?	?	
Häagen-Dazs	GMP	?	?	?	?	?	✗	?	?	Yes†	?	?	dolphins caught
Heaven	NEST	?	?	?	No	?	✗	No	Yes†	?	?	infant formula
Homestyle+	HOME	?	✗	✗	No	✓	✓	?	No	No	✓	✓	
Jell-O	MO	✓	✓	✓	No	✓	✓	✓	No	Yes	✗	?	cigarettes
Louis Sherry	BN	✗	✓	✓	No	✓	✓	?	No	Yes•	✓	✓	
Meadow Gold	BN	✗	✓	✓	No	✓	✓	?	No	Yes•	✓	✓	
Minimilk	UN	✗	✓	✓	No	✓•	✓	✗	No	Yes†	?	?	
Mrs. Smith's	K	✓	✓	✓	No	✓	✓	?	No	Yes•	✓	✓	
Nabisco	RJR	✓	✓	✓	No	?	✓	?	No	Yes•	✗	✗	cigarettes

✓ = Top Rating ✓ = Middle Rating ✗ = Bottom Rating ? = Insufficient Information
For a more detailed explanation see key on page 10 | Page 183

Whenever I think of do-gooding, I recall my grandmother's guilt-inducing comment regarding my rejected plate of spinach: "Think of the starving Armenians."(Armenia was in trouble at the time.) My defending grandfather then replied laconically, "Name two". He didn't believe in long-distance charity. As the proprietor of the modest pharmacy in a small Iowa town, he distributed what little largesse he could afford by refusing to take money from depression-stressed people who needed medicine.

His decision was easy; those folks were neighbors he'd known for years. Your decision is harder. How do you decide which of the hundreds of worthy environmental organizations gets your money? Grandfather offers us a clue: Let your heart tell you. Our house naturalist, Peter Warshall, recommends supporting favorite *projects*, rather than giving general support to an organization, some of whose divisions may engage in enterprises you don't agree with. Check an organization's brochure to see what they're up to these days. Look for projects that excite you. If you give to a biggie like the Sierra Club, earmark your contribution specifically for, say, beach clean-up or streambank improvement, or lobbying efforts. Some may be under the direction of a local chapter in your area. Many organizations will furnish you with a list of their current endeavors, their locations, and which are most in need. "I gave" isn't nearly as satisfying as being able to say "I'm involved in the Turtle Creek cleanup".

Even better is to support local organizations where you can actually participate. That way, you can keep an eye on how your money is being used, and you can enjoy the ultimate morale-boost of seeing real progress made by your own efforts. It's common to find small, local committees formed to accomplish a single project. You could start one. While a bit short on international prestige, they are often the most effective in solving problems directly affecting their members. Their low overhead means more action for the money. Once you have "your" project, you may find that mere checkwriting won't do anymore. You'll be in the thick of things, making your support an integral part of your life. Good place to make some stalwart friends, too.

Awkward Note: It would have been nice to list all existing environmentally righteous organizations here, but that's another book. No slight intended to any. You'll also find some scattered amongst various departments of the Ecolog. — JB

Earth Island Institute

*This is where David Brower hangs his hat these days. Earth Island is a bit different in that it coordinates and shares office space with other cooperating organizations (some featured in this **Ecolog**) — a power-increasing idea that also reduces needless competition on our side of the fence. There are also widely scattered "Earth Island Centers", other organizations that act more or less as local chapters. The **Earth Island Journal** is one of the better front-line magazines around. Earth Islanders still have the bloodboiling vigor and sass of a relatively new and tumultous group. —JB*

Earth Island Institute
$25/year (membership includes 4 issues of **Earth Island Journal**)
from: Earth Island Institute, 300 Broadway Suite 28, San Francisco, CA 94133-3312
(415) 788-3666

National Audubon Society

The strength of Audubon since 1905 has been its naturalist backbone. More than any other environmental organization, its members actually know the animals and plants they try to conserve. Not only that, they seem to love their knowledge with early naturalist enthusiasm. The educational aspects of Audubon are truly admirable. Their politics vary locally and, if you contribute, it's good to earmark your contribution for a particular purpose, especially for specific sanctuaries.
—*Peter Warshall*

National Audubon Society; **$30**/year (membership includes 6 issues of Audubon magazine) Join your local chapter or contact: National Audubon Society, P. O. Box 52529 Boulder, CO 80322 (800) 274-4201

Among the highly valued products of Louisiana's coastal wetlands are food and family recreation.

Sierra Club

*Venerable, powerful, and, to the impatient, excessively prone to compromise with The Good Old Boys, the Sierra Club carries on the work it's been up to for nearly a century. Nobody questions their effectiveness, that's beyond dispute. But there are plenty of questions about focus, policy, and willingness to cut a deal with the enemy. It isn't unusual to find different chapters or factions within the Sierra Club sniping at each other or even working at cross-purposes. While this may be distressing, it is no surprise to folks who are used to dealing with the realities of tough, ill-defined, emotion-stirring problems. Frontier work always engenders controversy while the best way of doing something is being extracted from a tangle of conflicting interests and philosophies. In any case, sneers are not in order. Earth First! (see p. 107), Greenpeace (see p. 106), and other dramatic activists have their place, and so do the Sierra Club forces — besneakered or besuited (sometimes simultaneously both) — who are past masters at getting things done in Washington as well as in the bush. And you might be surprised (I was) at the breadth of Sierra Club efforts. In addition to the expected media-attended action, the Club runs one of the best presses around (see p.112), a host of educational programs, tours and outings, and a system of networks organized to deal with specific problems requiring immediate attention. Check your nearby chapter and their newsletter for local action. A national membership gets you **Sierra**, a spiffy mag. —JB*

Sierra Club; **$33**/year (membership includes six issues of **Sierra**); contact local chapter or write to: Sierra Club, Dept. J-420 P. O. Box 7959 San Francisco, CA 94120

Friends Of The Earth

*FOE now include the Oceanic Society (see review p. 15) and the Environmental Policy Institute in their ranks, adding commendable breadth to their already considerable capabilities. 37 chapters and 50,000 members around the world take care of business. Your support is rewarded with a subscription to **Friends Of The Earth**, one of the best sources of eco-action news. You can also subscribe to **Atmosphere** -- an ozone newsletter and of course, FOE has a long list of other publications. —JB*

Friends Of The Earth; **$25**/year (membership, includes 10 issues of **Friends Of The Earth** newsmagazine and a membership kit)

Atmosphere Newsletter; **$15**/year (4 issues)

Publications list **free**

All from:
Friends Of The Earth, 218 D Street, SE Washington, DC 20003; (202) 544-2600
•

You need all the help you can get, so a further caution seems in order. While working on the side of the angels, you might actually detect contradictions in what people say and what they do. No kidding. You might hear, for example, some earnest fellow preaching a sermon on "cooperation and sharing as the key to the planet's salvation." He's so eloquent and sincere that it brings tears to your eyes. Later on, you discover that if his life depended on it, this guy wouldn't share so much as a pizza. What's more, you learn that he's just sold his grandmother for a chance to appear on the Today show. And now he wants to be named leader.

No wonder you opt for a collective. Social movements favor this notion (especially in their early stages), touting it as proof of their devotion to democratic ideals. But instead of reducing competition within the group, as claimed, collegial leadership actually increases it. When a throne is available, everyone imagines themselves king. I've found collegial leadership to be nothing more than a bad joke, utterly failing to disguise the frenzied conflict over power taking place backstage.

Among the righteous, this war of ambitions is certainly unseemly. But — to give the devil his — personal competition over leadership can benefit the cause. It does stimulate everyone to show their stuff.—Byron Kennard, *Friends Of The Earth*

The Trust For Public Land

Problem: a wonderful old building is about to be destroyed. There's no time for legislative action to save it. Problem: a couple thousand acres of pristine scenery has been put up for sale. Realty developers are eyeing it hungrily, but it really ought to be a park. Can the state get the money together in time? TPL specializes in the quick move. They arrange to hold the land or historical site until it can be purchased for use as a public resource — a process that typically takes considerable time. They've temporarily protected nearly a half-million acres so far. TPL is not an advocacy organization — you can't even join 'em! But you can contribute to their important work financially and by calling them in when things need to happen fast. True Earth-Saving, this is. —JB

The Trust For Public Land; Information **free**
Send donations to:
The Trust For Public Land
116 New Montgomery,
4th Floor, San Francisco
CA 94105; (415) 495-4014

The Nature Conservancy

The Nature Conservancy is responsible for preserving over five million acres of land, as well as innumerable rare and endangered plants and animals. For my money, they manage their purchases with the best network of volunteer and professional land stewards. The Nature Conservancy has gone international because many of the birds we protect here winter south of the border. "To save them here, they must be saved there as well." A fringe benefit of joining is a 4-color, top-notch bi-monthly magazine. —Peter Warshall

Nature Conservancy $15/year (membership includes 6 issues of **Nature Conservancy** magazine) Contact your local chapter or write to: Nature Conservancy 1815 North Lynn Street Arlington, VA 22209 (703) 841-5300

Two ingredients are essential to restoring the Conservancy's Tallgrass Prairie Preserve: grazing and fire. They are the primary natural forces, along with climate, that shaped and sustained the Great Plains of North America. Barnard Ranch, *(left),* whose purchase last fall (1989) laid a 30,000-acre cornerstone for the Conservancy's Tallgrass Prairie Preserve.

At the Audubon Society's request, TPL approached the landowner about selling the property. When the landowner resisted, the Audubon Society went to the public, talking-up their project, catching the attention of the media. They soon gained the support of half a dozen local groups, including Quality Forward, the French Broad River Foundation, the League of Women Voters, the Sierra Club, and the Asheville Council of Garden Clubs. In May of 1988, the developer optioned the property to TPL.

"The Trust for Public Land came along at a critical time for our organization. Without TPL's financial help and real estate know-how the public would not have a Beaver Lake Nature Center today."

Environmental Law and Lobby

Environmental organizations must approach politics with discretion; if they take a political stand, their tax-exempt status is revoked. While it's amusing to maintain that nature knows no politics (but always votes), politics — party and international — will have its way. Somebody has to insist that existing laws are enforced, and bring suit if they are not. (A favorite political deception is to make a big noise passing some impeccable eco-legislation, then quietly order authorities to ignore its enforcement.) Somebody has to "take it all the way to the Supreme Court". Such duties are performed by the several environmental legal organizations. Some are affiliated with, but separate from, nonpolitical parents. There is money involved — lots of it. You might be irritated at how some of it is spent, but it's gotta be done. Here are some of the courtroom and ante-room heavyweights you can support. They've been effective; without their work, things would be *much* worse. —JB

NRDC

*The **Natural Resources Defense Council** has been involved in demanding and then drawing up nearly every piece of positive environmental legislation extracted from a not-always-cooperative Congress and Senate. Strictly apolitical, they have the respect, if not the friendship, of governments worldwide. The excellent **Amicus Journal** accompanies your membership card. —JB*

Natural Resources Defense Council $10/year (membership includes 4 issues of **Amicus Journal** and 5 issues of **NRDC Newsline**) from: Natural Resources Defense Council 40 West 20th Street New York, NY 10011 (212) 727-2700

Sierra Club Legal Defense Fund, Inc.

This band of battle-hardened attorneys goes to bat anyplace they're needed, most often on behalf of organizations and citizen's groups other than their parent Sierra Club. When miscreants howl about nasty environmentalists violating the traditional American right to pollute and land-rape, this is who they usually mean. They're worried for good reason: the "Legal Defense Fund" usually wins. —JB

Sierra Club Legal Defense Fund (With minimum contribution of **$10** you will receive quarterly newsletter & information updates) from: Sierra Club Legal Defense Fund 2044 Fillmore St. San Francisco, CA 94115 (415) 567-6100

Environmental Studies Sought for North Cascades National Park

In 1968 Congress established the North Cascades National Park and adjacent Ross Lake and Lake Chelan National Recreation Areas to preserve the

Environmental Defense Fund

Supported by 125,000 members, EDF uses its formidable political and economic clout to influence major environment-affecting policy decisions all over the world. They deal with the World Bank, for instance, something that grassroots folks have not been able to do. Just the right size for the big lobbying tasks. —JB

Environmental Defense Fund, $20/year (membership includes 6 issues of **EDF Letter**) from: Environmental Defense Fund 1616 P Street, NW Washington, DC 20077-6048 (202) 387-3500

"By the Beautiful Sea" was the song of the day when the swimmers converged on this Staten Island beach in 1915. But recent summer weekends along the same stretch of sand have had a different look. Ocean pollution and beach closings have aroused public opinion against abuse of the seas.

outstanding scenery, wilderness, and outdoor recreation opportunities of Washington's North Cascades. Despite this mandate, the National Park Service has allowed private development to mushroom in the historic Stehekin River Valley, doubling the population of the Lake Chelan NRA. The service has also approved clearcutting of public forests to keep pace with the private demand for firewood. What's worse, the Park Service has prepared no environmental impact statements on these management policies. To redress this omission, on September 7 staff attorney Stephan Volker and Seattle lawyer Lynn Weir filed suit on behalf of the North Cascades Conservation Council to compel preparation of these studies.

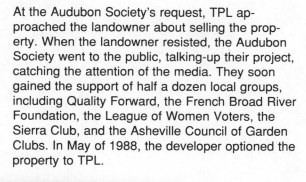

Environ, Garbage, and E.

These three keep up with all that's good and bad in the general field of popular environmental concern. **Environ** *was the first, though right now it isn't as flashy as the competition. Health is a major concern. (The same folks also publish* **The Wary Canary**, *p. 64.)*

To me, **E** *and* **Garbage** *are hard to tell apart. (I mean their editors no insult). They cover much the same news.* **E** *recently won a prize for good reporting; their articles are extensive and bite deeper than do those in many popular magazines.* **Garbage** *belies its name by reporting on lots besides solid waste management, using lots of color and upscale graphic design. It's great for a quick hit on an unfamiliar subject. Both magazines are loaded with advertising puffing "green" products, services, and organizations — hence are a good place to keep up with what's available. I'd say the choice of any of the three is a matter of personal taste.* —JB

Environ, Suzanne & Ed Randegger, Editors; **$15**/year (four issues) from: Environ, P.O. Box 2204, Fort Collins, CO 80522

E: The Environmental Magazine, Doug Moss, Editor; **$20**/year (six issues) from: E Magazine, Subscription Department, P. O. Box 6667, Syracuse, NY 13217-7934

Garbage, Patricia Poore, Editor; **$21**/year (six issues) from: Garbage, P. O. Box 51647, Boulder, CO 80321-1647

•

On nutritional tests, Organic Foods Production Association of North America concludes:

While there are studies indicating that some nutritional benefits may derive from excellent organic growing methods (versus conventional methods), adequate research has not yet been done to prove this, and such market claims are ill-advised at this time. Furthermore, the use in the marketplace of individual nutrient test results (even if no generalized claims are made regarding growing method superiority) is problematic and of questionable validity . . . Therefore, nutrient testing is seen as best relegated to the realm of research for the present.

Drafters of the OFPANA report included chemists, agronomists and nutritionists as well as organic farmers which adds to its credibility. —*Environ*

•

"Debt-for-nature" swaps pose other troublesome questions. The idea, conceived by the Smithsonian Institution's Thomas Lovejoy, is that big environmental groups buy up discounted debt certificates owned by foreign nations to U.S. banks in exchange for protection of forests and wildlife preserves. The World Wildlife Fund kicked this off, apparently successfully, in Ecuador. But in Bolivia, in the two years since Conservation International (CI) retired $650,000 of the country's debt, not a single tree has been planted under the required program, lumber companies have hacked down thousands more mahogany trees, and CI has ended up on the side of commercial logging interests in opposing the demands of indigenous peoples. —*E*

Ambio

Authoritative and glossy, this Sweden-based magazine is the voice of establishment international environmentalism. When I was working on a article about genotoxins — the flood of new chemicals that cause cancer and gene damage — **Ambio** *was my most indispensable source of up-to-date information.*
—Stewart Brand

Ambio
Arno Rosemarin, Editor
$44/year (8 issues) from:
Pergamon Press, Inc.
Maxwell House
Fairview Park
Elmsford, NY 10523

—Scott Willis, Garbage

Natural History Magazine

I use it two ways: The monthly column "This View of Life" by Stephen Jay Gould, who teaches Biology, Geology and History of Science at Harvard, regularly contributes to (or at least soundly reaffirms) my understanding of how the world works. He explains fundamental issues clearly and always sets them against a background of why anyone ever thought differently. Second, it is written and edited in such a way that our children seem to get as much out of it as we do. It is one of the few publications we've found that has this quality. A good magazine at a good price from a great institution. —George Putz

Natural History, Alan Ternes, Editor; **$22**/year (12 issues) from: Natural History, P. O. Box 5000, Harlan, IA 51537-5000; (800) 234-5252

A wild boar stands under the trees of Nordeifel Nature Park in West Germany. The species, originally widespread in Europe, is still found in numerous nature reserves.

Orion

How about a quarterly nature magazine that features as many pictures of people as of birds or trees? **Orion** *sees humans as part of the natural environment, and I find it a more believable nature magazine because of that. This full-color glossy has no political constituency to please (both* **Audubon** *and* **Sierra** *are straitjacketed by membership dogma), but simply raises interesting, intelligent topics, one per issue — such as "Architecture in relation to nature," "Sustainable agriculture," "Forms and patterns," or "Migrations." Every issue is a refreshing enlargement of what "nature" means.* —Kevin Kelly [Suggested by James Jackson]

Orion Nature Quarterly, George K. Russell, Editor; **$14**/year (4 issues) from: The Myrin Institute, Inc., 136 E. 64th Street New York, NY 10021 (212) 758-6475

Docks at Manaus, the transportation hub of the Amazon, shipping point for bananas, fish, and other produce of the region.

•

Resources everywhere

Eco-developers set out to prospect the broad range of life-supporting factors to assure the sustainability of yields over the long term. Through their glasses, numerous things and actions which so far had been taken for granted acquire a new, dramatic significance: they change into valuable resources. Cow dung, for example, kindled by the Senegalese peasant to heat water in the cooking pot, suddenly becomes an energy resource; the scrap metal used by a Peruvian squatter to build an annex to his hut takes on the dignity of a recoverable input; Kenyan women cultivating village fields are discovered to be human resources for boosting food production. Under Worldwatch eyes, more and more parts of the world assume a new status; they are disembedded from their local context and redefined as resources.

Resources count not because of what they are but because of what they can become. They are stripped of their own worth in the present in order to be stripmined for somebody else's use in the future. A resource is something that has no value until it has been made into something else. For more than 100 years the term "resource" has been used to survey the world for useful inputs into industry.

The Ecologist

Edited by the ebullient Teddy Goldsmith, this British mag is a nice mix of careful and radical. It has a strong point of view, lots of good ideas, and considerable effect. —Stewart Brand

The Ecologist
Edward Goldsmith
Nicholas Hildyard,
Peter Bunyard, Editors
$30/year (six issues)
from:
MIT Press Journals
55 Hayward Street
Cambridge, MA 02142
(617) 253-2889
•

An Open Letter to Mrs. Thatcher

Dear Prime Minister,

It is heartening that you should have chosen the occasion of your speech to the UN General Assembly to address the ecological crisis facing our planet. It was a timely speech and, given the global nature of the problems, a highly appropriate forum to make it.

That said, the contents of your speech are worrying. . . .

Nothing could demonstrate the wrong-headedness of your approach better than your decision to donate £100 million to the Tropical Forestry Action Plan (TFAP). As a publicity stunt, it is capital. However, in terms of saving the world's tropical forests, it is a disaster. The TFAP, as has been exhaustively documented in *The Ecologist*, is *not* a plan to save the forests. As its name makes clear, it's a plan to extend *forestry* — in effect, to promote commercial plantations. Indeed, its conservation programme consists of no more than assisting "in the establishment of a national network of protected areas designed to conserve *representative samples* of ecosystems." The forests will thus be reduced to ecological Disneylands — a few isolated islands to satisfy tourists and scientists but a little value in terms of the global ecosystem.

We urge you to withdraw Britain's support for the TFAP. We urge you too to broaden your choice of advisors to include those whom you refer to as "so-called greens". It is they who have correctly predicted the crisis and diagnosed its causes — not the industrialists, scientists and civil servants whom you have so far relied upon for advice. Much of what the greens have to tell you may at first appear unpalatable. But if we are to leave a world fit for future generations to live in, it is critical that you act on their recommendations. —*The Editors*

New Scientist

My primary source of scientific and technical information is the wide-ranging reporting in this British weekly. Droll wit abounds, and the sometimes rather nasty criticism and comment spares nobody, including the USA, thus integrating a useful political viewpoint not usually found in science periodicals. Technical articles are models of clarity, offering ready access to potentially difficult concepts. Environmental concerns are accented. At the Whole Earth offices, the latest issue grows legs immediately and is not seen again until months later, if ever. I have my own subscription. —JB

New Scientist
Michael Kenward, Editor
$115/year (51 issues)
from: New Scientist
Subscriptions, Freepost
1061, Oakfield House,
Perrymount Road,
Haywards Heath, West
Sussex RH16 3ZA
England
•

Drought and famine develop over months and years, yet details tend to emerge too late to avert death and suffering. But remote sensing by satellite can give us data that can warn of imminent disaster or provide effective emergency relief for remote areas. Depending on their orbits, satellites can produce images of the same area at intervals ranging from a few hours to a few weeks. Those images can pinpoint the extent and severity of sudden disasters, but long-term monitoring, over months and years can document changes that foretell drought and famine.

Cave painting of a bison at Altamira, Spain. **"Art has always been a crucial means whereby we establish our place spiritually in the macrocosm. Its meaning, purpose and origin lie in that deep strata of hope and terror with which our ancestors, facing an overwhelming universe, sought to communicate with it."**

Great Presses

Our staff and friends have learned that a book from any of these presses is likely to be the best on the subject and might even become a classic of its kind. —JB

Sierra Club Books

*A library made up of books from this press would be a fine library indeed. A look at their list will always prove enticing. (And, by the way, that library exists, in San Francisco. It's available to members of the Sierra Club.) For example, I just received a review copy of a new Sierra Club book, **Call to Action**. It's a well-named collection of rousing essays, mostly by well-known fighters for the Good & the True. Each section concludes with a list of specific actions you might attempt or join. If you've heard it all already, check the bibliography and source lists — they're among the most useful I've seen. And there's a wonderful glossary of Tools, Terms, and Tactics. This book may be the best introduction to environmental action around — just the place for a newcomer to start their homework, and just the place for an oldtimer to make sure they aren't missing anything. —JB*

Call To Action
(Handbook for Ecology,
Peace, and Justice)
Brad Erickson, Editor
1990; 250 pp.
$12.95 ($15.95 postpaid)
Sierra Club Books
Catalog **free**

Both from:
Sierra Club Books
730 Polk Street
San Francisco, CA 94109; (415) 923-5500

Island Press

"Ohboy, another new book from Island Press!" is our usual reaction — I think I've read every book they publish (and reviewed a good many). Their tasty catalog also stocks some of the best offerings from other good presses. —JB

Island Press; Catalog **free** from: P.O. Box 7
Covelo, CA 95428; (800) 828-1302

Peregrine Smith Books

Peregrine Smith Books *has made a business out of doing right by books on worthy subjects.*
—*Richard Nilsen*

They're gorgeous! —*Susan Erkel Ryan*

Peregrine Smith Books; Catalog **free** from:
P. O. Box 667, Layton, UT 84041
(801) 544-9800

The Workbook

One of the most significant developments in social-change movements in this decade has been the common perception among peace, environmental, and social-issue activists that their causes are inextricably linked: for example, "environmental" groups like Epoca are doing community development work in Central America with the belief that peace is the first step toward ecological restoration. And gay and lesbian organizations are joining the peace movement in greater force because they see the direct connection between military spending and lack of funds for AIDS research. The strength of Jesse Jackson's 1988 campaign indicates that these new coalitions are definitely coming of age.

The Workbook, *published by the Southwest*

Research and Information Center, has covered this broad, interrelated range of concerns for over a decade. Each issue features a long research article and related further-reading reviews, and a core section of reviews by their specialty editors of new books and publications in education, economics, nutrition, third world issues, the environment, women, work, and more. **The Workbook's**

The Workbook
Kathy Newton, Editor
$12/year (4 issues) from:
The Workbook
SRIC, P. O. Box 4524
Albuquerque, NM 87106
(505) 262-1862

greatest service is that their reviews include special reports from research institutes and universities that you probably wouldn't hear about anywhere else — with ordering information. Highly recommended. —Jeanne Carstensen
•

The Workbook cited. "Food Irradiation: Its Environmental Threat, Its Toxic Connection," published in the April/June 1988 issue of *The Workbook,* was selected as the fourth most overlooked news story of 1988. The *Workbook* article, written by Judith H. Johnsrud, Ph.D. and edited by Julie Jacoby, shared the honors in Project Censored's Ten Best Censored Stories of 1988 with "Update on Food Irradiation," a JoAnne Korkki article published in the December 1988/January 1989 issue of *Northern Sun News.*

The National Outdoor Leadership School

In simple terms, the NOLS goal is this: to teach you the skills necessary to survive in the wilderness — whether it's kayaking in Alaska, mountain climbing in the Rockies, or backpacking in Africa — and to pass through that wilderness without leaving any trace of your having been there. Unlike Outward Bound, NOLS is not into character development or proving yourself. Instead, it teaches only those skills directly related to the wilderness experience.

Both styles have their merits. The fundamental difference, I think, is between self-command and harmony. Me, I'll take harmony. —Joe Kane

NOLS also offers semester programs for credit
—JB

National Outdoor Leadership School
Courses $1200-$5800; Catalog **free** from:
National Outdoor Leadership School
P. O. Box AA, Dept WE, Lander, WY 82520
(307) 332-6973

•

ADVENTURE COURSE. *Age: 14-15; duration: 30 days; location: Ranges in Wyoming and Montana.*

An Adventure Course includes all the experiences and classes of a Wind River Wilderness Course for 14- and 15-year-olds. The course is education in action: students learn by doing, not just watching or reading about it.

Peak ascents, introductory rock-climbing, natural history instruction and fly fishing are among the skills taught on an Adventure Course. In addition to learning the basics of these activities, the course explores leadership roles and group dynamics.

Outward Bound

Now 30 years old, Outward Bound continues to offer challenging courses in such skills as climbing, whitewater running, and blue-water sailing. If you're a chickenheart, or think you are, one of these courses may be just what you need. Emphasis is on building self-confidence and leadership. Special courses can be arranged for executives, folks with substance-abuse problems, cancer patients unwilling to give up, and other special needs. Many participants are women and teens. I personally know a number of people who returned from Outward Bound courses noticeably changed for the better. —JB

Outward Bound; Courses $400-$2200; Catalog free from: Outward Bound/National Office, 384 Field Point Road, Greenwich, CT 06830; (800) 243-8520

•

Canoeing for the Disabled/Ablebodied

Dr. Kurt Hahn, Outward Bound founder, once said, "Your disability is your opportunity." This positive statement holds particularly true for persons with moderate to severe disabilities such as cerebral palsy, hearing impairment, paraplegia, amputation and congenital defects. Together with ablebodied persons who are interested in working with people with disabilities, you will have the chance to gain insights into yourself and others through canoeing, rock climbing and other activities.

CANOE EXPEDITIONING				VOYAGEUR OB SCHOOL
Date	No. of Days	Minimum Age	Tuition	Course No.
Canoe Expeditioning, Wilderness Camping, Rock Climbing: Minnesota/Canada Border Lake Region				
7/1-7/15	15	16	$1200	MD-469

NOLS Ranch Manager Paul Davidson explains the importance of properly balancing panniers when horsepacking.

Judgment and maturity can blossom in the backcountry, where the consequences of decisions are clear.

Though the Adventure Course curriculum is the same as the Wilderness Course, we offer each of them as a separate course for the benefit of the students. We find that 14- and 15-year-olds learn and experience more of the leadership aspect of a NOLS course in a group of their peers. College-aged and older adults who take Wilderness Courses are likely to dominate decision-making situations, keeping younger students from gaining the full benefit of a NOLS course.

Helping Out In The Outdoors

When people volunteer everybody is winning. Needed jobs get done (cheerfully!), and the volunteers go home with more than they gave. Like to partake? Our parks could use your help. Wanted are fire lookouts, craft instructors, trail crews, campground hosts, surveyors, and tree planters. Experience accepted, willingness preferred. Some jobs pay no money, others furnish groceries or lodging or gas money, or work clothes, and some even pay meagerly. Look over this semi-annual directory, decide who to give your love to, and write to them early. —Kevin Kelly

Helping Out in the Outdoors
$5 (single copy) 96 pp.; Published semi-annually in February and August; from: American Hiking Society, Attn.: Susan Henley, 1015 31st St. N.W. Washington, D.C. 20007; (703) 385-3252

•

SOUTH DAKOTA

BLACK HILLS NATIONAL FOREST
CUSTER DISTRICT

The famous Black Hills are located along the western edge of South Dakota. Custer District in the southern Black Hills offers a variety of opportunities for everyone.

WILDERNESS RANGERS to patrol trails in Harney Peak area and Black Elk Wilderness. TRAIL CREW to help with backcountry trails. GEOLOGIST-MINERALS ASSISTANT to manage mineral resources. RECREATIONAL AIDE to help with recreation sites. FORESTRY AIDE for indoor and outdoor timber management. RANGE AIDE for on-the-ground range management. CAMPGROUND HOST for several sites. Negotiable stipend, dorm-style housing, training, supervision, college credit by arrangement.

Contact: District Ranger
Custer Ranger District
330 Mt. Rushmore Rd.
Custer, SD 57730 Phone: 605/673-4853

The Tracker School

*Tom Brown, Jr. grew up in the desolate Pine Barrens of southern New Jersey. He was schooled mercilessly but compassionately in woodcraft by his best friend's father, a Navajo tracker named Stalking Wolf. With a consummate storyteller's skill, Mr. Brown tells us how he exchanged his small-town-boy's self-centeredness for the cunning, observant care, and sheer good heartedness of a true tracker. He does this in three books: **The Tracker** (which I like best), **The Search**, and **The Vision,** masterpieces of how to see and learn. These books are an outline for the many hands-on courses he teaches near his home (yes, that part of NJ is still pretty wild). The courses have inspired a whole stack of competent **Field Guides** that may be especially useful to urban dwellers and folks who have not been paying attention. There is some overlapping of subject matter amongst these books; that's inevitable since they are all manifestations of the same philosophy. And a commendable phioloosophy it is, in a time where it is increasingly difficult to tell realism from reality. —JB*

The Tracker School; Courses **$565**

The Tracker (The Story of Tom Brown, Jr., as told to William Jon Watkins) 1985 (8th ed.); 229 pp.; **$3.95** ($5.45 postpaid)

The Search, Tom Brown, Jr., with William Owen; 1982; 219 pp.; **$7.95** ($9.45 postpaid)

The Vision, Tom Brown, Jr.; 1988 241 pp.; **$7.95** ($9.45 postpaid)

Tom Brown's Field Guides (Wilderness Survival, Forgotten Wilderness) **$7.95** ($9.45 postpaid) each; (Survival for Children, Observation and Tracking, City and Suburban Survival, Wild Edible and Medicinal Plants, Living with the Earth) **$8.95** ($10.45 postpaid) each.

All from:
The Tracker,
Tom Brown, Jr.
P. O. Box 173,
Asbury, NJ
08802-0173
(201) 479-4681
✶WEA

•

He was so light and frail that I could hardly feel him. The remaining blood that dripped from his neck felt hot and heavy as it ran down my chest and back. I hated Grandfather and I felt bitter.

I wandered back to camp, my mind twisted with rage, and I knew what I had to do. I was going to walk into camp, drop the little deer at Grandfather's feet, and walk out of the woods forever. If this was what survival, what being a man, and what the doorway to the spiritual world were all about, then I wanted nothing to do with them. As I approached the camp, I noticed Grandfather leaning against a tree and watching me. A wry smile was held motionless on his face and penetrated my soul, causing me to despise him even more. As I neared him, he lost the smile and his face went blank, except for his piercing eyes. His look made me feel like he had been where I was once before, and his words shook my foundations and broke the back of my hatred. Before I could utter a word, he pointed that old gnarled finger at me and spoke. "Grandson, when you can feel the same way about a blade of grass plucked from the ground as you do for that little deer, then and only then will you be 'one' with all things." —The Vision

Foxfire

Foxfire is a quarterly publication concerned with researching, recording and preserving Appalachian folk art, crafts and traditions. A typical issue contains articles on quilting, chairmaking, soap making, home remedies, mountain recipes, feather beds and home-made hominy, plus regional poetry and book reviews. One issue was entirely devoted to log cabin building. These are not superficial "feature" articles, but definitive, detailed treatments of traditional skills and crafts that have come close to dying out of our culture.

Foxfire would be a credit to a group of professional folklorists. But when you consider that it is edited and published by high school kids at Rabun County High School in Clayton, Georgia, it becomes immediately diately around them for their inspiration, instead of taking cues from New York and California. In their own way, these people are as hip and sophisticated as any young people putting out a magazine on either coast. More so, even. They're cooler, more adult. *Foxfire*'s editors and writers (and some excellent photographers) seem to me as aware of what's wrong with the world as anyone. The thing that distinguishes them from their shrill counterparts in the cities is the absence of fad, slogan and cliche as they set out to improve the world. These kids in Georgia are living in a real world, studying real things, and in consequence they are creating a wonderfully real publication in *Foxfire.*
—Gurney Norman

Since Gurney wrote this review in 1969 *Foxfire* has grown and deepened with the years into a flat-out landmark of American education and folklore technique. It's been widely copied, always to good effect. Try it in your area. The old-timers tell things to youngsters they wouldn't say to anybody else.
—Stewart Brand

Foxfire
Eliot Wigginton, Advisor; $9/year (4 issues)

The Foxfire Book - Hog dressing, log cabin building, mountain crafts and foods, planting by the signs, snake lore, hunting tales, faith healing, moonshining, and other affairs of plain living. 1972.

Foxfire 2 — Ghost stories, spring wild plant foods, spinning and weaving, midwifing, burial customs, corn shuckin's, wagon making and more affairs of plain living. 1973.

Foxfire 3 — Animal care, banjos and dulcimers, hide tanning, summer and fall wild plant foods, butter churns, ginseng, and still more affairs of plain living. 1975.

Foxfire 4 — Fiddle making, spring houses, horse trading, sassafras tea, berry buckets, gardening, and further affairs of plain living. 1977.

PLATE 242 As all old wagon makers did, Jud "saws the joints" between the felloes to make the faces meet properly and to create a bit of slack space for the metal tire to pull together as it shrinks around the wheel and creates dish. According to Jud, it is also acceptable to saw out a three-eighths-inch space between two felloes and leave the other joints untouched.

Foxfire 5 — Ironmaking, blacksmithing, flintlock rifles, bear hunting, and other affairs of plain living. 1979.

Foxfire 6 — Shoemaking, 100 toys and games, gourd banjos and songbows, wooden locks, a water-powered sawmill, and other affairs of just plain living. 1980.

Foxfire 7 — Southern Appalachian religious heritage: baptizing, camp meetings, faith healing, snake handling. 1982.

Foxfire 8 — Southern folk pottery from pug mills, ash glazes, and groundhog kilns to face jugs, churns and rooster, mule swapping and chicken fighting. 1984.

Foxfire 9 — Wagon-making, general stores, Catawba potter, dogtrot house, quilting, home remedies. 1986.

Foxfire 1-9, $14.95 postpaid. ✱WEA

Sometimes A Shining Moment — Eliot Wigginton tells us about his teaching philosophy and how he started Foxfire. **$12.50** postpaid. ✱WEA

Foxfire also publishes **Hands On: A Journal for Teachers**, and produces tapes of folk music. And they put on a weekly radio show, produce videos, maintain a museum center, run a Teacher-Outreach program, lecture all over, and, as they like to say, "We haven't even started yet."

All from: The Foxfire Fund, Inc., P. O. Box B, Rabun Gap, GA 30568; (404) 746-5828

Martha Roane being interviewed in the Foxfire classroom. To her right is her grandson, Charles Dennis.

Planet Drum Foundation

*Since its start in 1974, Planet Drum has been a major influence in developing interest and action in bioregionalism and "reinhabitation." They are "now working to foster exchange among bioregional groups and projects — the growing number of people exploring cultural, environmental, and economic forms appropriate to the places where you live." You get the news — increasingly international — in their often provocative review, **Raise The Stakes,** sharply edited by the not-always-polite Peter Berg. It occasionally features a valuable updated directory of bioregional organizations. Other Planet Drum publications include several "Bundles" of essays, posters, poems and other materials celebrating individual bioregions, and a small selection of important books. This outfit is one to watch — their insights have often been years ahead of the rest of us.* —JB

Planet Drum
$15/year (membership includes two issues of **Raise the Stakes**, one bonus publication, 25% discount on all books, access to workshop facilities) from: Planet Drum, P. O. Box 31251, San Francisco CA 94131, Shasta Bioregion, USA

Audubon Expedition School

One of the more tempting and radical educational opportunities is aboard the Audubon Expedition school buses that spend summer on the road exploring the cultural and environmental wonders of our country. Students and professors camp out of the bus, taking due time to hike, bike, ski, boat and generally immerse themselves in the areas they study. Social and environmental matters are high on the list of subjects. Credit is offered for high school right up to advanced degrees (through Lesley College). Praise is high; the school gives that indefinable feeling of rightness that comes from involvement with reality instead of being cooped up in a classroom. I've actually interacted with several busloads (at New Alchemy Institute — one of their stops) and found these folks to be just what they claim. If they'd had this forty years ago, I would have pestered my parents until they let me sign on. Scholarships available. —JB

Audubon Expedition School; $5500/semester; **$9300**/year; Catalog **free** from: National Audubon Society Expedition Institute, R.R.1, Box 171, Sharon, CT 06069; (203) 364-0522
●

MARITIME CANADA EXPEDITION

Travel to the blue-green waters of the Bay of Fundy, the Gulf of St. Lawrence, and the island of Grand Manan. Canoe through the waters of Kejimkujik National Park and learn about Celtic music and the culture of Cape Breton Island.

The BioRegional Quiz

by Peter Warshall, Leonard Charles, Jim Dodge, Lynn Milliman, and Victoria Stockley

1. When you turn on your faucet, where does the water come from? (Can you trace it back to local storm systems?)

2. When you flush the toilet, where does the water go? (not just the treatment plant, but the final river or lake).

3. What soil series are you standing on?

4. How long is the growing season?

5. What are the major geological events that shaped your bioregion (faults, uplifts, downwarps, volcanics, sea floods, etc)? Does your community give them special attention . . . are they sacred, blessed, protected?

6. How did the original inhabitants eat, clothe, and shelter themselves? How did they celebrate the seasonal changes in times before you?

7. How many days until the moon is full?

8. From where you are sitting, point north.

9. What other bioregions of the planet have the most similar climate, culture, and analogous plants and animals? In other words, who are your Gaian cousins?

10. Name the major plant/animal associations that thrive in your bioregion. Name five resident and migratory birds; five grasses; five trees; five mammals and reptiles or amphibians. Which are native?

11. Name the plant or animal that is the "barometer" of environmental health for your bioregion? How's it doing? endangered? threatened? thriving? Has it become a symbol or totem of local power for your community?

12. Name the bioregions that grew each item of food on your dinner plate. Could you eat more locally? Support nearby farms?

13. Where does your garbage go?

14. What heavenly events most influence life in your bioregion? (fire? lightning? hail? tornadoes? fog? blizzards? drought? permafrost? chubascos? spring thaw?)

Earth Education

"For over twenty years the public has been led to believe that there is a serious educational response underway regarding the environmental problems of the earth. It is not true. The environmental education movement has been led astray: trivialized by mainstream education, diluted by those with other agendas, co-opted by the very agencies and industries that have contributed so much to the problems." With these fighting words, Steve Van Matre sallies forth with a comprehensive program for educating all of us. It's detailed right down to the language used, so will doubtless rankle many teachers who, however weary, would prefer their way to that of an outsider with all the answers. I recommend that you at least listen to what he has to say, not that he (or I, heh heh) has all the answers, but because I have noticed that most of the effective teachers I know use similar methods. This way of going at things gets results.
—JB

Earth Education (A New Beginning), Steve Van Matre; 1990; 334 pp. **$17.95** ($20.70 postpaid) from: The Institute for Earth Education, Box 288 Warrenville, IL 60555 (509) 395-2299

•

To assimilate something means to incorporate it into your own way of thinking. So we need to help our participants see the flow of energy, the cycling of materials, the interrelating of life, and the changing of forms in everything they do. Even though those systems have always been there, we have become so adept at covering them up in our societies that we no longer realize they operate all around us. By removing some of the disguises we have used to mask the actual workings of life, we can help participants see that humans are not really separate from nature; they have just hidden it away under layer upon layer of artificial glazing.

"We have had the experience, but missed the meaning."
—*T.S. Eliot*

Fortunately, opportunities for helping people peel away such disguises can be found in most every setting and situation. Years ago at the camp where our work began, there was a small chalkboard outside the main dining lodge. Each morning one of the cooks would write up what was coming for lunch, then return in the afternoon to put up what we would be having for dinner. By chance, I was watching the cook post the dinner menu one day when I suddenly realized that that wasn't what we were going to eat at all. It was a disguise. So after she had gone back inside, I went up and erased it. On the first line she had written "Roast Pork." I changed that to "Roast Pig" then decided that still wasn't clear enough and changed it again to "Roast Hoofed Mammal." The next line became "Boiled Orange Roots" followed by "Mashed White Tubers." And the last line read simply "Tossed Leaves." That is what we were really going to eat that evening — roots and tubers and mammals and leaves. You could do the same thing in your own setting today — at home or school or office or centre — just call your food by that which it is instead of by that which it is not. By peeling away such disguises we can begin to see our connections again with the systems of life around us.

Project Wild

Project Wild is an interdisciplinary, environmental and conservation education program emphasizing wildlife. There are three curriculum guides — elementary, secondary, and one called **Aquatic** *for grades K-12. Project Wild activities are organized around a conceptual framework comprising these major themes: awareness and appreciation of wildlife, human values and wildlife, wildlife and ecological systems, wildlife conservation, cultural and social interaction with wildlife, wildlife issues and trends, and responsible human actions regarding wildlife and ecological systems.*

Each Project Wild activity includes objectives, method, background for the teacher, materials needed, procedures, evaluation suggestions, recommended grade level, school subject area(s), skills, duration, group size, setting, concept, and key vocabulary. The guides include a glossary and several cross-referenced indexes (lists of activities by grade level, skills acquired, topics covered, etc.) to help teachers incorporate wildlife-related concepts into their daily teaching strategy.

Project Wild is a joint project of the Western Regional Environmental Education Council and the Western Association of Fish and Wildlife Agencies. —*Don Waxman*

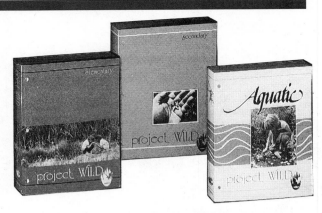

HOOKS AND LADDERS

Method: Students simulate Pacific salmon and the hazards faced by salmon in an activity portraying the life cycle of these aquatic creatures.

Age: Grades 3-9

Materials: Large playing area (100 feet x 50 feet); about 500 feet of rope, string, or six traffic cones for marking boundaries (masking tape may be used if area is indoors); two cardboard boxes; 100 tokens (3 x 5 cards, poker chips, etc.).

Procedure: . . . This is a physically-involving activity! Set up a playing field as shown in the diagram, including spawning grounds, downstream, upstream, and ocean. . . .

Assign roles to each of the students. Some will be salmon, others will be potential hazards to the salmon. . . .

Begin the activity with all the salmon in their spawning ground. The salmon then start their

Project Wild activity guides are available **free** of charge to participants in Project Wild workshops. Workshops are open to educators and youth-group leaders at nominal charge. For more information, contact Project Wild, P. O. Box 18060, Boulder, CO 80308-8060; (303) 444-2390.

journey downstream. The first major hazard is the turbines at the dam. . . .

At most dams there are escape weirs to guide migrating salmon past the turbines. The student salmon cannot go around the jump rope swingers, but they can slip under the swingers' arms if they do not get touched while doing so. A salmon dies if it is hit by the turbine (jump rope). . . .

NOTE: Any salmon that "dies" at any time in this activity must immediately become part of the fish ladder. The student is no longer a fish . . . .

Once in the open ocean, the salmon can be caught by fishing boats. The salmon must move back and forth across the ocean area in order to gather four tokens. Each token represents one year of growth. Once each fish has four tokens (four years' growth) that fish can begin migration upstream . . . . —*Aquatic*

City Safaris

Getting kids to be more aware of the world outside their classroom doesn't necessarily require a country setting or park; cities are amazingly rich in detail if you look closely. This book — a teacher's aid, really — prescribes a group of activities proven to engage young folks as they explore an urban landscape. The suggested games may seem a bit overstructured, but city dwellers know that without strong focus, things seem to get dissipated in the hustle and bustle. Looks good to me. Plenty of nourishment for adults, too. —JB

City Safaris, Carolyn Shaffer and Eric Fielder; 1987; 185 pp. **$9.95** ($12.95 postpaid) from: Sierra Club Bookstore 730 Polk Street San Francisco, CA 94109 (415) 923-5500 ✳WEA

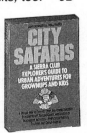

•

Can you tell what time of day it is by street sounds alone?

You can concoct many games using rubbings including guessing mystery rubbings from around the neighborhood.

Sharing Nature with Children

Smelling, feeling, listening, watching, guessing — imagining yourself to be a part of nature. Taking joy in it. That's what this extraordinary book is about. It's a far cry from the obedient line of kids marching along to the chirping of a bored teacher on a "nature walk." This is absolutely the best awareness-of-nature book I've ever seen. It works for adults, too. —JB

The 40 activities in this book are easy to use — for family or class outings. Kids actually like them. **Sharing Nature with Children** *was the most helpful book I found when doing research for a bioregional curriculum guide — Joseph Cornell knows how to talk about nature to kids without talking down to them.* —Jeanne Carstensen

Sharing Nature With Children
Joseph Bharat Cornell; 1979
142 pp.; **$6.95** (postpaid if payment accompanies order) from:
Dawn Publications, 14618 Tyler Foote Road, Nevada City, CA 95959; (800) 545-7475 ✳WEA

●

There is a bird call that you can easily do with no more equipment than your own mouth. It attracts many of the smaller species: sparrows, warblers, jays, vireos, chickadees, nuthatches, hummingbirds, flycatchers, bushtits, orioles, kinglets, wrens, and others. In the following section on predator calls, you will learn to attract some of the larger birds.

The call consists of a series of rhythmically-repeated "pssh" sounds. Different rhythms work with different birds. Here are a couple of simple rhythms you can start with:

> pssh . . . . . pssh . . . . . pssh . . . . .
> pssh . . . pssh . . . pssh-pssh . . . pssh . . . pssh

Each of these series should last about three seconds. Experiment to find the rhythms that work best for the birds in your area.

Sharing the Joy of Nature

Author Joseph Cornell's first book, **Sharing Nature with Children***, has become justly famous because it works; both kids and teachers have been happy to transcend the usual stultifying "nature walk." Now Mr. Cornell has added the depth and detail necessary to enthrall adults (the kids can come too, of course). The teaching method is a logical sequence he calls "flow learning": Awaken enthusiasm, Focus attention, Direct experience, Share inspiration. As both a giver and receiver of nature expeditions, I can vouch that it's an effective and up-beat way to get at things without being sappy.* —JB

Sharing the Joy of Nature
Joseph Cornell; 1989; 167 pp.
$9.95 (postpaid if payment accompanies order) from:
Dawn Publications
14618 Tyler Foote Road
Nevada City, CA 95959
(800) 545-7475 ✳WEA

●

Camera is one of the most powerful and enjoyable activities in this book. In a simple and natural way, it quiets distracting thoughts and restlessness and frees the attention for absorbing nature with unobstructed clarity.

One player takes the role of photographer, and the other plays the camera. The photographer guides the camera, who keeps his eyes closed, on a search for beautiful and interesting pictures. When the photographer sees something he likes, he points the camera's lens (eyes) at it, framing the object he wants to "shoot." Then he presses the shutter button to open the lens. . . .

Encourage the photographers to be creative in choosing and framing pictures. Tell them, "You can make stunning photographs by taking shots from unusual angles and perspectives. For example, you can both lie down under a tree and take your picture looking upward, or you can put your camera very close to a tree's bark or leaves.

Try looking down into a flower, or panning the horizon. Be open to the opportunities of the moment." . . .

Because the Camera Game uses nature experiences instead of verbal explanations, very young children can participate just as fully as adults. It's very touching to watch five-year-olds guide their parents or grandparents, taking pictures and sharing their delight in natural things.

Manure, Meadows and Milkshakes

This is a book full of wonderful games and activities that are every bit as creative as its title. The lessons effectively teach children the principles of ecology through hands-on exercises. One fifth-grader who participated in **Manure, Meadows and Milkshakes** *activities said, "You have to learn about nature in person. You have to taste it, feel it, see it and hear it."* —Don Waxman

Manure, Meadows and Milkshakes
Eric Jorgensen, Trout Black, and Mary Hallesy;
1986; 132 pp.; **$9.95** ($11.45 postpaid) from:
The Trust for Hidden Villa
26870 Moody Road
Los Altos Hills, CA 94022
(415) 941-6119 ✳WEA

●

Cinquains are a wonderful way to combine feelings and facts about our world into a poetic image. Easy to learn; easy to do! Here's how:

First line: one word, giving title

Second line: two words, describing title

Third line: three words, expressing an action

Fourth line: four words, expressing a feeling

Fifth line: one word, a synonym for the title

●

Ranger Game: Play this on a narrow trail when your children are pushing and shoving to be first. Number everyone off and start up the trail. No "cuts." Place yourself third in line. (You can talk to the two ahead and also keep track of the gang behind.) The first child is the ranger. When you or the children spot something of interest have your ranger stand by it and point it out to everyone as they walk by. "Ranger Dan or Ann" then becomes the caboose at the end of the line. Make sure everyone has a chance to be a ranger.

Hug a Tree

A workbook of more than fifty outdoor learning experiences for children in groups and individually. Especially good are the suggestions for aiding kids in recording the experiences in their own terms and for following up over time on the original activities. —Keith Jordan

Hug a Tree
Robert E. Rockwell,
Elizabeth A. Sherwood,
and Robert A. Williams
1983; 106 pp.; **$9.95**
($11.45 postpaid) from
Gryphon House, Inc.
3706 Otis Street
Mount Rainier, MD 20712
(800) 638-0928 ✳WEA

3 & UP: BURY THE SOCK

Things You Can Use

nylon sock
leaves
plants
grass
tin cans
glass
plastic
tissue
cellophane wrapper
gum
apple core
fast food containers

Words You Can Use

collect
litter
bury
change
time

We often hear that litter isn't biodegradable. Does this mean anything to a young child? Probably not. To an adult, it means that most litter does not break down biologically. What the child needs to know is that litter doesn't rot or decay very easily; it just stays where we leave it. In this activity the children discover what happens to cast-offs from people and from nature.

What To Do

1. Take a nylon sock and collect both natural materials and litter that you find in the yard. Try to get at least one each of the items listed in "Things You Can Use."

2. Make a record of your collecting by sketching the sock and its content.

3. Bury the sock so that it is completely covered by dirt.

4. Dig up the sock in a few months.

5. Compare what has happened to the organic materials with what has happened to the glass, plastic and metal. Talk about it. You can even moralize a little if you like. The idea that trash dropped on the ground doesn't just disappear is important—even for young children. Attitudes toward the world form easily. They ought to be good ones!

Want To Do More?

Keep the sock in the ground for one year. Repeat the procedure outlined and discuss changes.

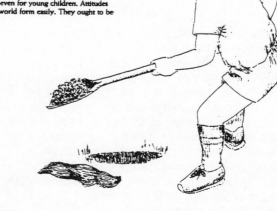

Shifting

One man, intentionally acting as an agent of Gaia, singleshoveledly attempts to reduce the rate of cattle-driven erosion in a desert stream system. He learns a lot, and so will you. —JB

Shifting
Paul Krapfel
1989; 185 pp.
$10 postpaid from:
Paul Krapfel, P. O. Box 1
Walla Walla, WA 99362
✱WEA

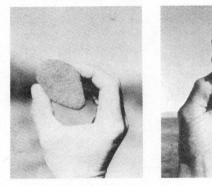

•

Animals will approach a sitting me closer than I can approach a sitting animal.

•

I stared across the *arroyo* at the runoff which was cascading down the opposite bank. The entire bank was washing away but the areas held together by grass were eroding more slowly than the unprotected bare areas. This slower erosion turned the clumps of grass into high points which diverged the runoff around them. Many clumps eventually washed down the slope and disappeared in the brown flood below. Yet for as long as each clump of grass remained, it created a divergence which reduced the energy of the cascade. Even if the grass washed away, it had reduced erosion during the time it stood. If those plants had not been growing on the side of the *arroyo*, the erosion would have been worse.

I am like the grass, I thought. My efforts prevent the erosion from being worse. Even if the flood washes my efforts away, my resistance will have absorbed some of the flood's energy and lessened the erosion that would have otherwise happened. Whether my efforts are enough to "win" depends upon the force I oppose. If the force is small enough, I shall "win." If it is large enough, I "lose." To be proud of "winning" is to be proud of encountering a force smaller than myself. I should forget about "winning" and, like the grass, simply resist the erosion.

I returned to my work. Twenty minutes later, the pounding rain subsided. So accustomed to that pounding had I become that its slackening sounded like stillness even though the waterfalls still shook the bedrock.

"Natural toilet paper" is an effective solution to one of the most common causes of wilderness trash. It's more comfortable than you might imagine. From left: stone, seaweed, moss, snow.

Soft Paths

How to enjoy the wilderness without harming it. We know, don't we? "Take only pictures, leave only footprints." Not that simple, folks. It depends on where you are, geography, weather, popularity of the area, and lots of other factors maybe you didn't really know that much about. This easily read and remembered book discusses the problems, then the attitudes and techniques essential for the preservation of wilderness attributes despite our potentially destructive presence. This is served up in a way that is intended to induce stewardship rather than guilt, just what you'd expect from the publisher, National Outdoor Leadership School (see p. 114). And all this time I thought I was doing O.K. (cringe). —JB

Soft Paths, Bruce Hampton and David Cole; 1988; 173 pp.
$10.95 ($11.95 postpaid) from: The National Outdoor Leadership School
P. O. Box AA
Lander, WY 82520
(307) 332-6973 ✱WEA

•

SANITATION

Since there is so little organic matter to provide sustenance for the microorganisms that eventually break down fecal material, sanitation in the desert presents a problem. Body waste won't decompose in this predominantly inorganic, often sandy soil, but instead dissipates, filtering through the ground as it follows natural drainages. In this respect, distance from water may be more critical than whether you bury your feces or deposit them at the surface.

•

Because the sun's heat penetrates desert soils,

shallow catholes are usually more appropriate than surface deposition. Visual contact by other visitors is kept to a minimum, and high temperatures near the soil surface (as high as 150 degrees Fahrenheit) destroy pathogens in a relatively short time. Not all burial methods work in the desert, however. Here, latrines are even less acceptable than in temperate climates, for burial deeper than a few inches eliminates the sterilizing effect of the sun's heat. The number of microorganisms is so low, and aeration is so reduced because of the compact nature of many desert soils, that deep, concentrated burial only preserves solid waste.

•

River users can camp on beaches, sandbars, or nonvegetated sites — somewhere below the high waterline. When the river floods, footprints wash away, and the site appears "new" to the next user. If you practice this floodplain camping, your impact will always be minimal.

•

If clear plastic is difficult to see in winter, toilet paper is even harder. Consequently, some winter visitors take only paper of a darker contrasting color. Regardless of color, however, toilet paper is always difficult to burn in snow. Even when the surrounding snow is cold and dry, the snow soon melts, soaking the edges of the paper and leaving some unburned pieces. The easiest solution is to avoid using toilet paper during winter. Snow — compressed and formed into a compact, oblong shape — provides a sanitary and surprisingly comfortable alternative. Best of all, when the snow melts, no evidence remains.

Eyewitness Books

Imagine yourself in Darwin's cabin on the Beagle surrounded by a fascinating array of specimens all neatly laid out and begging for further examination. Eyewitness books are infused with the same kind of wonderment that a naturalist's study might invoke. These beautiful books (21 in the series so far) visually convey many of the marvels of nature using narrative and captions to supplement the stunning photographs. Each two page spread introduces a new aspect to the general topic and the books end with ways to appreciate, care for, and protect the subject discussed.

Great books! A wonderful way to introduce nature to a child or budding-naturephile.
— Susan Erkel Ryan & Susan Crutchfield
[Suggested by Mary Law & Captain Walker]

—Pond & River

Eyewitness Books
Some titles: *Bird; Butterflies & Moths; Seashore; Plant & Flower; Pond & River; Rocks & Minerals; Tree; Shell;* **$13.95** ($15.95 postpaid) from: Random House
400 Hahn Road
Westminster, MD 21157
(800) 733-3000 ✱WEA

Backyard Safari

Jack Schmidling and Marilyn Schenk show how they created a mini-prairie in their Illinois backyard. First the how-to part: build a fence so neighbors won't complain about your "unkempt" yard; plant native plants (milkweed and thistle — weeds to us — are manna in the urbanized desert to goldfinches and monarch butterfly larvae); burn the "prairie" in early spring so grass and flower seeds will germinate. Then the safari begins — a trip through a yearly cycle in the backyard prairie ecosystem. Here the wildlife show the payoff for converting your backyard from barbecue patio to wildlife sanctuary. From lacewing beetle to the rabbit that visits this postage-stamp paradise, the diversity of life in a small backyard is astounding, entertaining, humbling — a good, doable project for homeowners everywhere.
—Corinne Cullen Hawkins

Backyard Safari, Video (VHS); **$32** postpaid Catalog **free** from: Jack Schmidling Productions 4501 Moody, Chicago, IL 60630; (312) 685-1878

Nature at Work

The subtle connections, cycles, and energy flows of ecology are wonderfully elucidated in this superior primer. Students and teachers will revel in it. —JB

Nature at Work
(Introducing Ecology)
British Museum of Natural History; 1978; 84 pp.; **$12.95** ($15.95 postpaid) from:
Cambridge University Press, 110 Midland Ave., Port Chester, NY 10573; (914) 937-9600 ✳WEA

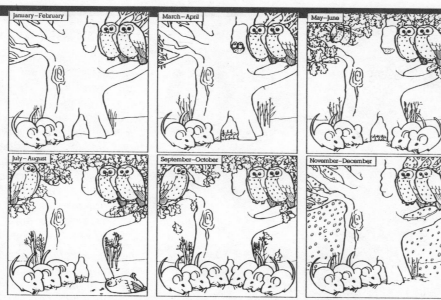

Light, temperature and rainfall affect the amount of energy stored by plants.

Woodmice eat mainly seeds, buds and insects. They store most energy (grow and reproduce) between April and September. At this time of year there is a good supply of plant food and they

use very little energy keeping warm.

Tawny owls eat woodmice and other small animals. They lay their eggs in late March and the young hatch at the end of April. So the young owls are growing when there is a good supply of small animals for food.

Chickadee & OWL

*If you are of the camp that thinks nature learning should be amusing, then you and any kids nearby will like these lively magazines. Better drawings than you might expect, and outstanding photographs accompany the lessons. Even the humor is pretty good. **Chickadee** is for the up-to-9 crew; **OWL** takes it from there. —JB*

Chickadee & OWL Magazines, Sylvia Funston, Editor, $19/year (10 issues) each from:
The Young Naturalist Foundation, 56 The Esplanade, Suite 304, Toronto, Ontario M5E 1A7 Canada
(416) 868-6001

Bullfrog Films

*From a mere tadpole sixteen years ago, this environmental film store has grown into one big bullfrog indeed. They sell 'em, they rent 'em, they provide free previews. They even provide replacement footage for portions of film eaten by your obsolete 1952 projector's gnashing sprockets. They deal videos. But most important, they have a great selection of films, the choice informed by a commendably wide definition of "environmental." These include some on enterprises featured elsewhere in this **Ecolog** (RMI p. 56 and New Alchemy p. 83, for example). In addition to a list of the very best films — I doubt if there's even one sappy offering — Bullfrog has begun to furnish entire schticks — a boon to teachers educated before environmental subjects took the stage. The **Energy, Technology and Society** kit is one of these. It's a complete course, with extensive teacher's guide, videos, and computer software.*

Despite the impression given in the catalogs of good-old-boy education supply companies, Bullfrog is without serious rival as a source for fare

that actually interests kids and adults. Even their catalog is interesting. And they're nice people to deal with, too. —JB

Bullfrog Films; Catalog **free** from: Bullfrog Films, Inc., Oley, PA 19547; (800) 543-FROG

• TOAST; 12 Minutes/Grades 3-Adult; Produced by Earth Chronicles/A film by Daniel Hoffman

One of the most effective energy films ever made, TOAST illustrates our underlying dependence on fossil fuels, and takes as its example the production and distribution of a commonplace item, bread. Using flowing images set to music, it documents all the fossil fuel inputs, from the oil well head (to make the fertilizer to grow the wheat, etc.) to the toaster. With Discussion Guide.

•

IN DEFENSE OF ANIMALS: A Portrait of Peter Singer; 28 Minutes/Grades 9-Adult (New!) Produced by Julie Akeret

What Martin Luther King was to civil rights and Gloria Steinem to women's lib, so Australian philosopher Peter Singer is to the animal rights movement. This is an excellent summation of both the philosophical and practical arguments that underpin one of the fastest growing political movements in this country and the world.

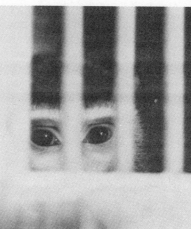

According to Singer, the heart of the argument lies in the recognition that we should not discount the pain and suffering of another just because the being that is suffering is not human.

Many believe this is a critical advance in the evolution of our moral thinking, and it is certainly time for all of us to familiarize ourselves with the arguments of the animal rights movement, arguments that are too frequently trivialized or deliberately misrepresented.

The Video Project

These folks produce and distribute films and videos on critical environmental issues, including some from the Soviet Union. Many are suitable for use on local PBS stations — Video Project offers a handbook on how to get the films that interest you aired. The high quality (Oscar-winners) selection

tends to emphasize dramatic presentations of things gone awry. Nothing wrong with that; it's a wake-up call. —JB

The Video Project (Films and Videos for a Safe & Sustainable World); Catalog **free** from:
The Video Project, 5332 College Ave., Suite 101 Oakland, CA 94618; (415) 655-9050

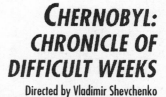

CHERNOBYL: CHRONICLE OF DIFFICULT WEEKS

Directed by Vladimir Shevchenko

VLADIMIR SHEVCHENKO'S FILM crew was the first in the disaster zone following the meltdown of the Chernobyl nuclear power plant in 1986. For more than two weeks they fought for the right to film. Then they shot continuously for more than three months. A lifeless city. Empty villages. A dead forest. A cemetery of abandoned cars. Wild chickens. The film itself is exposed with white blotches — a radiation leakage. After filming, the crew had to discard their camera and bury it, because it couldn't be decontaminated. While editing the film, the director was already fatally ill. Shevchenko was brought to the film's premiere from the clinic, accompanied by his physician. However, various agencies blocked its wider release. One agency demanded 152 changes in the completed film. The film lay on the shelf for four months. Filmgoers in the Soviet Union saw it only after the director's death.

☆ SPECIAL PRIZE, the International Film Festival in Cracow, 1987
☆ HONORARY GOLD PRIZE, 15th International Film Festival in Moscow, 1987
☆ AT THE 3RD INTERNATIONAL FILM FESTIVAL, PANTELLERIA, ITALY, THE JURY AWARDED A SPECIAL PRIZE IN MEMORY OF V. SHEVCHENKO.

Also with: 1986 • 53 Min. • Color

THE BAM ZONE
Portrays the harsh truth behind a major public works project of the Brezhnev era. 1987 • 18:30 Min. • Color.

VHS/Sale S59.95, Rent S35

shortly after the explosion

Transformations

City Building is the name of this game; build a real city, sort of, right in the classroom. In fact, the classroom becomes a city. Students organize themselves politically first, then they go to work, the classroom space and usual accoutrements serving as metaphors for special assignments and functions of a real city. By designing the whole thing, kids learn how the one outside really works and how it can be affected by their actions. Everyone participates. All of their schoolwork occurs in what they build. Much of the normal curriculum is integrated into the City Building program, giving opportunity to learn while using, the best way to catch and retain concepts. All the social forces that shape the built environment outside the school are represented. The effects of those forces on the natural environment are made plain. This is a great way to teach, though it takes a school board with nerves of steel to implement this program. Where it has been tried, it has worked well. Success has resulted in **Transformations**, a workbook (not a rigid set of pedagogical rules) guiding you through the program. Wish they'd thought of this in 1948.

Doreen Nelson's earlier book **City Building Education** is an easy introduction to the basic concepts. —JB [Suggested by Alan Kay]

Transformations
(Process and Theory)
Doreen Nelson; 1984
218 pp.; **$17.95** ($21.56 postpaid)

City Building Education (A Way to Learn)
Doreen Nelson, written with Kirsten Grimstad
1982; 65 pp.; **$4.50** ($6.05 postpaid)

Both from:
Center for City Building
Educational Program
2210 Wilshire Blvd, Suite 303
Santa Monica, CA 90403
(213) 208-1332

The Classroom/City Analogue

Classroom Functions Classroom Furniture	City Functions City Structures & Services
desks and chairs	private homes
aisles	streets and roads
doors	freeway ramps
book cases	libraries
art and musical instruments	cultural center
places where whole class meets	civic center
supplies storage and distribution area	commercial center
waste basket	utilities
Classroom Leadership Organization	City Government
overall leader	mayor
groups sitting together	council districts, commissioners
leaders of groups	council heads
class standards and rules	city charter, laws, building codes
Classroom Economy	Urban Economics
physical space	land/deeds
supplies	banks

Oakwood area of Venice, California redesigned by students from grades 3, 4, 5, and 6 in 1970.

Computer-Aided Environmental Education

"Rocky" Rohwedder, Ph.D., is an Associate Professor in the lively department of Environmental Studies and Planning at Sonoma State University in California. He also had a lot to do with the success of Econet (p.106). He is dismayed that the potential for computers in environmental education has often been ignored despite the availability of effective innovative programs and applications. Hence this book. It's a state-of-the-art collection of articles and critical essays on environmental interactive videodiscs and hypermedia, modeling/simulation teaching tools, on-line databases, and telecommunications projects for kids and their teachers. Rocky is a buddy, so I can't claim total total detachment; my only editorial comment is that there have been many times when I wished such a thing existed. —JB

Computer-Aided Environmental Education
W.J. "Rocky" Rohwedder, Ph.D., Editor
(Price was not available when we went to press)
North American Association for Environmental Education, P.O. Box 400, Troy, OH 45373
(513) 698-6493

The Ecosphere

The Ecosphere is a totally sealed, transparent glass globe about the size of a Civil War cannonball. Inside dwell four to six shrimp, a "twig" of burnt umber coral, a free-form mass of feathery green algae, and an invisible world of aquatic microbial life. The Ecosphere is quiet, doesn't advertise itself, and demands attentive peering. It has a jewel-like quality.

The Ecosphere must be kept out of direct sunlight or the shrimp molt so fast they consume themselves. The temperature needs to stay between 60° F and 90° F. A lighted support stand is provided for use in dimly lit rooms. Should the algae or shrimp die within the first year, the Ecosphere will be replaced free of charge. The makers give general support to all non-profit, educational organizations. Write them if your organization is interested in educational use or purchase of an Ecosphere. —Peter Warshall

Ecospheres have lasted 20 years under good stewardship. Our office has a rather less proud record: the first Ecosphere rolled off a slightly tilted desk during a photo session. The second lost its

The Exploratorium

In San Francisco, you don't say, "Let's go to the science museum," you say, "Let's spend the day at the Exploratorium." It's a place of discovery where you learn about light and sound and physics and biology and computers and whatever is being shown at the time of your visit, and whatever is being built for future shows (the workshop is visible so you can watch exhibits being made). Visitors are encouraged to poke, grab, and wiggle as they explore the amazing variety of fascinating stuff in the enormous space. It's what a "museum" should be. Even the store is wonderful. And you can book parties there if you're a member!

The Exploratorium publishes nifty items too: Posters, exhibit catalogs, and **The Exploratorium Quarterly**. Most interesting: three **Exploratorium Cookbooks** that tell you how to make your own exhibits. The whole bit is carried off with imagination, sass and humor in a way that makes most other museums of any sort seem sort of sad by comparison. —JB

Exploratorium; Membership **$35**/year individual **$40**/year family (includes subscription to **Exploratorium Quarterly** & monthly calendar)

Publications list **free**

Exploratorium Cookbook I, Raymond Bruman 1987 3rd ed.; 180 pp.
$70 ($78 postpaid)

Exploratorum Cookbook II, Ron Hipschman 1990 4th ed.; 180 pp.
$50 ($58 postpaid)

Exploratorium Cookbook III, Ron Hipschman 1987; 316 pp.; **$70** ($78 postpaid)

Set of Cookbooks; **$180** ($195 postpaid)

All from: The Exploratorium, 3601 Lyon Street
San Francisco, CA 94123

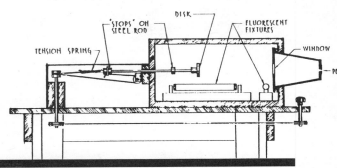

shrimp, parboiled by excess solar exposure. The remaining biota were launched to a shattered end on the floor of the editor's office during last year's earthquake. —JB

Ecosphere; **$80** (3.25", .25 liter); **$180** (5.25", 1 liter); **$250** (6.5", 2 liter) all from: Ecosphere Association, 9000 N. Oracle Road, Building C, Suite 4, Tucson, AZ 85737; (602) 297-4158

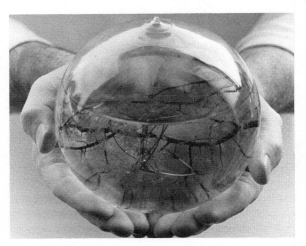

Secret House

MOMMY! There are about two million mites in my bed! On average, of course, and they're in your bed too. But yucky beings aren't the only interesting things you'll find in this 24-hour science tour of a typical home. Did you know that window glass is a thick liquid that glaciers slowly down the frame? That you shed veritable clouds of skin flakes as you walk around? That salting your food causes bacteria to explode? The tour talks of light bulbs, sneezes, lightning, ice cream and bathtubs. The explanations are bright, witty, and appealing to kids and adults alike. Eighty good photographs (you'll wish for more) illuminate the text. Wonderful! Aieee! —JB

The Secret House
David Bodanis; 1988
224 pp.; **$12.95** ($14.45 postpaid) from:
Simon & Schuster
200 Old Tappan Road
Old Tappan, NJ 07675
(201) 767-5937 ✱WEA
●

As the roar continues and the vacuum cleaner is moved back and forth directly overhead, the winds on the bottom get worse and worse. Not only are the dust pebbles being pulled up, not only are the broken matting fragments and other debris being hauled up out of sight into the sky, but even the living mite populations are beginning to be dragged away. At first it's only the stacked piles of mummified great-grandparent ancestors who go, swaying and rocking till they soar straight up in the suction wind, their hollow husks too light to resist. But then the smallest baby mites get tugged up, their eight legs grasping down as hard as they can to resist, but the vacuum pull is great, and their weight is slight, the feet pull loose, one by one, and then the young creatures are accelerated up and out of sight in the gale too.

It sounds horrendous, but we're not mites. The baby mites whooshed into the vacuum cleaner survive their high speed ascent without harm. Their tumbling and twisting in the air is safe enough, and when they do land in the cleaner's bag their touchdown will be cushioned by the piles and piles of dust already there. Nor is this just ordinary, run-of-the-mill, sneeze-producing and forget-about-it dust. Sucked up in the house this dust has a terrific number of human skin flakes in it, and skin flakes, remember, are the favorite food of these mites. They have landed in dust mite heaven. . . .

The human pushing the vacuum cleaner gets peppered with millions of high speed dust and mite pellets every minute. It's not a gentle pitter-patter either, but a wall of blasting shots, as if a fleet of miniature wooden sailing ships were blasting shells of hardened mite faeces and dust particles from their brass cannons in one broadside after another through giant nets (the bag) against him.

Physics

To have no understanding of basic physics in an industrial society is to be ignorant in a debilitating way; even if you don't like science and technology, there's no point in being blind. But learning physics is tough if you aren't adept at calculus. Until now. These three books are marvels of clarity — entirely free the of author ego-brandishing that so often clouds explanatory writing. **Conceptual Physics** *is the whole bit right up to a nibble of quantum physics.* **Thinking Physics** *is a set of fun and maddening questions that force you to use your noodle (and what you've learned in the first book).* **Relativity Visualized** *is just that, and a good job of it, too. You're unlikely to find an easier way to learn this stuff. —JB*

Conceptual Physics
Paul G. Hewitt
1985; 650 pp.; **$45.75** ($48.25 postpaid) from:
Scott Foresman
1900 E. Lake Ave.
Glen View, IL 60025
(708) 729-3000 ✱WEA

Thinking Physics
Lewis C. Epstein
1986; 565 pp.; **$19.95** ($22.90 postpaid)

Relativity Visualized
Lewis C. Epstein
1985; 200 pp.; **$15.95** ($18.90 postpaid)

Both from: Insight Press
614 Vermont, San Francisco
CA 94107 ✱WEA

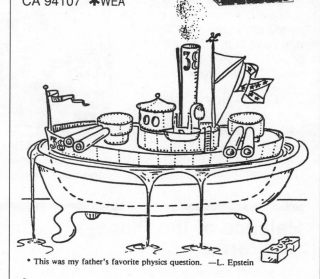

* This was my father's favorite physics question. —L. Epstein
●

Battleship floating in a bathtub

Can a battleship float in a bathtub?* Of course, you have to imagine a very big bathtub or a very small battleship. In either case, there is just a bit of water all around and under the ship. Specifically, suppose the ship weighs 100 tons (a very small ship) and the water in the tub weighs 100 pounds. Will it float or touch bottom?

a) It will float if there is enough water to go all around it.

b) It will touch bottom because the ship's weight exceeds the water's weight.

The answer is: a. There are a lot of ways to show why. This way was suggested by a student. Consider the ship floating in the ocean (sketch I). Next, surround the ship with a big plastic baggie — this is actually done sometimes with oil tankers — (sketch II). Next, let the ocean freeze except for the water in the baggie next to the ship (sketch III). Finally, get an ice sculptor to cut a bathtub out of the solid ice and you have it (sketch IV).

The question points out the danger of thinking in

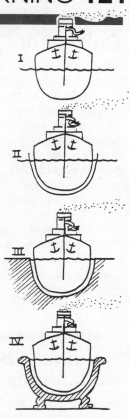

words, rather than thinking in pictures and ideas. If you just think in words you might reason: "To float, the battleship must displace its own weight in water. Its own weight is 100 tons, but there is only 100 pounds of water available — so it cannot float." But if you picture the idea you will see the displacement refers to the water that would fill the ship's hull if the inside of the ship's hull were filled to the waterline. And this displacement is 100 tons.

Don't rely on words, or equations, until you can picture the idea they represent.
—*Thinking Physics*
●

Galileo's explanation: The following is Galileo's explanation of why large and small masses (disregarding air resistance) fall at the same rate.

The acceleration of a large falling rock is the same as the acceleration of a small falling rock because a large rock is just a bunch of small rocks falling together.

This explanation is occasionally reinvented by people who think about these things. Though not the first to think this way, they walk in the footprints of the old master! —*Relativity Visualized*

How to Tell the Liars From the Statisticians

"Let's see the numbers" isn't enough. What you really mean is "Let's interpret the numbers." That isn't always easy, particularly if it's been a few years since your last stat class. This book makes it easy to see through the crap, including your own. (It is most embarrassing to be called out for tainted number manipulations, especially if you're trying to be good.) We liked a book on the same subject a long time ago, **How to Lie With Statistics.** *This one is similar, but more up to date. Thankfully, the reading is easy. Amusing, even. —JB*

How to Tell the Liars From the Statisticians
Robert Hooke; 1983; 173 pp.
$35 ($35.50 postpaid) from:
Marcel Dekker, Inc.
270 Madison Avenue
New York, NY 10016
(212) 696-6000 ext. 228
✱WEA

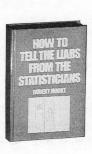

●

Let's take a utility company that wants to keep up with 10% inflation by raising its rates 10%. Suppose it has a million customers with an average monthly bill of $72. A business reporter can choose from these three headlines:

Utility Asks 1¢ Rate Increase

Utility Seeks 10% Rate Hike

Utility Asks for $86.4 Million Increase

The first of these is based on the hourly rate, as done when unions demand raises. The second is the reasonable way of describing the request. The third is an annual total and is calculated to encourage angry readership. It isn't necessary to point out which one of these three headlines is nearly always the chosen one.

College of the Atlantic

Most colleges and universities offer some short courses in environment and ecology, some have environmental studies departments. College of the Atlantic (COA) bases their entire curriculum on Human Ecology, attending the ramifications of that with a variety of interdisciplinary studies. This concept was considered radical when the college was founded twenty years ago, and it remains unique — COA is still the only college in the world dedicated entirely to ecological matters. It's a small school, with all that implies. Graduates I've talked to generally seem to appreciate their stay there, and the work it led to. —JB

College of the Atlantic
Information **free** from: College of the Atlantic
Bar Harbor, ME 04609; (207) 288-5015

National Geographic Educational Services

National Geographic — great magazine and "Oh boy, there's a Geographic Special on the tube tonight!" Their Educational Services are a bit less famous, but are, as you'd expect, done up in the impeccable Geographic manner. More of a surprise is the enormous selection and variety shown in their colorful catalog (most of it aimed at ages pre-K through 12, much of it interesting to adults): Science and social studies filmstrips galore (with teacher's guides); Videodiscs on American History (by Lucasfilm); Wonderful books of all sorts —hard to imagine nicer ones —toddler through adult; and of course, the Geographic's peerless maps. The renowned TV Specials are included in the prodigious list of videos (some available in French and Spanish). Most are available on film, too. Don't go away — that ain't all! The National Geographic Society is in the midst of a ten-year program intended to raise the level of geography education nationwide. It's too complex to even outline here, but the program includes teacher education, financial support and technical assistance (inquire to see if your school qualifies).

But most interesting, and even a bit unexpected from such a venerable institution, are the new Computer Courseware offerings and the Kid's Network®, telecommunications that hook participating schools together nationwide and worldwide, including in the Soviet Union. The program is hardly even weaned, but is already successful. Vigorously growing, it's obviously a taste of greater things to come. What better way to give kids a chance to be active world citizens! —JB
[Suggested by Jeannie Allen]

National Geographic Educational Services Catalog; **free** from: National Geographic Educational Services, Department 90, Washington, DC 20036; (800) 368-2728

THE WEATHER MACHINE

Courseware Kit components:
■ Three two-sided 5¼" disks, plus backups
■ One sound filmstrip
■ 15 copies of an 8-page full-color student booklet
■ Teacher's Guide with reproducible activity sheets
■ Library catalog cards
No. 80307 (ISBN 0-7922-0008-X) $159.95
Receive *today's weather today!* For purchasers of **THE WEATHER MACHINE** kit, this service transmits—via a modem—daily weather information prepared by National Geographic from National Weather Service data gathered from stations across North America.
Modem required: Apple®, Hayes, or Hayes-compatible. No additional software needed. Daily toll-free call; no hidden costs. Toll-free National Geographic hot line support. (ISBN 0-7922-0015-2)
One-time initiation fee $40.00
No. 80490 8-month subscription: 1/1/90-8/31/90 ....$125.00
No. 80492 1-year subscription: 9/1/90-8/31/91............$160.00*
price subject to change

SimCity

As mayor of an imaginary city I've constructed using a new Macintosh game, I finally understand why there is never enough funding for education, and how someone could bulldoze a park to build a high-rise.

Wearing the mayor's hat in SimCity I build parks, roads, fire departments, and mass transit. Sometimes I have to bulldoze. I can start a city from the ground up, or take over an existing city. Each improvement subtracts money from my limited city budget. Each improvement also has consequences down the road. I can zone the privately held land for residential use, but no Sims (computer-simulated citizens) will move in and build homes unless I also provide enough jobs, which entails building factories, which demand electric power plants and roads, which produce pollution and traffic, which cause Sims to change their minds and leave . . .

In one city which I built up over many Sim-years I had a 93-percent approval in the public-opinion polls. Things were going great! I had a nice balance of tax-producing commerce and citizen-retaining beauty. To lessen pollution in my great metropolis I had built a nuclear power plant. Unfortunately, I had inadvertently placed it in my airport's flight path, and one day by chance a plane crashed into the generators causing a meltdown. This set great fires going, and since I hadn't built enough fire stations in the vicinity (extremely costly), I could never gain control of the fires as they spread, eventually burning down the whole city.

I'm rebuilding, differently.

I love games and books that are able to create worlds of their own, and I've lived in nearly all of them. SimCity has been one of the most addicting of all.
                    —Alan Greene
                    and Kevin Kelly

SimCity, Copy-protected. Apple Macintosh **$49.95**, Brøderbund, 17 Paul Drive, San Rafael, CA 94903-2101; (800) 521-6263 (order); (415) 376-6434 (information)

The Folkecenter for Renewable Energy

This thoroughly professional Danish government-sponsored organization engages in renewable energy research and projects worldwide. Many of the machines and techniques developed there are now produced by commercial firms. Part of their mandate is to transfer their hard-won knowledge. One of the ways they do this is by means of a 12 week hands-on course in the several renewable energy technologies. It's a unique, concentrated shot intended for those who will be working in third world countries — seasoned pros adding you to their number. They encourage you to arrange a visit. —JB

Folkecenter for Renewable Energy
Training Programme; Information **free**
Course **$7000**,12 weeks (Fee includes board, lodging, excursions, and materials)

Renewable Energy Centres Worldwide
Newsletter, René Karottki & Jos van Beck, Editors; **$15**/year (four issues)

All from: Folkecenter for Renewable Energy, P.O. Box 208, Dk-7760 Hurup Thy, Denmark
Phone: +45 97 95 65 55

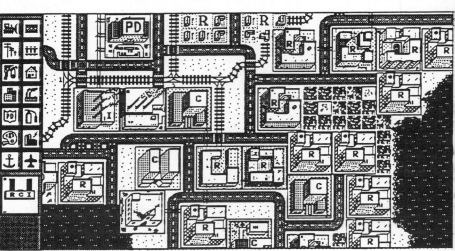

Tiny cars cruise SimCity's roads carrying citizens to work and home. Building structures are erected by Sim citizens as real estate growth conditions evolve.

Balance of the Planet • SimEarth

The closest we can come to demonstrating the web of relationships within ecology (and the environment) is through the many interdependent links possible in computer software. Both of these easy-to-use programs model the multiple complexities that make up our global environment. Each in its own way shows how small changes in one factor can result in large global effects, and how difficult it can be to find a good balance between competing interests.

In challenges like this, the best learning happens when you can make mistakes. But messing around with the only environment we have is not permissible. These two sophisicated software programs are tremendous eco-learning tools because, unlike nature, they allow mistakes.

In Balance of the Planet the goal is to design a world where environmental good things (such as biodiversity) outweigh the bad ones (pollution). In many cases there is a realistic trade off, say between use of pesticide and crop yields, or between more taxes and more forests. It's hard to make a world that is sustainable, and doesn't crash. One valuable skill Balance of Planet teaches is how to think ahead. It also is good for

learning to confront your biases, because there are biases, value judgements, and beliefs, built into the game at every turn. Much to designer Crawford's credit, one can alter the game's fundamental biases, giving advance modelling power.

SimEarth extends the fabulous game SimCity (see review on this page) to planetary scale. SimEarth considers the Earth as if it was a huge city of millions of organsims, animals, and raw resources like oxygen and ultraviolet light. Your job is to tweak resource parameters such that as many kinds of life live for as long as possible. You can play with carbon dioxide levels, rate of mutation, temperature, and impact of humans. Much like in the real world, "winning" is how you define it. The thrill is entering a rich, deep, and endless world.
                    — Kevin Kelly and Alan Greene

Balance of the Planet, (Macintosh Plus or greater w/hard disk and IBM PC or compatible w/ 512K RAM, CGA or better), **$49.95** from: Accolade, 550 South Winchester Blvd., Suite 200, San Jose, CA 95128; (800) 245-7744

SimEarth, Apple Macintosh, approx **$59**, for more information contact: Maxis, 1042 Country Club Drive, Suite C, Moraga, CA 94556; (415) 376-6434

David Orr has a wonderful idea: make the campus a model of ecologically sound policy, and use the accomplishing of that as a teaching tool. Obviously and importantly right, it's not so easy to do. He's doing it anyway. Watch this idea spread. How's your school doing? —JB

The Campus and the Biosphere

By David Orr

One of the greatest challenges facing environmental educators is to convey the seriousness of environmental problems without inducing despair and paralysis. The vital signs of the planet are not good: that fact cannot be avoided. But students must be given opportunities to think creatively and act constructively to solve these problems in ways that produce practical results. How might this kind of learning occur?

One possibility, with roots in the ancient Greek concept of *paideia* and the philosophy of John Dewey, is to regard the campus itself as a laboratory and as the source of a large part of its curriculum. Every campus is a resource-processing system that takes in food, energy, materials, and water and discards wastes. Typically no thought is given to how these flows affect the biosphere, the local economy, or the prospect of building a sustainable world. Nor are they regarded as a way for students to learn about the real world they inhabit. The "curriculum" concerns other, more abstract things. The institutional functions of the campus largely reflect the emergence of nation-wide and global marketing systems that are often environmentally destructive, highly subsidized, and socially regressive.

One obvious cost of this system is loss of the opportunity to consciously use the purchasing power of the institution to foster local and sustainable economies. Another cost is the educational opportunity missed. The analysis of campus rsource flows is interdisciplinary and combines abstract, theoretical knowledge with practical realities.

In the past two years the Meadowcreek Project, in Fox, Arkansas, initiated, funded, and conducted studies of the food systems of two liberal arts colleges: Hendrix College in Conway, Arkansas, and Oberlin College in Ohio. These studies were conceived as prototypes for a larger study of all resource flows that is to be started at St. Olaf College and Carleton College in Northfield, Minnesota. In the Hendrix and Oberlin studies Meadowcreek organized two teams of students to examine (1) where, how much, and at what cost food was purchased, and (2) what local and regional alternatives existed. Each team developed a documentary record of its results and a video that was shown to the campus community. In the Hendrix study, for example, students discovered that the college was buying only 9 percent of its food in Arkansas, a state that is primarily agricultural. Beef was being purchased from feed lots in Texas and Iowa and rice from Mississippi, although the college is just a few miles from cattle ranches and rice farms. The other team of Hendrix students, working with Meadowcreek staff members, discovered ample opportunities for the college to purchase a wide range of products locally.

As a result of the Hendrix study, completed in

January of 1988, the college has increased in-state purchases of beef and rice to 40 percent and has extended the idea to other purchases. The college has also hired a person to help in the transition to a more regional food system and in the ongoing effort to educate the campus community about the food system. More importantly, the study was educational in the highest sense. Students discovered, for example, that implementation of a college "wellness policy" was not independent of the college's purchase of feedlot beef which is laced with antibiotics and growth hormones. They also discovered that their wellness was related to that of migrant laborers in California and endangered species in Costa Rica. In this case, unthinking application of the industrial metaphor to biological systems had led to cascading undesirable effects that rippled through the system to the students on the Hendrix Campus. The fact that students themselves "discovered" this phenomenon heightened the educational impact.

The Oberlin study, completed in November 1988, produced similar results. Students developed a detailed analysis of campus food systems (one a student-run cooperative, the other operated by the Marriott Corporation), a workbook describing general methods of resource flow analysis for other colleges, and a video documentary. The college is now studying the recommendations.

The extension of this study at St. Olaf and Carleton to include energy, materials, water, and waste is designed to catalyze two immediate changes. The first is the development of campus policies for food, energy, architectural design, landscaping, water, materials, and organic and solid wastes that gradually shift the way the colleges spend their institutional budgets. Second, the study is intended to reinvigorate the liberal arts curriculum around the issues of the biosphere. This emphasis would become a permanent part of the curriculum through research projects, campus policies, academic courses, lecture series, and the establishment of interdisciplinary programs in conservation biology and environmental studies. The humanities, social sciences, and sciences all have important contributions to make in this dialogue.

The campus as a resource processing system is a laboratory that can contribute to students' intellectual breadth and practical competence. The study of resource flows combines theoretical knowledge across disciplinary lines with practical experience and introduces students to the art of solving real problems. Their participation in thinking through alternatives on their campus shows them that they can have a role in building a different kind of world.

Alfred North Whitehead once complained that "the secondhandedness of the learned world is the secret of its mediocrity." The study of the systems supplying the campus confronts students with firsthand knowledge and with the task of helping to create workable alternatives. Acquaintance with the mines, wells, forests, farms, feedlots, smokestacks, and dumps that service the campus confront students with firsthand knowledge of the most basic sort. Participation in developing alternatives can provide a dose of realism, hope, and skill in solving real problems.

Readers who have examples of projects in conservation education, at any educational level, and those with new ideas in conservation education, should send them to me at Oberlin College, Dept. of Environmental Studies, Oberlin, Ohio 44074.

Reprinted from: **The Journal of Conservation Biology** (see p. 33), Volume 3, No. 2, June 1989, by permission of Blackwell Scientific Publications, Inc.. The Journal comes with a membership in the Society for Conservation Biology, 3 Cambridge Center, Cambridge, MA 02141; (617) 225-0401, **$39.50**/yr U.S., **$51.50**/yr outside U.S. plus $13 airmail.

Meadowcreek

*David Orr is cofounder of Meadowcreek, an ecological education center in rural Arkansas. The notably beautiful campus is a model of the principles he suggests in this article, with energy-efficient buildings constructed from local materials, and food grown right on the land. The range of Meadowcreek programs and internships attracts people from high school (even some from the Soviet Union) through Elderhostel; the seminars are famous for tangling with difficult problems in applied ecology. Your support will bring you their excellent newsletter, **Meadowcreek Notes** — a good place to keep up with the pathfinders. —JB*

For more information contact:
Meadowcreek, Fox, AR 72051

Meadowcreek Publications

Meadowcreek publishes these materials to help you set up a campus system of your own. —JB

Local Food Production for Local Needs. A Manual for the Analysis of a College or University Food Service. $5 postpaid.

A Proposal to Supply the Hendrix Food Service with Locally Produced Commodities. This proposal was prepared by the student researchers and Meadowcreek staff. $5 postpaid.

Where Our Food Comes From: The Hendrix College Food System. This 45 minute video, developed by the Hendrix College student research team, documents Hendrix's role in the food system. **$35** postpaid.

Where Our Food Comes From. This 30 minute video, developed by the Oberlin student researchers, is more general than the Hendrix video and is geared to audiences on other college and university campuses. **$35** postpaid.

Where Our Food Comes From: The Oberlin College Food System; and **Where Our Food Comes From: The Oberlin Student Cooperative Association Food Service.** These reports were developed by the Oberlin student researchers and Meadowcreek staff. **$5** each.

All from:
Meadowcreek, Fox, AR 72051

•

RATIONALE FOR LOCAL BUYING

Economic

Reason 1: Avoided Transportation Costs

Reason 2: Hidden Transportation Costs

Reason 3: Economic Security

Reason 4: Direct Purchasing

Reason 5: Supports Local/Regional Farmers

Reason 6: Multiplier Effect

Health

Reason 7: Freshness

Reason 8: Chemical Residues

Environment

Reason 9: Fuel Efficiency

Reason 10: Waste Reduction

Community

Reason II: Food Origin

Reason 12: People and Land

—Where Our Food Comes From: The Oberlin College Food System

This index was compiled by David Burnor using Microsoft Works on the Macintosh. Books are shown in *italic*. Articles are indicated with "quotes."

This *Ecolog* is updated every three months
with a subscription to *Whole Earth Review*

Every three months, the authors of the *Ecolog* give you 144 pages of hard-to-find access to tools and ideas, delivered to your home. This on-going *Whole Earth Catalog* comes in the form of a quarterly magazine — the *Whole Earth Review* — filled with the same candid evaluations, resources, reviews and summaries of emerging ideas that you find here. If you had been a reader of *WER* you would have discovered some of these items in the pages of *WER* years earlier.

Like the *Ecolog*, there is no advertising in *Whole Earth Review*. You get 592 pages of solid news and information a year, untainted by advertisements. Since *WER* accepts no advertising, it is free from commercial interests and pressures, which gives us the freedom to tell you exactly how things are. Because we serve our readers first, we can cover unusual and controversial topics while they are still unusual and controversial.

Also like the *Ecolog*, *WER* covers both the "Big Picture" and the little-reported details that you really need to make something happen. *WER* keeps you up-to-date on solar hardware, political resources, computer software, non-toxic materials, do-it-yourself building, sustaining agriculture, personal communication technology, new economics, radical communities, and living lightly.

Would you like to know what's happening on the cutting edge? Not only in North America, but in our global culture? *Whole Earth Review* is years ahead of the mainstream press in its trailblazing coverage of unorthodox solutions. We'll give you art, cartoons, unconventional technical news, first-hand reports of works-in-progress, excerpts from hard-to-find books, and all the tools you need for self-education.

You can take up where the *Ecolog* leaves off by subscribing to *Whole Earth Review*.
— Kevin Kelly

RECENT COVER STORIES

THE GLOBAL TEENAGER:
Most of the world's population is under the age of 20. These kids are all listening to the same music, wearing the same clothes, seeing the same movies. What kind of world are they making for the rest of us? Winter 1989.

BIOSPHERE II:
In Arizona, eight people locked themselves for two years into an airtight glass ark with 1,000 other species of wildlife. In their 2.5 acre bottle there's a rain forest, a desert, a coral reef lagoon, and a garden where they grow their own food. The air, water, and solid matter are all recycled. Summer 1990.

RESTORATION:
Stories of success in restoring the natural environment. Practical advice on helping nature heal the messes we've made. Nitty-gritty details on how an ailing savanna, old mine, and forest creek bed were each brought back to good health. Spring 1990.

PLANTS AS TEACHERS:
In the rainforests and wayside vegetation of the world are thousands of plants that will be sources of new medicines. The indigenous people who know how to use these plants are dying off even faster than the plants are being chainsawed and burnt. This issue calls for a Botanical Peace Corp to help save plant power. Fall 1989.

WHOLE EARTH POSTCARDS
Classic shot popularized by the Whole Earth Catalog. The same postcard we use for our correspondence. Taken by Apollo 17 astronauts. Package of 12; $6, plus $2 per order for postage and handling.

THE ELECTRONIC WHOLE EARTH CATALOG
CD-ROM VERSION.
A computerized version of the Essential Whole Earth Catalog. You use a Macintosh to navigate through 4,000 electronic images and 6,000 screens of text. There is also a mini-Whole Earth Music Catalog built inside so you can hear more than 400 excerpts of music from around the world, while reading the review and ordering information. (Needs a Mac with 1 Mb., and an Apple Compact Disc SC drive.) $153 postpaid.

SIGNAL
ACCESS TO COMMUNICATION TOOLS AND INFORMATION FRONTIERS. Recommendations on the best personal communication tools and techniques, such as making low-rent camcorder movies, backyard satellite TV, free computer networks, low-cost software, xerox art, smart phones, hacker ethics, information viruses, fax stuff, fractals, artificial life, home recording, public speaking, writing to learn, and cassette culture. Over 900 items; 228 oversize pages. $18 postpaid.

THE FRINGES OF REASON
A FIELD GUIDE TO NEW AGE FRONTIERS, UNUSUAL BELIEFS & ECCENTRIC SCIENCES.
Weird stuff like ball lightning and spontaneous human combustion. How to follow conspiracy theories, access to brain machines, the truth about crystals, advice for being a skeptic, all sides of the UFO mysteries, the science of "unknown" animals like bigfoot, contacts for believers of perpetual motion, a flat earth, dowsing, bigfoot and things stranger than you thought possible, all with names, addresses and phone numbers. 224 pages. $16 postpaid.

A BRIEF HISTORY OF THE WHOLE EARTH CATALOG

WORLD BIOGEOGRAPHICAL PROVINCES

1968 Stewart Brand initiates **The Whole Earth Catalog** as "a Low Maintenance, High Yield, Self Sustaining, Critical Information Service." Self-published, with no advertising, it sold 1000 copies at $5 each.

1969 Now published quarterly with **Supplements** in between, The Catalog has also become an exchange for interesting ideas and heresies — mostly from readers. Sales reached 60,000 by Fall.

1971 Whole Earth and Stewart are internationally famous, with Catalog sales in the hundreds of thousands. Stewart expects that the many specialized Catalog-inspired publications will take over the job we have started. He publishes the fat **Last Whole Earth Catalog** as a farewell performance. The non-profit POINT Foundation is founded to disburse whatever funds have accumulated.

1972 Stewart Brand wins the National Book Award. POINT money is distributed to the Jonah Project (a whale-saving operation), New Alchemy Institute (see p. 83), and Trust for Public Land (p. 111), among others. Sales of the now obsolete **Last Whole Earth Catalog** continue at 5000 a week.

1973 Demand for the Catalog continues unabated. Recognizing that nobody has grabbed the ball, POINT resumes publication with **The Updated Last Whole Earth Catalog**.

1974 Stewart inaugurates the **CoEvolution Quarterly**, a reader-supported journal featuring long articles on unorthodox subjects, some considered unacceptable to magazines restricted by advertising. Reviews of tools and books let the **"CQ"** replace the Supplements as Catalog updates, but the deluge of new information forces POINT to augment The Updated Last Whole Earth Catalog with the **Whole Earth Epilog** in the Fall.

1976 Working with pioneer bioregionalists, POINT produces the first **World Biogeographical Provinces** map.

1977 POINT produces two books: **Space Colonies**, a serious consideration and critique of proposals for living in space, and **Soft Tech**, a look at applied state-of-the-art appropriate technology.

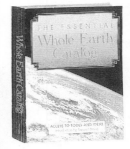

SPACE COLONIES

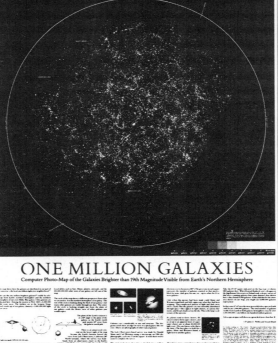

ONE MILLION GALAXIES

Computer Photo-Map of the Galaxies Brighter than 19th Magnitude Visible from Earth's Northern Hemisphere

1978 We celebrate our tenth year with the **Whole Earth Jamboree**, and publish "**One Million Galaxies**", a poster showing for the first time the large-scale textures of the Universe.

1980 POINT "pushes paper technology to the limit" with the 608 page, 5 pound, 2,700 item, **Next Whole Earth Catalog**.

1981 And updates it with an even heavier 3,907 item second edition.

1984 Stewart leads POINT into a new era with **The Whole Earth Software Catalog 1.0**, and a companion magazine, **Whole Earth Software Review**. With reviews still unsullied by pressure from advertising, the two are a critical success, but inevitably out-of-date before they hit the newsstands. After just three issues, the magazine is assimilated by CQ to become the **Whole Earth Review**.

1985 POINT convenes the first "Hacker's Conference," the **Whole Earth Software Catalog 2.0** appears, and a regional computer teleconferencing system, the **Whole Earth 'Lectronic Link** (**WELL**) is born.

1986 We distill the best we've found in eighteen years and decant it as the fat and chunky, urban-oriented, **Essential Whole Earth Catalog**.

The vigorously growing WELL breaks even.

1988 After a year of development supported by Apple Computer, Inc. the Essential Catalog is redeployed on CD-ROM as **The Electronic Whole Earth Catalog** (Available from Broderbund Software, 17 Paul Drive, San Rafael, CA 94903-2101; 800/521-6263; $153) A taste of things to come, it features music catalogs with sound.

SIGNAL

THE FRINGES OF REASON

1988 POINT produces two books using desktop publishing techniques: **Signal: Communication Tools for the Information Age**, and **The Fringes of Reason: A Field Guide to New Age Frontiers, Unusual Beliefs and Eccentric Sciences.** The Well now has more than 2000 paying users.